Justin Winsor

The Mississippi Basin

The Struggle in America Between England and France, 1697-1763...

The Mississippi Basin

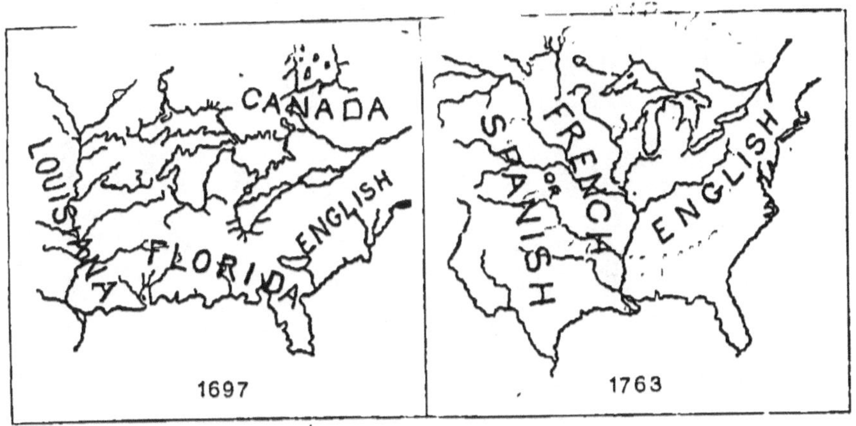

THE

STRUGGLE IN AMERICA BETWEEN ENGLAND AND FRANCE

1697—1763

WITH FULL CARTOGRAPHICAL ILLUSTRATIONS FROM CONTEMPORARY SOURCES

BY

JUSTIN WINSOR

BOSTON AND NEW YORK
HOUGHTON, MIFFLIN AND COMPANY
The Riverside Press, Cambridge
1895

To

CLEMENTS ROBERT MARKHAM, C. B., F. R. S.

President of the Royal Geographical Society, London.

Dear Mr. Markham, —

Such an observer as you are knows how the physiography of a continent influences its history; how it opens avenues of discovery, directs lines of settlement, and gives to the natural rulers of the earth their coign of vantage. I would not say that there are not other compelling influences; but no other control is so steady. If we appreciate such a dominating power in subjecting the earth to man's uses, we cannot be far from discerning the pith of history, particularly of those periods which show the work of pioneers.

The society over which you hold so signal an authority gives itself to the study of geography as elucidating many problems in man's destiny. There is, then, a fitness, I trust, in your accepting this homage from one who is enrolled in that society's foreign membership, and also is your friend and servant,

Justin Winsor

Harvard University,
March, 1895.

CONTENTS AND ILLUSTRATIONS.

CHAPTER I.

CHAPTER II.

CHAPTER III.

CHAPTER IV.

CHAPTER V.

CHAPTER VI.

CHAPTER VII.

CHAPTER VIII.

CHAPTER IX.

CHAPTER X.

CHAPTER XI.

CHAPTER XII.

CHAPTER XIII.

CHAPTER XIV.

CHAPTER XV.

CHAPTER XVI.

CHAPTER XVII.

CHAPTER XVIII.

CHAPTER XIX.

CHAPTER XX.

CHAPTER XXI.

CHAPTER XXII.

CHAPTER XXIII.

EXPLORATIONS IN THE MISSISSIPPI BASIN.

CHAPTER I.

THE MISSISSIPPI BASIN AT THE END OF THE SEVENTEENTH CENTURY.

THE seventeenth century closed with France prepared to profit by the results and influences of more than a hundred and sixty years of exploration in the interior of North America.

On the eastern seaboard of the continent the claims of France arising from the voyage of Verrazano had availed little, though Louis XIV. had strenuously asserted them. The Spaniards of those days guarded their capricious rights from Florida northward. The English, taking advantage of the close attention bestowed by France upon intestine affairs during her civil wars, had begun a settlement on the North Carolina coast. This was almost coincident with the defeat of the Great Armada, that first serious setback to Spanish pride. The century which followed saw the English well established along the Atlantic shores of North America. In 1688, the revolution which put William of Orange on the English throne opened the way for a long conflict with France, nowhere more warily pursued than in the New World. By the close of the seventeenth century, England was prepared to defend her territorial claims from Spanish Florida on the south, with limits in dispute, to Acadia on the north, where there was a like uncertainty of boundary. The English claim thus covered an extent of coast, with an indefinite extension inland, of so varied a climate that the average temperature ranged from 42° to 75° Fahrenheit.

1700. The rival claimants.

In the struggle for the possession of the region about the

Gulf of St. Lawrence, though France had contested it with England and with Portugal, she had practically obtained the mastery, and now held without dispute that grand northern portal of the continent, so essential in pressing her claim upon the great interior.

The St. Lawrence and Hudson's Bay.

Farther north, about Hudson's Bay, her rivalry with England was brisk, — for it was necessary there to protect the flank of her main enterprise on the St. Lawrence, — and at the close of the seventeenth century it was at its height. It was a claim for and against, on both sides, stoutly advocated and as stoutly defended. Between the rivals it was not only a question of trade for peltries, vital for France in her system of colonization, but it was to decide with whom rested the coveted chance of finding in those high latitudes the long-sought passage to the western ocean. Already in the closing years of the seventeenth century, the leader whom France had most trusted in this northern conflict was gaining skill and hardihood for a career which was soon to be transferred to the mouth of the Mississippi.

Iberville and Bienville.

In 1641, Charles Le Moyne, leaving Dieppe, had come to Quebec to cast his lot for a while with the Jesuits. Here he raised up a family of distinguished sons, and the oldest and youngest bore the appellations respectively of Iberville and Bienville. The elder was a man of nearly thirty when he appeared in command of an expedition sent from Quebec to attack the remaining English forts on Hudson's Bay. He failed in his purpose, and learning on his way back that the Yankee Phips was in the St. Lawrence (1690), he bore away his ships to France with what plunder he had secured. In the years immediately following, fortune varied in the north, — now the French, now the English, got the ascendency. In the winter of 1694–95, Iberville gained what had been lost, and a like fortune followed him in a measure in 1697.

Stories told by the Indians, and some papers captured by him in Fort Nelson, had inspired him with the hope of finding his way through these northern waters to the great western sea, but in this he failed, leaving the problem to be intermittently attacked with little cessation even to the present day.

Peace of Ryswick. 1697.

The peace of Ryswick, negotiated in ignorance of the French conquests hereabouts, restored in 1697 to the

English all they had lost about Hudson's Bay, and Iberville was left to final adventures in a new field.

The death of Frontenac had deprived Canada of a conspicuous leader, and active spirits, subject to the influence of that rugged soldier, turned to other allurements. So Iberville appears on the Mississippi.

English sea-to-sea charters.

The charters which the English king had given, while parceling out the Atlantic seaboard of the present United States, carried the bounds of the several grants westward to the great ocean supposed to lie somewhere beyond the Alleghanies. Though Drake and others had followed the Pacific northward to Upper California, the determination of longitude was still so uncertain that different estimates prevailed as to the width of the continent. When the charter of Virginia was confirmed in 1609, there was just dying out a conception which had prevailed among geographers, but which the intuitions of Mercator had done much to dispel, that a great western sea approached the Atlantic somewhere midway along its seaboard. This theory had come down from the voyage of Verrazano. To prove it, various explorations had been made inland from the ramifying waters of the Chesapeake and the Hudson. It was with this determination in view that Francis I. of France had commissioned Cartier to pierce the continent from the great gulf back of Newfoundland; and Cartier's success, followed by the later developments made by Champlain, Nicollet, Grosseilliers, and Joliet, had proved on the contrary the extent of the two great interior valleys of North America, and that they stretched over the latitudes and longitudes supposed to have been the bed of the Verrazano Sea. These explorations had also shown how slight a ridge separated the basins of these continental valleys. St. Lusson and Duluth had gone through the formalities of taking possession for France of these enormous watersheds near their upper springs, and La Salle had planted the arms of France at the mouth of the Mississippi for a similar purpose. Thus, by 1665, the French had proved the vast westward extent of the St. Lawrence water-system, and had made extremely probable the existence of the Mississippi. The ultimate discovery of this latter basin could not be avoided

The Sea of Verrazano.

The interior valleys and France.

when the English, in 1663, insisted in the charter of Carolina on territorial rights which reached to the New Albion of Drake. This region of the Pacific coast was no longer generally thought to lie just beyond the Alleghanies, as British disregard of foreign intelligence, exemplified in the Farrer map of 1651, had recently asserted.

Rights of discovery.

The principles which underlie the rights of discovery were sure to bring these rival claims of sovereignty over the same territory to a sharp encounter, as soon as the French had proved that their lines of exploration crossed these charter bounds of the English. This impending conflict was made inevitable by the passage of Joliet and Marquette down the Great River to the Arkansas, in 1673, and of La Salle to the Gulf of Mexico, in 1681. It was the establishment of military posts throughout this vast valley that eventually brought on a life-struggle between the English and the French. The English pretension was an alleged territorial right derived from charters formulated for the most part when the world was ignorant of the limits they conveyed. These charter extensions were propped by claims bought from the Iroquois, only less substantial, which prompted England to push her pioneers toward the setting sun and athwart the French course. A large part of the history of the Mississippi valley during the eighteenth century is the record of a conflict of races which these opposing claims engendered.

The Mississippi basin.

The prize contended for was a noble one. In Europe the Alps and in Asia the Himalayas shake off as from central buttresses the streams of human life to a verge of ocean waters. A continental condition that the Old World had not known was now found in this magnificent interior basin, over which the frontiers of a great republic were yet to be rapidly pushed from one mountain wall to and beyond the other. It is a territory in its central water-shed of more than a million square miles, and with its tributary areas of no less than two and a half millions. It is, perhaps, as fertile a space for its size as the globe shows, and capable of supporting two hundred millions of people. It has a breadth of tillable valley remarkably free from impassable mountains, and modern engineering can easily overcome all physical obstacles in the way of a united people holding it.

It is threaded by a central water-way that begins amid an average temperature of 40°, and meets the sea with the mercury at 72°. This lordly current passes through belts of corn, cotton, sugar, and oranges. It is shaded successively by the willow and the sycamore, by the locust, persimmon, and ash, and at last by the bay-tree, the magnolia, and palmetto. With forty or fifty considerable tributaries and a hundred thousand affluent streams in all, the great current carries off to the Gulf a marvelous precipitation. These water-ways offer sixteen thousand miles of navigable waters, and it has been said that its great body of tributaries is more generally serviceable for transport service than that of any other river, except perhaps the Amazon. Vessels of good size are thought to be able to traverse at least ten thousand miles of channel for most of the year. The voyager stemming the current from the Gulf must pole his bateau nearly a thousand miles to the Ohio. At the Falls of St. Anthony — the first serious obstruction — he finds himself about seven hundred feet above the sea, and this elevation is more than doubled when he reaches the source of all in Itasca Lake, more than twenty-five hundred miles from the deltas in the Gulf. If he follow the Missouri from its junction with the main stream, he can reach the Rocky Mountains, near four thousand miles from the sea, and the sinuosities of his course will double the length of his passage.

Descending, as was ordinarily done in these early days of the French occupation, from the portages about Lake Michigan, the canoeist found a declination of nearly six hundred feet in twenty-five hundred miles. In the floods of the early summer it took him about a month to make the descent, and hardly less than three months at any time to mount against the stream. A season of freshets would have raised the surface of the Gulf a foot and a quarter but for some oceanic compensations.

The surging current.

Moreover, there was something commensurately grand in the surging of this vast current through the years athwart an average width of forty or fifty miles of alluvial bottom, on its way to find the level of the sea. Franquelin, in 1684, gave the Taensas lake as immediately opening into the Great River. Iberville, in 1700, found it a league to the west, and Thomassy, in 1859, put it several miles still farther from the main stream. Again, Cahokia was founded in 1699, but it was not long before the shifting current left its habitations far inland. Charlevoix, in 1721, speaking of the region about the mouth of the Red River, found evident proof that "the Mississippi casts itself here from the east," — a condition to be considered, he thought, in making settlements thereabouts. To counteract these and other hydrographical vagaries along the great current and its largest affluent, the government of the United States is now expending five million dollars a year.

The discoverers.

For over a century after the European contact this great river had waited for recognition. It sometimes rose fifty feet in its bed, and yet this immense outflow in the Gulf had failed of adequate notice. Pineda, in 1579, did not comprehend it. Twenty years later, De Soto had crossed the river at the Chickasaw bluffs without a suspicion of an immense drainage, of which the consequent cartography took no note.

It was not till 1673 that Marquette and Joliet found the "great water" of the Indian report, so long familiar, to flow neither into the Gulf of California nor into the Sea of Virginia, but to run south to the wide semi-tropical Gulf. The future of the Great River was now assured. The luckless La Salle had fallen by the assassin's bullet while endeavoring to make it the imposing southern entrance to the interior of the continent.

The trough of the continent.

Nature had, indeed, made the entrance from the Gulf more than the portal of a single basin. The south winds which are swept in from its tropical waters, uniting with other currents drawn thither from the regions bordering on the Pacific, course northward together to be precipitated at the sources of the Mississippi, Saskatchewan, and Mackenzie rivers. Thence passing up those boreal valleys, reinforced by the Chinooks from the North Pacific, they make the soil fairly tillable almost to the Arctic circle, and agriculture profitable as far north as the 62° of latitude. There is another natural cause of the cultivable power of these high latitudes in the depression of the average altitude of the land, as shown in the eight thousand feet of elevation where the Union Pacific Railroad runs, and the four thousand on the line

NOTE. The opposite map is from the *Carte de la Louisiane, par le Sieur D'Anville, dressée en mai, 1732; publiée en 1752.* It shows the country of the Natchez and Tonicas, and the position at that time of the Lac des Tainsas.

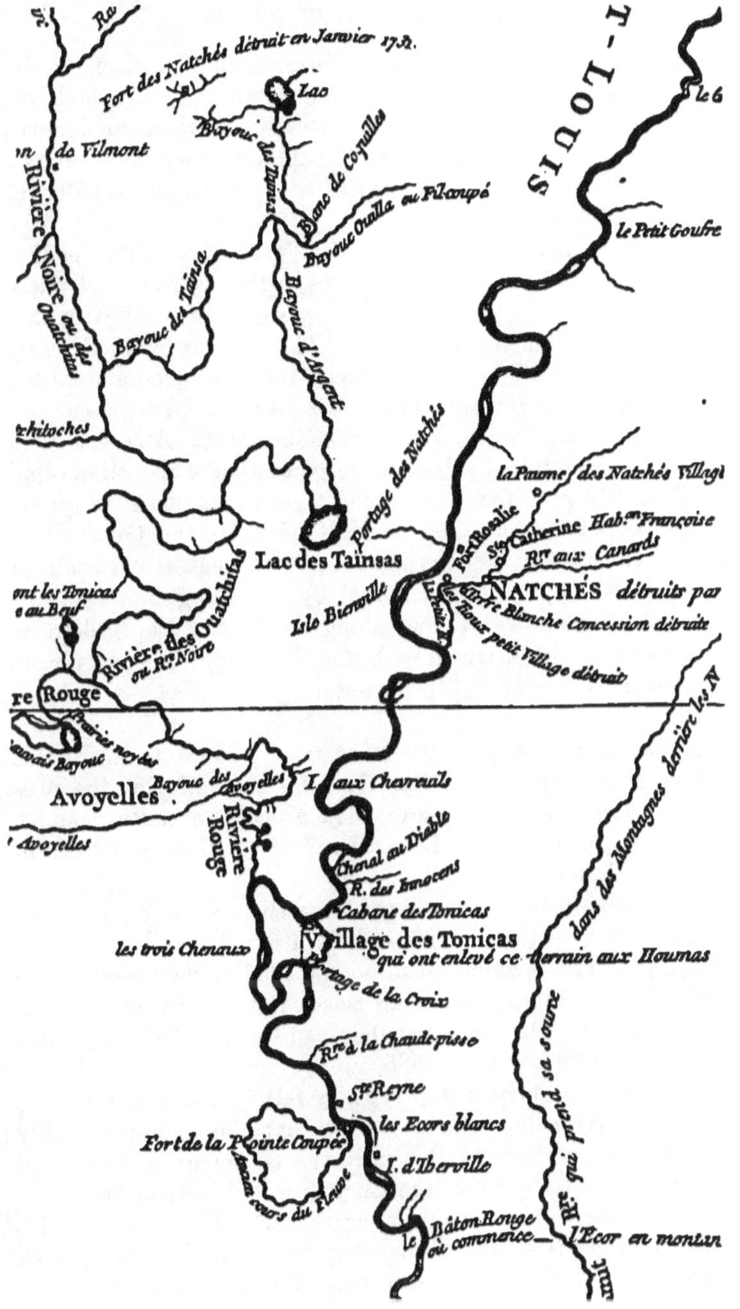
Fort des Natchés détruit en Janvier 1732.
Lac
Bayouc des Tainsas
Blanc de Coquilles
de Vilmont
Rivière Noire ou des Ouatchitas
Bayouc Oualla ou Fil coupé
Bayouc des Tainsa
Bayouc d'Argent
ST-LOUIS
le Petit Goufre
Portage des Natchés
la Pomme des Natchés Village
Fort Rosalie
Ste Catherine Hab.on Françoise
Rr aux Canards
NATCHÉS détruits par
Lac des Tainsas
Isle Bienville
Terre Blanche Concession détruite
les Roux petit Village détruit
Rivière des Ouatchitas ou Rr Noire
re Rouge
Prairies noyées
Bayouc des Avoyelles
Avoyelles
I. aux Chevreuils
Rivière Rouge
Chenal au Diable
R. des Innocens
Cabane des Tonicas
Village des Tonicas
qui ont enlevé ce terrain aux Houmas
les trois Chenaux
Portage de la Croix
Rre à la Chaudepisse
Ste Reyne
les Ecors blancs
Fort de la Pointe Coupée
I. d'Iberville
Ancien cours du Fleuve
le Bâton Rouge où commence l'Ecor en montan
Rr qui prend sa source dans des Montagnes derrière les N

of the Canadian Pacific. It has been computed that the depression of altitude from Wyoming to the Mackenzie River would counteract climatically a northing of thirteen degrees. Furthermore, the greater length of sunlight everywhere characteristic of high latitudes conduces at least to the rapidity of botanic development.

All these causes put spring on the Peace River ahead of that season on the Minnesota, and the ice in the river at Fort Snelling near St. Paul is said to break up simultaneously with that at Fort Vermilion in Athabasca. Thus it was in these early days that the buffalo ranged among the copsewood and on the prairie extending from the lower Mississippi to Athabasca.

So the great longitudinal trough of North America, with scarce a perceptible divide in some places where the Mississippi and Red River of the North head together, stretches in graduated aspects from the Mexican Gulf nearly to the Great Slave Lake. In this way the enormous interior trough is not confined to the Mississippi, but is increased by something like two millions of square miles of land along the Mackenzie, Saskatchewan, and Red rivers, which with the Mississippi form an almost continuous course of fertilizing water.

It was obviously now the mission of France to make this watery portal by the Mexican Gulf for the valley of the Mississippi what French explorers had already, a century and a half before, made the St. Lawrence Gulf for the lower basin of the Great Lakes.

The French had two rivals to be feared in fulfilling this mission, — the Spanish and the English.

Rivals of France, — Spanish and English.

The Spaniards had not profited as they might have done by the incursions across this lower country made by Narvaez and De Soto; but they had founded St. Augustine, on the Atlantic coast, in 1565, twenty years and more before the fatal stroke to Spanish prosperity fell in the destruction of the Great Armada. Spain was at that time unquestionably dominant everywhere in this northern continent, and she had not yet begun to fear that the English would in time dispossess her of the New Mexican mines, or that the French in the Illinois would get from the Comanches horses bred from Spanish ponies. She had little to dread from Raleigh's colony at Roa-

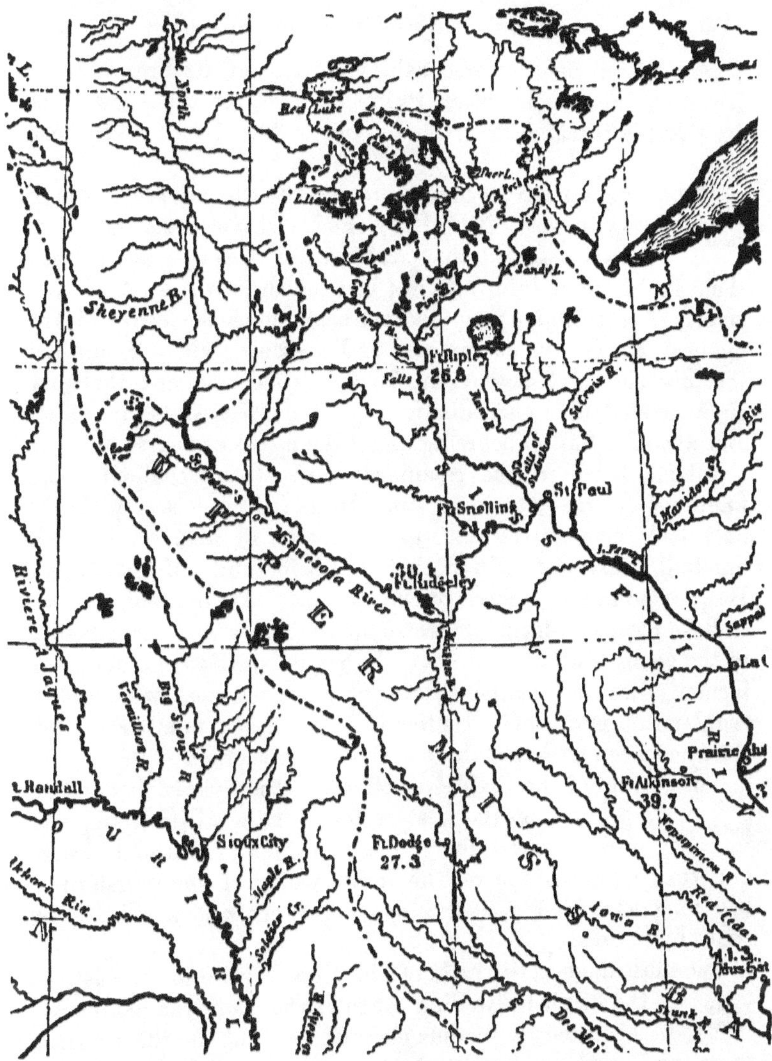

[From Humphreys and Abbot's *Basin of the Mississippi*, etc., War Department, 1861. It shows the Mille Lacs region, the upper Mississippi basin, and the sources of the Red River of the North.]

noke, or from the scattered fishing stations of the French about Newfoundland. But when Philip II. died, the time had come for Spain's threatening rivals to contest her claim to American soil.

Texas.

France on her part was not prepared to dispute the rights of Spain west of the Rio Grande del Norte, for the Spaniards asserted that Antoine du Miroir, who had led their explorations from Mexico, had never passed east of that river. Accordingly, from that stream along the coast of the modern Texas and as far east as Pensacola (where Spain had recently settled a colony, in 1696) France claimed that her rights rested upon her discovery of the Mississippi by Joliet, and upon La Salle's coursing along the adjacent coasts.

Inland, however, the Spaniards had already gained some knowledge of this Texan region. In 1575, Francisco de Urdinola had reconnoitred the upper reaches of its rivers, and a hundred years later (1675) an expedition under Fernando del Bisque had again penetrated the country. There seem, indeed, to have been wandering Spanish missionaries at certain points in the country at a later day. What is now San Antonio had formerly been a Spanish military post, and was considered a regular station of their frontier in 1690, and a number of settlers had been gathered there under its protection.

Red River.

The current of the Red River offered to the Spaniards another approach on the western flank of the Mississippi; but it would lead them to a low country, without mines, and this characteristic of the lower valley of the Mississippi had long kept that gold-seeking people out, and was likely to continue to do so.

English colonies.

The most dangerous rivals of the French were in the east, — the English dwelling north of the Floridean peninsula, separated by bounds claimed in 1663 by the English to be the 31° of north latitude, but never settled till the obliteration of 1763. Living under their sea-to-sea charters, these English were nevertheless walled in on the Atlantic slope by the Appalachian range. Though in some regions much conglomerated of stock, they were in the main dominated by unmistakable English principles which the French little understood. This difference of character always kept the two people mutually unattractive. There was a fundament of English policy which at first blush seemed to place the English on a better footing with the aborigines, but events hardly showed a constant advantage in it. This was the policy of claiming only sovereignty over the natives' land, and requiring the purchase of the fee before occupancy. The French and the Spaniards, on the other hand, claimed both sovereignty over and the fee in all heathen lands which they occupied.

The English, moreover, were a trading people in a sense that the French were not. They founded their communities on family life, which bound them to the soil, so that they abided whereon they entered. The practice of the fur trade, the sole support of the French, was opposed to such kind of domesticity. The English, too, had proved themselves a seafaring folk beyond what their rivals on the St. Lawrence were. They had flourished on the ocean in spite of a survival of mediævalism in the narrow policy of imperial navigation acts. By this failure of the mother English to recognize a public policy advancing inevitably, the colonies were hardened to ways which eventually deprived England of them.

The Dutch, during their rule on Manhattan, had organized an Indian trade in peltries, and the English, who succeeded in their pursuit of the same trade, outbid the French in their own policy. Their rivals in this were touched in their sorest spot. From the beginning this emulation engendered and kept up a sort of guerrilla warfare between the traders of both races. In 1685 Governor Dongan of New York had invited the "Ottawawas, a people on the back of Maryland, Virginia, and Carolina, to come and trade at Albany," and the next year the French captured some Albany traders who had gone to these Indians "on a lake."

Their political character.

The British colonists were drawing apart from the feudal and manorial systems of the Old World, as the French were not. In New England, the early adoption of the Mosaic code had banished primogeniture and entail. The Quakers in Philadelphia had already sounded the knell of slavery, and Samuel Sewall, in Boston, was soon to inveigh against it in his *Selling of Joseph*. The future union of the States was noticeably prefigured in the plans of confederation which William Penn, Lord Culpepper, and others were considering. The people were everywhere divided into "patriots" and "prerogative men."

The class lists of Harvard, soon to be followed by those of Yale, ranked students by social position, so that a strong infusion of Old-World sentiments in family distinctions was still prevailing, but on political questions it was easily remarked that growing convictions were sundering the colonies from the mother country. It was significant of the geographical divergencies of these sentiments, that in the sequel the southern gentleman was oftenest to stand for a new future, and the northern to be conservative.

Other races.

To the people of pure English stock other hardy races had been added. Cromwell, through his navy under Blake, had prepared the way for the downfall of Spain; but he exercised quite another influence on the destiny of America when he sent over the Scotch prisoners captured at Dunbar and Worcester. It was the thrift and premonitions of these exiles which had established at Boston the oldest of American mutual-aid associations, vigorous and rich to-day. The Scotch-Irish which followed later to Pennsylvania, Maryland, and Virginia, were to make the most enduring of pioneers, and to stamp their virile nature upon the early history of Tennessee and Kentucky. This spirit was in due time to permeate the Great Valley. A body of Germans, sent over by a society in Frankfort-on-the-Main, had already settled in Pennsylvania and on the tide-waters of the Chesapeake, — redemptioners, for the most part, — who were in fit time to move along the valley of Virginia and play their part in the great western march. It was unfortunate for New York that she did much by her large manorial grants to repel the Germans, who might have pushed her settlements westward much faster than was done. Those who came to seek an independent life in the New World did not take kindly to anything like tenant servility, and seldom tarried in a province that denied them the best results of emigration.

The Appalachians.

Such were the peoples kept back for a while from the watershed of the Mississippi by a mountain barrier of peculiar impenetrability for one of its climate and height. " The woods of the Appalachian district," says Professor Shaler, a distinguished student of our American physiography, " were in all respects the finest of those found in any region beyond the tropical parts of the earth." With an undergrowth of brushwood and vines they long retarded the English progress to the west, and such was their density that ten to twenty years followed the deforesting before the land became wholly arable.

Cartier, in 1535, when he was laying open the great St. Lawrence route into the heart of the continent, saw the extreme northern end of this mountain wall in the highlands of Maine. Four years later (1539), De Soto found that its southern end turned westward in upper Georgia. Mercator, in 1569, using the reports of these two explorers, and observing from the stories of those who had been along the coast that none of the streams entering the Atlantic between the Gulf of St. Lawrence and Florida flowed in very large volume, was the first to divine the true nature of the Appalachians as a coast range, and he so delineated it on his great mappemonde. That intuitive geographer erred, however, in turning this coast range at its southern end to the west, so as to make it serve the same purpose in shortening the rivers which flowed into the Gulf of Mexico. He was led to this mistake by the little importance which Spanish explorers had so far put upon the Mississippi. To the geographical sense there was yet no suspicion that this still obscure river had a volume equal to the water-shed of the larger part of the continent. To Mercator's mind this great inland region — for he had discarded the Verrazano theory — was all one with the basin of the St. Lawrence. The character of the Great Lakes was not yet comprehended, and Champlain had not begun their development. So it seemed natural to Mercator to place the springs of the St. Lawrence in Arizona and make the central depression of the continent run nearly east and west, rather than north and south.

Mercator.

It is curious that so late as the close of the seventeenth century what was true in Mercator was neglected, and what was false was adopted. The maps of Hennepin, the Frenchman, and of Edward Wells, the Englishman, fail to delineate any coast range along the Atlantic side, but from upper Georgia they extend a mountain range due west, making only a break in it for the Mississippi.

In the seventeenth century, the intercourse of the Iroquois with the French and English had taught these rivals what a commanding position those native confederates held to dominate the passage to regions beyond them. At the very close of that century, Bellomont, governing New York and New England for the English, had suggested the barring out of the French from the Iroquois country by the occupation of Oswego. Already hamlets were appearing along the Mohawk, and the Palatines of that German stock which was to push up the valley of Virginia were leading the way. The French had got a strong hold upon the Iroquois as early as the middle of the seventeenth century. At its close, Robert Livingston was warning the English that their alliance with the Iroquois would be imperiled if they did not send their own missionaries among them. The New York Assembly tried to checkmate the Jesuits by making it death for a papist to enter their borders. The French acted more adroitly, and on September 8, 1700, deputies of the Iroquois signed, at Montreal, the earliest written treaty — not a mere deed of land — between Europeans and the aborigines. Under its terms Jesuit missionaries were once more dispatched to the region south of Ontario and within what New York claimed as a part of her jurisdiction.

The Iroquois and their country.

All these years had shown both to the French and to the English that there was little difficulty in running trails for trade or war from the valley of the Mohawk and Genesee to the springs of the Alleghany River, and leading the way to the Ohio and the Mississippi.

The basin of the Ohio, with which there was thus easy contact at its northeastern limit, was the same inviting country which after the American Revolution drew away, under Putnam and Parsons, from the Atlantic States so large a proportion of their best blood. It was an area of more than two hundred thousand square miles, through which the vitalizing river, gathering its affluents along a course of more than a thousand miles, sped on its way with an almost even flow. Only at the modern Louisville was there a fall of something like twelve to fifteen feet in the mile. The ripple on its banks had a far from constant level. It has been known to sink to a depth of a very few feet in its channel and to rise to fourscore and more. Evans, on his maps, puts the ordinary freshet rise at twenty feet, and says that the stream scarcely ever overflows its upright banks. Modern gauges have shown

The Ohio basin.

that for about a hundred and sixty days in the year boats drawing six feet of water can find a free passage. In his day, Evans reckoned that during full water boats could be rowed from Pittsburgh to the sea in sixteen or seventeen days; and that from Mingo-town, seventy-five miles from the Forks, an ordinary stage of the flood would carry a draught of four feet. The river sweeps on amid a variegated flora, and the oak and hickory, the maple and black walnut, sheltered in these older days vast herds of buffalo.

Iroquois conquests.

It was along this valley that the Iroquois in the seventeenth century had pushed their westward conquests. On their route they had scattered the Eries dwelling south of the lake of that name. La Salle had heard of the Ohio through some Senecas who visited Montreal in 1669, and in following its current some years later, he had found that the name of the Iroquois could create alarm even as far as the Mississippi.

At the close of that century these confederated tribes were at the height of their power, — a domination that had taken more than a century and a half in the making. Their influence extended on the east into New England. They were feared at the north in the upper parts of Canada. They were a terror on the Mississippi, and they enforced a savage law as far south as the Potomac. They had nearly scoured away all human life between the Ohio and Lake Erie, so that a territory marked as a vantage-ground for man's endeavor — with its moderate elevation separating the streams that were ultimately delivered into the gulfs of St. Lawrence and Mexico — was simply a hunting-ground for their young men, or was continuously traversed by marauding bands of Shawnees. By the close of the seventeenth century, the foes of the Iroquois were gaining courage. It is a traditon gathered by Loskiel that the Delawares, fleeing before the whites, now crossed the Alleghanies, drove the Cherokees before them, and pushed into the Ohio valley. In 1693, the governor of New York had endeavored in vain to entice the Miamis, bordering on the western end of Lake Erie, to break their bonds with the French. Three years later, by English instigation, the Iroquois advanced against these Miamis, with the Senecas in the van. The confederates now received their first check. They were defeated

The Ohio tribes.

the next year (1697) and driven back, and ultimately (1702) forced to a peace.

Senecas and Mingoes.

At the opening of the eighteenth century, the Senecas maintained the westernmost outposts of the Iroquois in northeastern Ohio. Their congeners the Mingoes — as the English called them from a Delaware usage — were in the southeastern parts. Later the Shawnees came back to their old haunts, and some of them settled farther west on the Scioto, leaving their friends the Minnisinks on the forks of the Delaware.

Shawnees.

It has been suggested by Parkman and others that the Shawnees were remnants of the devastated Eries; but the evidence is not conclusive. Their villages extended south of the Ohio into Kentucky, perhaps as far as the Savannah River, since Delisle placed them there in 1720. The most populous of their towns appear to have been situated on the Shawanee (Cumberland) and the Cherokee (Tennessee) rivers, whence in time the Cherokees and Chickasaws were to push them back.

The vagrancy of the Shawnees — Chaouanons, as the French termed them — renders their history the most perplexing of all tribes of the Great Valley. We find traces of them as far south as the Gulf shore, and as far east as Pennsylvania and perhaps Virginia. Mr. C. C. Royce, of the Ethnological Bureau at Washington, has tried to trace their wanderings. He is inclined to the Erie theory of their origin, and thinks them not unlikely the "Massawomekes," of whom Captain John Smith, in 1608, heard as living over the mountains "upon a great salt water, which by all likelihood is some great lake, or some inlet of some sea that fitteth into the South Sea." They were thought to make their approach to the tide-water tribes, their enemies, by streams entering Chesapeake Bay from the northwest.

When Marquette was at his mission on Lake Superior in 1670, he encountered the Shawnees there, and he knew from the glass beads which they wore that they had traded with the English, then only possible by packmen who had passed the Alleghanies. Again we find Marquette, while on his eventful voyage down the Mississippi three years later, speaking of the Ohio, when he passed its mouth, as coming from the country of the Shawnees. At the very close of the century, Father Cosme tells us that the Shawnees were still bartering with the people east of the Alleghanies.

Beyond the Scioto lay, as the century went on, the Wyandots, — a fragment of the old Huron people, — and neighboring to them were the Ottawas on the Sandusky and the Maumee of the north.

As to this eastern affluent of the Mississippi, the French had introduced a confused nomenclature, which needs to be borne in mind in reading the early narratives. What they often called the Ouabache (Wabash) was the present stream of that name, continued in the modern Ohio below their junction. The Belle Rivière, or the Ohio, was the larger stream above the Wabash, and the name was extended to cover what we now call the Alleghany. James Logan of Pennsylvania early (1718) discriminated: "Some call both these rivers [Ohio and Wabash] by the same name, and generally Wabache; but they ought to be distinguished, because the head of Ohio comes much more easterly [in the Alleghany], extending even to the government of New York."

Ohio and Wabash.

The French and the Dutch had knowledge of this Alleghany ingress into the Ohio regions as early as the middle of the seventeenth century, and the English came later to know it. Champlain had been the first to invade the Iroquois country, the natural gateway to the west. His maps are the earliest we have. The Jesuit missionaries added further information, and the warring inroads of Tracy and Denonville still increased it. But the almost steady adherence of the Iroquois to the English gave these rivals of the French an advantage, increased much in the eighteenth century by the remarkable personal influence of William Johnson, when the final struggle came for the possession of the valley.

The Alleghany River and the Iroquois country.

As the English settlements moved back from the sea, all along the Appalachians, it became apparent, from time to time, that there were gaps in the mountains which could be passed, and water-ways beyond to be found which led to the Ohio valley. The Pennsylvanians opened such a passage by the west branch of the Susquehanna. Evans later describes it as "interlocked with branches of the Alleghany, making a portage of forty miles, and from thence to Shamokin [at the forks of the Susquehanna] the traders are usually seven days coming down with a fresh." One of the legends on Evans's map of 1744 speaks of the Susquehanna as having no "sea navigation" because of its obstructions, but, it adds, "by its length and large branches, communicating with the country beyond the mountains, it makes amends in conveniences for Indian navigation with canoes." Of the "Endless Mountains" (Appalachians) it further says that "back of Pennsylvania there are a hundred miles right across, scarce an acre of ten of which is capable of culture."

Pennsylvania gaps of the Alleghanies.

There was also from Pennsylvania another portage from the Juniata to other affluents of the Alleghany, a route which knew much devastation in the later wars. The Virginians found still shorter portages to the Monongahela and Ohio from the upper waters of the Potomac, and observers were not slow in discovering that the climate on the two slopes of the mountains was not much changed by the elevation which was to be passed.

Gaps in Virginia.

The passage west in upper Georgia by an almost level route around the mountains had long been known. The information which De Soto had acquired was confirmed by the Spanish miners, who worked here at intervals for a long time after 1560. The Carolina traders, however, did not depend alone on this more practicable route in maintaining their Indian traffic. The Carolinians were a conglomerate people from the beginning. Beside the pure English, there were strains of other blood, — Scotch and Protestant Irish, Swiss, Palatines, and Dutch, the last coming down from the Iroquois country after the English occupation. The cultivation of rice was even yet looked upon among them as a staple, and created with the increase of its crops a scattering plantation life, so that towns were not the rule.

The Carolinians and their Indian trade.

Trade had already begun with the Cherokees, a race in the south much like the Iroquois in the north. Indeed, Horatio

NOTE. The opposite map is from Humphreys and Abbot's *Basins of the Mississippi*, etc., War Department, 1861. It shows the Ohio basin, and how the rivers on the southern side of the Ohio are separated by the Alleghanies from the Virginia and Carolina waters.

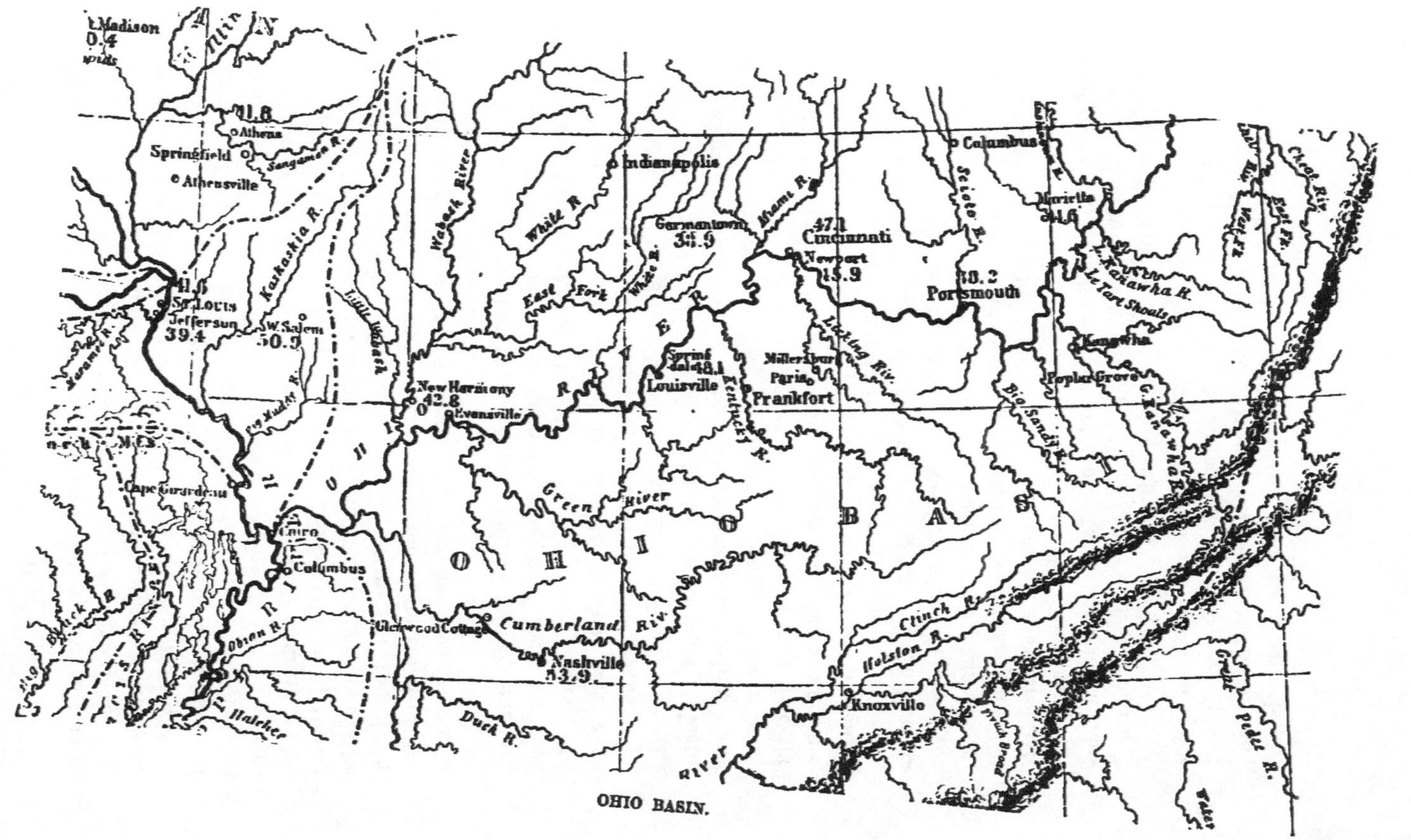
Springfield
Athens
Athensville
Sangamon R.
Kaskaskia R.
St. Louis
Jefferson
39.4
W. Salem
50.9
Little Wabash
Wabash River
White R.
Indianapolis
Germantown
East Fork
White R.
Miami R.
Cincinnati
47.1
Newport
45.9
Columbus
Scioto R.
Portsmouth
Marietta
L. Kanawha R.
Le Tart Shoals
Kanawha
Poplar Grove
G. Kanawha R.
Big Sandy R.
Licking Riv.
Millersburg
Paris
Frankfort
Kentucky R.
Louisville
New Harmony
42.8
Evansville
Cape Girardeau
Cairo
Columbus
Obion R.
Green River
Glenwood Cottage
Cumberland Riv.
Nashville
53.9
Duck R.
Clinch R.
Holston R.
Knoxville
River
Cheat Riv.
East Fk.
West Fk.
Pedee R.
O H I O B A S I N
O H I O R I V E R
OHIO BASIN.

Hale and other philologists have seen in the Cherokee tongue certain linguistic relations to the language of the Iroquois, though there are some investigators who connect them rather with the Dacotahs. The Cherokees were a skillful people, made pipes deftly, and constructed mounds of earth. They were much more inclined to agriculture than the tribes which the French had known in Canada, and their sustenance depended rather on vegetables and fruits than upon animal fats and oils used in the north. Their villages stretched all along the mountains southward, from the headwaters of the Holston and Clinch in Tennessee to the sources of the rivers in Carolina, and they built their lodges on either slope of the Appalachians and in their valleys. De Soto had found them in much the same situation.

Cherokees.

It is very likely that in the latter half of the seventeenth century the Virginians had some knowledge of their northern villages. In 1690, one Daugherty, a Virginian trader, had gone among them. In 1693, a deputation of their chief men had come to Charleston to ask aid against the Tuscaroras.

In May, 1699, Bienville, the French commander on the Gulf, reports an attack of Indians on the north shore of Lake Pontchartrain, and among the assailants were some whites; and he supposes they were English from Carolina. Even as early as La Salle's time, it seemed evident to that explorer that the English in Carolina were sending traders over the mountains, for he could not otherwise account for the articles of European make which he found among the Mississippi tribes.

Carolina Indians and traders.

The inter-tribal traffic which was carried on by the Yamassees on the Savannah, by the Catawbas on the river of that name, and by the Tuscaroras on the Neuse, with the Indians over the mountains naturally opened traders' trails for the English. Delisle, in his map of 1701, shows the routes of the Carolina traders to the Chickasaws; in that of 1703 he makes a river, evidently the Tennessee, a thoroughfare for such trade, and in 1707 he calls it the "Tinnase," making it rise among the Cherokee villages.

The Creeks.

The Creeks, more easily reached around the southern spurs of the mountains, occupied the territory south and west of the Savannah River and thence to the Mobile, and they included in their tribal associations the Seminoles of

Florida. The line between the Cherokees and the Creeks followed the Broad River, and ran roughly along the 34° of north latitude. The English were already beginning to establish their factories among this people, and a legend on Mitchell's map (1755) says that such stations are scattered through the country, except among the Alibamons on the Alabama River, who had come under French influence in 1715, though the English had been among them as early as 1687. The "route of Colonel Welch in 1698," given in the same map as that followed by the Carolina traders, crossed westward the upper waters of the Appalachicola, past the Alabama and Chickasaw rivers (the main forks of the Mobile), and so reached the country of the Chickasaws.

La Salle and Iberville.

When La Salle turned trader, he was confined in his enterprise, by royal edict, to those parts of the upper Mississippi valley which did not supply furs to the Montreal market. Finding the peltries of this region heavy, — for they were largely buffalo-skins, — he had been prompted, after his discovery of the outlet of the Great River at the south, to organize a plan of shipping his furs down the Mississippi on their way to Europe, rather than to trail them over the northern portages on the way to the merchants' ships at Montreal. Apprehensive of English interruption, he had at the same time urged that the eastern tributaries of the Mississippi should be occupied, to close them against any such rivalry. It was left for Iberville to open this ocean route to France.

La Salle and Tonty.

Even after La Salle had reached the Illinois and had begun to covet their trade, the Montreal merchants had been jealous of the interference which it would cause with the commerce of the northern Indians. Royal decrees had recognized the diverting of this trade of the Illinois Indians to its natural channel down the Mississippi; but when La Salle's patent fell to his faithful henchman, the picturesque Tonty with the silver hand, an exception was made in the latter's favor because of his signal services, and he was allowed (1699) to dispatch two canoes and twelve men yearly from the St. Lawrence to his Rock on the Illinois. This indulgence did not long continue, and in 1702 it was withdrawn. Tonty, as we shall see, was thus driven to join Iberville at the mouth of the Mississippi.

The obstacles of these Canadian routes to the sea were great, involving the passage of divides, which were scattered from the extreme end of Lake Superior to the Niagara River. To the common apprehension of the average European geographer, these multiplied connections were simply evolved in the conception of a river by which the Mississippi was united with the St. Lawrence. This is seen in the *Introductio in Universam Geographiam* of Cluverius, and in an edition published so late as 1729. Even Bowen, the English geographer, so late as 1747, makes the Wisconsin River an unbroken link connecting Lake Michigan and the Mississippi.

The northern portages.

The earliest known of these portages were those farthest away from the Canadian settlements, and principal among them was that starting from the country about Green Bay, where the Winnebagoes, an isolated tribe of the Dacotah stock, first introduced these Iroquois of the west to the early explorers. This carry was known from Indian report to Nicollet as early as 1634, but Joliet was probably the first to pass it, in 1673. It was a somewhat tedious, but not a difficult portage, and it is said that even to-day, in wet seasons, the waters of the approaching streams sometimes mingle. Passing up the Fox River from the Bay, the canoeist traversed Lake Winnebago, along the sites of the now populous towns of Fond du Lac and Oshkosh. Twisting along the upper Fox for sixty or seventy miles, at what is now Portage City, he passed not much over a mile by land to the Wisconsin with its umbrageous banks and shifting sands.

Green Bay.

The course of the trader thus threaded the country of the Foxes, a people who were never brought wholly to succumb to French blandishments, and often rendered this route dangerous and even impassable. They were a tribe who, in alliances with the Dacotahs on the one side and the Chickasaws and Iroquois on the other, did much to resist the westward movements of the French.

The Foxes.

Driven from this route by Green Bay, the French trader sometimes resorted to another carry, at the extreme western end of Lake Superior, where he entered the St. Louis River, and found himself in that Mille Lacs region, the arena of many a conflict of the Chippeways and Dacotahs. The variegated forests of this passage are still mirrored in its innu-

Lake Superior.

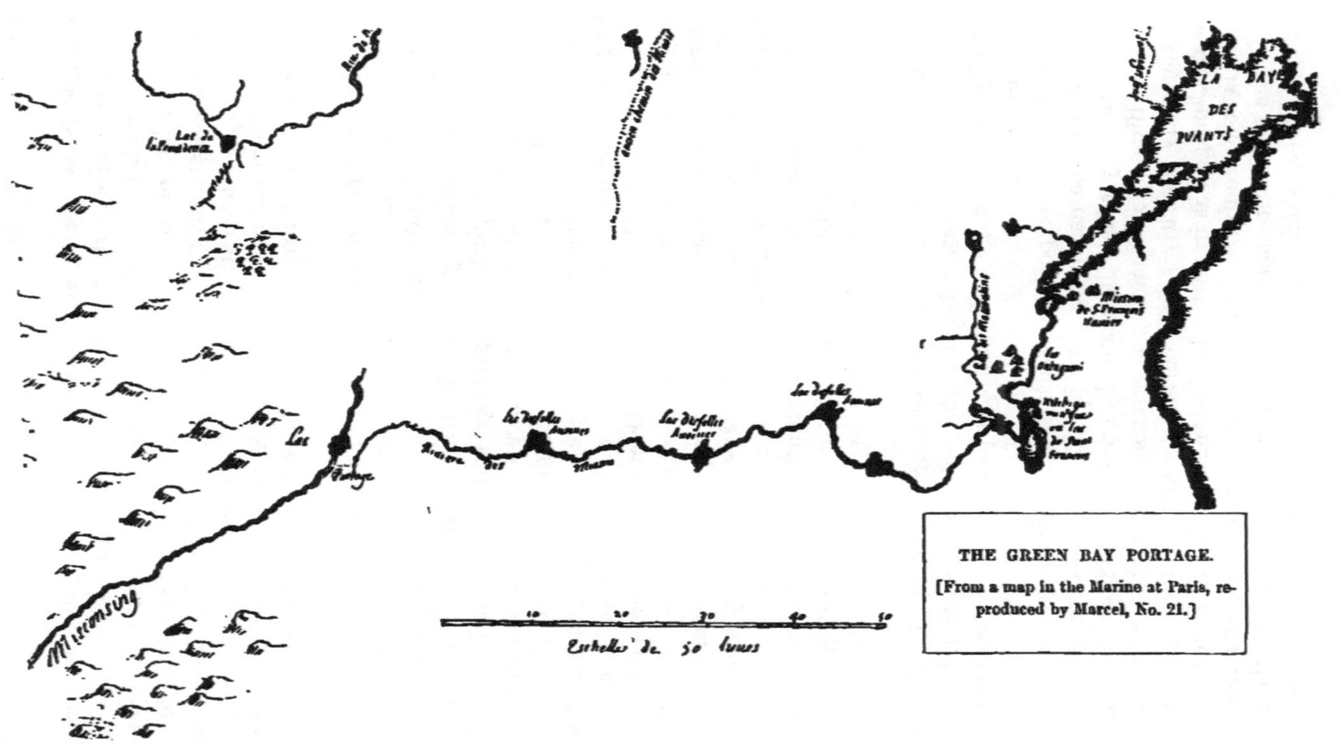

THE GREEN BAY PORTAGE.

[From a map in the Marine at Paris, reproduced by Marcel, No. 21.]

merable lakes, ponds, and streams, clear and pebbly, and the wild rice rustles as the paddle bends its tottering stalks. It was through such a country that the woodsman sought the uppermost reaches of the Mississippi, where that river was first seen by Europeans, and whence Duluth, in 1680, had hoped to find a way to the Gulf of California. Where the pioneer two centuries ago stranded his canoe, the twin cities of an ocean lake now rival Chicago as a distributing centre of produce and trade.

Lake Michigan portages.

Before the end of the seventeenth century, the portages at the head of Lake Michigan had become the best known of all, and there had been a trading-post for something like fifteen years at the Chicago River. What Herman Moll, the English cartographer, called the "land carriage of Chekakou" is described by James Logan, in a communication which he made in 1718 to the English Board of Trade, as running from the lake three leagues up the river, then a half a league of carriage, then a mile of water, next a small carry, then two miles to the Illinois, and then one hundred and thirty leagues to the Mississippi. But descriptions varied with the seasons. It was usually called a carriage of from four to nine miles, according to the stage of the water. In dry seasons it was even farther, while in wet times it might not be more than a mile; and, indeed, when the intervening lands were "drowned," it was quite possible to pass in a canoe amid the sedges from Lake Michigan to the Des Plaines, and so to the Illinois and the Mississippi.

It is along this route that the drainage canal of the city of Chicago is now constructing for the joint purpose of relieving the city of its sewage and opening a passage for its commerce with the interior.

There were other portages south of the Chicago River, and at the southwest corner of the lake by the lesser and greater Calumet rivers, by which the Kankakee and Des Plaines branches of the Illinois were sometimes reached. It is not always easy, in the early narratives, to determine which of these portages about Chicago was in particular instances used, and in the maps there is some confusion in the Chekagoua and Calumet rivers.

In the southeast angle of the lake was the portage of the St. Joseph River, which La Salle was much accustomed to trav-

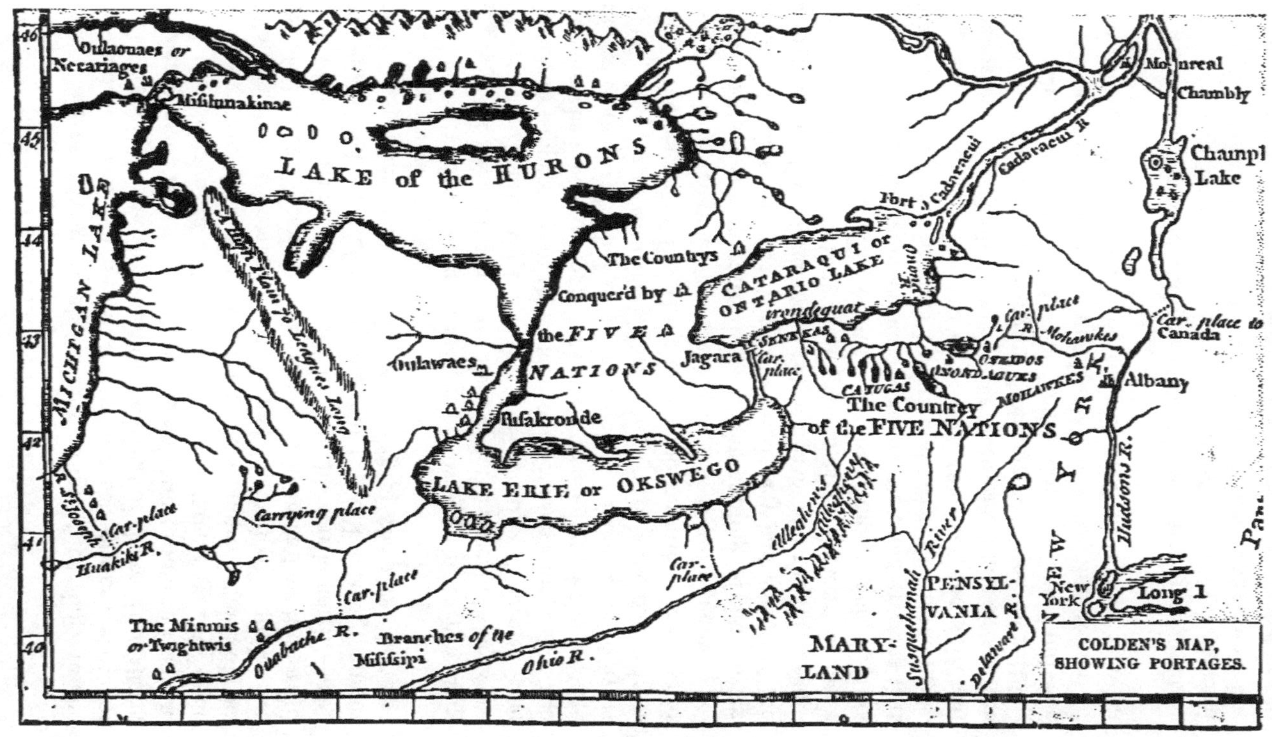

COLDEN'S MAP, SHOWING PORTAGES.

erse. There was by it about four miles of carriage to the Kankakee. The northward current of the eastern shore of Lake Michigan, and the southward current of the western shore, naturally made the St. Joseph portage a return route to Canada, and the Chicago an outward one. At a later day, this same river was found to afford a carriage to an upper branch of the Wabash, and it became the principal channel of supplies for the settlers at Vincennes. One can well imagine how this broad prairie land struck the Canadian from his sterile north, — the flower-studded grass of the spring and the tall waving bannerets of the later season, with the luxury of the river bottoms and their timber margins.

There was still a series of portages crowning the narrow strip of the southern water-shed of Lake Erie, but they were little used till the eighteenth century. There is some reason to suppose, from the evidence of Sanson's map, that the Maumee had been explored as early as 1656, and the portage thence to the Wabash had been known to Allouez as early as 1680. A year or two later, La Salle says it is the most direct of all the routes to the Illinois, but too hazardous because of the prowling Iroquois. It remained almost unfrequented because of these confederates till after the settling of Detroit in 1715. By this time the Miamis' confederacy had possessed the region about the affluents of the Wabash, and the three thousand warriors which they could put in the field were a check upon the Iroquois. The country was an attractive one, with its undulating landscape of meadow and upland, and streams that alternately lingered in calm repose and twirled with the foaming rapid. Animal life was brisk with the deer, the wolf, and the bear. The rivulets were alive with the white swan, the crane, and the heron, springing from the wild rice or settling along the grassy isles. On the gentle slopes of the land one heard the turkey and the quail. It was a meeting-ground of the savages, and the ashes of their council fires were seen on the knolls.

Lake Erie portages.

This portage varied with the state of the water from eight or nine miles to even thirty. For two hundred miles downward from the carry the Wabash was more or less interrupted, but

NOTE. The opposite map is from Humphreys and Abbot's *Basins of the Mississippi*, etc., War Department, 1861. It shows the line of the divide intersecting the portages between the Great Lakes and the Ohio and Mississippi basins.

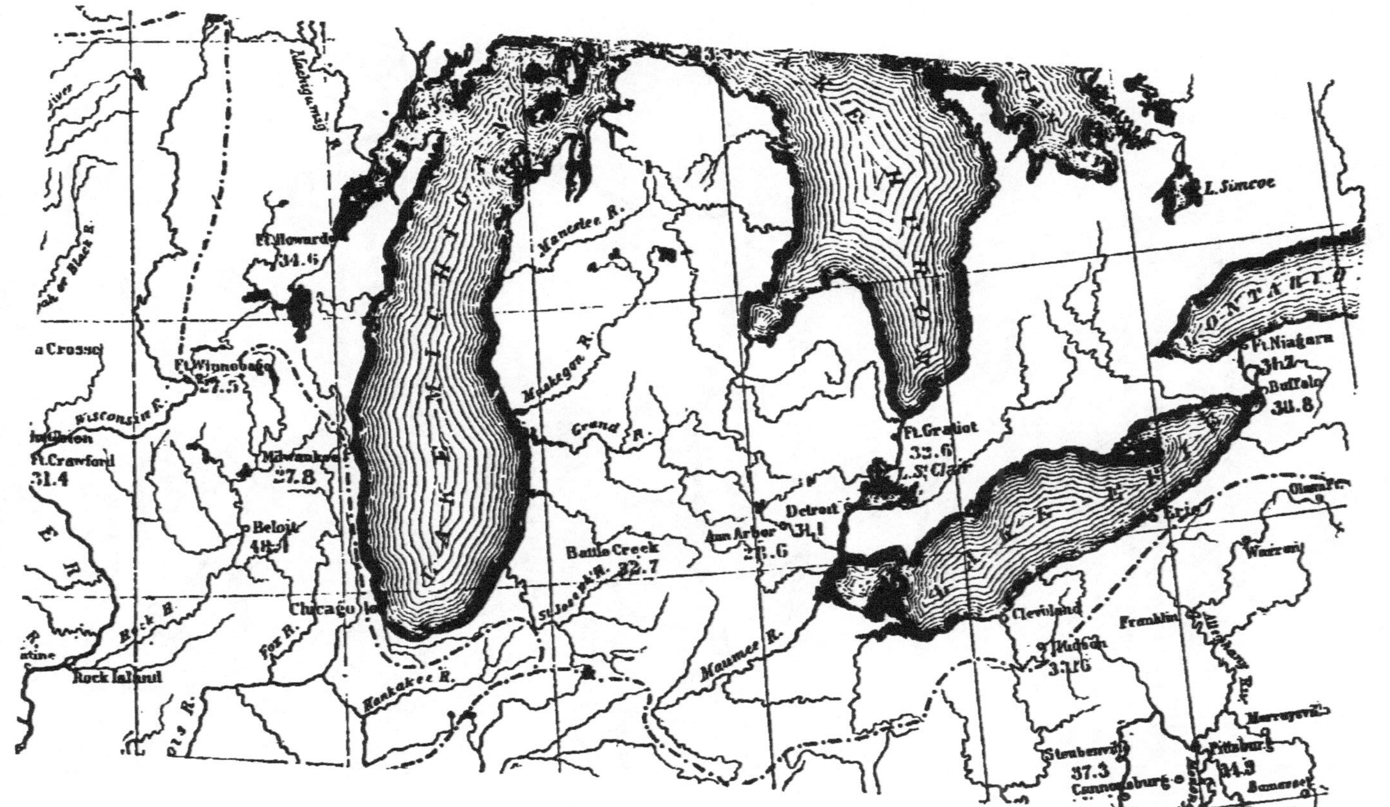

Ft. Howard
34.6
Ft. Winnebago
Wisconsin R.
Ft. Crawford
31.4
Milwaukee
27.8
Beloit
Chicago
Rock R.
Fox R.
Rock Island
Kankakee R.
Manistee R.
Muskegon R.
Grand R.
Battle Creek
32.7
Ann Arbor
Detroit
Maumee R.
Ft. Gratiot
L. Simcoe
Ft. Niagara
Buffalo
30.8
Erie
Cleveland
Franklin
Warren
Steubenville
37.3
Pittsburg

Kilistinons
Riuiere par ou lon ua aus
poualac a 120 lieues uers le couchant
Supe
Riuiere pour aller aus Nadoue a 60 lieues uers le couchant
Mission du S. Esprit
La pointe du St Esprit
Riuiere Nantounagan
Chemin aus Ilinois a 150 lieues uers le medy
Riuiere
La Colbertie ou Amerique Occidentale
Pierres sanguines
Riuiere diuine
Par une de ces grandes riuieres qui
De Louest et se dechargent dans la
Colbert, on trouuera passage pour entrer
vermeille, iay ueu un uillage qui nestoit
parterre dune nation qui a commerce auec
la Californie, si iestois arriué 2 iours plutost
en. estoient ueeues et auoient apporté 4 haches pour present
Riuiere par ou
Riuiere Colbert qui se decharge dans le sein Mexique

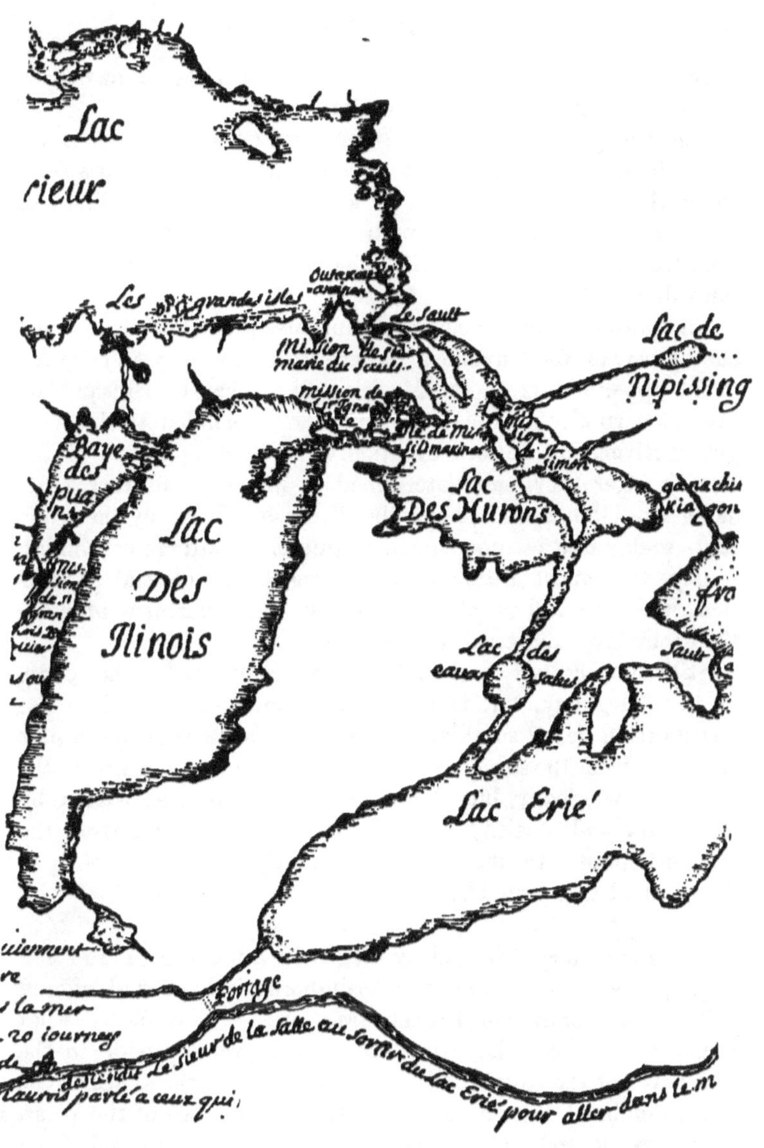

Lac
Les grandes isles
Le Sault
Lac de Nipissing
Baye des
Lac Des Ilinois
Lac Des Hurons
Lac
Lac Erie'
Portage
descendit Le Sieur de la Salle au sortir du Lac Erie' pour aller dans le m

beyond that there was about four hundred miles of navigable course for boats not drawing over three feet.

Another portage from the Maumee to the west branch of the Big Miami became later the traveled route of the traders from Pennsylvania and Virginia. A short carry from Sandusky to the Scioto became the warpath of the French Indians about the Detroit River against the Choctaws and flat-headed tribes towards Carolina.

The portages farther east came into use much later. A short one by way of the Cuyahoga (where Cleveland now stands) led to the upper waters of the Muskingum. That by Presqu' Isle (the modern city of Erie) and French Creek led to the Alleghany River, and became eventually the chief approach of the French after they had determined to maintain military posts along the Ohio and bar out the English. It is by the same route to-day that commerce and engineering skill are combining in hope to connect Pittsburgh, the great centre of coal production, with the Lakes, already coursed with steamers of more than four thousand tons displacement.

Still more easterly was that to Chautauqua Lake, the source of the Alleghany, but it proved too much of an incline for transporting heavy supplies. It was also quite possible to pass from the sources of the Genesee to the springs of the Alleghany, but the route was hardly used except by wanderers and stealthy war parties. The portages from the Iroquois country to the south were mainly of use in passing to the Susquehanna and Delaware.

Lake Ontario portages.

There is a story reported by Bégon in a memoir (1716) that as early as 1688 the Assiniboine Indians had offered to conduct a French traveler, De Noyen, by what seems to have been the Minnesota River, over a divide to the Red River of the North, and so to Lake Winnipeg. Thence, the memoir claimed, the way was open to the great Sea of the West, where people rode on horseback. The journey to and from would occupy, he said, five months. These are the earliest intimations of an overland discovery of the Pacific, by a definite

The Sea of the West.

NOTE. The map on the preceding pages shows the northern portages as understood at the time of Joliet's discoveries. From Marcel's *Reproductions*, following a map in the Archives of the Marine at Paris.

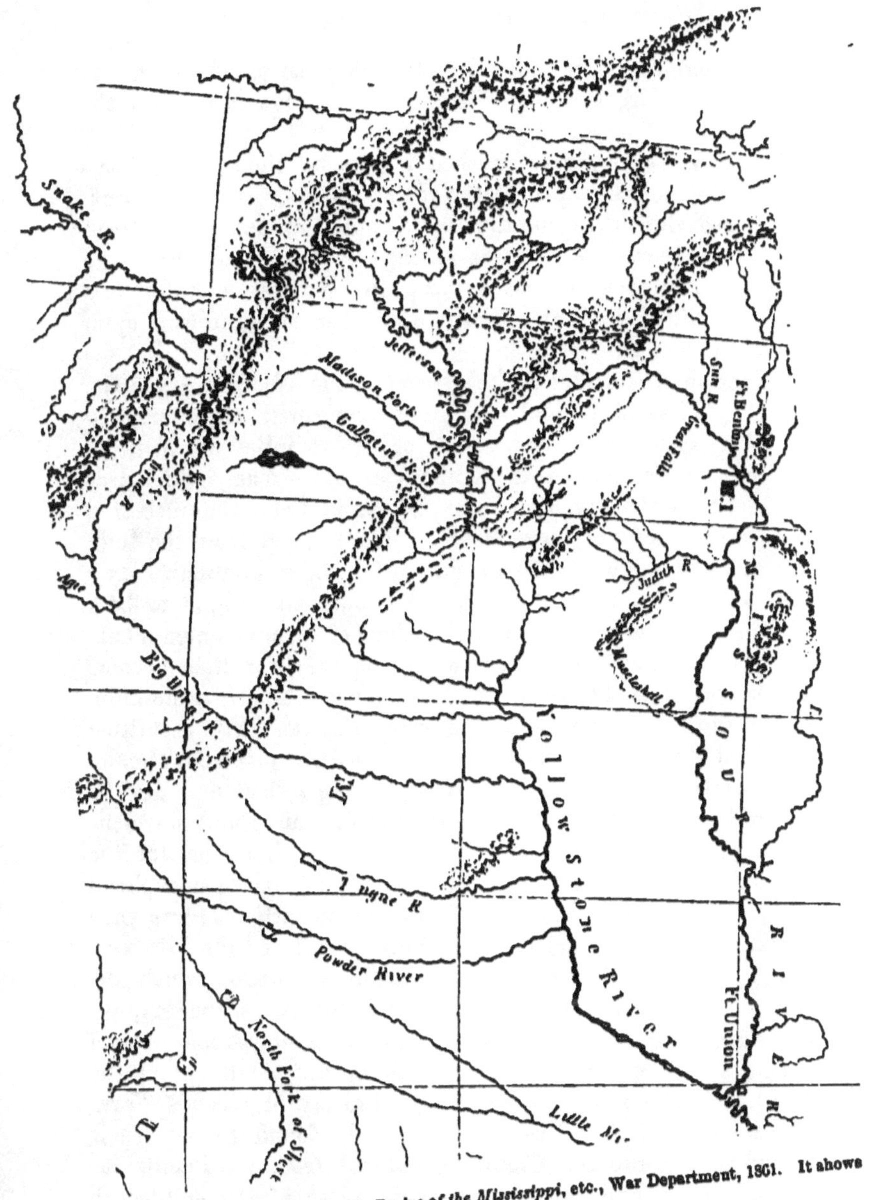

[From Humphreys and Abbot's *Basins of the Mississippi*, etc., War Department, 1861. It shows the divide between the Yellowstone River and Snake River.]

course, and the first indication of the passage which was to connect the Great Valley with the Mackenzie basin and the polar sea.

In 1695, Le Sueur established a post on the upper Mississippi, and acted as a pacificator of the Chippeways and Sioux. In his search at the same time for a copper mine on the Green River, — which was reached by the Minnesota, — he had, it is supposed, been the earliest to know this affluent of the Mississippi, when he bestowed upon it the name of St. Peter.

La Sueur, and St. Peter River.

When, in 1673, Marquette descended the Wisconsin and the Mississippi, and was going along with the current in clear water at a speed of twelve miles an hour, he noticed a great change in the body of the stream, which was produced by the much more rapid influx from the west of a great volume of eddying sediment. He learned from the Indians that this polluting stream was called the Pekitanoüi. At a later day, when the tribe of the Missouris was found to be a leading race among the fourteen nations of savages which inhabited the banks of this great river, it was easy for it to become better known as the Missouri, thus distinguishing it as an affluent of the Mississippi, when the volume of its current entitled it, rather than the Mississippi, to be called the principal stream. At this time Marquette indulged the hope that one day he might be permitted to ascend its turbid course and solve the great problem of the west. It was reserved, however, for the eighteenth century to begin the solution of that geographical riddle which was made clear in the nineteenth. It was then found that the springs of the Platte, which fed the Missouri, were adjacent to those of the Colorado, which debouched into the Gulf of California. Other explorers discovered that the sources of the Yellowstone opened portages to those of the Snake, while an upper affluent of the Missouri was contiguous to the headwaters of Clark's Fork. The Snake and this fork were ultimately found to pass their united waters into the Columbia, entered from the Pacific for the first time by a Boston ship at the close of the eighteenth century, and draining a country richer and larger than the combined area of the Atlantic seaboard commonwealths from Maine to Virginia.

The Missouri River, and its portages.

CHAPTER II.

IBERVILLE'S EXPEDITION.

1697–1700.

THE treaty of Ryswick, in April, 1697, left France in possession of the two great valleys of North America. Tonty was now at his Rock on the Illinois, a sort of privileged character in the valley, respected by Indian and white whenever they came within his influence. Whoever has followed the career of La Salle needs not to be told of the services of this faithful follower. It was well known how valorously and devotedly he had gone down the Mississippi, hoping to rescue his bewildered leader. A journal which Tonty had kept, falling into irresponsible hands, had only just been published in Paris, but there was so much of interjected error and foolish untruth in it that the hardy adventurer promptly disowned it. The publication, however, had served to increase his fame in France. Before this he had asked that he might be permitted to follow up the discoveries of La Salle at the mouth of the Great River and confirm its possession to the king, but the man of action was not yet thought to be needed.

Tonty.

In October, 1697, Louvigny preferred the same request, and held out the hope of invading Mexico successfully, from the Mississippi as a base, — a view of the river's usefulness that was not lost a few years later. In December, De Remonville argued in a *Mémoire* that the development of Louisiana was of great importance to France. He catalogued the variety of products which the country could be made to yield, — game, peltry, wine, silk, and hemp. The territory, he said, was rich in mines. Its oaks could more than supply the royal navy with masts. He pointed out that a colonizing expedition ought to be sent speedily, lest the English should gain possession in advance. Moreover, he added, a considerable military

Louisiana.

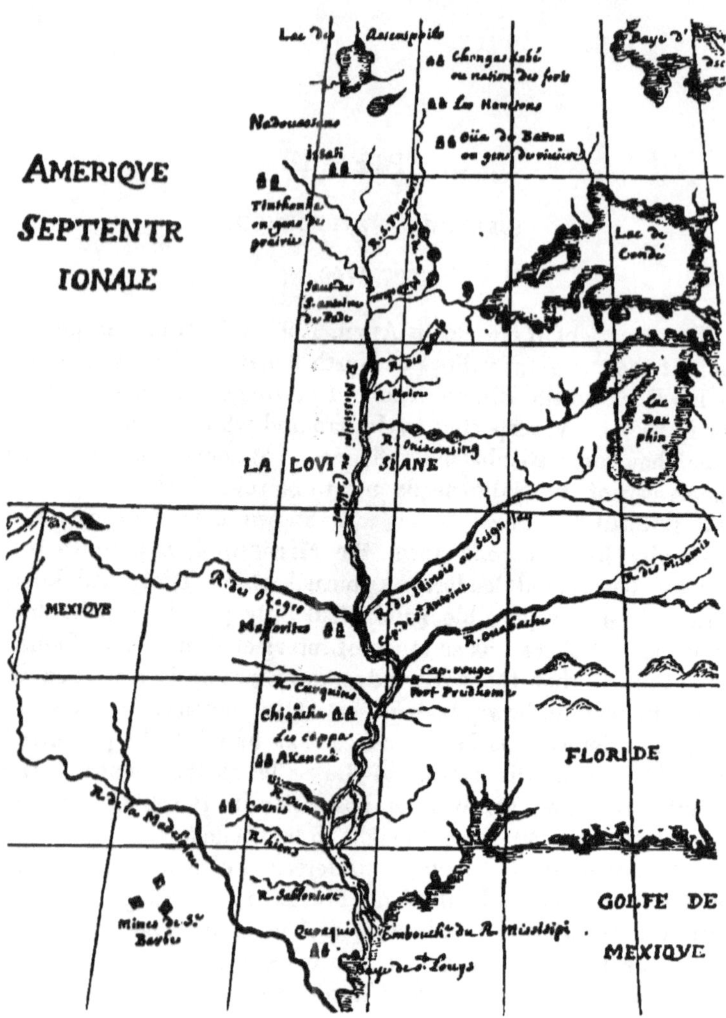

THE MISSISSIPPI.

[From a map in the Bibliothèque Nationale, given in Marcel's *Reproductions*. It was made by the Abbé Gentil and given to that library in 1713. It shows the early explorations of La Salle, and represents the knowledge previous to Iberville's voyage.]

force was necessary to protect the expedition from the English buccaneers, who infested the coast from New York to Florida. He adduced a rumor that the governor of Pennsylvania had already dispatched fifty men to settle on the Wabash (Ohio),

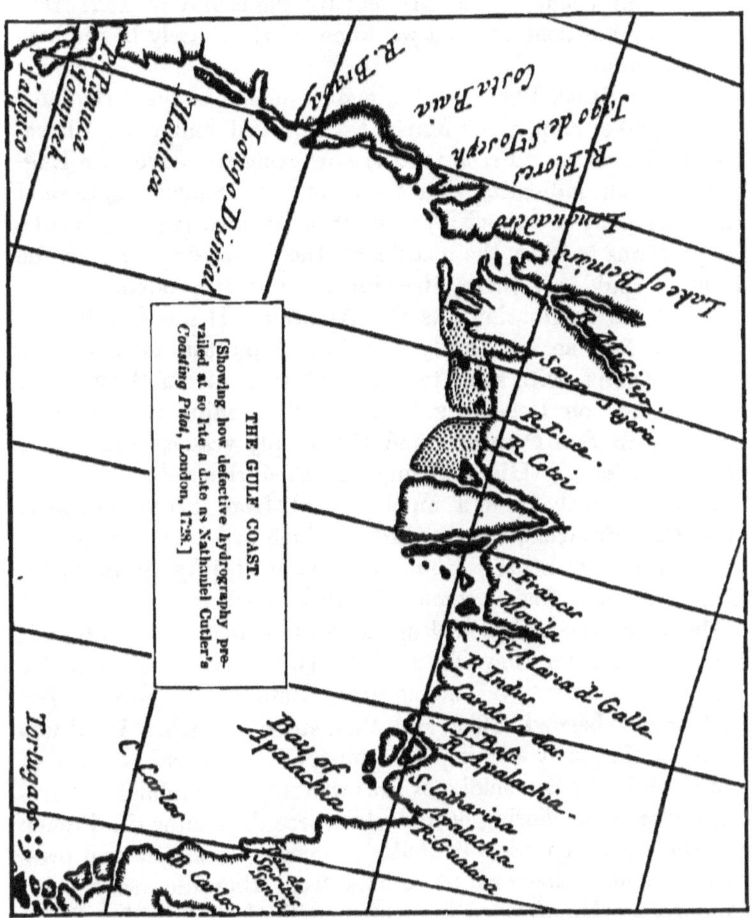

THE GULF COAST.

[Showing how defective hydrography prevailed at so late a date as Nathaniel Cutler's Coasting Pilot, London, 1728.]

and such an occupation could be but a distinct threat to the French control of the Mississippi.

This memoir was addressed to Pontchartrain, who as minister had already been importuned by Iberville, just now released from service in the north by the treaty of Ryswick. The urgency was great, and the des-

Pontchartrain and Iberville.

tined actor was restless. The government yielded, and Iberville gathered for the undertaking a company of two hundred emigrants, men, women, and children. It is from Penicault, a carpenter in the company, who kept a running account of events up to his leaving the colony in 1721, that we get a great deal of what we know of these early beginnings of Louisiana.

Penicault.

In June, 1698, Iberville obtained command of the "Badine," while another ship, the "Marin," was placed under the Chevalier de Surgères. Fresh reports now came from over the English Channel, indicating that their rivals were planning to send out a company of French Protestants. While the government's purpose was to seize the mouths of the Mississippi before the English could get there, Iberville thought it prudent to give out that his destination was the Amazon. It was October before he was ready to sail, and on the 24th his two ships, with some tenders, put to sea from Brest. Six weeks later, on December 4, the leading ships reached Cap François in San Domingo, and the supply vessels came safely in one by one. His company refreshed themselves, but not always prudently, and a number died from over-indulgence. Here the "François," having orders which had been sent ahead, joined the expedition. She was a ship of fifty guns, under Chateaumorand, and became a faithful escort.

Iberville sails.

Iberville, who had picked up some filibusters as recruits, left San Domingo on New Year's Day (January 1, 1699), under the piloting of a wild adventurer, Laurent de Graff. The fleet passed beyond Cuba and then steered north. Land was made in the early evening of January 23. It was a coast of white sand, and the smoke of fires was seen far inland. Turning west and anchoring each night, three days later the French saw the masts of vessels behind a protecting sand-spit, and presently a sloop came out to reconnoitre. Iberville was now off Pensacola. He avoided intercourse with the inquisitive Spaniards, and crawled away, still westerly, along the coast. On January 31, he was opposite Mobile Bay, but the weather was foul and he did not stop. Ten days later his ships glided under the lee of an island, which was later known as Ship Island.

Iberville soon started (February 27) in a boat towards the mainland, where he cautiously tried to open communication with the natives. He hoped to get guides from them to aid him in finding the Great River. Some wandering Bayagoulas, whom he encountered among the Biloxi Indians, told him of a great river farther west upon which their tribe lived.

IBERVILLE. [From Margry.]

There was fortunately among the French the priest, Anastase Douay, who had been a companion of La Salle. Moreover, Iberville himself was well informed of what La Salle, Membré, Tonty, and even Hennepin had said of the Mississippi, and counted on their descriptions as aids in identifying the stream.

Following the shore south and west, it was on March 2 that

Iberville entered a large river, and struggled up against its turbid flood. His range of vision was bounded by canebrakes and willows. As he went on, he began to doubt if it was the river which Hennepin, Joutel, and Tonty had known. Wherever he encamped he marked a tree with the cross. The youthful Bienville, a younger brother of Iberville, usually pushed his boat ahead of the rest. They saw fires in the distance, and occasionally got a sight of the neighboring bayous. Whatever Indians were seen possessed canoes fleet enough to escape, but one day a savage was cajoled into coming to them to receive gifts. This enticed others, with whom the French traded trinkets for meat. Whenever they fired a cannon, the amazed natives fell as if struck.

The Mississippi found.

The French reached the spot where New Orleans was later built, and here discovered the portage which led to inner waters, by which they could reach their ships. Leaving the examination of this for another occasion, they passed on and landed among the Bayagoulas, who lifted the peaceful calumet as the strangers approached. With this tribe they feasted, and presents were distributed. Its chief wore a serge cloak, which he said had been given to him by Tonty. This was the first incident which went far to convince them that they were at last stemming the current of the Mississippi. They got some fowl from the Indians, and were told that the original stock came from the shores of the western ocean. To increase their confidence in their identification of the river, they turned to the text of Hennepin, but failing to find all that this priest said of the river, they grew more and more satisfied that the Recollect was the liar which Europe was inclined to believe him.

Site of New Orleans.

Some of the narratives of those who had been before them on the river mentioned the villages of the Houmas, and they actually came to one of these. They found a palisaded camp. Iberville says that it had a sort of temple, built of upright logs, and smoothed with mud in the chinks. A conical roof made of canes was covered with painted figures. They counted about two hundred cabins around the temple, and saw a glass bottle which Tonty had left there. The French again raised a cross on the river-bank, and hung up the royal arms.

The Houmas.

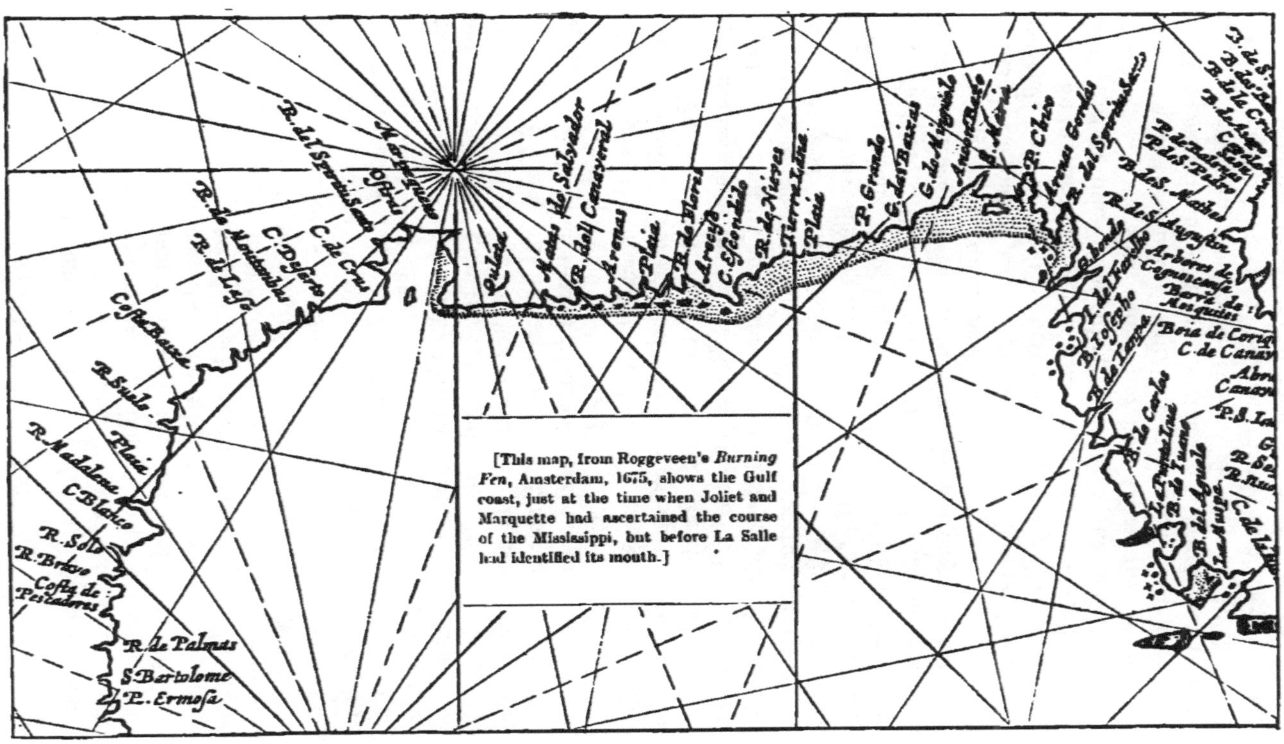

[This map, from Roggeveen's *Burning Fen*, Amsterdam, 1675, shows the Gulf coast, just at the time when Joliet and Marquette had ascertained the course of the Mississippi, but before La Salle had identified its mouth.]

Some of the Houmas went along with the French as guides. They told Iberville that the Ascantia, a stream on the right, could be followed to the sea. At one place on the shore was a red-tree trunk, ornamented with the heads of fish and bear, indicating, it was said, the bounds between the Houmas and the Tonicas. Our modern Baton Rouge marks the spot. They were put to great labor in turning the bends against the current, and where they could they struck across the bayous. Their Bayagoula chieftain acted as an intercessor when they came to a new village, to which they usually announced their approach by the discharge of a gun. In some of these native hamlets they were entertained by chanting choirs and dancing-girls; in all they were feasted. In their turn the French distributed presents. Sometimes gifts of corn and meat were made on the part of the tribes. They heard of a people called the Quinipissas, and Tonty was known to have been among such a tribe.

Red River.

A Taensas Indian spoke of a large affluent on the left, which proved to be the Red River. The journal of Membré gave the order of the tribes to be encountered, but they found it difficult to make their observations agree with it. Presently they learned that an Indian chief, who dwelt somewhere near the mouth of the Great River, possessed a letter, intrusted to him by Tonty a good many years before, with injunctions to give it to a Frenchman who was expected to enter the river. It was in fact the letter, dated April 20, 1686, which

Tonty's letter.

Tonty, turning back from the Gulf after his failure to find his chief, but hoping that La Salle might yet appear, had left with the natives. If this letter could be found, or its existence proved, there would be scarcely a doubt that the Mississippi was discovered.

Membré's journal seemed to indicate that he and Tonty had descended one of two channels where the river divided. They could find no such parting of the stream, and the Indians said there was no other descending river than the one they were following. With this doubt puzzling them, the boats were turned with the current, and they were soon gliding on in a way that made their progress a recreation. When they reached

The Ascantia or Iberville River.

what in prehistoric times was very likely the main channel of the river, but was now a diverging outlet, already indicated to them on their way up as the

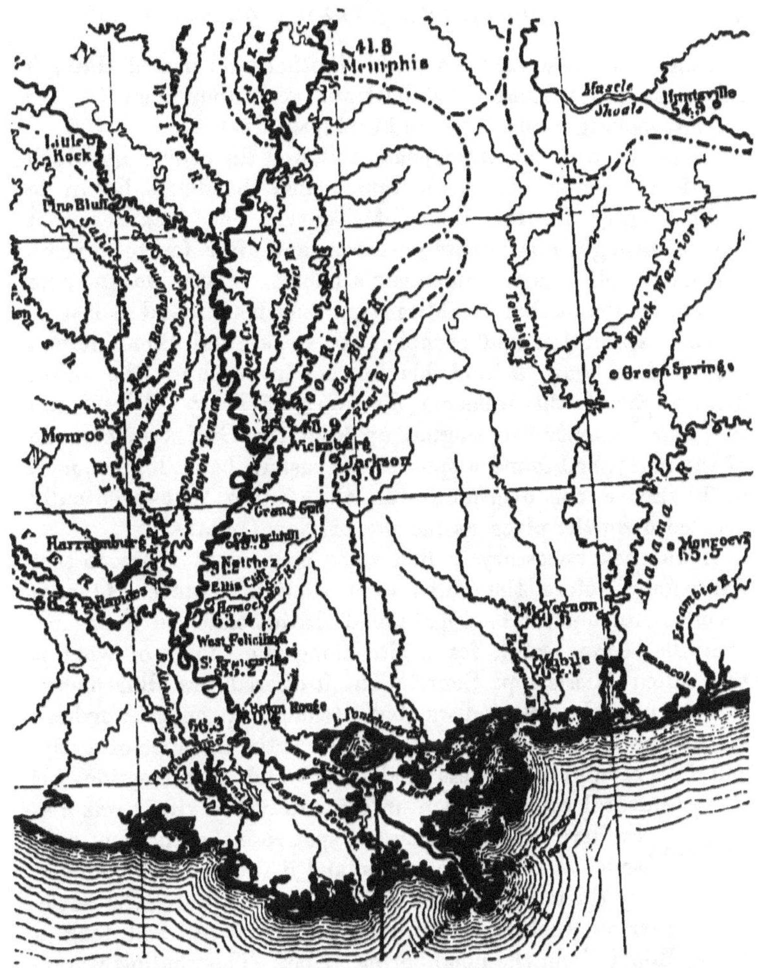

[From Humphreys and Abbot's *Basins of the Mississippi*, etc., War Department, 1861. It shows the lower Mississippi and the Gulf coast. The water-shed of the rivers flowing into the Gulf east of the Mississippi is bounded by a dotted line.]

Ascantia, Iberville parted with his brother, and passed through this passage to Lake Pontchartrain, with four men in two canoes, seeking a new route to his ships.

Bienville, with the other boats, followed the course by which they had ascended, and as he approached the deltas began to make inquiry for the letter of Tonty. The promise of a hatchet brought forward its possessor, and after fourteen years the paper fell into a Frenchman's hands. There was now no reasonable doubt that the Mississippi had been found at last.

This exploration had occupied six weeks, and Bienville was only a few hours behind his brother in reaching the ships. They reported the welcome discovery of Tonty's letter, and that about twenty-five leagues up from the Gulf, Sauvole, one of the party, had found a spot on the eastern bank, high enough to be above the overflow, — an observation that eventually decided upon the place as the site of New Orleans.

It was now necessary to find some convenient shore to seat the colony before the ships went back to France. One of them, Chateaumorand's frigate, had already sailed in February. Iberville began search for a site along the shores of what is now called Mississippi Sound; but it offered few allurements, and the place he selected was but a sand-heap on the northern side of the sound. It was a peninsula at the entrance of a bay, and its prevailing aridness could have had no attractions for an agricultural colony, which unfortunately Iberville's was not.

Fort Maurepas at Biloxi.

So here in an ungenerous spot rose the nine-foot palisades of Fort Maurepas, and it was soon surrounded by the temporary huts of the little colony. The settlement, garrison included, numbered ninety souls, and took a name, Biloxi, from the neighboring tribe. The shallow waters of the sound prevented the near approach of the ships, and it proved a weary task to ferry the guns, forges, and the heavy stores a long distance from the vessels to the shore. There were a few patches of poor soil where they could plant beans and grain; but their thoughts were much more upon the mines to the westward, of which some Spanish deserters had already told them.

When the fort and habitations approached completion, Iberville and Surgères prepared to depart. It was arranged that Sauvole should be left in command. Bienville was to be his deputy. This ardent fellow, though but eighteen years of age, had already shown the courage which was yet to face years of trial in Louisiana. The chief and his associates left the fort on May 2, 1699, and proceeding to Ship Island, on the next day, sailed thence. During the voyage, Iberville worked on a report of his operations, to be presented to Pontchartrain, and dated it at Rochefort after his arrival July 3. He took occasion in it to berate "the Recollect [Hennepin] whose lying story had deceived every one. Our sufferings and lack of success," he adds, "were owing to the time we spent in fruitless search for things which had no existence but in his imagination."

Iberville's return and report.

Meanwhile, life at Biloxi was far from pleasant. The heat and blinding reflection from the sand were intolerable. The worms were ruining their boats. The water was nauseating. Famine looked at them in a ghastly way, and vessels sent to San Domingo for supplies were still absent. With gloomy prospects before them, they were startled on July 1 to see some strange canoes. They brought nearly a score of other mouths to consume their fast decreasing supplies. The visitors were some Canadians who had accompanied two priests, Montigny and Davion. These fathers, with a third, St. Cosme, had entered the Illinois country from the Lakes the preceding year, and had come down the Mississippi under the escort of Tonty. St. Cosme tells us how helpful this faithful friend, "loved by all the bushrangers," had been to them. He adds that to have Tonty with them was a sure way to escape insults from the Indians. It shows how the Iroquois were terrorizing the shores of Lake Michigan at this time, when the missionary says that his party made a long detour to avoid them, while they were also obliged to take the Chicago portage, because the Foxes were rendering that by Green Bay unsafe.

Canadians find them.

Tonty had parted with his friends near the mouth of the Arkansas River, and returned to his Rock, in the previous December. Since then the priests had been on the lower Mississippi, ministering to the Taensas and Tonicas, and from them had heard of Iberville's arrival in the river. There was now for the much-tried colony a hope that the news of their coming would yet reach Tonty and the French of the upper valley.

Their intercourse with the natives at Biloxi was now getting upon something like a friendly footing; but there was a source of uneasiness when they learned that in a recent attack by the Chickasaws upon their savage neighbors these dreaded warriors had been led by white men. It showed

Dangerous neighbors.

COXE'S MAP,

them that the English, probably from Carolina, were securing the country to the north. Other signs of dangerous rivals soon followed. Bienville had found it not a long march to the east to reconnoitre the Spaniards at Pensacola. Later in August, he started west across Lake Pontchartrain to the Mississippi.

Leaving the Ascantia, he turned down the stream, and on September 15 met an English ship of twelve or fifteen guns. It was at a bend of the river known to this day as the English Turn. Bienville boarded the stranger, and found the commander — Barr or Bank, for the statements

Bienville finds English on the Mississippi.

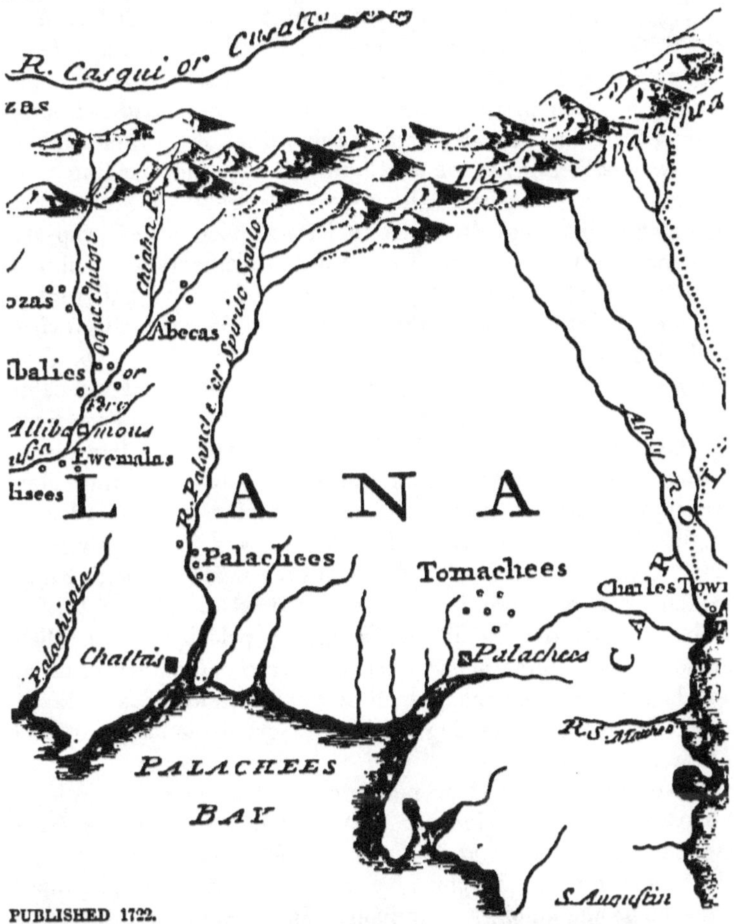

PUBLISHED 1722.

are confused — one whom Bienville had encountered in Hudson's Bay. The Englishman said he was searching for the Mississippi. It does not seem to be satisfactorily shown that the usual story is true, in which Bienville is represented as deceiving the visitor by telling him that the Mississippi was farther to the west. The English captain was not over urgent for his rights, and yielded to the French claim of prior possession, though not without intimating that he might return later.

The occasion of this English visit is now to be accounted for. Heath's and Coxe's grant. There had been a royal grant to Sir Robert Heath in 1627, covering a stretch of the Carolina coast from 31° to 36° north latitude, and extending westward under the sea-to-sea principle for which the English contended. Doctor Daniel Coxe had recently bought this patent of "Carolana," — as it was called in honor of Charles I., — understanding that it did not cover within those parallels what the Spaniards occupied at St. Augustine and in New Mexico. The property had come to Coxe directly from Lord Maltravers, the original purchaser from Heath. A year before, 1698, Coxe had sent a Colonel Welch to explore the country, and it was claimed that he had traveled from Charleston to the Mississippi. We find his route laid down on English maps, and a son of Coxe, in 1722, published journals which were alleged to have been kept by those who made these inland trips. This publication was at a time when the younger Coxe was seeking to make the country known, and was trying to induce immigration in order to render his heritage profitable. These, and other things in this "Carolana" book of 1722, have been much doubted, being looked upon as mere inventions contrived to bolster Coxe's claim against the French by asserting priority for English explorations. Some such pretensions were palpable invention, as when, to antedate the French occupation under La Salle, it was claimed that some English had traversed the length of the Mississippi in 1676.

Coxe, the father, had proposed to found a commonwealth on his patent, and had talked of a stock company to back it with eight thousand shares at five pounds each. He sought at the same time to catch the pious by an avowed intention to propagate the gospel among the Indians. In 1698, he had fitted out two armed ships, which took a company of French Huguenots and some English gentlemen, with the alleged object of settling

NOTE. The opposite map is from Mitchell's *Map of the British Colonies* (1755). It shows the westerly part of the supposed route of Colonel Welch through the Chickasaw country to the Mississippi. The route leaves Charleston, S. C., crosses the Savannah at Fort Moore (Augusta), and extends to the west.

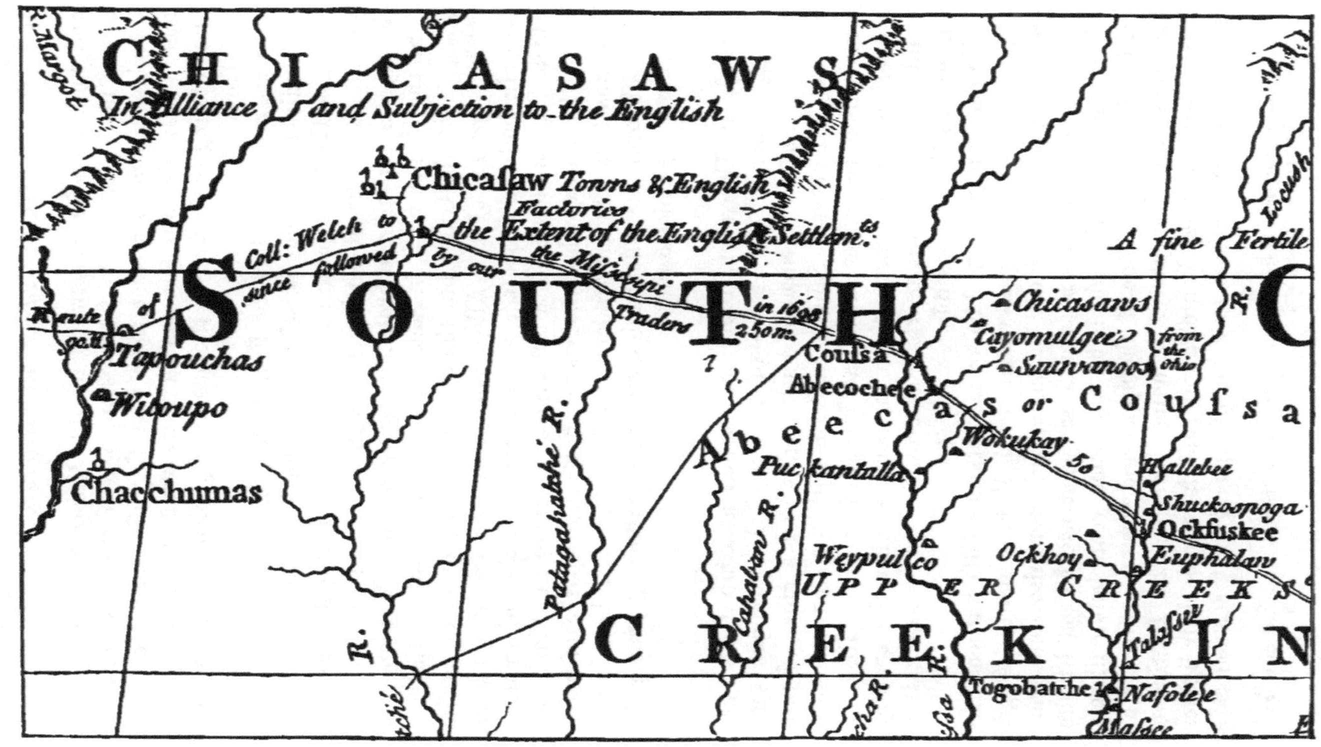

R. Margot
CHICASAWS
In Alliance and Subjection to the English
Chicasaw Towns & English Factories
Coll: Welch to the Extent of the English Settlem.ts the Missisipi in 1698
since followed by our Traders 250m.
Route of
Tapouchas
Witoupo
Chacchumas
SOUTH
A fine Fertile
Locush
Chicasaws
Cayomulgee
Sauvanoos
from the Ohio
R.
Coufsa
Abecochee
Abeecas or Coufsa
Wokukay 50
Puckantalla
Patagahatche R.
Cahaban R.
R.
Hallebee
Shuckospoga
Ockfuskee
Euphalaw
Weypulco
Ockhoy
UPPER CREEKS
CREEK IN
Talasee
Togobatche
Nafolee
Masaee

and building a fort somewhere on the Mississippi. The expedition made its way to Charleston, where the new colonists found so much to attract them that they did not proceed farther. A single ship, however, actually went ahead to explore, and entering the river was the one met by Bienville at the English Turn.

It seemed to all but the French that this stray ship was the first really ocean-going vessel to enter the Great River from the sea. The English captain never carried out his threat to return, and all the plans of settlement which Coxe had formed with the royal approval were broken up by the death of William III.

English traders.

So the French were, in fact, without a contestant on the side of the Gulf; but the future necessity of blocking the passes of the Alleghanies, to check the English as La Salle had contemplated, was prefigured in the information which Davion imparted to the anxious company at Biloxi, and which the Pascagoulas who visited Fort Maurepas confirmed. This was that English traders had for some time been using the trails over the Alleghanies, and were trafficking among the Choctaws and Chickasaws.

Iberville's arrival.

Early in December, 1699, the cannon at Ship Island announced the return of Iberville. He brought with him sixty Canadian bushrangers and a store of provisions. He cheered Sauvole and Bienville with new commissions which the government had intrusted to him. Iberville himself was under instructions to discover what the country could furnish in furs, pearls, and ores, and to ascertain if a culture of silk were possible.

St. Denis and Le Sueur.

He had brought with him an adventurous fellow, Juchereau de St. Denis, of whom we shall hear more. A geologist, Le Sueur by name, had been also sent over, and it was his mission to see what use he could make of the "green earth" which he had some years before discovered while exploring one of the upper and western affluents of the Mississippi. A party, including Iberville and Le Sueur, started towards Lake Pontchartrain, and here took their lighter boats across the morass to a bit of upland that seemed safe

NOTE. The opposite map is from Danville's *Carte de la Louisiane*, 1732–1752, showing the position of the Bayagoulas, Houmas, etc.

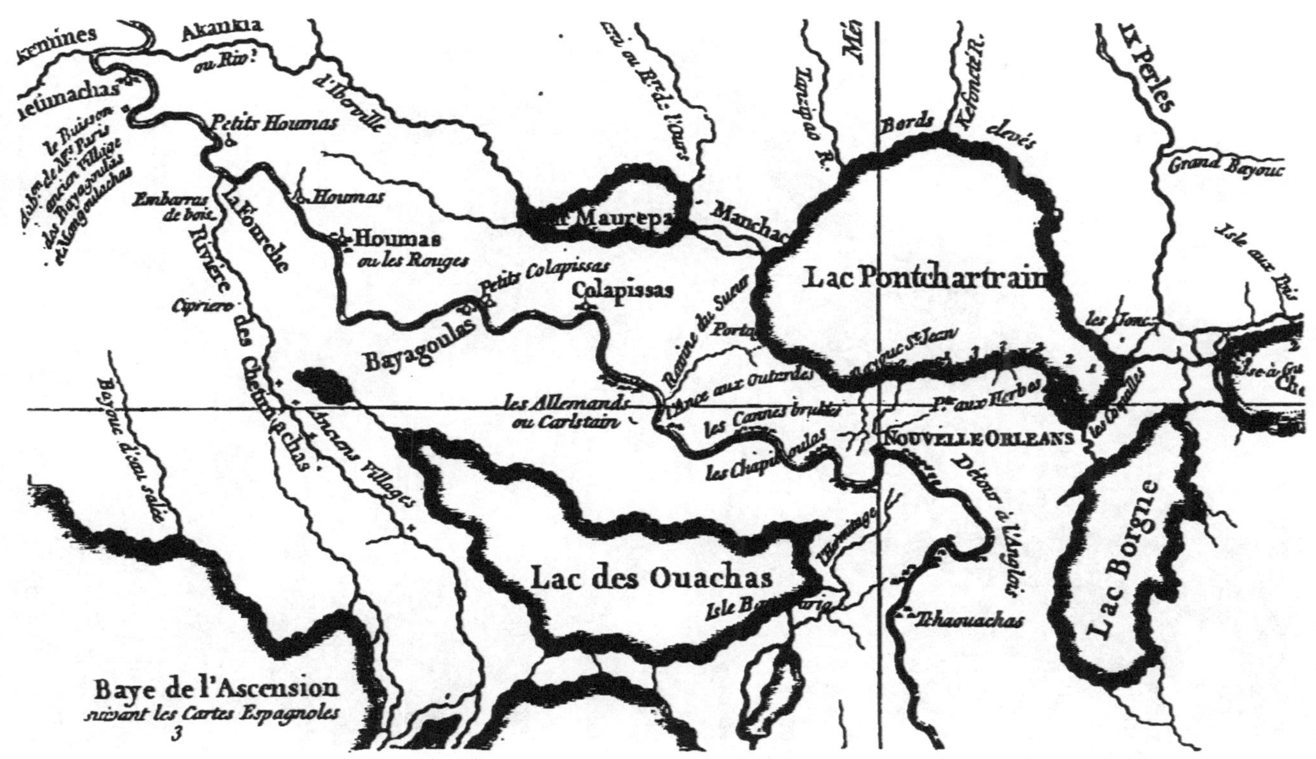

Akankia
ou Riv?
Petits Houmas
d'Iberville
Embarras de bois
La Fourche
Houmas
Houmas ou les Rouges
Riviére des Chetimachas
Cipriere
Petits Colapissas
Colapissas
Bayagoulas
Manchac
Lac Pontchartrain
Bords
Kefoncté R.
elevés
Tanzipao R.
Grand Bayouc
Isle aux Pois
les Joncs
Bayouc St. Jean
Portage
Ravine du Sueur
l'Ance aux Outardes
les Allemands ou Carlstain
les Cannes brulées
les Chapitoulas
Pte. aux Herbes
NOUVELLE ORLEANS
les Cocquilles
Détour à l'Anglois
Lac Borgne
Anciens Villages
Bayouc d'eau salée
Lac des Ouachas
l'Hermitage
Tchaouachas
Baye de l'Ascension
suivant les Cartes Espagnoles
3

[From Jefferys' *Course of the Mississippi River from Bayagoulas to the Sea*, 1759, showing the site of Fort La Boulaye and the first settlement on the river.]

HOMANN, 1720(?).

[Showing the route of Tonty from the Chickasaw country.]

from overflow. The episode of the English ship and the stories of English traders rendered it necessary to be prepared against attempts to eject them, and on this higher land Iberville determined to erect a fort. It was about fifty-four miles from the Gulf, and the site is marked on later maps.

Fort on the Mississippi.

It was now January, 1700, and when the palisades were up, Bienville was put in command. In February, while they were still at work on the fort, they were surprised by the appearance of Henri de Tonty, who came with boats loaded with peltry and manned by Canadian boatmen. He had left his Rock on the Illinois, and had stopped on the way to trade with the Arkansas Indians.

Tonty appears.

While the tidings which Tonty brought were still fresh, Le Sueur, with twenty men and some Indian guides, started to find his mines of green earth. He was no stranger in the country at the north, having spent six or seven years among the Sioux. During this period he had been a strong advocate of measures to frustrate the English attempts at opening trade along the Ohio. He had taken some chiefs of this distant nation to Quebec, and Frontenac had formally placed the Dacotah tribes under French protection.

Le Sueur's expedition.

Concerning the expedition of which Le Sueur was now in charge we have a good account in Penicault's narrative, which is given more consecutively by Margry than in the uncertain English version by French, and this may be supplemented by the memoir of the Chevalier de Beaurain, also given in Margry.

There was a new cause for disquiet when the party reaching the Arkansas found a Carolina trader at work. In August, they were at Lake Pepin, and saw the stockade built a few years before by Nicolas Perrot left standing for chance traders to occupy. In September, they had passed the Falls of St. Anthony and entered the St. Peter, now the Minnesota, River. Canoeing into one of its tributaries, the Blue Earth or Green River, as it was indiscriminately called, at a point a little above 44° north latitude, as he supposed it, Le Sueur built a stockade, and called it after the royal farmer-general, Fort l'Huillier. This was in October, 1701.

Slaughtering buffalo and freezing the flesh, Le Sueur's men began to lay in provisions. There was need of it, for seven

Canadian traders soon joined them and spent the winter, depending on Le Sueur's stores. The mine they had sought was close by, and they began to work it. Wandering Sioux passed, and they accumulated some skins by barter.

When Callières at Quebec heard of these doings of Le Sueur,

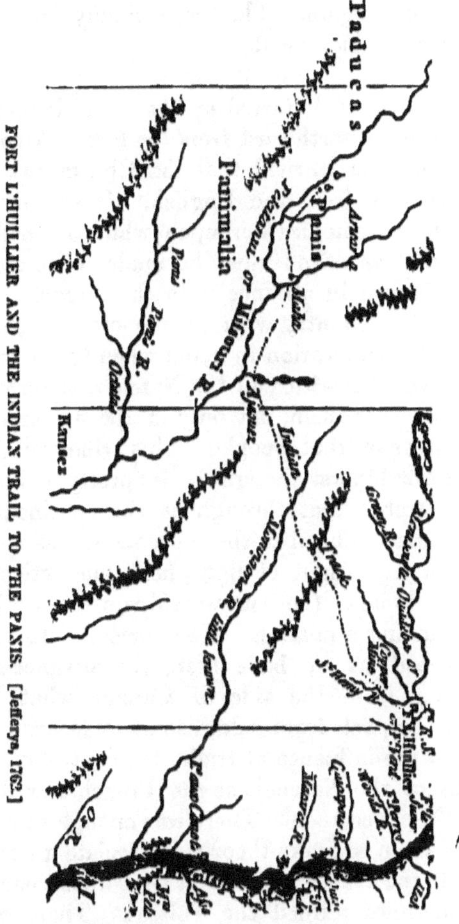

FORT L'HUILLIER AND THE INDIAN TRAIL TO THE PANIS. [Jefferys, 1762.]

by which the trade of the far west was diverted to the Mississippi, he wrote complainingly to the ministry, and asked what was to become of poor Canada if such a course was to be permitted. It was hard, if not impossible, to enforce edicts in the wilderness, and, as Tonty's ventures had shown, trade had already indicated its future channels.

In May, 1701, Le Sueur, loading his canoes with a portion of the green earth which he had dug out, — about four thousand pounds, — descended to the lower stations, leaving a garrison to hold the fort. Misfortune overtook him, and he never saw his fort, or his mine again. The Sioux finally drove off his men, and the fort was abandoned.

After Le Sueur had started up the river, Iberville proceeded leisurely northward from his fort. Among the Bayagoulas he learned that the Chickasaws were getting firearms from the English. It was more than ever apparent, if the colonization upon which he had started was to succeed, that an effort must be made to combine the tribes of the Mississippi in alliance with the French. The passing through the low country with its monotonous canebrakes had little exhilaration in it, but when the party reached the elevated territory of the Natchez, there were new sensations in store for them, not only in the air and scenery, but in the character of that people. This tribe were, perhaps, distinctly sun-worshipers, though it is pretty evident from the modern researches that throughout the continent all Indians were accustomed to bend to the supreme orb, as recent scientists turn to it for the origin of light, heat, magnetism, and electricity. Here, among the sun-worshipers, Iberville found St. Cosme conducting a mission. This priest, with Montigny and Davion, formed, as we have seen, the advance-guard of the church, doing from the side of Canada what Iberville was hoping to accomplish from below, so as to secure by the church, as well as by the influence of trade, the control of the valley.

Iberville ascends the Mississippi.

The Natchez.

The rites of the Natchez, as the French saw them, both attracted and repelled them. There was enough of a sort of mock grandeur in them to make theorists associate these children of the sun with the Aztecs, and even with those early peoples of Mexico sometimes termed the Toltecs. There was the same constructive energy in raising earth mounds for their buildings which the native American showed almost everywhere. This

NOTE. The opposite map, from the Bibliothèque Nationale at Paris, is given in Marcel's *Reproductions*, No. 17. It shows results of the explorations of La Salle, corrected by those of Iberville.

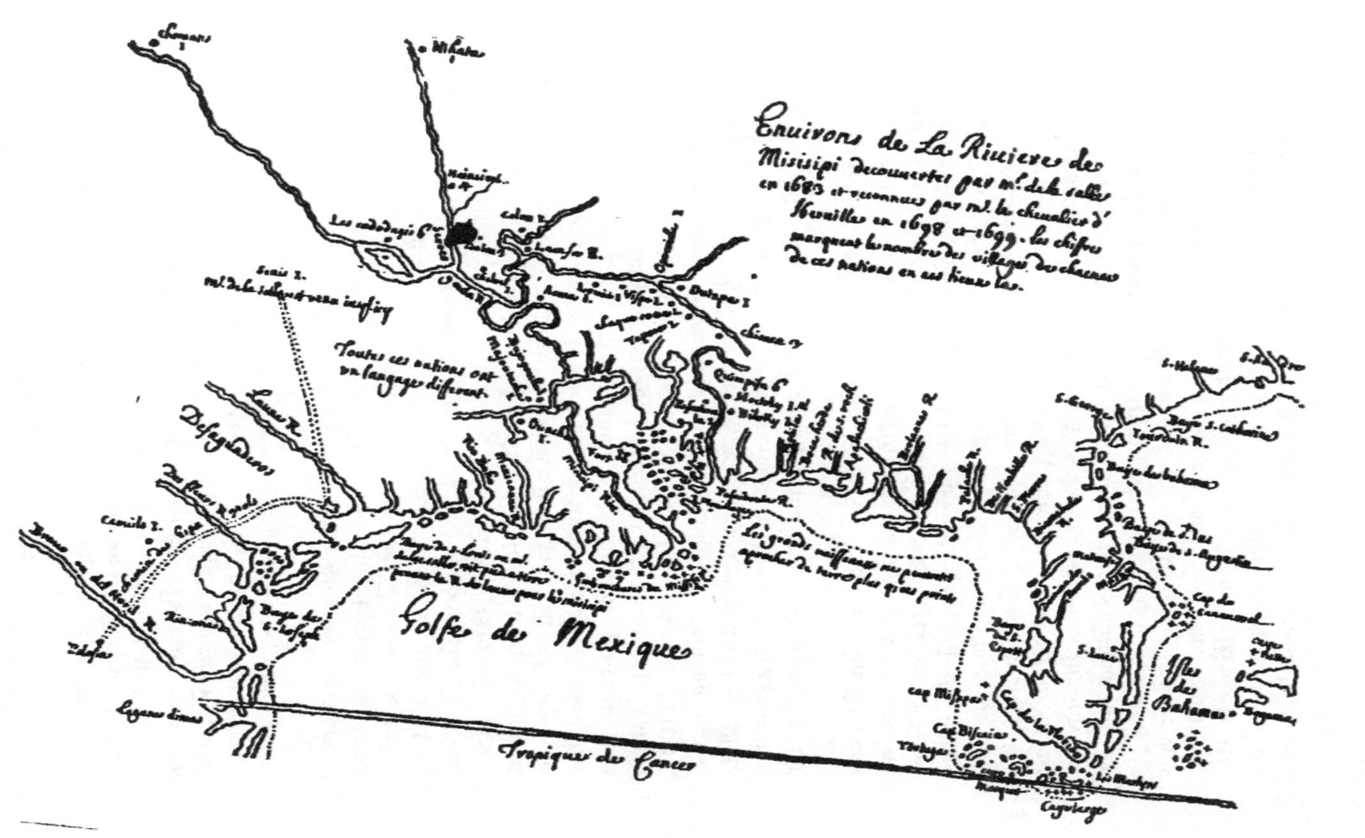
Enuirons de La Riuiere des
Misisipi decouuertes par ml. dela salle
en 1683 et reconnues par ml. le cheualier d'
Iberuille en 1698 et 1699. les chifres
marquent le nombre des villages de chacunes
de ces nations en ces lieux la.
Toutes ces nations ont
vn langage different.
Golfe de Mexique
Tropique du Cancer
Les grands vaisseaux ne peuuent
aprocher de terre plus que ce point
Isles
des
Bahamas
Desaguadero
Apalachicoli
Bocalanes R.
Cap de Canaueral
Cayo largo
Los Martyres
Tortugas
Cap Bisçaia
Baye de S. Catherine
S. George
Lauaca R.

has influenced some ethnologists of a later day to trace a connection for them with the so-called mound-builders. Their government had some features which induced a belief in the despotism of their headmen, but American Indians were as much committee-ridden as the American people are to-day; and it is doubtful if their polity varied from that of the rest of the aborigines of the continent in giving a kind of representative character to their civil control.

Montigny, whose visit to Biloxi has been already mentioned, had accompanied St. Cosme to this region and was conducting a mission among the Taensas, a tribe upon one of that link of lakes which lay just west of the Mississippi. While Bienville stayed among the Natchez to prepare an expedition for the Red River, Iberville made Montigny a hurried visit. On his return, he found Bienville had his party well organized. Tonty and St. Denis were to accompany him, and the chief object of the undertaking was to reconnoitre the Spanish posts in that direction, for as they understood the Indians, these rivals were established up the Red River. It was now March (1700). The country being naturally swampy and the spring not a favorable season, they returned without accomplishing their purpose. They went apparently about a hundred leagues beyond the Natchitoches, the leading tribe upon the lower parts of the Red River.

Montigny and the Taensas.

Bienville on the Red River.

Tonty soon left his new friends, to go back to the Tonicas with presents. It was now agreed that Tonty and Davion should undertake to keep the Indians on the upper river from forming an English alliance, while Iberville guarded the lower river with a similar purpose. There was need of precipitate action at the north, for the English were becoming active, since Robert Livingston was striving to bring about the occupation of Detroit as a vantage-ground for forcing a peace between the Iroquois and the western Indians, and in that way to bring them into support of the English schemes.

The Indians at the north.

In the Illinois country the dread of the Iroquois had driven the mission, where Father Pinet had been working, from the old Kaskaskia on the Illinois River to the site of the modern town of that name on the peninsula between the Kaskaskia River and the Mississippi, and two miles away

Kaskaskia mission.

from the latter river. This transference, made under Jacques Gravier and Gabriel Marest, had probably been accomplished in the autumn of 1700. The mission thus became one of the earliest permanent settlements near the banks of the Great River, within easy support of the increasing traffic of the French up and down the stream. This

Traffic on the Mississippi.

BIENVILLE. [From Margry.]

traffic was soon to grow perceptibly under the policy which Callières, the governor of Canada, was pursuing in consequence of orders from France; namely, to diminish the number of posts in the western country, so as to avoid the cost of garrisons. It was thought that as a result the peltry would be taken down the Lakes to Montreal. As it turned out, the injunction worked quite as much to the advantage of the new trade springing up along the Mississippi, since the bushrangers, pursuing a contraband trade with the Indians, better escaped police observations by carrying their skins down the Mississippi. All this soon improved the prospects of the new Louisiana colony.

Source of the Mississippi.

It was about this time, also, that Du Charleville, a kinsman of Bienville, sought, as we learn from Le Page du Pratz, to extend trade connections farther to the north by following up the Mississippi to its source. The story indicates that, leaving the Illinois, he went up to the Falls of St. Anthony and a hundred leagues beyond. Here he met a party of Sioux hunters, who had some reason for telling him that the distance from the falls to the source was equal to that from the falls to the sea. The exaggeration discouraged him, and the springs of the Great River were for a long period to remain unknown.

The Iroquois.

At the source of the Ohio, the western outposts of the Iroquois Confederacy were held by the Senecas, mainly in the French interests, while the English supremacy was still maintained among the eastern portion of the league, nearer Albany. These remoter Indians had, in the summer of 1700, been induced through French agency to make peace with the western tribes, not quite in the spirit of Livingston's project, and through this conciliation there was to be an exchange of prisoners. This bore hard on the Iroquois, as their incessant wars had depleted their fighting force, which they had sought to replenish by the adoption of these same prisoners. The result was that the exchange was unequal, since the confederates could only produce six warriors whom they had not adopted against the much greater number brought down to Montreal by the western tribes. Furthermore, the conference gave Callières the opportunity which he desired of extolling French faith and denouncing English perfidy, and he made the most of it. He had good abettors in the Jesuits, for whom the way was now clear to settle in the Iroquois country. It was a question how long the Canadian governor could maintain the hold upon the confederates which he flattered himself he had now acquired.

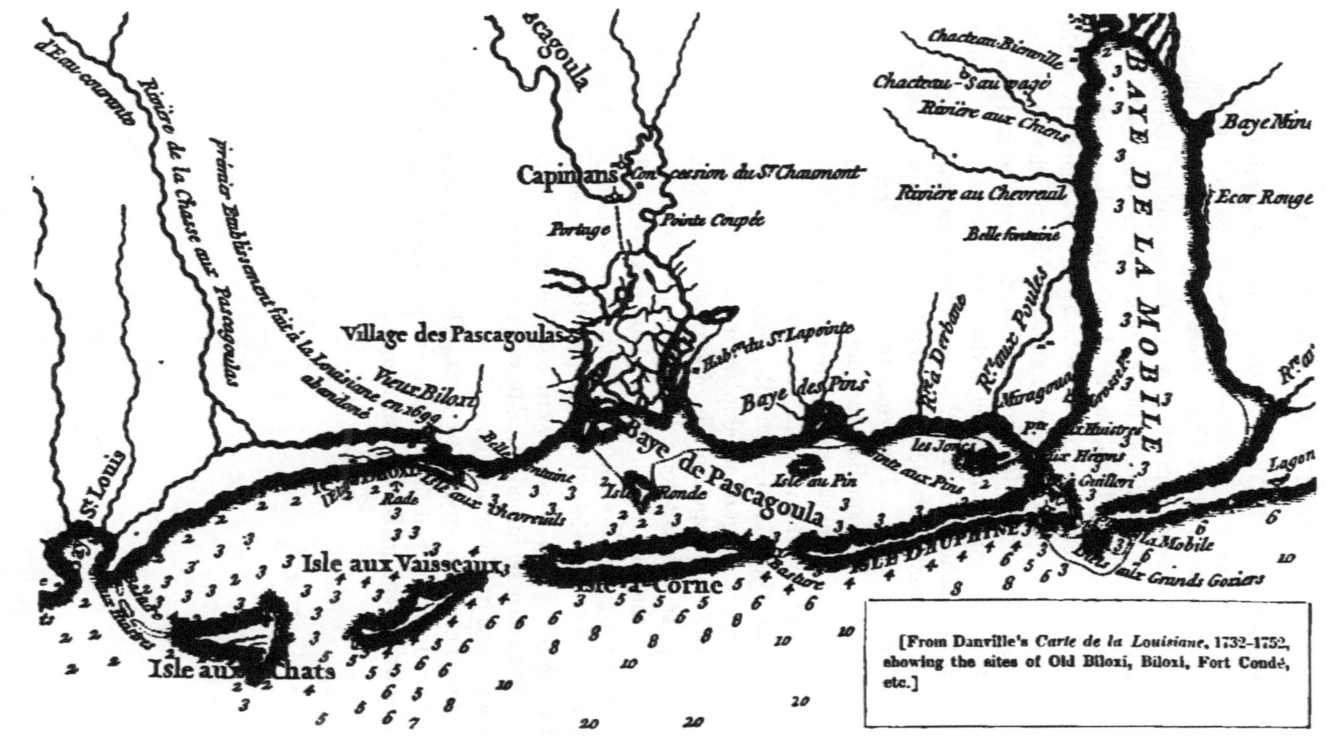

[From Danville's *Carte de la Louisiane*, 1732–1752, showing the sites of Old Biloxi, Biloxi, Fort Condé, etc.]

This condition of things at the north and northeast and the purposes of the local governments, as well as the views entertained at Paris, were important aids to the new movements on the lower Mississippi. Iberville, as we have seen, had pushed far enough to meet the traders and missionaries coming from the St. Lawrence valley. Moreover, he had derived encouragement from Tonty's conceptions of the drift of trade. He was consequently able, on the same day that Bienville started for the Red River, to turn back from the Natchez with some confidence in the future of the Great Valley. When he reached Biloxi, his impressions were again confirmed, since the policy of Callières was such that Louisiana would get most of the profit. This reassurance came from finding that another party of Canadian rangers had come with peltry for a market, flying from the restrictive measures which the Canadian government was enforcing at Mackinac.

Iberville and the Mississippi trade.

Late in May, 1700, Iberville, leaving Bienville to manage the colony, was again on shipboard bound for France, having apparently little apprehension of any trouble with the Spaniards. It was not long, however, after he had gone before the governor of Pensacola appeared at Biloxi to protest against the French occupation of any territory along the Gulf shore. His claim foreboded peril, inasmuch as he asserted that Florida and Mexico were contiguous, and were not to be wedged apart by intruders. He was content at present to couch his protest in words merely.

Spaniards at Biloxi.

On the return voyage to Pensacola, the Spanish ships were wrecked, and such of the crews as escaped the waves were shortly afterward back in Biloxi, suppliants for relief.

CHAPTER III.

THROUGHOUT THE VALLEY.

1700–1709.

Iberville's movements on the lower Mississippi had so much aroused the Illinois tribes that they showed a disposition to move down the river to be nearer the new-comers. Father Gravier, who had left the Miami mission on September 8, 1700, encountered the Kaskaskias, a group of the Illinois, well on their migrating way; but he finally prevailed upon their chiefs to stop at the modern Kaskaskia. The priest himself then started down the stream to see what was going on. Some Frenchmen accompanied him in five canoes. They went on, killing buffalo upon the banks and leaving their carcasses for the wolves. Passing the mouth of the river now called the Ohio, Gravier mentions how that stream, known to him as the Ouabache (Wabash), is formed by three tributaries, the present Wabash, the Ohio (above the confluence of the Wabash), and the affluent which comes from the southeast, upon which live the Shawnees, who trade with the English of Virginia and Carolina. The Indians at this time called the main river, debouching into the Mississippi, the Akansea, after a tribe formerly dwelling there, but which was now seated farther down the Mississippi.

Gravier and Kaskaskia.

Gravier descends the Mississippi.

As Gravier went on, he tells us that he actually boxed the compass with the windings of the current. In one place he found some Mohegans, of that New England race which had fled west after Philip's war, and who had been faithful some years earlier to La Salle. They were still trading their commodities with the English, and the English guns, which he soon after found among the Akanseas in their new home, told of further inter-tribal traffic, if not of direct contact with the Carolina traders. The priest found among these Akanseas some who recollected the advent of Marquette, then nearly a score of years gone by. The party stopped awhile for a visit to Davion and St. Cosme among the Tonicas, and it was late in November when they left the Natchez. They saw cocks and hens in their villages, and conjectured that the progenitors of these birds had been saved from the wreck of some Christian vessel on the Gulf coast.

It was December 17 when the voyagers reached the French fort at Poverty Point, as it has since been called, having been sixty-eight days in coursing the Mississippi from the Illinois to its lower curves. In the following February, while still at Iberville's fort, Gravier wrote the letter which is our main authority for his descent of the river, and of which Dr. Shea has given us a translation. In the preference which Gravier expressed for the advantages of Biloxi — which he next visited — we have a premonition of the final abandonment of this desolate Mississippi stockade.

1700-1. Iberville in France.

During the autumn of 1700, and in the following winter, Iberville was in France, considering future plans. He was urged to push his explorations westward towards New Mexico, and he drew up a plan for reaching the Gulf of California. He had his eye, too, on the Spanish fort at Pensacola, — a vision seldom obscured to his successors, — and above all he urged upon Pontchartrain the military defense of the Mississippi banks as making all these projects sure, and as giving a base for a still more important purpose. This was to push the English back upon Carolina and prevent their selling arms to the populous villages of the Cherokees.

Fort at Mobile.

A population for Louisiana of a hundred and fifty all told, and an unhealthy camp at Biloxi, — where Sauvole soon died from the fever — was not promising, unless the home government was prepared to give large succors. At all events, a more salubrious post seemed a necessity, and a site, thought to secure it, was soon found at the head of Mobile Bay. Boisbriant was now sent thither, with a party, to construct a fort.

Iberville returns. December, 1701.

Sauvole's death had brought Bienville from the Mississippi fort to take the general command in the dreary waste of Biloxi, with its burning sands and noxious damps, and here Iberville found him when, on December 15,

1701, accompanied by another brother, Le Moyne de Serigny, he reached the colony. The change to the post at Mobile was at once ordered, but Iberville did not remain to see the new position in complete order, for another hurried visit to France intervened before, in March, 1702, he took again the control, and the course of events once more felt his influence.

Tonty had come (March 25, 1702) from the up-country with a band of Choctaws and Chickasaws in his train, and it gave Iberville the opportunity to warn these jarring neighbors that the English purposed to stir up inter-tribal distrust till they exterminated each other. He urged them to a defensive alliance. At the same time he sent to Quebec to ask for missionaries to be sent among them as the best antidote to English intrigue. Turning to the other hand, he equally sought to work upon the fears of his Spanish neighbors by representing to them that the French occupation of this region meant in reality giving the Spaniards a barrier against the English.

The Indians and the French and English.

With complications on all sides, the founder of Louisiana, with his health undermined, was not destined to see his work completed. His northernmost outpost, Le Sueur's Fort d'Huillier, even before Delisle, using, as he says, the memoirs of that adventurer, signified its position on his new map of Louisiana (1703), had been abandoned for fear of the Sioux, and its destitute garrison were just now come to report their failure. It was not a grateful outcome of all Iberville's hopes of far-reaching influence throughout the Great Valley. Burdened with such disappointment he returned to France, never to see his colony again. Pontchartrain, indeed, recognized his merit, when he made him "Commander of the Colony of the Mississippi," but he felt that the title and the authority failed to carry with it the material aid, in concessions of land, in mines, and in negroes, which was necessary to make his control successful.

Le Sueur's fort abandoned, 1703.

Iberville's last years.

He had intended to return, but the ship on which he was expected in August, 1703, brought word that he was too ill for the voyage. He lived for three years, and died July 9, 1706, at Havana, whither he had gone in command of a fleet for the purpose of driving the English from the West Indies, and harrying the Carolina coast.

Bienville in command. 1702.

After the departure of his chief in 1702, Bienville was left to his own resources. The Indians in the up-country above Mobile were active, and it was thought that the English were inciting the Alibamons to pillage. To chastise them, Bienville, taking Tonty and St. Denis as lieutenants, marched against them. His party suffered much, and got no real help from some Choctaws and Mobilians, who pretended to act as allies. The movement, therefore, failed; but later he attempted another by water, and succeeded in burning the enemy's camp in the night.

His relations with the Indians,

Not long after, Bienville determined to abandon the fort on the Mississippi and concentrate his force at Mobile, where Fort St. Louis had already been built, above the modern city. This union of his forces was not made too soon, for the tribes north of Mobile were becoming turbulent; and it was convenient, if not just, to charge their uneasiness upon English machinations. There was perhaps more certainty in the Spanish intrigues to set the Chickasaws upon the Choctaws, and as the latter were generally inclined to the French interest, Bienville tried to make the two tribes friends as the surest way to gain immunity from the enmity of the Chickasaws. The mediation did not prove long successful, for the Chickasaws found their profit in disposing of Choctaws taken in battle as slaves to the Carolinians. Later, when they drove the Tonicas upon the Houmas, there was thought to be another manifestation of English intrigue. Colonel Moore, with a body of Carolinians, was making the English name a dreaded one to every Indian who looked to the French for protection.

and English.

Life at Mobile.

Distractions like these, as rumors came in, served at least to turn the poor colonists at Mobile from their miseries. These were not unmixed with apprehensions all the while lest the English should strike them by sea, supplementing the land attacks upon their Choctaw allies. A vessel arriving with marriageable damsels relieved life somewhat by a month of weddings. The poor craft, however, had touched at San Domingo and been infected with yellow fever. The fearful malady soon got a foothold, and among those who succumbed was the valiant Tonty, — not such an end as one would wish for his chivalrous nature. The ship which was the source of all these loves and woes had not enough men escaping the fever to navigate her away, and some who had come to stay as soldiers, and were sorely needed, were obliged to return as seamen. Clothing ran short, and attempts were made to supply it by spinning-bees. New ships would come, but somehow through the weary months the old miseries would recur.

There was some relief when Spain became the ally of France in new hostilities, and there was an interchange of civilities between Mobile and Pensacola, while certain courteous graces brightened life; but Bienville never forgot that Pensacola was a threat, though he had the skill to hide his hostile hopes. France had too much to do in Europe to grant the aid that was vital in Louisiana, and immigration did little to repair the losses of the colony. With all such symptoms of decadence, nothing but a united and respected government could give a hopeful turn to affairs, and this was wanting. Commandant and priest disagreed, and violent religious factions arose. Squads of bushrangers came down from the upper country with peltry, but it was rather the promise than the fulfillment of trade. La Salle, the commissary, was intractable, and defied Bienville till the commander's life was hardly less unbearable than that of the meanest hind who slunk away to the Indians to avoid starving.

French and Spaniards.

When tidings came in October, 1706, of Iberville's death at Havana, faction became rampant, and before many months had passed Bienville's friends had deserted him, and the poor man was powerless. The distressed colony possessed now less than three hundred inhabitants, and more than two thirds of these were soldiers and slaves, and nearly all, in some way, were pensioners of the public chest. It was apparent that the enemies of Bienville had triumphed, when orders were received for his recall. Presently, Diron d'Artaguette reached the colony (February, 1708). He was a man fit to shape a policy; but a treacherous future confronted him, for there were ugly stories in the air of a projected combination of the Cherokees and the Alibamons against the French and their Mobilian allies. It was of course a disguise for English hostility, or at least was thought so.

Condition of Mobile. 1706.

For some years, the rival interests of the French and English centred in the region between the Ohio and the Lakes, which ever since the extinction of the Eries by the Iroquois in the middle of the preceding century had been almost untenanted except by savage hunters. Of late, there had been a movement among the aborigines to reoccupy this region. The danger forced the Virginians on the Atlantic slope to push settlements up toward the mountains, so as to hold the Appalachians like a barrier against the threatened and barbarous inroads.

The Ohio country.

The easy portages which connected this Ohio territory with the basin of the St. Lawrence, and the natural tribute which the region could pay to the lower Mississippi, had soon caused an eager rivalry between the governments of Canada and Louisiana for its control, and made them suppliants in turn to the home government for the jurisdiction of it.

Iberville's policy had far better grounds than that which Callières had demonstrated in the St. Lawrence basin. In a communication to the minister at Paris, the Louisiana leader had pointed out the mistakes of the Canadian system in yielding to the hunter and excluding the tiller of the soil. This was a fatal blunder, he contended, if France had any hope of maintaining the country against the English. Iberville's plan for the control of the upper Mississippi basin was to establish posts near the mouths of the Missouri, the Ohio, and the Arkansas, and to make these stations permanent centres of French influence. He urged also at a later day to have the tribes of the Illinois settled along the banks of the lower Ohio. All this was a distinct denial of the English claim to this region, and just at the same time Governor Penn was expressing the views of the colonial governors, when he said that "we take the south side of the river [St. Lawrence] and lakes of Canada to be our just and reasonable boundaries." Bellomont of New York was also at this time planning a reconnaissance through the Iroquois country along the verge of the Great Valley itself, and gave instructions to that end to Colonel Römer in September, 1700, bidding him particularly "to go and view a well or spring which is eight miles beyond the Sinecks' [Senecas'] farther castle, which they have told me blazes up in a flame when a light coal or firebrand is

Iberville and Callières.

put into it." These burning springs are over the divide, and their waters flow into the Alleghany.

Meanwhile the rival powers of London and Paris were planning counter movements to secure the aid of the Iroquois for their respective purposes. Robert Livingston, in May, 1701, while warning the Lords of Trade of the French purpose to "encompass the English" by possession of the Mississippi basin, represented the Iroquois as a "constant barrier of defense between Virginia and Maryland and the French, and by their constant vigilance they had prevented the French making any descent that way." He further reports that the French were using the best artifices they could to weaken this alliance with the English, and complains that the selfish purposes of the Albany tradesmen were a check upon pioneering towards the west, because they thought that their own peltry trade would be intercepted by it.

English and French counter claims.

To counteract all such adverse influences, Lieutenant-Governor Nanfan of New York is said to have entered upon a treaty July 9, 1701, with the confederates at Albany, by which the region north of the Ohio and stretching to the Mississippi and Illinois rivers was ceded to the English king. The same treaty covered also a similar cession of the territory north of Lake Erie, stretching east to the Ottawa. The Iroquois based their right in this northern portion on their driving the Hurons out of it in 1650, and their hold on the southern part to their conquest of the Eries and others at a later period. The whole cession constituted what the Iroquois called their beaver-hunting grounds. What purports to be this deed of 1701 has been printed in the *New York Colonial Documents* (iv. 908), setting forth that the grantors in return expected "to be protected therein by the crown of England;" but there has been a suspicion that the document was in some part at least a device, trumped up at a later day, to antedate a treaty which the French made at Montreal in the following August, and it is not easy to see how both can be genuine. The Montreal treaty was made under the urgent appeal of the Canadian company, who complained of the English inroads by the Alleghany and Ohio rivers. Callières, as has been already indicated, had brought about the conciliation in it of the Iroquois and western tribes,

Nanfan's treaty. 1701.

Montreal treaty. 1701.

and had bound the confederates by a promise to prevent the erection of English posts throughout their country. The French claimed, and not without warrant, that they had thus made themselves actually the arbiters of the entire Indian question, to which not only the Iroquois but the western Indians were parties. But Indian faith was dependent on annual gratuities, and, as the French soon found, not always sure at that. They had, however, secured what they most needed just at present, and that was the neutrality of the confederates in an impending war with the English. They were not quite as successful with their own woodsmen, for the Canadian bushrangers were fully inclined to profit by the better opportunities of trade which were offered at Albany. Bellomont had been petitioned by two of them to be allowed to come to the English mart, and these applicants said they were but the forerunners of others, — "thirty brave fellows laden with peltry," as they said; and one Samuel York, who had been a prisoner in Canada, testified to the eagerness of these northern rangers to cast in their lot with the English.

English trade with French bushrangers.

When, in September, James the Stuart exile died, and the French king acknowledged the Pretender, war between England and France was inevitable. King William died in March, 1702; Cornbury, the royal governor of New York, arrived in May, but Queen Anne was not proclaimed there till June 17. War meanwhile had been declared on May 4, and when the news of the opening conflict reached Canada, Callières strengthened the fortifications of Quebec, and set to work at the same time to turn the assured neutrality of the Iroquois into pronounced hostility to the English. Neither he nor Vaudreuil, who upon Callières's death (1703) became governor, was able to do more than hold the confederates to their neutrality.

War. 1702.

It was important for England that the union of the French and Spanish crowns should not close the trade of the New World to English merchants; and it soon became evident that a struggle was at hand. The French dreamed of the conquest of New York and Boston, and their emissaries had for some years been clandestinely making maps of the approach by sea to those ports. The English hoped that a small army and a few frigates would drive the French from Canada, and Dudley was urging such an undertaking upon the Massachusetts Assembly, for it was these Canadian French who stood most in the way of the English in efforts to penetrate to the Mississippi by the Ohio route.

The war meant all this, but even more, to the English colonies; for it implied a better acquaintance of one colony with another, and New England was already, in the *Boston News-Letter* (1704), superseding the old manuscript methods of communicating intelligence from one government to another. The war was likely also to furnish common opportunities of defying the parliamentary navigation laws. It was the chance to teach the colonists the advantage of making their own woolens, and thus to emancipate them from the domination of the British merchant.

War and the English colonies.

It meant still more. Robert Livingston of New York looked forward to the time when, if supineness were allowed, the French, "by forts and settlements in the heart of the country and keeping a constant correspondence and communication with Missesepie," would be able "to make daily incursions upon our plantations." The remedy, to his mind, was some scheme of intercolonial confederation. Livingston's views were not without supporters in Cornbury, the local governor, and to some extent in a certain royal emissary, Colonel Quarry. The chief anxiety, however, of this attentive observer was lest the colonists, in cementing themselves together by common aims, should dare to arrogate to themselves the prerogatives of Parliament. He was pretty sure this was the tendency in the Virginia Assembly. Quarry, nevertheless, was not blinded to the treacherous nature of an Iroquois alliance. "They are a very uncertain people to trust to, and do lie under very strong temptation from the French," he said. His remedy in the case was to drive the French from Canada, and he did not think the effort one of insuperable difficulties. It would bring to the English, he said, "the whole trade of the main, which will be of vast consequence." He little thought that the project would take sixty years.

Cornbury and Quarry.

While Cornbury and the New Yorkers were thus dreaming of success and laying plots, Vaudreuil kept his trusty lieutenants among the Iroquois to watch the intrigues of the English. The Lords of Trade had been for some time urging Queen Anne to send Protestant missionaries among these confederates, as the best means of circumventing the Jesuits now in possession of the field. Robert Livingston at the same time complained that "the Jesuit priests by their insinuations and false pretenses were decoying a great many of our Indians, and have raised a great faction in their castles [palisaded villages], and it is feared a great many more will follow unless they have ministers to instruct them in the Christian faith, of which they seem very fond." He adds that French emissaries were among them "all last winter, endeavoring to corrupt their affections from the English, and make ill impressions in their minds, to the apparent prejudice of our trade with them, which decays daily more and more."

The Iroquois and the missions.

While the Iroquois were uncertain, it was the Canadian policy to spare the New York frontiers; but there was no hesitancy in harrying the borders of New England, and the story of Deerfield and the ravages of the coast attest their ghastly success.

The Senecas, the most westerly of the confederates, soon patched up a peace with the Miamis, and to keep these and the more distant Hurons and Ottawas in subjection, Vaudreuil continued to dispatch to them his quieting messages. These "speeches," nevertheless, had only partial effect. The English influence was not quelled, and the rival suits, as urged by the emissaries from Albany and Quebec, only divided the Miamis. Those who favored the English soon drove away a colony which Juchereau of Montreal had settled near the site of the modern Cairo in Illinois. It had been the purpose of this pioneer to open thereabouts mines of copper and lead, and to establish a barrier against any adventurous English daring to pass that way.

The western Indians.

It was the determined policy of the Canadian government to withdraw from the distant west such posts as interfered with the bringing of furs to the market farther down the St. Lawrence valley, and it was equally a satisfaction to the royal government to suppress any manufactures which infringed the monopoly of the home producers. Juchereau's proceedings were hardly in harmony with such principles, for he not only was gathering skins, but had established a tannery to

Juchereau's colonies.

turn them into leather. The irruption upon him, therefore, of the English faction among the Miamis was not altogether the sacrifice of French interests which it seemed. The English sympathizers among these Indians did not accomplish all that Governor Cornbury had wished, for they failed to carry the tribe as a whole over to the English side.

Vaudreuil, though he managed the Indian interests skillfully, did not hesitate to use coercion with any recalcitrant tribe. Nor did his efforts to square accounts with the English lead him beyond a courteous and seeming willingness to negotiate a peace with Dudley of Massachusetts. These interchanges of diplomatic suavities were protracted through many months, and in 1708, when nothing had come of them, the New England frontiers were again ravaged.

Vaudreuil and New England.

Once again aroused, the English compelled the entire Iroquois confederacy, except the Senecas, to rise against the French, and the Jesuits were at last expelled from their country (1708), never to return.

The English emissaries now pushed beyond the Iroquois country, and the Miamis were induced to send some chiefs to Albany and enter into a pact for trade. Five years of strenuous efforts for this object were thus crowned at last with success, and Cornbury, in congratulating himself, gave a young halfbreed, Montour, much of the credit for it. The French showed quite as much evidence of their belief in his agency by compassing his destruction the next year. This traffic with the Miamis was the formal beginning of a reorganized English trade in the northeastern parts of the Great Valley; but it was destined to be maintained with difficulty against the incessant plottings of the French.

Trade with the Miamis.

Samuel Vetch, an active man, who had been much on the St. Lawrence, picking up information to be useful in case of an attack on Quebec, was shortly after (1708) in England, urging such an incursion. His pleas were reinforced by Cornbury's representations, and Quarry warned the government that to delay the movement would very likely make it too late. The victories of Marlborough disposed the public to the undertaking. The rumors of the intention which reached Quebec induced the Canadians to concentrate their forces, and this had much to do with their withdrawal from the Iroquois country, as already related.

Vetch and Quebec. 1708.

England, as it turned out, found enough to do in Portugal, and the troops which were promised did not come over. The colonial forces lacking this support, the campaign of which so much was expected proved a failure, and the Boston government did not hesitate to believe that the apathy of New York arose from this desire to preserve the Canadian trade.

In view of such a fiasco, Jeremy Dummer's ambitious argument, that even Canada of right belonged to the British crown, seemed all the more ridiculous, and served rather to outrage the French than to mollify the disappointment of New England.

Palatines.

Better than such pretense and the treaty of 1701 was the sturdy influence of the German Palatines, now begun to be felt along the Mohawk, and still more to be felt when, later on, they constituted the advance-guard of the Teutonic race in pushing towards the headwaters of the Alleghany and Monongahela. There was at the same time a movement of the Swiss to purchase lands "beyond the Potomac and in Virginia," where it was supposed there were mines.

Swiss.

Cadillac and Detroit. 1701.

We have seen that Livingston, in 1699, had been urging Governor Bellomont to seize upon the straits at Detroit, as the fittest place from which to control trade with the western Indians. The advantages of this post had been equally apparent to Lomothe Cadillac, and he had the spirit to anticipate the English.

Cadillac was a Catholic of Franciscan associations, who hated the Jesuits now and in the times to come, and he looked with a sinister eye upon their mission at Mackinac. A Jesuit was assigned to found a mission at the new post; but Cadillac chose a Recollect for his chaplain. It was thirty years since St. Lusson, with ambitious parade, had formally attached to the French crown all this upper region of the Lakes. The first civil and military government was now to be established in this great domain.

In June, 1701, Cadillac left Three Rivers with a hundred soldiers and colonists in twenty-five canoes. He took the Ottawa route to hide his movements from the Iroquois. By July 24, the expedition was at the straits, and at the end of August his stockade was completed and named Fort Pontchartrain.

The movement raised up enemies hard to conciliate. The

Jesuits never liked to have settlements near their missionary fields. The traders found a diminution of profits, if stores of merchandise were made too accessible to the savage. The opposition of the Canadian packmen before long inured to the benefit not only of the English on the Atlantic, but of the French in Louisiana, for it prompted one Jean Pacaud to lease for seventy thousand francs a year the privileges of the old Compagnie des Indes, out of which was organized speedily a new Compagnie du Canada, under a concession of October 31, 1701. The new company thus secured the exclusive trade at Frontenac and Detroit, the latter post deriving no advantage except that the company set up the establishment there and the king maintained the garrison.

Compagnie du Canada. 1701.

Cadillac did not hear of this project till the following July (1702). He protested, and got some modification of the company's power. He even importuned Pontchartrain for the abolishment of the company and a separate government for Detroit. The organization still had enough of prescriptive rights to incense the old traders. This class would not have been averse to bring on an Iroquois war, if Detroit was to disappear in the conflict. In this they were at one with the English at Albany, and it is sometimes alleged that a fire in the Detroit stockade was a consequence of English influence.

A natural result followed. An illicit traffic in peltries sprung up, and the French down the Mississippi and the English at Albany were soon profiting more than the company. Cadillac was hampered; but the company was more so.

Callières died, and political power in Canada passed into the hands of Vaudreuil, who was so connected by ties of blood with some of the directors of the new company that the prospect, in Cadillac's eyes, grew gloomier still. The end, however, was nearer than he thought, and Pontchartrain proved powerful enough to displace the company. That minister, in June, 1704, wrote from Versailles, placing Cadillac in power, and gave him some good advice to ponder over.

Vaudreuil governor.

The Jesuits were still a thorn. Cadillac wrote to Pontchartrain that the only way to keep peace with them was to do their bidding and hold his tongue. If relations in this way were jarring, it was hopeful to find the western tribes becoming amenable to French influence to such a degree

Cadillac in power.

that they were flocking to settle along the straits. Cadillac had need of their attachment before long; and they served him well in repelling an attack of the Sauks and Foxes. The hostility of these warlike allies was and remained a serious impediment to the success of the French about the upper reaches of the Mississippi, and we have already noted how Le Sueur's followers on a branch of the Minnesota were driven away by the Sioux, ever a treacherous foe.

Hostile tribes.

The years that ensued under Cadillac's rule at Detroit were passed in continuous efforts to keep peace, with the Ottawas on the one hand, and with the Miamis on the other, who were always watching for opportunities to strike a blow. Detroit failed in the competition with Mackinac as a mart for furs, and the English for the most part got the advantage with cheaper goods and better offers of skins. The Albany traders were quite content with profits that were not lessened by the cost of maintaining the posts.

The Bay of St. Louis or St. Bernard, on the Texan shore, is well round the northwestern curve of the Mexican Gulf, and towards the south. It is the spot where La Salle had sought to found his colony. His belief that he was near a western outlet of the Mississippi influenced the views of Minet, his engineer, in delineating the southern bends of the Great River, and gave Franquelin the incentive to make a false course for its lower current. Even so late as the close of the eighteenth century, we find a survival of La Salle's mistake in the *English Pilot* (1794), of Mount and Page. It was left for Delisle, opportunely coming forward and proving himself the real founder of modern geographical science, to correct this misconception, but not wholly to eradicate it from the stock notions of the lesser cartographers. Indeed, it is surprising how prevalent the views of half a century before remained with the mere copyists. The maps of Jaillot, De Witt, Schenck, Allard, and Danckerts continued for ten years after the new developments under Iberville to present the views of Sanson of fifty years aback. Their maps pertinaciously represented incomplete outlines of Lakes Michigan and Superior, unmindful of the explorations of La Salle and the Jesuits. All that stood for the principal affluent of the Mexican Gulf on its

Texan coast.

Its cartography.

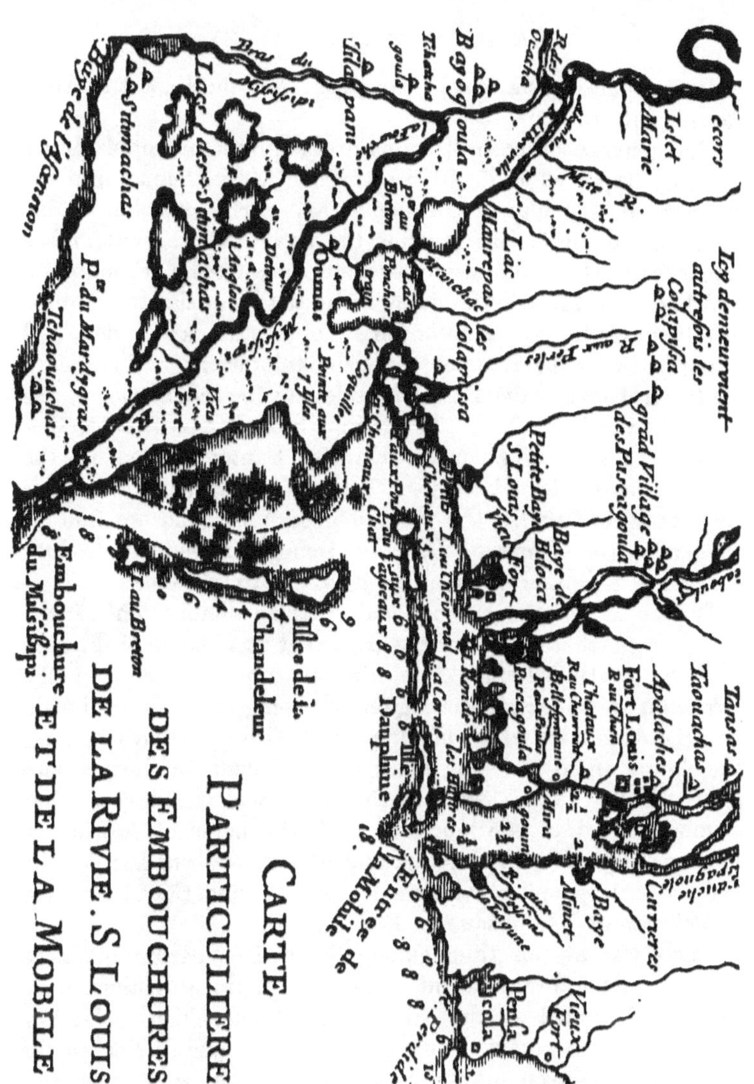

SITES FROM PENSACOLA TO THE MOUTHS OF THE MISSISSIPPI. [After Delisle.]

[It shows the site of the old fort on the Mississippi, abandoned for the new one at Mobile.]

northern shore was a looped bay with a few short coast streams flowing into it.

Maps of the Mississippi.

The general southern direction of the great current as Joliet reported it in 1673 was accepted by Hennepin in the dotted line of his honest and early map, but in his later dubious draft, disregarding the surveys of Iberville, if he knew them, Hennepin swung over to the views of Franquelin, and had been preceded in doing so by the Englishman, Edward Wells, in his maps. Another error of a still earlier day, and going back to the remoter Spanish explorations, had caused a confusion between the Bay of Mobile and the indentation of the Gulf shore, of which the Mississippi Sound of our day makes a part. The name Espiritu Santo, applied in the early days both to a bay and a river, is not always easy to identify with the modern geography, and we find it, even after the advent of Iberville, sometimes made to do duty for one or the other of such half-inclosed stretches of water.

Espiritu Santo.

Florida.

It was a relic of the original Spanish domination of the northern shore of the Gulf that their name of Florida continued for some time to apply, even with the French map-makers, to the region extending from the peninsula and St. Augustine to the confines of Mexico. Notwithstanding the claims which Iberville made for Louisiana bordering here on the Gulf, Delisle, who all the while was working on that commander's data, continued to apply the name of Florida to the territory between Carolina and Texas. It was left for the Belgian cartographer, Nicolas de Fer, to give the alternative appellation of "Louisiane ou Floride."

French claims and maps.

There was at this time, among the French cartographers, a general agreement that the national claims were bounded on the east by the Appalachians. De Fer so recognizes the extent of French jurisdiction in his maps, and was even more liberal than Delisle, who at a later day was forced to reclaim for his king a region along the western bounds of New York and Pennsylvania, which he had been content in some of his earlier maps to give to the English. Delisle even then did not attempt to push the French claims beyond the mountains into Carolina; but, for some reason,

NOTE. A portion of Franquelin's map (in the Marine, reproduced by Marcel, No. 40), which shows his misconceptions, is opposite.

POU ALACS
DES
ASSINIBOUELS
NATIONS
NATION DES
N O U V
NATIONS
DES SIOUX
SON-
GATSKITONS
DES SIOUX DE
DE L'EST
L'OUEST
F R A
NATION DES
TINTONS
NATION DES
OTOCTATA
PAIS DE LA
NATION
DES PANIS
PAIS DE LA
NATION
LAC SUP
PUANS
PAIS DE LA NATION
QUICAPOUX
NATIONS ET
PAIS
DES
ILINOI
PAIS DE LA
NATION
PAIS DE LA
NATION DES CHE
NATION DES MISSO
DES PANAS
C E
PAIS DE LA NATION
DES
ANALAOS
LA FLO
PAIS DE LA
NATION
DES PANAMOS
GOLFE DE MEXIC
PANUCO

Schenck, the Dutch map-maker, in reissuing Delisle's map, stretched Florida or Louisiana far up toward the modern Virginia.

It shows how diverse interpretations could be put upon the same reports, when Delisle is always correct in making the Ohio and Wabash confluent streams, while De Fer puts them down as parallel affluents of the Mississippi.

In his map of the upper Mississippi, published in 1703, Delisle profited by the information collected by Duluth, Perrot, and Le Sueur. Through such channels he obtained the stories of Indians who professed to have followed the Mississippi to its source, and placed it in latitude 49°, in a marshy region where it was linked with three small lakes, — a configuration which was continued in the maps well down through the century, and misled the American negotiators in the treaty of 1782. It was repeated by De Fer, though some contemporary cartographers, like the Dutchman, Schenck, were pretty sure in all their maps to carry the fountains of the great river as high as 54° or 55° north latitude. They had about as little warrant for this as the French traders wandering among the Upper Sioux had when they detected Chinese sounds in the savage gutturals.

Source of the Mississippi.

There were stories often repeated by adventurous traders, and tales credited to the Indians, which gave hopes that west of the Mississippi some productive trade could yet be opened with the Spaniards in New Mexico, and a way be found to a great western-flowing river. From the time when, in 1673, Marquette was inspired with the hope of carrying the gospel westward by the turbid current of the Missouri, there had been in many an adventurous breast a longing to face its unknown dangers. That there was beyond a divide somewhere in these temperate latitudes a practicable passage westward was readily accepted. Lugtenberg, in 1700, while illustrating his belief in the peopling of the New World by the Lost Tribes, had imagined a water-way from Lake Superior which connected with the fabled Straits of Anian. Delisle had placed a lake near the Missouri, from which the "Meschasipi ou Grande Rivière" flowed west. We know that in 1703 a party left Kaskaskia to follow up the Missouri, but we are ignorant

Trade with Spaniards.

Missouri River.

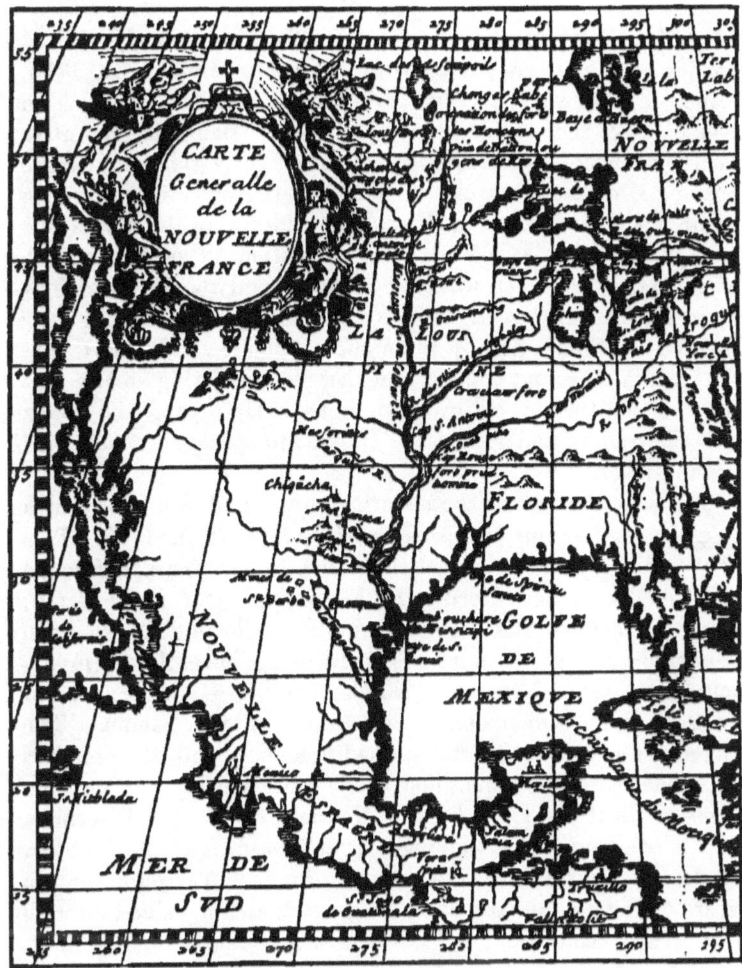

[From La Potherie's *Histoire de l'Amérique*, 1722, showing how the mouth of the Mississippi was misplaced, forty years after La Salle originated the error.]

of its fate. A year later, some Canadians on that river heard stories of a western stream over the upper divide. In 1705, some miners went up the Missouri, and built a fort on an island above the confluence of the Osage. Bienville soon after heard stories of the possibility of reaching by this route some nations who used horses. Sometimes the stories referred to white men; and some of Bienville's officers, in 1708 and the year following, were planning an expedition to reach a source of the Missouri which was said to be beyond the three or four hundred leagues already followed without encountering any Spaniards. Somewhere in this upper region it was believed that the Spaniards found copper, and there were floating stories that they carried the ore off on pack-mules. Up among the Sioux also the traders understood the Indians to speak of a westward flowing river.

The most distinct of these stories were found in a book which Lahontan published at The Hague in 1703. This story-teller claimed that some fifteen years before he had found a stream entering the Mississippi near Lake Pepin, which came from the setting sun. By following its sluggish current he had come to a large lake, lying beneath the mountains, and beyond these highlands there were the sources of another river, which could be followed to the Pacific. The statement was specific and gained credence, and the wonders of it had doubtless something to do with causing the multifarious publication of the book in French, English, and German, which was put upon the market at The Hague, in London, Hamburg, Amsterdam, and Leipzig, for the next eight or ten years. For a while the story prospered, and it gained a qualified assent from De Fer. Delisle was inclined to believe it, but at a later day, importuned to discard it, he yielded to the arguments of Bobé against it. Homann, in 1706, puts this "Rivière longue" on his map. The English cartographers, Moll and Senex, gave it full play in their maps, though Senex finally rejected it.

Lahontan. 1703.

The impressions produced by what is now known to have been a studied deceit were hard to dispel, and in certain quarters the illusion did not vanish till the century was near its end.

NOTE. The opposite map, taken from the U. S. Topographical map, of the region west of the Mississippi (1850) shows the Mille Lacs region and the continuity of the central trough of North America through the upper Mississippi and the Red River of the North.

N
E
S
DACOTAHS
CHIPPEWAS
Little Salt R.
Salt R.
Park R.
Big Salt R.
Turtle R.
Red Lake River
Red L. River
Opashwa L.
Turtle L.
Pemidji L.
Kitchi L.
Sandy L.
L. Dodge
Long Prairie R.
Winnebago Agency
Crow Wing R.
Rum R.
Vermillion L.
Shayen oju R.
Tchampahu Wita L.
Pejihu or Wild Rice R.
Wild Rice R.
Buffalo R.
Otter Tail L.
L. Lyell
L. Sibley
St. Croix R.

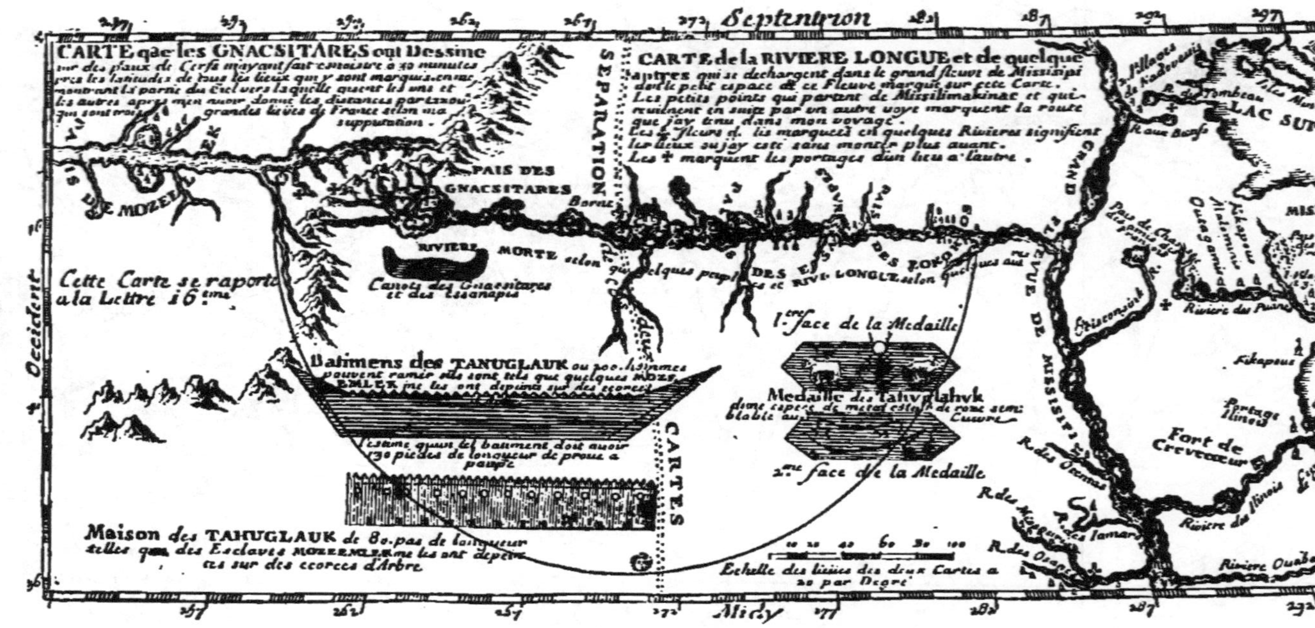

LA HONTAN'S RIVIÈRE LONGUE.

CHAPTER IV.

CROZAT AND TRADE.

1710–1719.

It had been determined in Paris to place La Forest in charge at Detroit, and to transfer Cadillac to Louisiana. On May 13, 1710, Pontchartrain notified the new governor of his appointment. He received the message through Vaudreuil in September. A man of Cadillac's disposition was neither happy nor at his best under the restraints which he had felt at Detroit. In June, 1711, he was ready for his journey, and asked for an escort. He was obliged, however, to return to France, and reëmbark for his new post, and various delays prevented his reaching it before May, 1713. He had left a discouraging prospect at Detroit, and the one he found before him on the Gulf was hardly less disheartening. The colony had been reduced by disease to scarcely more than four hundred whites and about twenty negro slaves. For two years there had been a succession of miseries. D'Artaguette, before his return to France, could do nothing but give the home government good advice; and it availed little. His better associates had died or returned to Europe. Food was so scarce that the men wandered off among the Indians for a livelihood. The English made an attack on Dauphine Island, and the community was in constant apprehension of other inroads. They had not infrequent grounds to fear that deserters disclosed their weakness to their enemies. The Choctaws professed to be friendly, but if the Chickasaws and their allies failed of their purpose with these neighbors of the French by friendly solicitation, they were always ready to use the tomahawk, and they trusted to the English leadership in any event.

Cadillac governor of Louisiana. 1710.

In Louisiana. 1713.

Condition of the country.

With all these environments of danger and distress, it was

not strange the colony suffered from the loss of some of its best members, who sought better fortune up the Mississippi. Vincennes had been founded on the Wabash by Father Mermet, and held out lures for settlers. The missions in these upper regions were beginning to thrive, and habitations were increasing about them. There was one at St. Joseph's for

The Illinois country.

FRENCH SOLDIERS, 1710.

the Miamis and Pottawattamies. Another was at Peoria; but the most successful was among the Kaskaskias, at their new settlement near the Mississippi. The effect of this priestly influence had become perceptible among the Illinois Indians, and they had grown far less barbarous than any other tribe. They used ploughs, and in other practices were assuming habits of civilization. The Jesuits taught them the use of windmills, and the Kaskaskias, one of the Illinois tribes, constructed treadmills, and ran them by horses. They obtained these animals by inter-tribal exchanges from a stock reared among the distant Spaniards of New Mexico. The little

Illinois tribes.

settlement at Kaskaskia quickly took on an air of permanence, and we very soon find that they were adopting permanent land records.

All these amenities of life were in sorry contrast to the absence of them near the Gulf, and in D'Artaguette's day that commander had urged a military post on the Ohio, to confront any advance upon Louisiana by the English, who might be tempted to take advantage of their weakness. The conditions were not changed now that Cadillac held the reins. His petulancy and imperiousness were to prove ill calculated to atone for the defects of his people and the sorrows of their life.

Louisiana.

When, in May, 1713, La Jonquière in a fifty-gun ship startled Mobile with his booming cannon, there was much beside the new governor, whom he had brought, to throw the poor colony into a condition of expectation. There was a new invoice of marriageable damsels for one thing. There were also the tidings of the peace, settled at Utrecht. There was the promise of a fresh policy of trade for the colony, by virtue of a contract signed at Paris, on the 14th of the previous September.

Cadillac arrives. 1713.

This instrument gave to the Sieur Antoine Crozat the right to farm the trade of Louisiana for fifteen years. In the month following the arrival of the news, Crozat's agents came to carry out the undertaking. The territory defined by the document as the field of Crozat's operations gave the French claim to the limits of Louisiana, and is a starting-point for the pretensions of the French in this regard. It is described as including all the territory between Carolina and New Mexico, while at the same time it extended from the Gulf of Mexico to the Illinois. Its area towards the east included the basin of what was called the Wabash or the St. Jerome, that is, the modern Ohio; and towards the west it went up the St. Pierre or the Missouri. It made no claim to go beyond the sources of that river, though there has sometimes been a doubt if France, in ceding Louisiana in 1803 to the United States, did not touch the Pacific between the bounds of England on the north and Spain on the south. Thus Louisiana, as mapped at this time, took the entire water-shed of the Mississippi, except between the Illinois and

Crozat and his plans. 1714.

Limits of Louisiana.

the sources of the Great River on its eastern side. At the south it also included the valleys of the coast streams which flowed into the Gulf, but it respected the rights of the Spaniards in the southwest, though it was sometimes claimed that the French territorial rights on a more northern parallel stretched to the Gulf of California.

There was a disposition, moreover, on the part of the French government at this time not to be too definite in their descriptions of limits. A year or two later (January, 1715), Raudot, in charge under Pontchartrain of the colonies, requested Delisle to remove the dots from his map which marked the limits of Louisiana, "as the court wishes it left indefinite, and does not want French maps to be quoted by foreign nations against us." Delisle generally marked the limits of Canada by the divide which bounded the St. Lawrence basin on the south, and drew those of Louisiana by the mountains which on the east confined the streams feeding the Mississippi. There is hardly exact correspondence in these respects among any of the contemporary maps delineating the interior of North America.

Crozat's rights.

Crozat had in antecedent years been very helpful to the French king in replenishing his treasury with gold and silver, and that sovereign hoped his subject's prosperous ways might inure to the benefit of his American province. He was willing accordingly to give him manifold advantages. He allowed him to open mines, with a due reservation of the crown's share; but he was compelled to recruit the colonists, and to send two ships with supplies every year. He was permitted, also, to send a single ship each twelvemonth to the coast of Guinea for negroes. Further, the charter provided that French law and customs should prevail in the province, "with the usages of the mayoralty and shrievalty of Paris."

The country explored.

Crozat's agents at once began to establish posts upon all the principal rivers, and explorers were sent out to search for mines. Lead ore was found in southeastern Missouri, and the miners got their supplies from the Illinois country, where a trading-post was set up. Another station was placed at the modern Natchez, and De La Tour was sent four hundred miles up the Alabama River at the junction of the Coosa and Tallapoosa, to build a stockade, which was named Fort Toulouse. Some of Crozat's traders penetrated to the

Tennessee country, and built (1714) among the Shawnees a storehouse on a mound near where the modern Nashville stands. An old deserted stockade of the Indians, close by, was occupied as a dwelling.

Deerskins and other peltries in large quantities were soon going down the Mississippi. With no competitors in the colony, Crozat counted on large profits. His aims, however, were soon thwarted. The traders got better prices from the English and Spanish, and the skins found their way to Carolina and Pensacola. Crozat was soon complaining that the English were seducing the natives from the French interests both on the Red River and on the upper Mississippi. To add to his disappointments, the Spaniards, playing into the hands of the English, warned Crozat's ships away from their Gulf ports, and the demand in that direction for his skins was cut off. A grinding monopoly could but create discontent in the province. Before Crozat's plans were fairly organized, the operations of the treaty which had just brought peace debarred him from the importation of Africans. Its provisions had, in fact, transferred the control of the slave trade to England, a plan far-reaching enough to make the mother country responsible for the long bondage of the negro in America.

Slave trade.

The treaty of Utrecht, after a truce which Bolingbroke had made, and which the victories of Marlborough had induced, was signed March 31 (April 11), 1713. France did not by it yield all that four years earlier she might have been compelled to grant. At that time the English, who by the treaty had permission for a yearly ship to trade with the Spanish colonies, might very likely have enforced free trade. The South Sea Company might doubtless have secured a monopoly of the Spanish trade in America. Though the treaty when actually negotiated failed in this, it gave England enough to make her at once the first power in Europe, — a place which France had held for nearly fifty years. The Pretender was forced out of France, and the Protestant succession in England was recognized. The English king became sovereign of Newfoundland and Acadia. In gaining these provinces, the British negotiators were not as wary as they should have been, since they fixed the bounds of Acadia by its "ancient limits," which

Treaty of Utrecht. 1713.

had all the vagueness that France delighted in, when she found occasion to define her own boundaries. Nor did it prove wise to leave Cape Breton in the hands of the French. The questions involved were indeed difficult and awkward, but perhaps less so than the contention which ensued.

Bounds of Canada.

Previous to this the French would hardly have admitted that the northern bounds of Canada — still theirs by the treaty, and with a population not much over eighteen thousand — stopped short of the north pole. Now the Hudson Bay Company and the British government got the larger part of the basin of that inland sea. There was at last a definite line, where the French had studiously avoided having one. It ran west from the Labrador coast on latitude 58° 30′, but from Lake Mistassin it struck 49°, and so continued westward, — the origin of the line which forms the present boundary of the United States on the north along the westerly half of its extent.

The Iroquois and the treaty.

On August 18, 1713, Governor Hunter proclaimed the peace at New York, and on September 20 he communicated it by messenger to the assembled confederates at Onondaga. He warned them not to intercept the far nations of the Mississippi and the Lakes, coming to trade at Albany. The Indians on their part implored forgiveness for the Tuscaroras, who had been driven north by the Carolinians, and had now become a sixth nation in the Iroquois Confederacy.

In the struggle of the French and English for the Mississippi valley, the language of the treaty of Utrecht respecting the Iroquois was by interpretation made of large importance in the future. The contracting nations agreed to respect the country of the tribes allied to each, and the Iroquois were taken under the protection of England. It soon became evident that the English intended to assume a protectorate over all the territory which the Iroquois claimed to have subdued. This included the country lying beyond the Alleghany River, within which the Iroquois had destroyed the Eries, and from which they had driven other tribes, and which in the English interpretation stretched to the line of the Mississippi and Illinois rivers. The earliest delineation of such a line we find at a later period, and after the English and French had made preparations for the great struggle. The

Country subdued by the Iroquois.

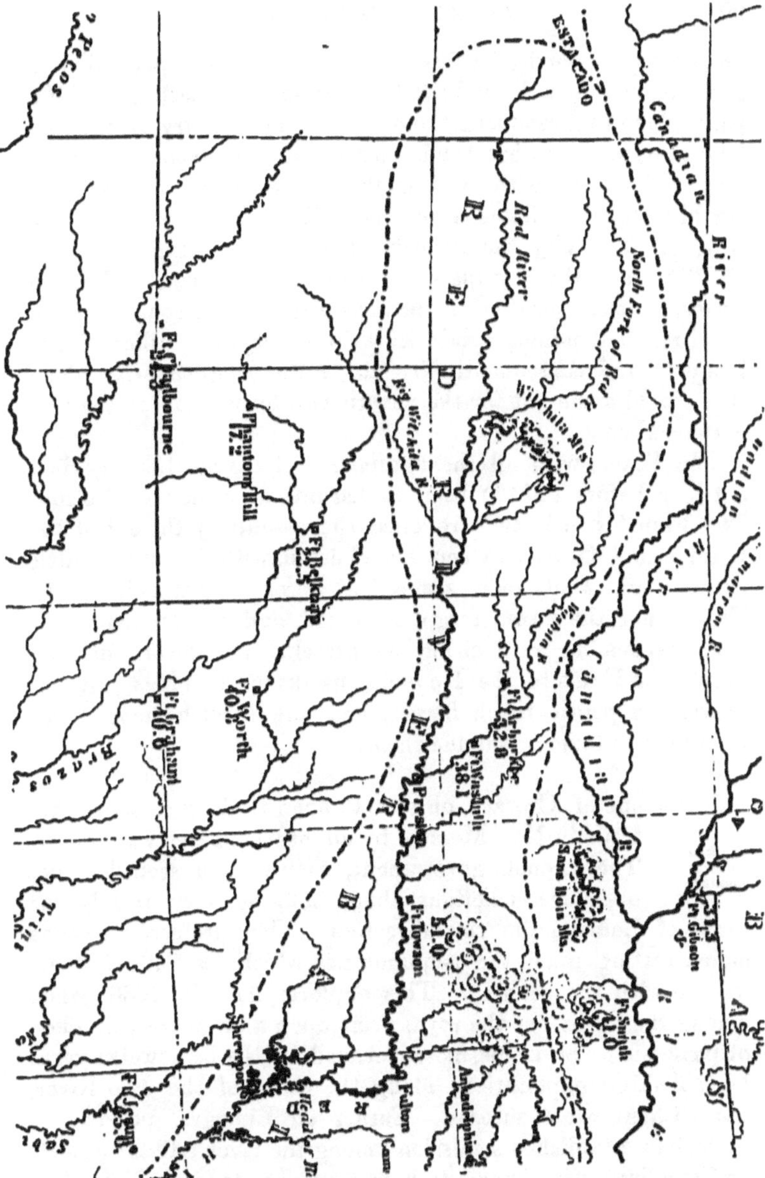

[From Humphreys and Abbot's *Basins of the Mississippi*, etc., War Department, 1861. It shows the Red River basin and its connection with the Texas rivers on the south, and the Canadian and Kansas rivers on the north.]

record as it stands, for instance, on Evans's map (1755) is accompanied by a legend: "The author has been something particular in representing the extent of the country of the confederates, because whatever is such is expressly conceded to the English by treaty with the French." The extent of this claim would bring the Illinois tribes under English jurisdiction, while in reality the French were seated among them and held their sympathies. On the other hand, it left the Foxes, or such portion of them as were in Wisconsin, within the French dominion, while they in reality were allies of the Iroquois, and consequently friends of the English, with whom they would trade but for the vexatious interposition of the ubiquitous French.

The Illinois and Foxes.

The Foxes, with all the appliances of savage knavery, had not long before (1712) been forced into an attack on Detroit. The French had in turn repelled the assault by the aid of the Hurons and Ottawas, when Du Boisson, with his sturdy little garrison of twenty men, secured a victory. But neither the French nor the Foxes forgot the event, and the Iroquois were held responsible for inciting the attack. Charlevoix, in comparing the Foxes to the Iroquois, speaks of them as just "as brave, less politic, much fiercer, and the French have never been able to tame or subdue them."

It was one of Crozat's objects to open trade with the Spaniards in New Mexico by an overland westward route. The French government, as we have seen, had not been over-solicitous about defining very exactly the limits of Louisiana in this direction. They preferred a vague claim, resting upon the acquaintance which La Salle had acquired with the country. This explorer had, in 1686, when among the Cenis, cut the royal arms upon a large tree, in token of possession. St. Denis, moreover, had for the last twelve years been making explorations along the valley of the Red River, but without great success. Father de Limoges, as early as 1702, had established a mission among the river tribes. Squads of Canadians were known to have wandered towards New Mexico in the hope of finding mines.

The Red River country.

When the Crozat rule began, it had been reported at Mobile that the Arkansas River had been followed to its source; but

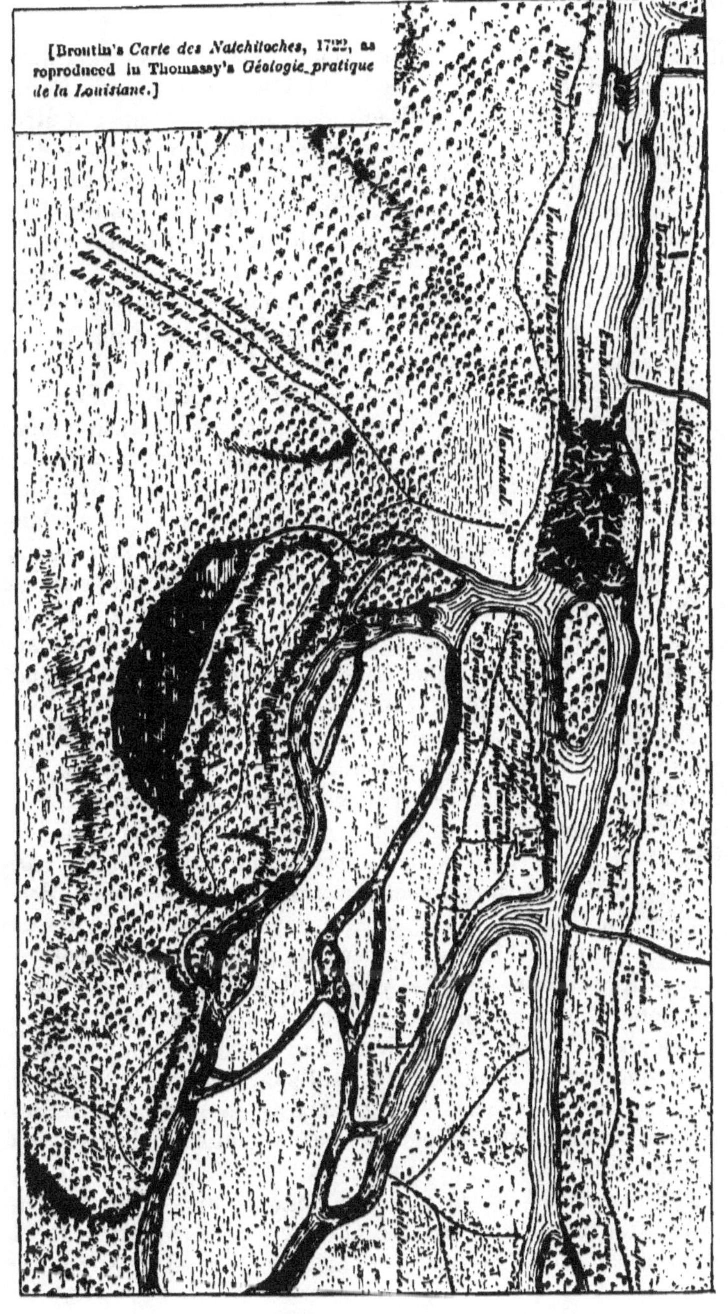

[Broutin's *Carte des Natchitoches*, 1722, as reproduced in Thomassy's *Géologie pratique de la Louisiane.*]

it was scarcely probable at that time. The secrets of the west were indeed still to be probed, and Cadillac was ready to attempt it. So St. Denis was dispatched up the Red River to Natchitoches, whence he struck across the land to the region of the Cenis. Here he took formal possession of the country. Finding some savages ready to follow him, he pushed on towards the Rio Grande del Norte. In August, 1714, he found welcome at the mission of Saint Jean-Baptiste, near its banks, which had been founded by the Spaniards. Here St. Denis fell in love with the daughter — or, as some accounts say, the niece — of Raimond, the commander of a small body of Spanish troops, stationed there to protect the priests. This officer had already dispatched a messenger to headquarters with tidings of this French intruder, when the love affair happened, and rendered the situation rather embarrassing for the vigilant Raimond. After a while St. Denis was sent to the city of Mexico to render an account of himself. Here he agreed to go back with some missionaries to the Texan country, and he faithfully did so, finding it a convenient opportunity to seek Raimond's post once more and marry his love. This done, he made his way to Mobile, and reported there in August, 1716.

St. Denis's exploits. 1714–1716.

The adventure, if it had accomplished little for Louisiana, had satisfied the successful gallant. It had done more for the Spaniards, for it instigated greater alertness to save the Texan country for his Catholic majesty. The Spaniards had, in the days of La Salle, set up a claim that the inlet in which he had built his fort, sometimes called the Baye de St. Bernard or St. Louis, or the Baye du Saint Esprit, was quite within the Spanish bounds. The question of ownership was now manifestly to be determined by actual occupation. The Spaniards had already placed a force among the Cenis to secure that position, and they were only waiting the coming of the annual fleet from Spain to have an available force to send to the bay. They hoped by its possession to control the Indian trade along the rivers which have their outlets in its waters.

Baye de St. Bernard and La Harpe. 1718.

The Spaniards dallied, and had done nothing when, in August, 1718, the directors of the Company of the West ordered that the bay should be seized. This was followed in November

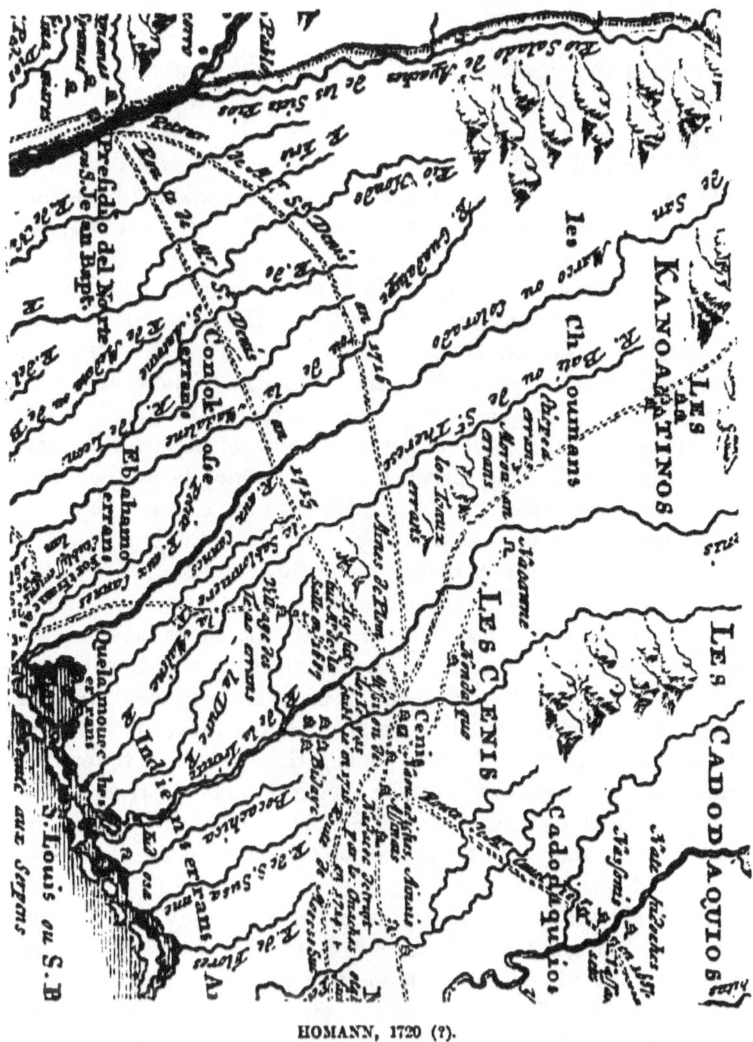

HOMANN, 1720 (?).

[It shows the routes of St. Denis.]

by a royal order, which further commanded that force should be used to retain possession if the Spaniards interfered. Margry gives a relation of one Simars de Belle-isle, who claims that in 1719 he had been shipwrecked near the bay, and had been kept in captivity by the Indians. But such chance adventures served little more than to keep the French claim in mind, till in August, 1721, La Harpe was sent with instructions from Bienville to occupy the bay. He found the natives hostile, and the difficulties of maintaining a post so far from succor were so great that, on La Harpe's report, Bienville, in December, announced that the post had been abandoned. There were still those, however, who held that this was the true ingress to the Texan country, and Margry gives us a document in which Derbanne regrets that St. Bernard's Bay had not been the chief port of the province instead of Mobile. He claimed that the Spaniards had so alienated the savages about the bay that the French could easily ally them against their rivals.

The river approach to this disputed Texan territory was more promising. In October, 1716, St. Denis, now in Mobile, and forming a partnership with others, bought a large quantity of goods from Crozat's stores. With a train carrying these supplies, he made a new move up the Red River. At Christmas he was among the Cenis, and found the Spaniards in possession. In the spring of 1717, he reached the mission where he had met his Spanish bride, and thence he passed on to the city of Mexico to reclaim some of his goods, which had been seized.

St. Denis on the Red River. 1716.

St. Denis was a man of vain manners and heady temper, and soon found himself in a Spanish prison. In December he was released; but his tongue was too free for his safety, and his wife's friends helped him escape the country. During the next spring (1719) he found his way to Isle Dauphine.

Meanwhile Cadillac, fearing that the Spaniards would be before him, sent a force to occupy Natchitoches island in the Red River (January, 1717). Cadillac felt it a matter of life and death to maintain this station, and he wrote full of gloomy forebodings lest the Spaniards should force the French back here. He was equally apprehensive that the English on the east would dislodge his interior settlements and leave the French little beyond Isle Dau-

Natchitoches. 1717.

Spaniards at Adaes.

phine. The Spaniards, on their part, had stoutly taken post at Adaes, and this outpost of the Spanish and that of the French at Natchitoches faced each other across a broad interval. The Spanish government hoped to recruit their settlement from the Canaries; but few emigrants came.

THE RED RIVER REGION.

[From Danville's *Louisiane* (Venice).]

It was soon apparent that Natchitoches was not well situated to allure the Spanish trade, and so, to picket the country beyond and open more direct communication, La Harpe was sent out with a small force. He had a wide region to traverse, and the country was infested with

La Harpe at the Red River country.

hordes of hostile savages, so that the transportation of merchandise and treasure was dangerous. La Harpe was armed with a letter from Bienville, addressed to the Spanish governor, in which the French commander declared it his wish to live in amity with his Spanish neighbors. Early in 1719, La Harpe built Fort St. Louis de Carlorette, not far from Natchitoches. Thus securing a new fortified base, he pushed toward the upriver tribes, hoping to make new alliances with them. He had heard of the Padoucas, said to be seated near the springs of the Arkansas, Red, and Colorado rivers, and he was in hopes to reach their country. Just where the sources of the Colorado might lie was not so certain as of the other rivers, but it seemed probable that the whole region, assigned in common report to the Padoucas, was the country which the map-makers had long designated as Gran Quivira. Efforts to reach this country which lay beyond the Panis (Pawnees) were still going on by way of the Missouri. The English geographer, Herman Moll, in a map of this time (1720) had put a legend upon this region to indicate that "many wandering nations of Indians are at the head of these rivers, who use horses and trade with the French and Spaniards." There had been enough chance contact with this people for La Harpe to know them to be powerful, counting something like two thousand horsemen. The Spaniards under De Soto had first encountered them, and they were said to adorn their persons with gold and silver ornaments, which, as well as their horses, they had obtained from the Spaniards.

Padoucas and Gran Quivira.

La Harpe's party went on under great difficulties. The carries were swampy and infested with noxious animals. At last he reached the Nassonites, and began a fort among them, as he had been instructed to do. In June (1719) he received from the Spanish governor a reply to Bienville's letter, which he had dispatched in April, while among the Cenis. This answer resented the French invasion of Spanish territory. La Harpe, in his rejoinder, referred to the prior occupation of Texas by La Salle, and the later explorations of St. Denis. Further, he argued that there was no question about the French rights to the Mississippi basin, and the Nassonites, among whom the French were now sojourning, were dwellers on an affluent of the Great River.

Nassonites.

THE EXTREME WEST.

[From a map by Palairet, improved by Delaroche, after Danville, Mitchell, and Bellin. It shows "Quivira;" the "River of the West;" the supposed connection of the Mississippi and Red River of the North; the country of the Padoucas, Panis, etc.]

Not deterred by the Spanish protests, La Harpe, getting some horses from the Indians, still pushed on, and September 3, he found himself beside the Arkansas River. A part of his purpose had been to discover the sources of the Red and Arkansas rivers, but in this he had failed. He learned that other Spanish settlements were higher up the Arkansas, and he believed that both rivers rose somewhere in New Mexico. With this information or impression, he began his backward journey.

The Arkansas River. 1719.

CHAPTER V.

THE MISSISSIPPI BUBBLE.

1714–1720.

"CADILLAC always says the opposite of what he believes," said Bienville, who had scant respect for his superior. The governor found others could practice the same art. Towards the end of 1714, he received from the Illinois what was represented to be ore from mines of that region. Shortly afterwards, Cadillac was on his way up the river to inspect the wonderful deposits. It proved a deceit, and the specimen of silver had been carried there from New Mexico. After an absence of nearly a year, Cadillac returned to Mobile in October, 1715.

Cadillac and silver mines in Illinois. 1714-15.

Louis XIV. had died a few weeks before, and France was left with an enormous debt. There was need of eighty million livres to meet the obligations, and the royal treasury could only command about nine millions. Mines or something else were needed, and the possibilities of Louisiana were soon to be made the most of by an extraordinary personage.

The debt of France.

John Law stands in European history as the creator of one of the most marvelous crazes ever known. This strange manifestation was as much a wonder to Law's contemporaries as it is to us. A tract (1720) purporting to emanate from an Englishman in the colonies, and reflecting upon the consequences of the French occupation of the Great Valley, speaks of Law's success, before he reached the precipice, as "one of the most prodigious events of any age," and sniffs at the skeptics.

John Law and his scheme.

A Scotchman, extremely nimble of mind, but destitute of sane principles, nurtured a rake and a gambler, Law had fled from London to Amsterdam to avoid arrest. Here his quick perceptions seized on some methods which he observed in the bank of Amsterdam as affording such great and possible developments as are ever attractive to those holding vagabondish

JOHN LAW.

[From *Het Groote Tafereel*, etc.]

notions of finance. He accordingly laid before the Scottish parliament a plan for alluring his countrymen to the glorious capabilities of paper money. The canny Scots were not so easily captured, and he fell back to his old ways and sunk himself once more in dissipation. His hour was not yet come.

Events in Louisiana.

Meanwhile the leaders of Louisiana, ignorant of what was in store, had enough to occupy their attention. The flat-headed Choctaws, instigated by Bienville, had pillaged some English traders, and brought them to Mobile. The French at this time had become particularly anxious over the increase of the English trade, and had been much alarmed with reports of what Young and other English emissaries were doing along the Mississippi banks to gain the sympathy of the natives. The action of the Choctaws was simply an effort to show their steadfastness to the French interests.

To keep all this region under closer surveillance, the French authorities had already given orders to construct some new stockades, — one above Mobile, another near the Natchez, and a third at the mouth of the Ohio. Bienville was making ready to go up to the Natchez when word reached him of the fearful devastation which that tribe was making among the French, trustfully scattered in their neighborhood. It was the beginning of the ruthless Natchez wars, and we have the story in the narratives of Richebourg and Penicault. It should be remembered that both of these chroniclers are partisans of Bienville in his quarrels with Cadillac. They both say that what had angered the tribe was the governor's impulsive rejection of the Natchez calumet, offered to him while passing up and down the Mississippi in his recent search for mines. Crozat in France sided with the enemies of Cadillac, and set in motion the influence which soon led to his recall.

The war with the Natchez.

Bienville started up the river with such a force as the governor would spare. All overtures of atonement which the Natchez offered him were rejected, unless they were accompanied by the surrender of the murderers or their heads. His persistence prevailed; obedience was rendered, and he even got their help in building a stockade to awe them for the future. This was the beginning of Fort Rosalie, the earliest permanent station of the French in the Great Valley south of Kaskaskia.

Fort Rosalie.

Bienville, on his return to Mobile, learned of Cadillac's recall. A new governor, L'Epinay, was to be sent out, but until he arrived Bienville held the chief power. This control lasted from October, 1716, till March, 1717, when L'Epinay came, in company with some soldiers and emigrants. He had instructions to carry out stringently the monopoly of Crozat.

Bienville succeeds Cadillac. 1716-17.

Louisiana had now a population of about seven hundred, for Crozat had done little to increase their numbers. He had neglected even to augment the laboring population by the importation of blacks. The agricultural condition of the province had not, therefore, improved, and Crozat was in reality bankrupt after four years of unsuccessful commercial effort.

Crozat surrenders charter. 1717.

The renewed instructions to L'Epinay had been merely a last gasp of power. Indeed, Crozat was already prepared to seek relief by surrendering his charter, and this he actually did in August, 1717, before he could have known anything of the effect of his last injunctions.

All the privileges which Crozat had enjoyed were now vested in a new organization known as "The Company of the West," or more popularly as "The Mississippi Company." This body received its charter September 6, 1717. Its capital stock was fixed in December at a hundred million livres. It was expected to restore the shattered finances of the kingdom by funding as *rentes* the outstanding *Billets d'Etat*, the government guaranteeing four per cent. on its capital. This was to be Law's opportunity.

Company of the West or Mississippi Company. 1717.

An engrossing search for mines was no longer to imperil the prosperity of Louisiana, and the Spaniards were to be suffered to get on as best they could without the aid of French trade. Bienville was understood to represent the best spirit in the province, which was to do for Louisiana what the Canadian leaders had failed to effect for Canada, — develop its agriculture and at the same time work its mines. In being constituted by the company the governor-general, Bienville felt that he was now to have his opportunity to make manifest the possibilities of the province. Through him the company could regulate all civil matters; could build forts and arm vessels for its defense. It was claimed that frigates of thirty guns could patrol the Mississippi for six hundred leagues.

Bienville governor of the company.

This new life for Louisiana had a lease of twenty-five years, and it was to be invigorated by bringing into the country six thousand whites and half as many blacks. In five years the company did actually send over seven thousand settlers beside six hundred slaves from Guinea.

Law had already attracted the attention of the Regent, and was given the chief control of the company. If inevitable disaster overtook his stultified adherents in Europe, Louisiana at least got a start in something like the right direction. Under these impulses the life of the colony began to assume the character which comes from settled labor, and lost many of the haphazard turns which come from vagrancy. Law's influence in Louisiana.

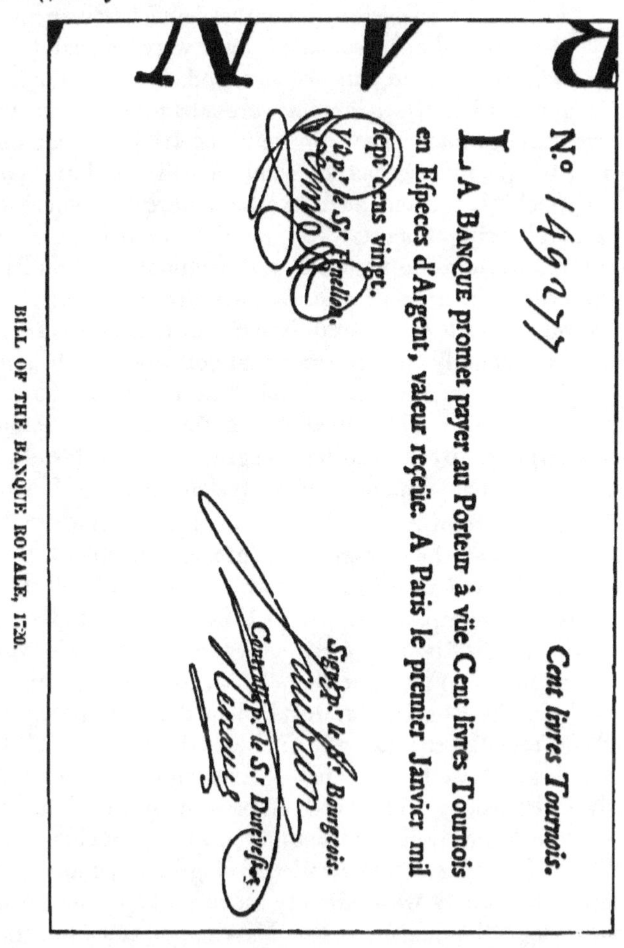

No 149277

Cent livres Tournois.

LA BANQUE promet payer au Porteur à vüe Cent livres Tournois en Especes d'Argent, valeur reçeüe. A Paris le premier Janvier mil sept cens vingt.

Vû p.r le S.r Fenellon.

Signé p.r le S.r Bourgeois.

Contrôlé p.r le S.r Durevest.

BILL OF THE BANQUE ROYALE, 1720.

About sixteen months before the new company received its charter, Law had opened in Paris (May 2, 1716) a private bank of issue, which the government had favored as a means of absorbing in its capital seventy-five per Law in Paris. 1716.

cent. in its *Billets d'Etat.* Law treated it as an experiment, hoping by his success to induce the government to make it a royal bank. The forming of the new company was an opportune help to that end, and Law's position in it served to make it subservient to the wider interests of the kingdom.

The main thing was to populate Louisiana, and create an apparent prosperity by numbers and labor on the soil. To this end concessions of land were offered to those who could send out settlers, and as a greater inducement to speculation the grantees were not required to accompany the immigrants. Law himself received a tract on the Arkansas River, and agreed to send out fifteen hundred persons. Unluckily, neither he nor others were compelled to be careful in choosing tenants. So we find a good part of the comers for a while to be vagrants and criminals, but on May 9, 1720, an order was issued forbidding such recklessness.

Concessions of land in Louisiana.

There was no lack of general interest in these measures, and one finds occasionally in cartographical collections a "Cours du Mississippi ou Saint Louis," as the map was called, prepared in 1718, to abet the fever, at the command of the company, by a leading geographer, Nicolas de Fer. Across the English Channel there was an echoing furor, and an old plate of John Senex's "Map of North America" was revamped to meet the demand for information about the new El Dorado. It was inscribed to Law. Herman Moll, the rising English cartographer, inserted (1720) in his map a legend athwart the trans-Mississippi region, saying that "this country is full of mines." At a later day, 1755, Mitchell, in his great map made in the English interests when the final struggle was impending, recalled the fever in the legend: "Mines of Marameg, which gave rise to the famous Mississippi scheme, 1719."

Maps of Louisiana.

Early in February, 1718, three ships sent by the Company of the West arrived at Dauphine Island. They brought to Bienville a commission, giving him the authority of commandant. There were already movements in progress for new surveys of the mouth of the Mississippi, so as to establish an entrance from the Gulf more practicable than that by way of Lake Pontchartrain. Bienville, with his new powers, now sent a party to clear the ground for a trading-post at a spot on the river about a hundred miles from the Gulf, which had

Ships arrive. 1718.

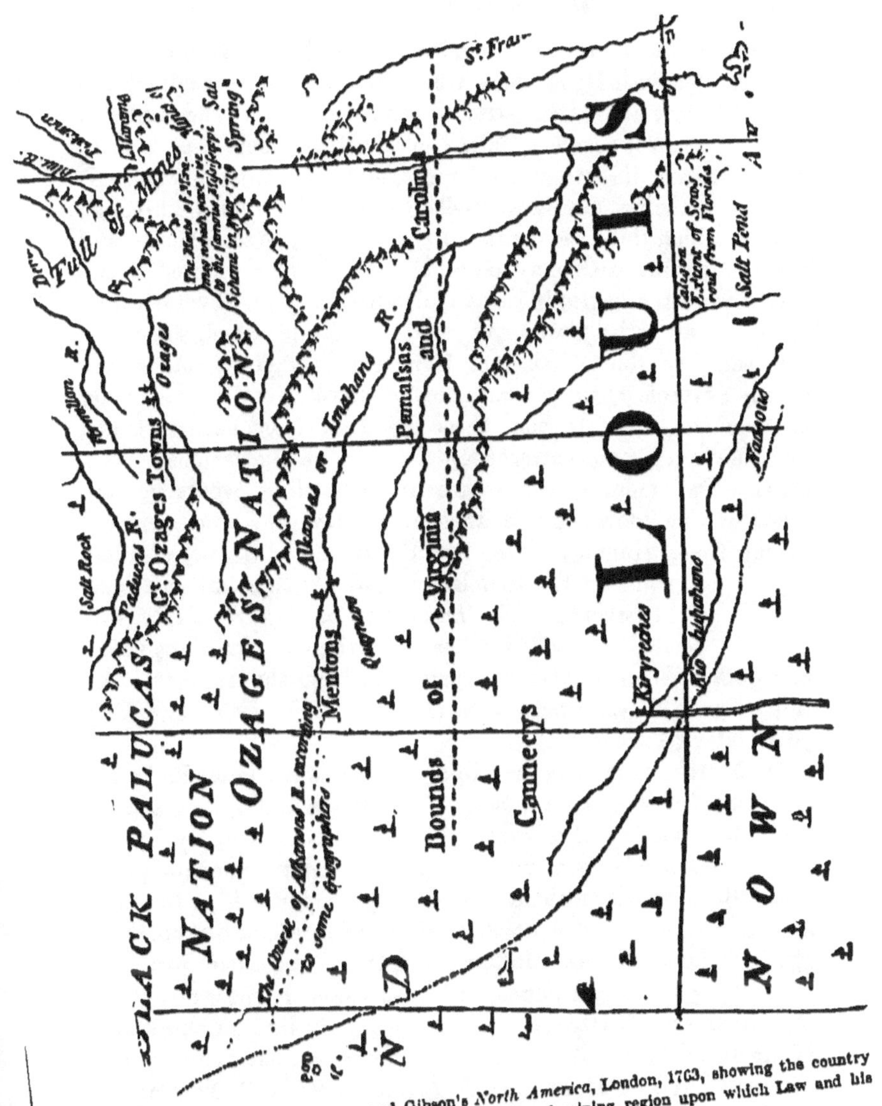

[This map is from Bowen and Gibson's *North America*, London, 1763, showing the country of the Black Padoucas, the Osages, and the alleged mining region upon which Law and his followers based their expectations of wealth.]

already attracted the commandant's attention. This was on a curve of the shore where the banks were about ten feet above the stream. Back from this the land fell off, and when it reached Lake Pontchartrain there was but little to prevent its waters breaking over the swampy margin. It was nevertheless the most inviting site in the almost universal morass which lined the course of the river. The storehouses and traders' cabins with clay chimneys which soon showed themselves were the beginning of the destined city of New Orleans.

New Orleans. 1718.

While everything was yet crude and unfinished, some vessels sent by the Mississippi Company landed in this infant colony (March 9) three companies of infantry and a small body of colonists. In August, three hundred more settlers came, and they were soon scattered up the river on the various concessions. Two men, to whose care in chronicling events we owe much of our knowledge of these early days in Louisiana, were among these grantees. One was Benard de la Harpe, who had a grant on the Red River, and who has left us a journal of events. The other was Le Page du Pratz, who settled near the Natchez, where he lived for eight years, and gathered much curious information from the Indians. All this he gave to the world in a *Histoire de la Louisiane* forty years later (1758).

La Harpe and Du Pratz.

In March, 1719, five hundred negroes were landed; in the following October, a large body of Alsatians and other Germans arrived, a portion of whom at least had been sent by Law as settlers upon his own grants. If these developments promised well, a check to them was already prepared in a war with Spain. In August, 1718, the representatives of England, France, Holland, and the Empire had formed a quadruple alliance, with the avowed purpose of upholding the treaty of Utrecht and forcing Spain into an observance of its provisions. A declaration of war against Spain proved necessary, and on December 17 (January 9, 1719, New Style), hostilities were decided upon. The news reached Mobile in April, and Bienville at once organized a force to surprise Pensacola. After a brief investment by sea and land, he took the place and sent the prisoners to Havana. The Spaniards seized the ships which had brought the prisoners, and during the summer returned and retook the

Quadruple alliance and war with Spain. 1718.

Pensacola taken and lost. 1719.

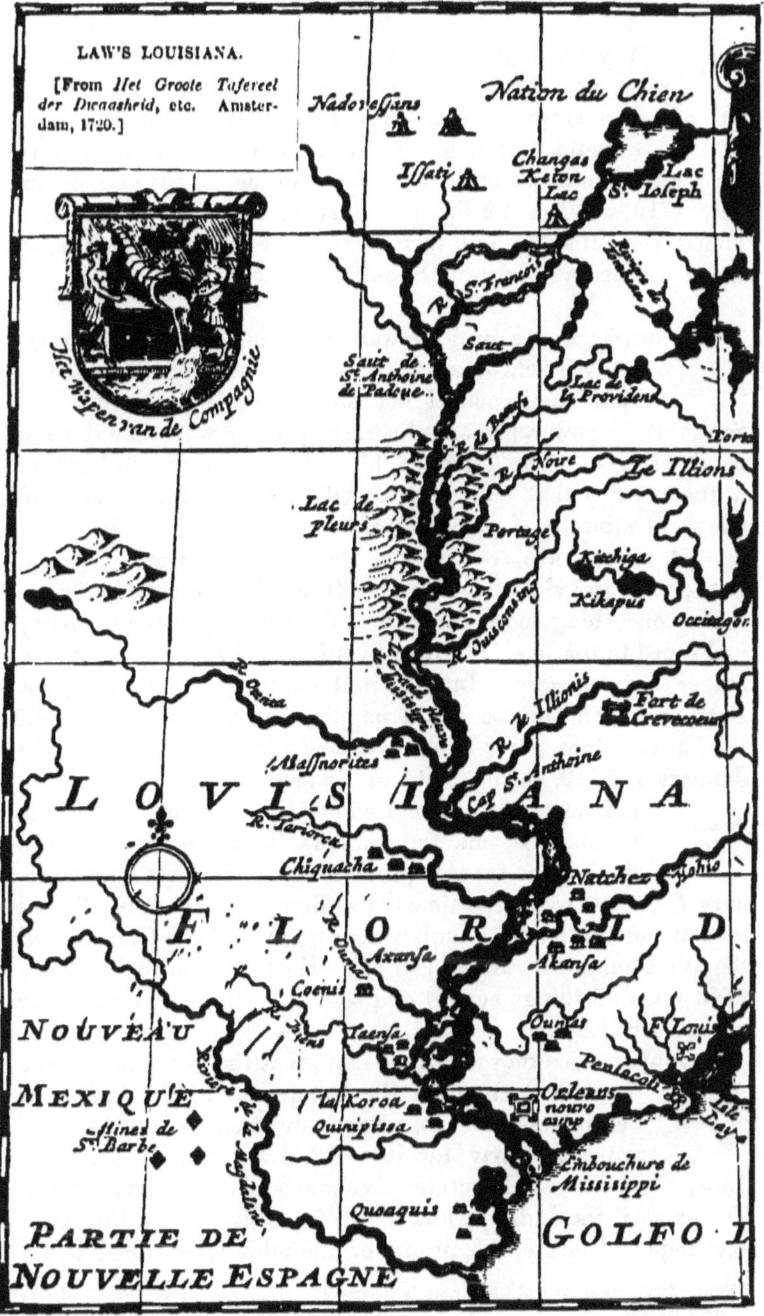

LAW'S LOUISIANA.

[From *Het Groote Tafereel der Dwaasheid*, etc. Amsterdam, 1720.]

town. They tried at the same time to make an impression on the French post at Dauphine Island, but the opportune arrival of some ships from France completed the discomfiture of the assailants, and they withdrew. It was again Bienville's turn, and Pensacola once more fell, into his hands in September, 1719. When Philip, the Spanish king, succumbed and joined the alliance, and there was peace in 1721, Pensacola was confirmed at last to its Spanish founders.

Meanwhile, Law's projects were ripening for good, as everybody seemed to think, — at least for everybody's individual good, if not for the public good. The Regent, then in power, placed all sorts of privileges in the extended hands of Law. The shares of his company became so buoyant in the market that nobody dreamed of a precipice. The old stories of mines in Louisiana were revived, and their sites were figured, as we have seen, in the maps. Ingots were produced at the mint in evidence, — coming from Mexico, very likely.

Law's Company.

The one thing more for Law to do was to get all the money in France into a bank of royal prestige. Then loans would no longer be necessary. Interest and taxation would disappear. Both crown and people would happily discover that true credit is what the state gains by an excess of paper over bullion. On January 1, 1719, such a state of financial bliss came in with the new year. The Banque Générale of the Scotch prophet became the Banque Royale of France, with the Regent for sole proprietor. A few days later (January 5), Law was proclaimed its director. He was allowed to make an unlimited circulation of notes, and the Company of the West existed to work them off. He was permitted to put a tariff upon all things bought and sold. In this way everything was absorbed by it.

Banque Royale. 1719.

In May, it was known in Louisiana that the Company of the West had engulfed the Companies of the East, and before long the colony was directed to receive more paper and pay for it with all the coin it had. In June, 1719, the conglomerated companies took the name of the Company of the Indies, while the frenzy still grew on the Paris exchange. In July, the profits of the mint were added to its

Company of the Indies. 1719.

NOTE. The opposite view of Quinquempoix is from *Het Groote Tafereel der Dwaasheid*, etc. Amsterdam, 1720.

resources, and this privilege was to run for nine years. The stock gave a new bound upward, only to be temporarily depressed, upon a rumor of Law's illness. An installment plan was introduced, and so the circle of victims was inordinately widened. By the end of the year (1719), there were half a million foreigners gesticulating in the streets of Paris, eager for something. "Paris," says the English pamphleteer already cited, "like the temple of Fortune among the heathen, is resorted to by innumerable crowds of every nation, quality, and condition, and the dirty kennel of Quinquempoix has for some time been more frequented than the Royal Exchange of London."

The capital stock, increased to six hundred thousand shares, rose to fifteen thousand francs a share and even higher, — some thousands per cent. advance in the end. It came to be known that three thousand millions of livres were borne on the face of its aggregated paper.

In January, 1720, Law became comptroller-general of the kingdom. In February, the company absorbed the Banque Royale with all its privileges. The entire money power of the country was now at Law's disposal, and every tax came into his hands. But the fabric had begun to totter. Law was at his wits' end to keep this from being known. In May, he tried a hazardous expedient, and issued a royal decree to reduce values. Within a week he saw he had made a blunder, and the decree was revoked. It proved too late. Shrinking hope had succeeded to buoyant exhilaration. Law worried through the summer and autumn, uncertain how to turn. By December, he was sure that no one could be longer deceived. He put eight hundred livres in his pocket one day and disappeared. The end had come.

Law comptroller-general.

Law disappears.

As soon as the news of Law's flight reached Louisiana (June, 1721), the Germans who had been sent to occupy his concession became alarmed, and in the following November Charlevoix saw their deserted villages. To pacify them, a new grant was made by the authorities, twenty miles up the river from New Orleans, and what is to-day known as the "German Coast" along the stream marks where they settled. They began a new industry in supplying vegetables for the young capital of the province.

Germans in Louisiana.

CHAPTER VI.

THE BARRIERS OF LOUISIANA.

1710–1720.

If La Harpe and St. Denis had failed in finding in the southwest an overland way to the South Sea, there was a vague hope that it might yet be revealed in the northwest. If Lahontan's story of his Rivière Longue was now generally discredited, since Delisle, the leading geographer of France, had pronounced against it, there were, however, still a few credulous cartographers, like Homann of Nuremberg, and Moll the English map-maker, who placed it on their maps. The common opinion among those interested in this problem of a western way to the Pacific pointed rather to the Missouri, or perhaps to some way from Lake Superior by a higher latitude. It was a report that explorers had gone four hundred leagues up the Missouri without encountering any Spaniards, but that a hundred leagues farther tribes were reached who were warring with them. It was a natural apprehension that Spanish success in an Indian war in this direction might enable these rivals to slip in before the French in this western route. Cadillac shared this fear, and was watchful to report all rumors from the far country to his superiors at Paris.

Lahontan and a passage to the western sea.

A priest at Versailles, Father Bobé, who had a correspondent at Mobile, was acting just now as an intermediary between Raudot, one of the secretaries of Pontchartrain, and Delisle the cartographer, in the rectification of the latter's maps. He tells the geographer that his letters from Louisiana speak of a populous country, which the Spaniards had discovered, towards the western sea, and suggests that Bourbonia would be a good name for it on the maps.

Bobé and Delisle.

In October, 1717, the Sieur Hubert made a report to the minister of the marine upon an alleged route by the Missouri, through a rich mining country, and he supposed it to lead to a mountain barrier, where the springs of eastern and western flowing rivers could not be far apart. The notion was not a novel one, but it had always been veiled in conjecture. Delisle and others put near the eastern edges of their maps a lake, with an outlet towards the Pacific, but they avoided any direct presentation towards the west of the mouth of such rivers. Intimations in the book which Tonty discarded, and in the *Carolana* of Coxe, had more or less familiarized the reading public with like notions, which were soon to be reinforced in the great English map of Popple.

Bourgmont, a trader who had been for fifteen years trafficking on the Missouri, was responsible for a story that the Panis (Pawnees) and their kindred in the remote west were trading with other peoples living about a great lake. This far-away race were represented as small of stature and dressed like Europeans. There was a suspicion that they might prove to be Chinese.

The Missouri route to the western sea.

It was thought by some to be a favorable condition of a route by the Missouri, that the tribes along its current were represented to be more tractable than Indians generally were, while more to the north the mutual hostilities of the Sioux and Christineaux rendered exploring peculiarly dangerous. Begon, the Canadian Intendant, informed (October 11, 1718) the Paris government that all hopes of a successful search for the western sea must be abandoned unless these savages could be forced into peace with each other.

In a memorial which was prepared at Paris in 1718, outlining a plan for giving Louisiana a dominating position in North America, it was made a part of the means to that end that the mines on the Missouri should be worked, and commerce with Mexico established from that base. Inasmuch, it went on to say, as the Missouri has one branch leading to the South Sea, trade can also be opened with Japan and China.

La Harpe on the Missouri.

In the summer and autumn of 1719, there were two adventurers, incited by such stories as these, endeavoring to discover the meaning of them. One, La Harpe, had gone up the Mississippi in August with a small escort, and was soon among the Osages on the Missouri, finding

NOTE. The opposite cut is a section of Popple's great *Map of the British Empire in America* (1732), showing the supposed lake and its outlet towards the west.

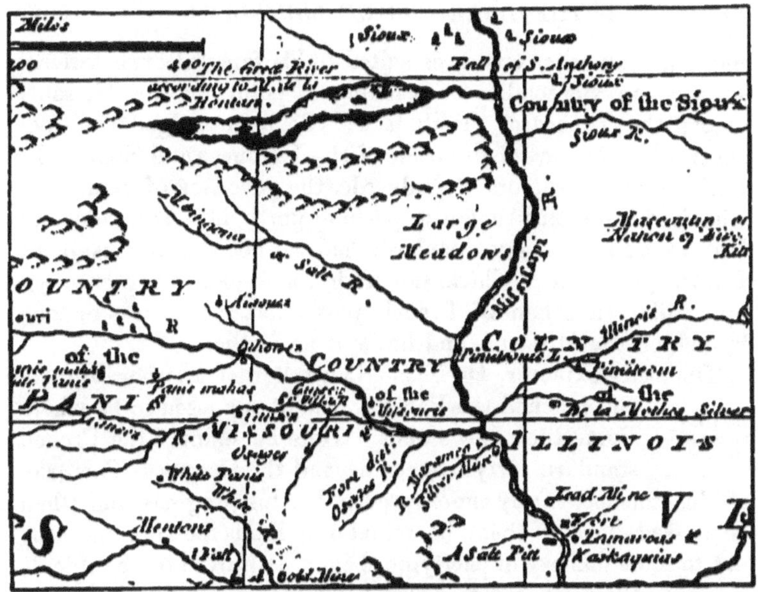

GENTLEMAN'S MAGAZINE, JUNE, 1763.

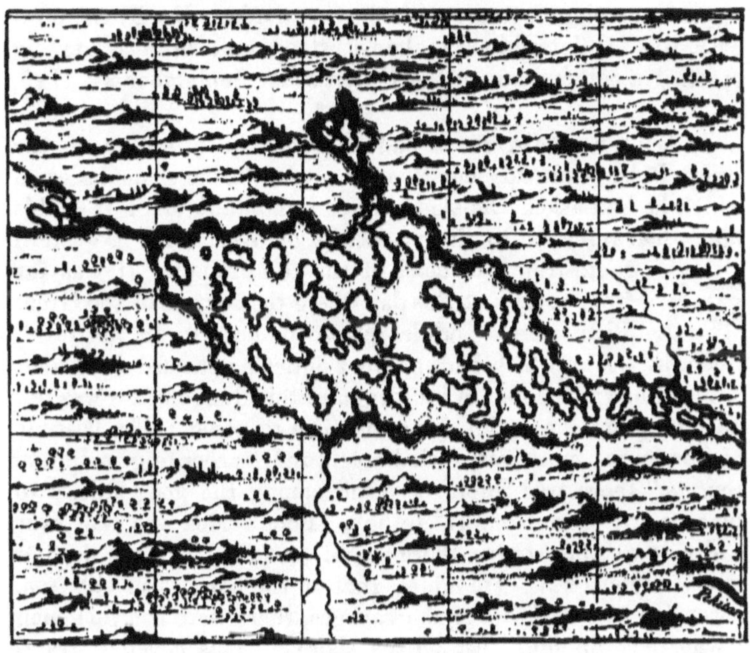

POPPLE, 1732.

unicorns and other creatures suited to his fanciful expectations. Finally, on September 6, reaching a point on the Missouri among the Tonacaras (latitude 37° 21′), he judged the spot favorable to command the trade of the Padoucas and Spaniards. Perhaps he got rumors of Valverde, the governor of Santa Fé, who just about this time was pushing north into Colorado and Kansas, as far as any Spaniards had yet been. At this point La Harpe found a Chickasaw trader, and in his presence set up a pillar in token of French possession. This was on one branch of the Missouri, and he went no farther.

Du Tisné on the Missouri.

The other explorer, Du Tisné, had followed another branch, and reached the Panis at a point supposed to be where Fort Riley now stands. Here he planted the French standard forty leagues beyond the Osages. This people had unsuccessfully endeavored to bar his progress, and when he passed beyond them he found the Panis hostile, and was put to some anxiety in pacifying them. It proved to be difficult to obtain their consent to going farther to reach the Padoucas, whom they looked upon as foes, saying that they stood in the way of carrying on trade with the Spaniards. Du Tisné, however, was too determined to be withstood, and he succeeded in erecting a column among the Padoucas on September 27, 1719.

Source of the Mississippi.

A more northern route had engaged the attention of the priest Bobé — already mentioned, — who, in the same letter in which he had asked Delisle to efface Lahontan's river from his maps, had referred to the possibility of discovering a western route from the head of the Mississippi. It was far from certain at this day where the sources of the Great River were. Cadillac placed its head in 48° north latitude, in a lake which had another outlet northward into what is now known as Lake Winnipeg, and this dual outflow was not an infrequent conception for some time to come. The latitude of this source, moreover, varied much, and, "according to Indian reports," there was found occasion among the geographers to place it anywhere from 47° to 55°. Bobé's idea was that over a divide at this source there would be found a river flowing to the western sea. He added that on the borders of this sea, according to the report of the savages, there were bearded men "who pick up gold dust on the shore." This coveted strand lay, in his belief, far beyond many other nations, to whom the French had not yet come. These stories, as he affirmed, had been picked up among the Sioux.

The passage, meanwhile, which had most engaged the attention of the government was one lying beyond Lake Superior, in the direction which Iberville had followed from Hudson's Bay, twenty years before. It was the route by which ultimately Vérendrye reached the Rocky Mountains. Vandreuil had recommended this route, and it was approved by the Regent, June 26, 1717. It was recognized as too far distant from bases of supply to be sustained by the Indian trade, and that the government must consequently support an exploration by grants. De la Noüe had already been dispatched to Lake Superior to gain information, and in 1717 he had reëstablished Duluth's old fort at the head of the lake. In September, 1718, Vaudreuil, under the orders he had received, sent forward a party to begin operations in earnest. These explorers soon found how pestilent the Sioux could be, and the Indians allied with the French in the exploration were under constant irritation at the difficulties which the Sioux interposed. The movement resulted in placing two new forts in this country, one upon the Lac des Christineaux or Lake of the Woods, and the other upon the Lac des Assinipoiles. This last was the water later known as Lake Winnipeg, which, as we have seen, was connected with the Mississippi in Cadillac's judgment. Homann, Van der Aa, Jaillot, and other secondary cartographers, were constantly representing it as the source of the Mississippi.

Passage beyond Lake Superior.

Lake Winnipeg and the Mississippi.

The establishment of these forts served two purposes. They gave advanced positions for further progress. What was perhaps of more importance, they interposed a barrier to prevent the English from pushing west from Hudson's Bay, where they were now well established under the treaty of Utrecht. The forts might possibly sustain themselves by the Indian traffic; but it was thought that the government would have to make an actual outlay of something like fifty thousand francs, before this occidental sea could be reached. This was not, nevertheless, an adequate calculation of the great cost which would have to be incurred in transporting goods from the ships at Montreal to so remote a region.

In the original grant to Crozat, the Illinois region had been left within the jurisdiction of New France, as the Quebec government was officially called. This took all the country, roughly speaking, lying about the Illinois River and eastward to the Wabash, while the lower peninsula of Michigan fell naturally under the oversight of the commander at Detroit, though Lemaire and others extended Louisiana up to the straits. La Salle had crossed this peninsula along its southern edge at a perilous time, but we have little record of any acquaintance with its interior. The map-makers, like Senex, drawing upon report or imagination, represented the divide between Michigan and Huron as an elevated terrace, along which stretched "a walk above two hundred miles in length." So much ignorance, in fact, prevailed, in spite of familiarity with the neighboring portages of Chicago and St. Joseph, that Jaillot, in 1719, in a map dedicated to the king, slavishly followed the geography of Sanson (1656) and obliterated entirely Lake Michigan, putting in its place the Bay of the Puants (Green Bay) as a pocket of Lake Huron.

Michigan peninsula.

The years which followed the treaty of Utrecht made an opportunity for France, but the chance was lost. Rivalry with England had failed to teach her government the secrets of successful colonization. It appears, however, from some of the memorials presented to the crown, that the lesson was not lost upon all her subjects. She was content with her greater power over the savages. For the most part she continued to maintain this, despite the fact that in all articles of trade, except firearms, powder, and a few trinkets, she charged the Indians more than the English. The French had failed, nevertheless, to discern what Champlain had clearly seen a hundred years before, that the very qualities which made their character attractive to the Indian unfitted it for the real life of a pioneer, if such an existence meant the subduing of the soil.

French colonization.

When Louis XIV. died, on September 1, 1715, he told his grandson that he was conscious of his failure to be a solace to his people. The history of the French in America, indeed, gives constant tokens of his baleful influence in the colony, which might have been the brightest jewel of his crown. New France had been crushed by grinding monopolies,

Louis XIV. dies. 1715.

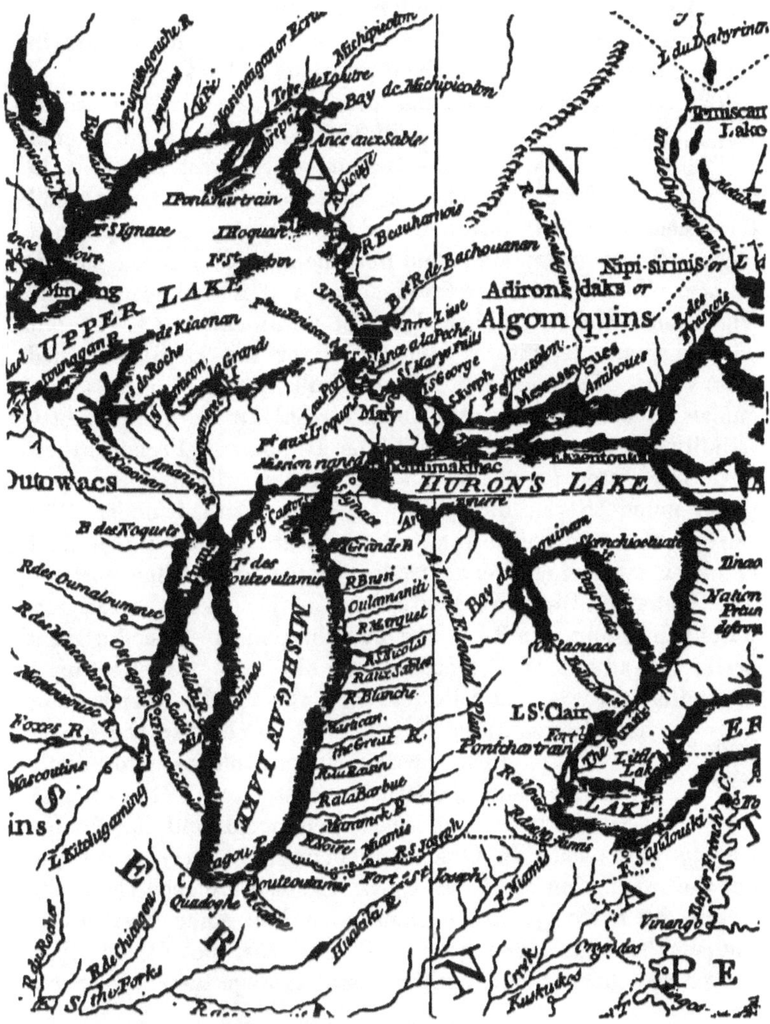

[From Sayer and Jefferys' reproduction of Danville's *North America* (London), showing the current conception of the Michigan peninsula.]

and Louisiana was now undergoing the same degradation. This monopoly diverted energy from building up a state in order that it might sustain the aspirations of hucksters.

The Iroquois and the western tribes.

The Iroquois played fast and loose with this Gallic instinct, to gain what they could, and to let the English gain more. To keep the Indians of the west steadfast in the French service, it was necessary either to bind these nearer tribes in peace, or raid their country to keep them at home. Truces were made and unmade according to the savage humor. The western fur trade ebbed and flowed accordingly. The French had reëstablished a post at Mackinac (1714), but without great benefit to their trade, for the English gained most by it. Through the Iroquois influence the Foxes (Outagamies) and their associates about Green Bay were kept pretty steadily on the English side. The Illinois, as French allies, were fair game for them, and they occasionally pounced upon them, much to the annoyance of their white friends. The Foxes had not forgotten their disasters at Detroit, and had of late been waylaying French traders at the Green Bay portage. The Sauks and Sioux were with them in spirit, and the Iroquois waited their opportunity. The combination threatened a great peril; the advice of Perrot, now an old man, for effecting a reconciliation, was not followed, and the Quebec government sent Louvigny in March, 1716, to chastise the Foxes. He was enjoined further, if possible, to exterminate them for being the ferocious instigators of the conspiracy. The campaign was vigorously conducted, and in October Louvigny was back in Quebec, reporting, not the destruction, but the submission of the savages. He had clinched their subjection by a treaty, and brought with him some hostages to compel the observance of it. The Foxes, notwithstanding, proved treacherous, and nothing could assuage their implacable hostility.

Louvigny and the Foxes.

The northern portages.

These dangers besetting the older portages led to a more general use of the passage by the Maumee and Wabash, as Coxe in his *Carolana* informed the English public in 1722. The post at Vincennes probably became a recognized station at this time, though it was nearly twenty years before it can be said to have ripened into a social community. This line of contact by the Maumee between the

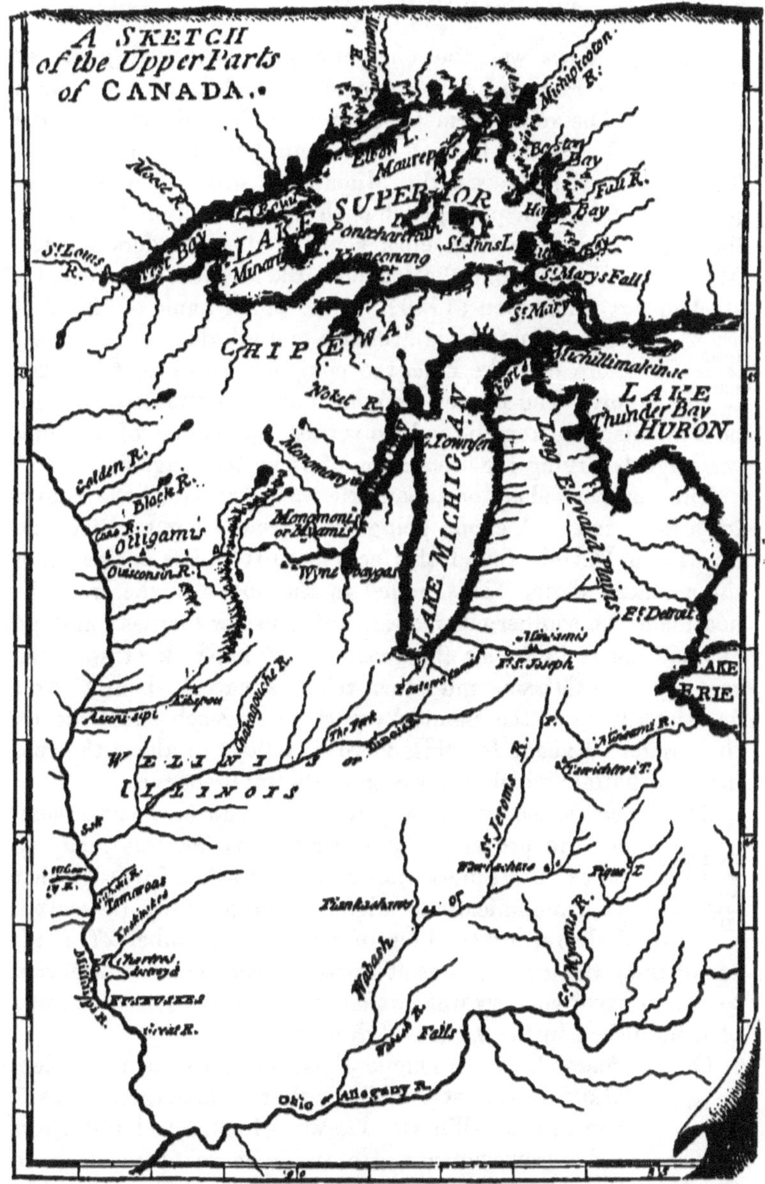

THE ILLINOIS COUNTRY.

[From a corner map in the large *General Map of the British Middle Colonies*, as corrected after Pownall, 1776.]

two great valleys was the only one just now well guarded. That by the Fox and Wisconsin rivers had become well-nigh deserted. The routes near Chicago were also subject to savage raids, and La Salle's fort of Crèvecœur had been abandoned. The French tried to draw the Miamis to settle about and protect the St. Joseph portage; but the English offered superior inducements for them to cluster about their traders on the Maumee. To keep out the Iroquois, the French constructed a stockade at Ouiatanon (1720), on the north bank of the Wabash. East of the Maumee and all along the southern shore of Lake Erie, the confederates were still a terror. The French had not dared to establish a single post in this wide region, and Governor Spotswood of Virginia was eagerly urging the occupation of it by the English.

South shore of Lake Erie.

This southern shore of Lake Erie was to remain little known for a long time. A canoe going west from Niagara River, on its way to Detroit, found this course thirty miles longer than the northern shore. This, added to the terror of the Iroquois, had made the southern banks an untracked wilderness, and no one had dared to follow the footsteps of La Salle athwart the region. The Ottawas and other tribes squatted about Detroit occasionally used the Sandusky portage to reach the Ohio on their raids. Except for this, there was little to alarm the vast herds of buffalo which roamed amid its water-courses.

There were reasons, then, why the French government, reversing the provisions of Crozat's charter, was ready to annex the Illinois country to Louisiana, in order that its communications might be more easily preserved. A decree of the king in council, September 27, 1717, establishing this union, came at a period when renewed attention to that up-river country was awakened because of fresh accounts of it published in the *Lettres Edifiantes*.

The Illinois country joined to Louisiana. 1717.

On February 9, Pierre Dugué Boisbriant, a cousin of Bienville, arrived at Mobile with a commission to command in the Illinois. He was directed to build a fort in his government. He was also to keep watch on the English, who might be attracted by the mines which he was expected to open. In October he started up the Mississippi in canoes, carrying a hundred men, and in December he was at Kaskaskia. He began his fort sixteen miles above that

Boisbriant in the Illinois. 1718.

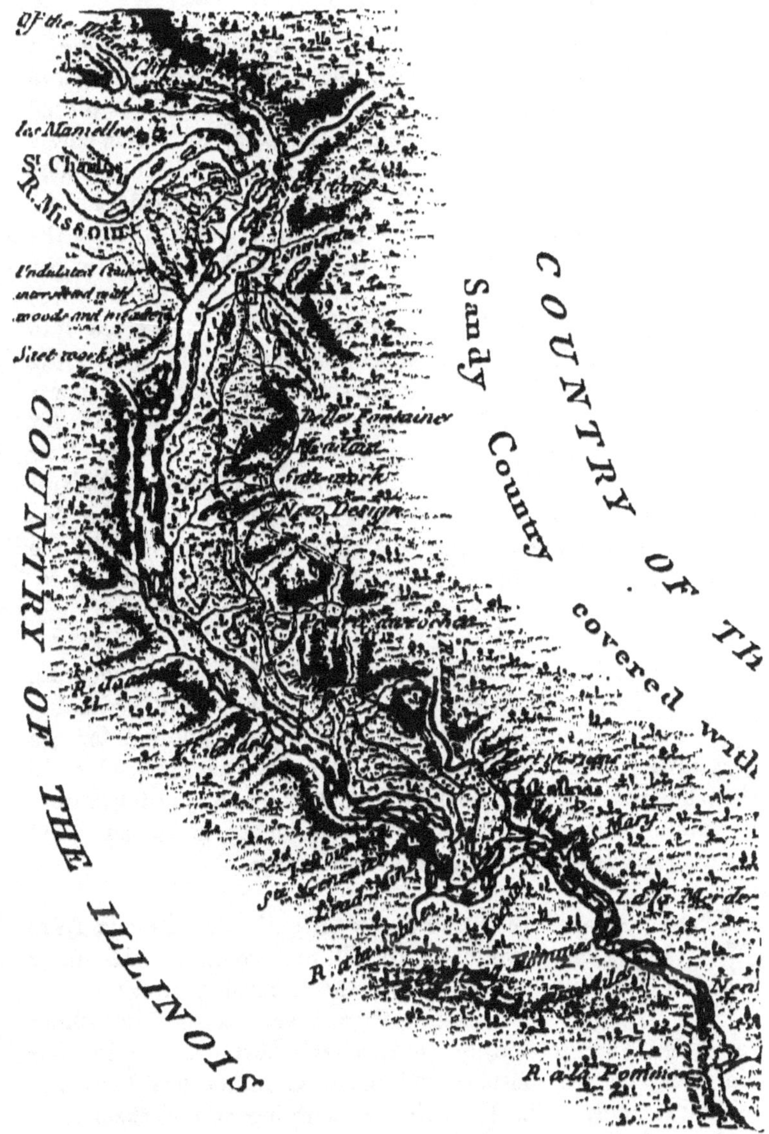

KASKASKIA AND KAHOKIA.

[Part of a *Map of the Course of the Mississippi, gravé par Tardieu.*]

place on the left bank of the Mississippi, and in the spring of 1720 it was completed, and named Fort Chartres in compliment to the Regent of France. It was placed one mile from the river; but to-day its site is partly covered by the current. The United States land commissioners at Kaskaskia, December, 1809, reported that the neighboring village, which originally stood "a small distance" below the fort, "had been mostly, if not wholly, washed away by the river."

Fort Chartres. 1720.

The next year, the mission at Kaskaskia was converted into a parish, — a sign of permanence in the life of the upper valley which had been slow in coming. It was helped, doubtless, now by a temporary passion for mining, instigated by the fever which, as we have seen, Law was spreading in Paris. One Philippe François Renault brought thither at this day some two hundred miners and five hundred slaves; but Kaskaskia profited in the end more by the families which came in his train. The lead mines of the modern Galena were opened, and life was active for a while.

Kaskaskia and the mines.

Canada had now a population of about twenty-three thousand. Some manufactures of coarse fabrics were beginning, and the merchants of Quebec were allowed for the first time to open an exchange, and enjoy partial freedom in their business. It was a slight sign that new ways of life were beginning to operate; but they were to be too much hampered for a generous competition with the English.

Canada.

There was need to withdraw the attention of Canada from this new activity in the Illinois country. All along the Appalachian range, the natural bulwark of the English colonies, the French were constantly looking for English aggression, but only at the northern end in New York, and at the southern end below Carolina, was there imminent danger. The English had long ingratiated themselves with the Indians who guarded those approaches. Here, as Moll in his maps designated them, the "Charakeys and Iroquois" formed efficient outposts for the English.

The Appalachian border.

Though New England was territorially apart from this extended frontier, she had a decided mission in helping to sustain the efficacy of the barrier. This mission was to disconcert any western aggression of the Canadians by keeping their attention upon the northeast. To this end, in 1710, Nicholson's fleet had sailed from Boston, and in October it took Port Royal in Acadia. All the colonies north of Pennsylvania only looked upon this success as an earnest of something more. Their governors accordingly held a meeting at New London, and established their respective quotas for a more serious attack the next year. The English government, in the mean while, promised to help them with a naval contingent. Sir Hovenden Walker with a fleet reached Boston in due time. With Samuel Vetch commanding the provincials, the armament sailed at the end of July, 1711, to carry out the confident plans of St. John, the English minister. New England bore the odium of the failure, though, if Jeremy Dummer is to be believed, she did not deserve it. A royal favorite, General Hill, in command furnished quite enough incapacity to relieve the Yankees of the responsibility. Canada was, indeed, ill prepared; but, fortunately for her, she was not put to a severe test. The elements needed no ally, and shattered Walker's fleet in the St. Lawrence (August). Everybody's courage oozed out, and no one dared to repair the loss which the gales had caused, and proceed to the attack. Sir Hovenden, with what was left of his fleet, turned and fled; and in October the disgraced general was in England charging the New Englanders with his misfortunes.

New England.

Sends armament against Quebec. 1711.

A land force, which had meanwhile gathered at Albany, waiting for happy tidings of a naval victory before advancing by Lake Champlain, never got farther, and Canada breathed freer.

Thus New England in this chance failed to do her part in the general attack, and New York remained inert. There was, perhaps, a too narrow policy of self-protection prevailing at Albany. At any rate, Massachusetts thought so, and (May 11, 1711) complained to Lord Dartmouth "of the criminal neutrality maintained by New York with the French Indians."

Robert Hunter had shortly before (June 14, 1710) been transferred as governor from Virginia to New York. He knew that the southern colonies felt as bitterly toward New York as New England did; for while the Iroquois,

New York.

unchecked, raided down the Appalachians to Carolina, the New Yorkers treated them tenderly along the Mohawk. Logan of Pennsylvania, in a memoir to the home government, a little later, recognized this; but at the same time he insisted that the safety of the colonies as a whole depended on their maintaining the good-will of the Iroquois in New York. To this end, Governor Hunter, while he felt there was no effective union of the colonies, was hanging the silver crowns of Queen Anne about the necks of the Iroquois warriors in token of their obligations to fight on the English side. All the while, Hunter's assembly was earnestly representing to the throne that the French were securing all the back country and misguiding the Indians. "He ought to be a cunning man who treats with the Indians," says an English writer at this point, "and therefore the French leave it to the Jesuits." Fortunately, the English had a match for the priest in Madame Montour, who was usefully employed occasionally in conferences with the confederates. She was the daughter of a French Canadian by a Huron woman, but had been captured in youth by the Iroquois, and had since lived among them, married to an Oneida chief. The French never forgot her unnatural defection.

Madame Montour.

It was in some respects a more striking influence upon the Iroquois which Schuyler exercised when he took five Mohawk chiefs to England, and let them see the evidences of British power. They had their portraits taken, and a series of mezzotints following those pictures were favorite prints among our ancestors. Addison and Steele made the sachems play conspicuous parts in the scenic weeks of the *Tatler* and *Spectator*.

Mohawk chiefs in England.

It was not the policy of the French to let the provisions of the treaty of Utrecht have all their effect on the Iroquois; and the English made steady complaints of the insidious schemes of Joncaire and other French intriguers to draw the confederates over to the French interests. It grew to be a constant assertion that "the French were debauching the Iroquois through the Jesuits and by other means."

The French and the Iroquois.

In July, 1715, Colonel Heathcote notified Governor Hunter that the French had entered the Onondaga country in force, for the purpose of erecting a fort there. He urged the colonial governments to build a line of posts along the frontier, "to answer the line of settlements the French have for some time been, and are now, making from the Mississippi to Canada." Schuyler, as acting governor, tried in return, but unsuccessfully, to induce the Onondagas to drive Joncaire from their villages. All the while, the confederates were not chary of their professions of friendship, and in August, 1715, the record of one of their councils with the English represents them as saying, "We must acquaint you that we have a hatchet of our own, which we have had of old, and which has always been very successful and fortunate. It has subdued a great many nations of Indians, and we have made their habitations a wilderness and desolate, and that hatchet is still lying by us ready, and it is yours as well as ours."

These rival bids for the confederates' alliance naturally divided the tribes, and at least a third of them had before this been drawn away to the St. Lawrence and fallen under the direct influence of the French. So we find Logan of Pennsylvania rather pitifully complaining, in 1718, that beyond what was left to them of the Iroquois, the English had hardly fifteen hundred Indians in their interests north of Carolina.

The Iroquois on the St. Lawrence.

The great Iroquois trail passed west from Albany, by successive "castles" of the confederates, and so on to the Niagara portage. Another path branched off among the Senecas and passed down the upper streams of the Alleghany to the Ohio. This was one of the routes along which occupation must be pressed, and the passage made familiar, if the traders from Albany were to join those from Pennsylvania and Virginia, and make good in the end the occupation of the Ohio valley.

Iroquois trails.

In these years, large numbers of Lutheran Palatines were seeking asylums in England, and near three thousand of them came to swell this westward tide along the Mohawk. Among them were the orphaned Zenger, who was later to champion a free press in Pennsylvania, and the parents of Conrad Weiser, who was to become the conspicuous intermediary with the Ohio Indians when the decisive epoch came.

Palatines.

The French were making ready to check this advance, and at a later day (1721), when Joncaire fortified a post at Niagara, the act was promptly resented by the English as an encroachment. It was, however, as the occupants of

Niagara.

the post contended, nothing more than a natural result of the possession of that strategical point by La Salle in the previous century.

Oswego.

The English sought to counteract this movement, and preserve their trade with the remoter tribes, threatened through this occupation of Niagara, by planting their power at Oswego. Burnet, now the governor of New York, strove to make his assembly authorize the construction of a fort at that point; but failing in this, he used his private means to do it. The governor at Quebec protested. He did not dare to eject the intruders, as he called them, but resorted to new intrigues with the Iroquois to make those Indians drive the English off. The ultimate result of this bold step of Burnet was that the French put two armed vessels on the lake, and tried to intercept the Indian trade by a post at the modern Toronto. The English, on the other hand, hoped to put a stop to the clandestine trade by which Albany supplied goods to the Montreal traders, now prohibited by law (1720). To effect this, they constructed Fort Lydius on the Hudson, fourteen miles from Lake George, — later to become better known as Fort Edward.

The Scotch-Irish.

While the rivals were playing off one measure against another along the Iroquois route, there was no inaction farther south. Along the Pennsylvania border, the Scotch-Irish were receiving new currents of their valiant blood. This North Irish people had been paid for their devotion to the Protestant succession in England by so much persecution for their non-conformity that they had sought relief by coming to the American colonies in large numbers. Governor Shute had tried to settle a part of those who had come to Massachusetts along the Maine coast and throughout the northern frontiers, hoping to make them bear the brunt of the Canadian onsets. The first immigration had landed in Boston in 1712. Continued raids of the Indians had so unsettled some of their abodes that a part of these northern frontiersmen were instigated to join their kindred in Pennsylvania. Some Palatine

Germans.

Germans, discontented with the aristocratic preëmptions of lands about them, followed not long after from the Mohawk country, and thus the pioneer blood of the communities pressing against the Alleghanies was doubly reinforced. The tide of emigration which was yet to surge through the mountain passes could have no hardier stocks for the task before it.

All the while that these people and others, chiefly servants released from contracts, were spreading up the streams toward the mountains, the authorities of Pennsylvania kept out some adventurous youths, wandering afield, so as to observe what the French were doing along the Ohio. In 1718, Governor Keith of Pennsylvania was transmitting the reports of these scouts to the home government. At the same time he urged the Lords of Trade to establish a fort on Lake Erie. In his *Caroluna*, Coxe was enforcing the dangers of delay, and picturing the risks which would unhappily result if by connivance of the Iroquois the French got foothold on the lake. He pointed out how the portages to the Susquehanna and the Juniata would open a way for an attack on Pennsylvania and Virginia.

Fear of the French.

A bustling, active man was now ruling in Virginia. Governor Spotswood had been a soldier, and had been wounded at Blenheim. To show his career in Virginia his many letters are fortunately preserved. He had early made inquiries of the Indians about the springs of the Potomac, and had been informed that they were in a lake beyond the mountains, whence the current issued and forced its way through the hilly barrier. Spotswood argued that by pushing up this valley and through this gorge, there was a fair chance of being able to cut the line of French communications from Canada to Louisiana. He thought that the English would have an advantage in maintaining posts in this trans-montane country over the French, inasmuch as their supplies would be carried by a shorter line.

Spotswood in Virginia.

Spotswood was a loyal supporter of the English sea-to-sea charters. He claimed that the grant to Penn went to the borders of Ontario, as some contemporary maps represent it. The Virginia charter, he contended, included all other territorial rights to the west, north of Carolina. In this he formulated the Virginia claim, which was only abandoned by her cession of the northwest lands at the close of the Revolutionary War. Under Spotswood's interpretation, this charter covered the Great Lakes from Erie west, and took in a large

Limits of Virginia.

part of the country bordering on the upper branches of the Mississippi.

In announcing this, Spotswood showed abundant ignorance of what the French had done. "In which space westward of us," he says, in 1720, "I don't know that the French yet have any settlements, nor that any other European nation ever had. Neither is it probable that the French from their new plantations will be able in some years to reach the southern boundaries mentioned in the charter of Virginia." He then contends that the French posts on the lower Mississippi are within the charter limits of Carolina. By the last advices, he adds, the French have a settlement at "Habbamalas," as he calls the Alabama region, where in fact the French had been seated for more than a decade.

In one of his letters (December 10, 1710), Spotswood records that some adventurers had recently gone not above a hundred miles beyond the farthest settlements, and had ascended a mountain, before deemed inaccessible, where they had looked down into the valley of Virginia. Though the descent on the farther side seemed easy, they had not tried it because the season was late. Not far from the same time, De Graffenreid described ascending Sugar Loaf Mountain, near the sources of the Potomac, and said that he saw from the summit three distinct ranges, one higher than the other, with beautiful valleys lying between the nearer hills.

The valley of Virginia.

There is little doubt that an occasional trader had for a long time before this pushed through gaps hereabouts, but without making public record of it. The Shawnees were in the lower parts of the valley, and are known to have received, and to have passed west, various products of English manufacture. Such adventurers could scarcely have missed observing the well-defined traces of the buffalo between gap and gap. A few years later (1715), the movement of the English in this direction was exciting alarm among the French. Father Mermet, at Kaskaskia, even reported that the English were building forts. The French were trying to induce the Indians of the Wabash to avoid the English traders who were coming among them. These pioneers were in part from Virginia, which had become, next to Massachusetts, the most populous of the English provinces. The great influx of Germans into Virginia had already begun, and they were pushing back towards the mountains.

In 1716, Spotswood made his famous reconnaissance with his Knights of the Golden Horseshoe, for such was the insignia with which he later decorated his companions on this jaunt of jubilation. We have the journal of John Fontaine, who accompanied the governor, — meagre enough, but with Spotswood's letters it constitutes most of the knowledge which we have of the undertaking. Robert Beverly, the historian of Virginia, was another companion, but he was not so regardful of posterity.

Spotswood and his Knights of the Golden Horseshoe. 1716.

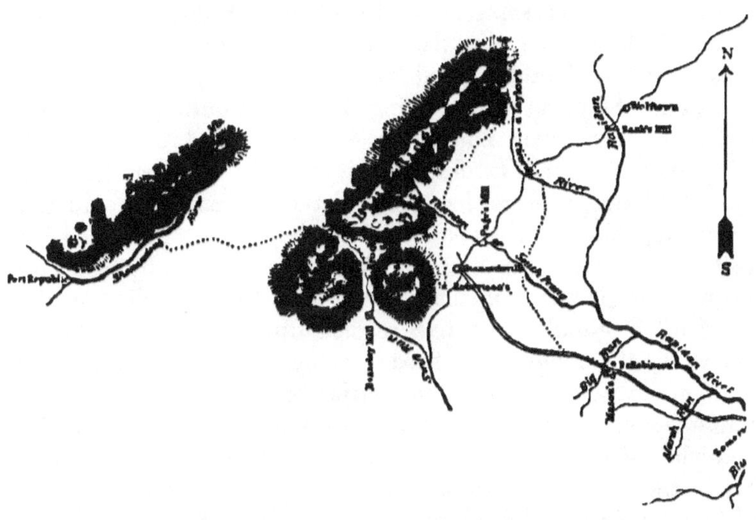

SPOTSWOOD'S ROUTE, 1716. [According to Fontaine's Journal.]

It lay upon Spotswood's mind to probe the secrets of this western barrier, and find the sources of the rivers which formed the great highways of the tide-water districts. He wished to discover if it were practicable to reach the great western lakes by passing these Appalachian gaps. The stray hunters and traders who had essayed the task had done nothing to make their routes known. Fontaine's entry of August 20, 1716, is that at Williamsburg he "waited on the governor, who was in readiness for an expedition over the Appalachian Mountains." On September 5, he writes: "We followed the windings of the James River, observing that it came from the very top of the mountains," and reached "to the very head, where it runs no bigger than a man's arm, from under a large stone. We drank King George's health, and all the Royal Family's, at the very top of the Appalachian Mountains." It seems evident that the party, which consisted of fifty persons and a train of pack-horses, were now in the Swift Run gap, which they had reached in thirty-six days from Williamsburg. "About a musket-shot from the spring," says Fontaine, "there is another which rises and runs down the other side. It goes westward, and we thought we could go down that way, but we met with such prodigious precipices that we were obliged to return to the top again. We found some trees which had been formerly marked [blazed], I suppose, by the northern Indians, and following these trees we found a good safe descent." Going on seven miles and observing "the footing of elks and buffaloes and their beds," a large river flowing west was reached and crossed. They named it the Euphrates; it was the modern Shenandoah. "The governor had some graving irons, but could not grave anything, the stones were so hard. . . . He buried a bottle and a paper inclosed, on which he writ that he took possession of this place in the name of and for King George the First of England. We had a good dinner, drank the king's health in champagne, and fired a volley." Fontaine next goes on to enumerate an abundant variety of liquors in which they drank the health of others. The return trip was made leisurely, and when they reached Williamsburg, in September, the itinerary of their busy days showed that they had traversed a distance of four hundred and forty miles.

Spotswood later made a report to the Lords of Trade, and said that "by the relation of the Indians, who frequent those parts, from the pass where I was, it is but three days' march to a great nation of Indians, living on a river which discharges itself in the Lake Erie; that from the western sides of one of the small mountains which I saw that lake is very visible, and cannot therefore be above five days' march; and that the way thither is also very practicable, the mountains to the westward of the Great Ridge being smaller than those I passed on the eastern side, which shows how easy a matter it is to gain possesion of these lakes." The governor then proceeds to consider the danger from the French occupation of this trans-montane region. He apparently had not heard, as a contemporary English map-maker had, of the "Tionontateecaga," who beyond the mountains inhabited caves, so as "to defend themselves from the great heat"!

Spotswood's knowledge of the French beyond the Alleghanies had grown of late, and he now began to have a better conception of the problem which the English had to solve. He says further: "The British plantations are in a manner surrounded by the [French] commerce with the numerous nations of Indians settled on both sides of the lakes. They may not only engross the whole skin trade, but may, when they please, send out such bodies of Indians on the back of these plantations as may greatly distress his Majesty's subjects here. Should they multiply their settlements along these lakes so as to join their dominions of Canada to their new colony of Louisiana, they might even possess themselves of any of these plantations they pleased. Nature, 't is true, has formed a barrier for us by that long chain of mountains which runs from the back of South Carolina as far as New York, and which are only passable in some few places; but even that natural defense may prove rather destructive to us, if they are not possessed by us before they are known to them." He then urges that settlements should be formed on the lakes, and that the passes on the way to them be securely held. Above all he urges settlements on Lake Erie, "by which we shall not only share with the French in the commerce and friendship of these Indians inhabiting the banks of the lakes, but may be able to cut off or disturb the communication between Canada and Louisiana, if a war should happen to break out . . . and we are nearer to support than they to attack. As this country [Virginia] is the nearest, . . . and as I flatter myself I have attained a more exact knowledge than any other Englishman yet has of the situation of the lakes, and the way through which they are most accessible overland, I shall be ready to undertake the executing this project if his Majesty thinks fit to approve of it."

Spotswood was complaining in 1711 of the exactions put by the Carolina government upon the Virginia traders. These impositions had forced the packmen to pass by preference south into Carolina, and thence to follow

Carolina and the traders' trails.

well-established trails to the Cherokee and Chickasaw villages. These routes are shown by pricked lines in a map by Moll (1720), and the paths connecting the several tribes are shown on a map made at this time by the Indians themselves. The contemporary maps often put a legend along the Tennessee River to the effect that it formed the usual route from Carolina to the Illinois.

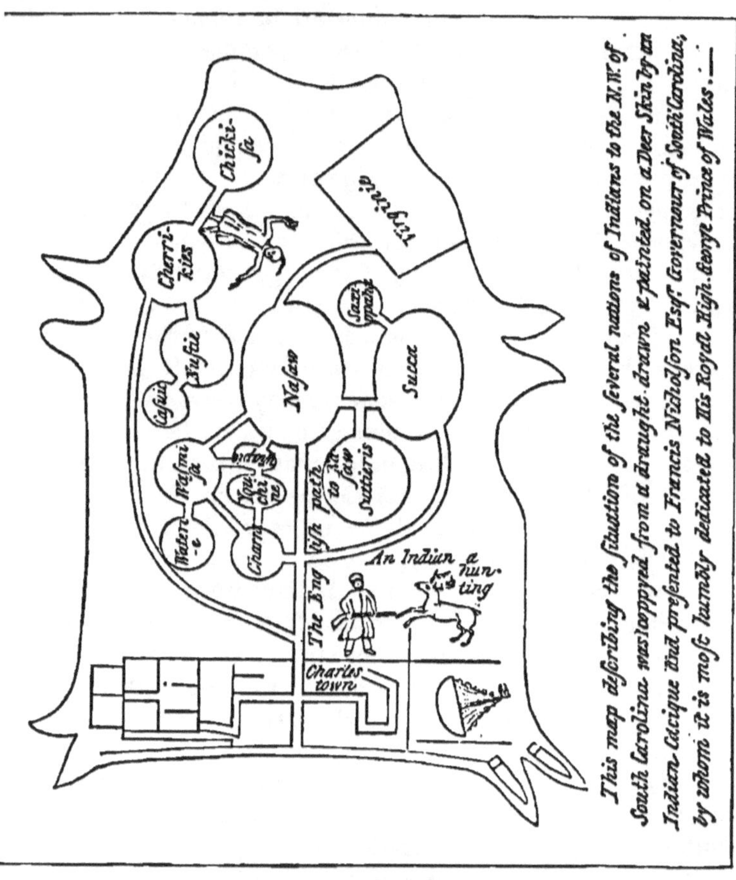

INDIAN MAP OF TRADERS' PATHS.

The western routes had, however, suddenly become dangerous. The Tuscaroras, Yamassees, and other tribes, all along the frontier, had risen (1711) against the English, and the exposed settlements of Swiss and Palatines

Indian war. 1711.

under the Carolina jurisdiction had begun to suffer. The conflict lasted for more than two years, and checked the westward movement up the Neuse River. Colonel Moore, by a successful campaign, forced the Tuscaroras out of the country, and they joined, as has already been stated, their kinspeople, the Five Nations in New York, making a sixth in the Iroquois Confederacy. Quiet followed in 1713, and the traders were once more on their travels. Penicault encountered three of them among the Natchez in 1714. An Englishman, Young by name, is said to have gone beyond the Mississippi to arouse the more distant tribes against the French, and at one time Bienville strove to embroil the Choctaws with the Chickasaws, simply because these latter Indians were manœuvring in the English interest. The French averred that it was the policy of the English to set one tribe against another, so that they could profit by buying the prisoners to work as slaves on the Carolina plantations. This practice became so prevalent that in 1720 it was made a punishable offense. The English, on their part, charged the French with instigating the savages to pillage the traders. It is to be feared that no accusation of any kind can be safely denied against either nation. Rivalry in the American fur trade has always been the source of inhumanity north and south.

Indians as slaves.

The English traders, in pressing their debtors among the nearer Indians and inciting new enmities, provoked the Yamassee war, which again in 1715 involved the Carolina borders in devastation, not without the suspicion that vagrant Virginia packmen supplied the marauders with guns and powder.

Yamassee war, 1715.

Next to the rivalry of the French, that of the English colonies among themselves embittered the colonial life. It became a steady complaint in Carolina, as it did in Massachusetts, that the New Yorkers did not do all they could to prevent the ravages of the Iroquois on other borders than their own. It was now a grievance in Charleston that the confederates, through such remissness at Albany, were raiding south along the Appalachians and harassing the tribes friendly to the Carolinian interests. The Iroquois might have the ostensible purpose of carrying out Governor Hunter's injunction to attack the hostile tribes in the French interests;

Carolina and the Iroquois.

but they were pretty sure to be loose in their discrimination when on their southern warpath. The complications were many which marked the deplorable conditions of the English in this Yamassee war. They might have secured immunity from its evils if they had leagued themselves with their new enemies against the hated northern confederates, but this would have brought fresh disasters along the Appalachian borders in the alienation of the Iroquois. The confederates had already harbored the Tuscaroras, enemies of the south, and the Iroquois had no hesitancy in charging the war upon the Carolinians failing to recompense those tribes who had assisted them in expelling the Tuscaroras. Despite these difficulties, the Iroquois were in the main kept to the English interests. They professed that their messengers went "with their lives in their hands," to urge the Choctaws to keep the peace, and followed the warning up with active participation on the English side. "If the war does not end soon," said Governor Hunter, "the confederates will go south in still greater force."

The French were of course at the bottom of all these border hostilities, or at least the English never failed to think they were. The government of South Carolina, in 1716, was repeating these stock charges against the French to the Lords of Trade. All the while the increased activity in Louisiana, under the influence of Law's system, was creating new grounds of anxiety in Carolina. "It is obvious," said the memorialists, "how formidable the French will grow there during peace, considering how industrious they are in frequently supplying their settlements with people." Late advices from France, they add, show how many colonists are going from Brest to their new colony of "Luciana in Mississippi, which by the small number of inhabitants in Carolina, the French had the opportunity to begin, and by the present troubles with the Indians are encouraged to increase." The memorial then proceeds to advise that military posts be placed in the Bahamas and on Port Royal Island, supported by cruising vessels. These will be safeguards, it adds, which perhaps the gold mines in the Appalachians will suffice to maintain, if only explorations are made to discover such ore.

Louisiana.

Just at this juncture (1717) a movement was made to push settlements into the Appalachians on the grant made to Sir

Robert Montgomery. This territory, which was designated as the Margravate of Azilia, lay between the Savannah and Altamaha rivers, and along the southern banks of the latter stream. The project was to make such settlements a barrier against the French; but settlers failed, and after three years the grant was reclaimed. As an alternative means of protection, Fort King George was now built at the forks of the Altamaha, where the Oconee and Ocmulgee rivers unite. This fort, however, was not long maintained, and it was, in part at least, because the province was not able to defend the colony against its enemies, that South Carolina now changed its proprietary government for a royal one. At the same time, claimants under the old "Carolana" grant were petitioning the Lords of Trade to settle disputed bounds with the French by making the "Mischacebe by them styled Messisipy" the division between the two crowns.

Azilia. 1717.

CHAPTER VII.

CHARLEVOIX AND HIS OBSERVATIONS.

1720–1729.

THE student feels a certain confidence in facing the problems of New France as her leaders learned to know them, if

Charlevoix and the Sea of the West.

he keeps before him the impressions which an intelligent observer like Charlevoix was receiving in passing from Mackinac to the Gulf. Not one of these questions was older or of steadier recurrent interest than the riddle of the west. When Charlevoix heard that the climate was less severe at Lake Winnipeg than on the St. Lawrence, though it lay farther to the north, he did not fail to conjecture

The trough of the continent.

that a neighboring sea softened the rigors of a boreal region. There was as yet no comprehension of that central longitudinal trough of the continent which could conduct the southern winds even as far north as the Arctic circle; and exploration towards the west by Lake Winnipeg had as yet revealed nothing.

The Duke of Orleans had interested himself in geographical questions, and it was in large part to satisfy his curiosity in regard to a route to the Sea of the West that Charlevoix had been dispatched to gather such information on this point as he could. This Jesuit priest landed in Canada in 1720, and proceeded to Mackinac to begin his inquiries. A journal of his

Charlevoix's writings.

movements and observations was published in his well-known *Histoire de la Nouvelle France* (1744), and we have an official report, including his recommendations, in a letter addressed by him to the Count de Toulouse, January 20, 1723. From Mackinac, July 21, 1721, he informed the minister that he had visited every post in the upper country except those on Lake Superior. He had made up for that

[From Lafitau's *Mœurs des Sauvages*, Paris, 1724, showing the prevailing view as to the extreme northern position of the source of the Mississippi, and how the springs of the Missouri approached the western sea.]

omission by studious inquiry of priest, trader, bushranger, and Indian as to what he could have learned had he gone there.

Transconti-nental passages.

Charlevoix's tendency was to be skeptical. He had heard the story of a ship working eastward from the Pacific through northern water-ways till she reached the Atlantic above Newfoundland; but he found, as he thought, that the story originated in a bad French translation of a Spanish book. Everywhere the Indians told him that there was a western-flowing river over the great divide which confined the sources of the Mississippi, Missouri, and St. Pierre rivers; but he found the details so wild and contradictory that he never quite thought the story-tellers honest. Scouring along the Missouri appeared to him to unfit every one for a truthful statement. La Harpe seemed to suspect that if Charlevoix had been a little more credulous he might better have divined the truth. What the Jesuit did believe seems to have been in a general way that the Missouri, somewhere in its springs, did interlock with other waters which sought towards the west an unknown sea near which there were white men. As it was evident the Sioux knew more than anybody else about these contiguous fountains, missionaries among them might elicit the secret, if the church would only take the matter into its hands.

The Missouri route.

This belief was, indeed, not unshared by many, layman and priest. French and English tracts, in 1720, quote Indian testimony that the source of the Missouri is in "a hill on the other side of which there is a torrent that, forming itself by degrees into a great river, takes its course westward and discharges itself into a large lake." Coxe, in his *Carolana* (1722), seems to have better conjectured the exact geographical relation of the Missouri, when he makes one of its branches interlace with a stream that we may now safely identify with the Columbia, while another branch, opening the way among the Spaniards, led the explorer near the sources of other rivers which we may now believe to be the upper waters of the Colorado, the Arkansas, and the Rio Bravo del Norte.

Spaniards from Santa Fé, 1720.

It was from Santa Fé, on the latter stream, that the Spaniards, in 1720, had started to join the Padoucas (Comanches) near the Kansas River and raid toward the Missouri. Their ultimate destination was thought to be Fort

[From De Fer's *La Rivière de Missisipi et ses Environs*, 1718.]

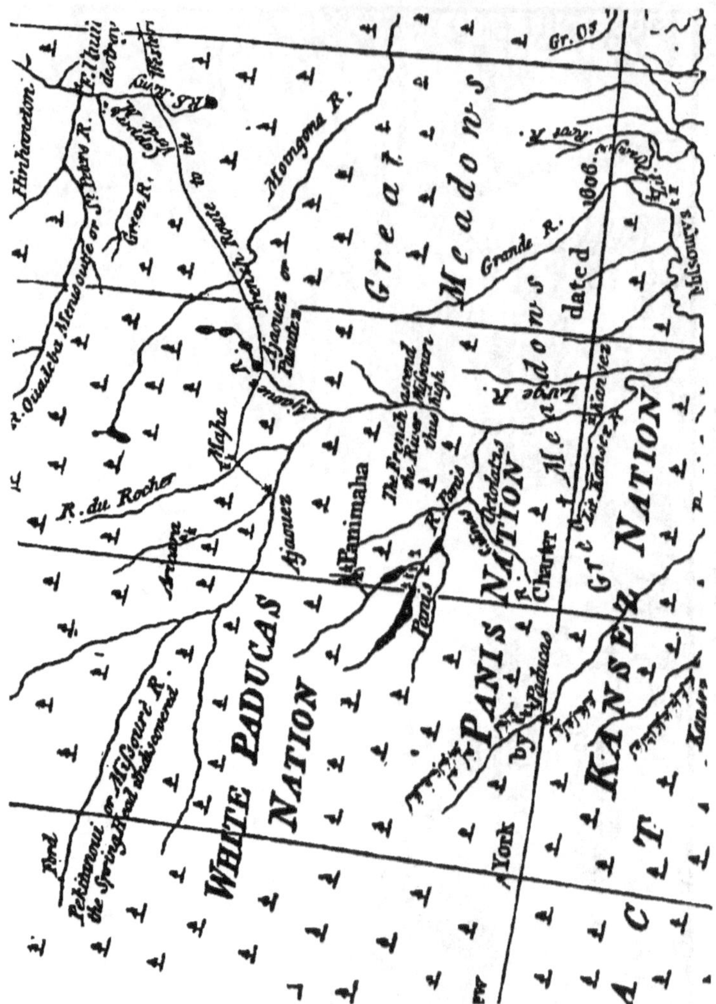

[This map is from Bowen and Gibson's *North America*, London, 1763, showing the upper branches of the Missouri and the supposed country of the Padoucas, Panis, and Kansas tribes. The "French route to the western Indians" touches the Mississippi opposite the mouth of the Wisconsin [Ouisconsing], whence Canada was reached by the Fox River portage and Green Bay.]

Chartres, and Boisbriant, then in command there, had timely notice of their approach. The purpose, doubtless, was to divert the Indian trade from the Illinois to Santa Fé. Boisbriant was relieved of anxiety when, in May, 1721, he learned that the invading Spaniards had fallen into a trap among the Osages and had been massacred. The question then of interest was: Could the route laid open by these raiders now be found?

On January 17, 1772, the Company of the Indies instructed M. de Bourgmont (Bourmont, Boismont, Bournion), who was already somewhat familiar with the country, to do what he could to hold the line of the Missouri against such inroads of the Spanish. He came to Louisiana, and passed up the Mississippi and Missouri, with the hope of establishing friendly relations with the Indians. This done, it might be easy to find a practicable route for traders to reach New Mexico. There was already some irregular trafficking in that direction. Exploration seemed to be turned toward this channel of trade in preference to discovering the "mountains of monstrous height," that were reported to be somewhere up the river near that source, which Penicault says no one had yet found.

Bourgmont on the Missouri. 1722.

Bourgmont's first movement was to build a stockade on an island (since disappeared) in the Missouri, which he called Fort Orleans. It was a base for further progress, and already settlers were passing up the stream. A body of Germans was thereabouts in 1723, and in the same year the earliest grant on the river was made to the Sieur Renard. During the year before, Bienville had ordered Boisbriant to interpose somewhere on the Kansas River a fort against Spanish intrusion, and later (August, 1723) he transmitted through Boisbriant to Bourgmont orders (dated January 17, 1722) to ascend the Missouri from his new fort, and establish another post better situated to engage the Spanish trade. He was directed to defend it, if necessary, against any force which might be sent from Santa Fé. To secure the Indians, he was ordered to dole out gifts to them, but in small quantities, in order to hold them in allegiance by the hope of more.

Fort Orleans.

Starting from a point near the modern Atchison, and pro-

NOTE. The map on the two following pages is from Dr. James Smith's *Some Considerations on the Consequences of the French settling Colonies on the Mississippi.* London, 1720.

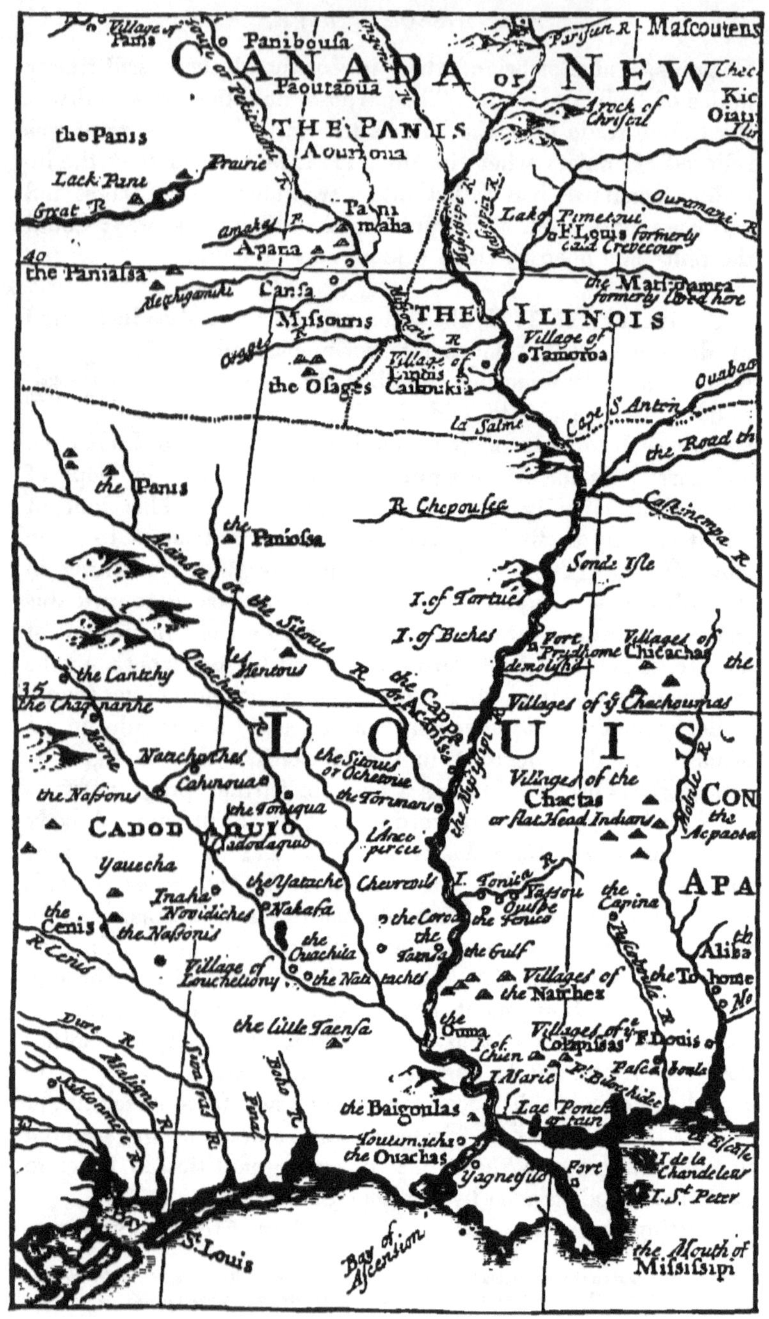

Village of Panis
Paniboussa
Mascoutens
CANADA or NEW
Paoutaoua
A rock of Christal
THE PANIS
Aourtoua
the Panis
Prairie
Lack Pane
Great R
Pani maha
Apana
Ouramani R
Lake Pimeteoui
F. Louis formerly call'd Crevecoeur
40
the Paniassa
Cansa
the Maroa formerly lived here
Missouris
THE ILINOIS
Village of Tamoroa
Osage R
Village of Ilinois
Caoukia
the Osages
Ouabache
la Salme
Cape S. Anton
the Road th
the Panis
R. Chepousea
Casquinempa R
the Paniassa
Acansa or the Sitoues R
Sonde Isle
I. of Tortues
I. of Biches
Port Prudhome demolish'd
Villages of Chicachas
Ouachita
the Cantchy
the Capa or Acansa
15
the Chaquanhe
Villages of ye Chachoumas
LOUIS
Natchoches
the Sitoues or Ochetoue
the Mississipi R
Villages of the Chactas or flat Head Indians
Mobile R
Cahinoua
the Nassonis
the Torimans
CADODAQUIO
the Tonniqua
Cadodaquio
the Acpaoba
Yauecha
l'Anse percee
Chevreuils
Tonica R
Yassou
Ouispe
the Capina
APA
the Yatache
Nakasa
Inaha
Novidiches
the Cenis
the Nassonis
R. Cenis
the Coroa
the Taensa
the Gulf
the Ouachita
Village of Louchelioney
the Natchitoches
Villages of the Natchez
the Tohome
Aliba
the little Taensa
the Ouma
Villages of ye Colapissas
I. of Chien
I. Marie
F. Louis
Pascaboula
Pt. Biloxi
the Baigoulas
Lac Ponchartrain
Ouachas
Yagnetsito
Fort
I. de la Chandeleur
I. St. Peter
St. Louis
Bay of Ascension
the Mouth of Missisipi

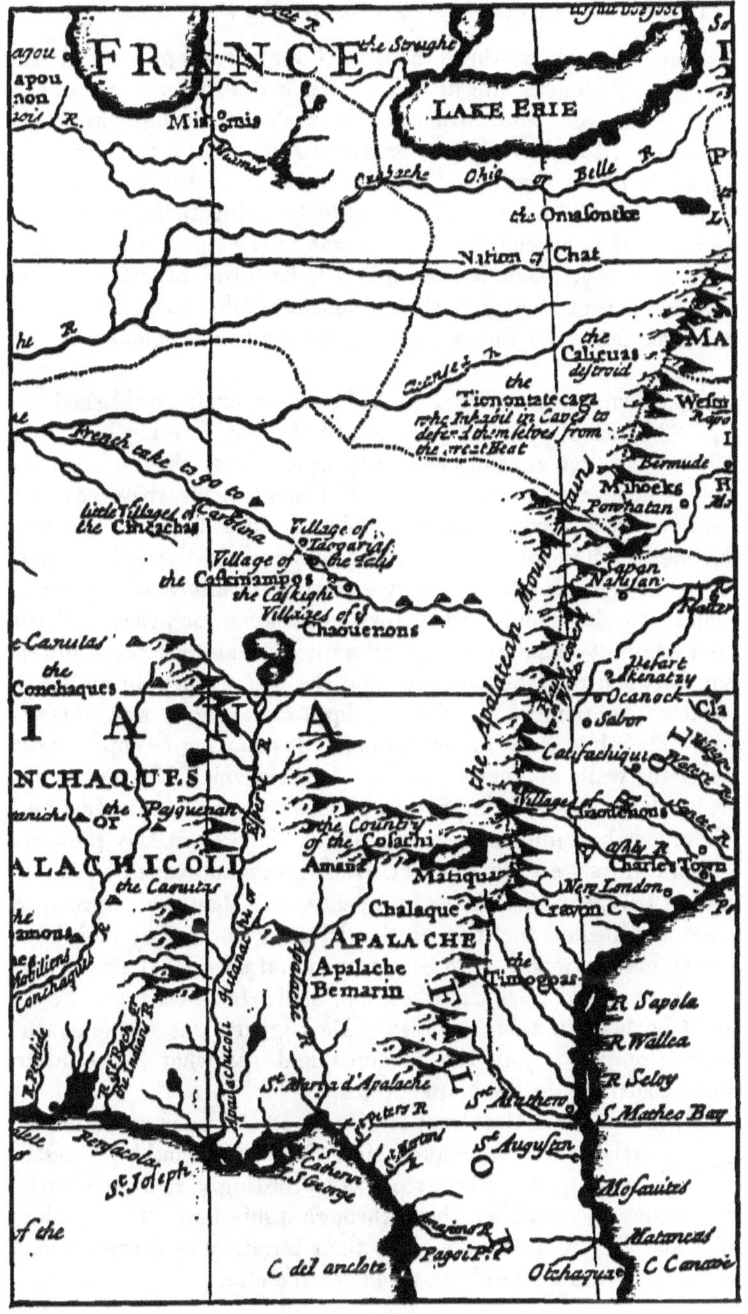

ceeding through northern Kansas, Bourgmont approached the Padoucas late in June. He had broken down on the march, and turned back, without accomplishing his purpose. Ill and dispirited, he reached his fort on the Missouri. Another effort succeeded better, and in November he was among the Padoucas, and was able to bring them to a pact, by which they agreed to open the way to the Spaniards through their territory. Suavity and a lavish bestowal of gifts accomplished all that Bourgmont's instructions called for. The question was, how long the savage consent would hold good.

Padoucas, or Comanches.

Charlevoix tells us that in 1721 the French established an armed post at the mouth of the Fox River. They had as yet encountered no people whom they needed so much to overawe as the Foxes. For some years, these savages rendered it a fearful risk for trader or adventurer to traverse the country lying between Lake Michigan and the Mississippi. Allied with the Kickapoos, they seemed determined to bar every avenue to the Sioux, either for the packman or priest. With such vigilant enemies, every attempt to maintain communication between the St. Lawrence and the Mississippi through any territory frequented by these ubiquitous savages was dangerous. They had been known to make devastating swoops almost under the walls of Fort Chartres. A crisis which Charlevoix apprehended seemed to impend in 1726, when the Mascoutins and Kickapoos had put a stop to the use of the Green Bay portage. When affairs were the darkest, De Lignery succeeded at Mackinac in bringing the Foxes to a peace, and they even agreed to spare as allies of the French the Illinois, whom they had been accustomed to worry. De Siette, who had succeeded Boisbriant in command at Fort Chartres, had little faith that the Foxes could be held to their promise. De Lignery was suspicious of their attempts to join the Iroquois, and did what he could to block their way to the confederates.

Fox Indians.

With the Foxes thus temporarily, at least, under surveillance, there was a chance that the Sioux could be better managed. Recourse was accordingly had to Charlevoix's plan of reaching them through a mission. The borders of Lake Pepin, near enough to their territory to attract them, seemed the most eligible position for the effort.

The Sioux.

Father Guignas was selected for the work of the church, and René Boucher de la Perrière (or Périer), who had an evil name among the English for his merciless inroads upon the New England borders, was put in charge of the secular part of the undertaking.

The party left Montreal in June, 1727, and trusting to the pacification of the savages near the Green Bay portage, passed that way. We can follow them in the priest's journal. They met friendly greetings among the Winnebagoes on the pretty little lake where this people dwelt, and on August 15 they arrayed themselves in the village of the Foxes, "a nation," as Guignas describes them, "much dreaded," but without reason, as he thinks, since they are reduced to only about two hundred warriors. He became confused with the perplexing tortuousness of the river, and found the actual portage little better than half a league of marsh mud. Once upon the Wisconsin, he counted thirty leagues to the Mississippi. Turning up this river, their course lay northerly for fifty-eight leagues, as he measured it, winding among islands, till they reached a widening of the stream, destitute of islands, which was known as Lake Pepin. Here, about the middle of September, the party staked out a stockade, a hundred feet square, with two bastions, and in four days completed it, and called it Fort Beauharnois. It was the first settlement on the Mississippi north of the Illinois. They had trusted the Indians' advice in placing it, as they supposed, above the highest level of the water, but in the following April a freshet forced the reconstruction of it on higher ground. In due time nearly a hundred cabins of the Sioux sprang up about the fort.

Green Bay portage.

Lake Pepin.

The Foxes had proved, however, far less tamable than the Sioux. Their treacherous maraudings still continued. The two hundred warriors whom Guignas had thought so placable were still true to the same instincts which, a hundred years and more later, their descendants manifested under Blackhawk. De Siette was inclined to renew the war and exterminate them, if he could; but when the king heard of it, he remembered the sad results of past attempts to annihilate the savages, and wrote to Beauharnois, April 29, 1727, to call a halt. The governor counted on help from Louisiana, which

The Foxes.

was much more exposed to ravages than Canada. He was only anxious to strike the blow before the savages could fly to the Iroquois or to the Sioux of the prairies. In the spring of 1728, it seemed no longer possible to desist from a war, and De Lignery led a formidable force against them; but the wily savages eluded their pursuers, and little was accomplished.

Such were the impediments to western progress which were developed during the years following Charlevoix's study of the problem. We must now follow his observations on other points. From Mackinac, where Charlevoix pursued these inquiries as to a western way, he passed by the St. Joseph portage to the Kankakee, and so to the Mississippi, reaching Cahokia October 10, 1721. There had been a settlement here for a score of years or more. Charlevoix says that its inhabitants told him they had originally built their cabins on the bank of the river. In three years the current had moved so far to the west as to leave them half a league inland. He found the French at Kaskaskia living in ease and taking on the habits of settled life. Boisbriant was shortly afterwards (1722) to sign the earliest land warrant which is on record there, the product of the settlement was increasing, and before long supplies were to be regularly sent down to New Orleans. The travelers heard stories of mines; but though considerable bodies of San Domingo negroes had been brought to the region to work these deposits, the French never profited much from mineral wealth. Neither Canada nor Louisiana was quite content with the divided interests of this whole region. The Canadian bushranger took advantage of the uncertain control, and passed from one to the other jurisdiction to escape punishment for his mischief. It was from these roving miscreants that the Sioux and Foxes obtained their guns and ammunition.

Charlevoix in the Illinois. 1721.

Kaskaskia and the mines.

The fact was, that the northern limits of Louisiana were never definitely determined. The makers of maps drew the division line according to caprice, shifting it up and down between the Natchez and the Ohio. Delisle was still applying the Spanish designation of Florida to the whole northern coast of the Gulf of Mexico, between the Appalachians and New Mexico. In 1722, he stretched the province up the

Limits of Louisiana.

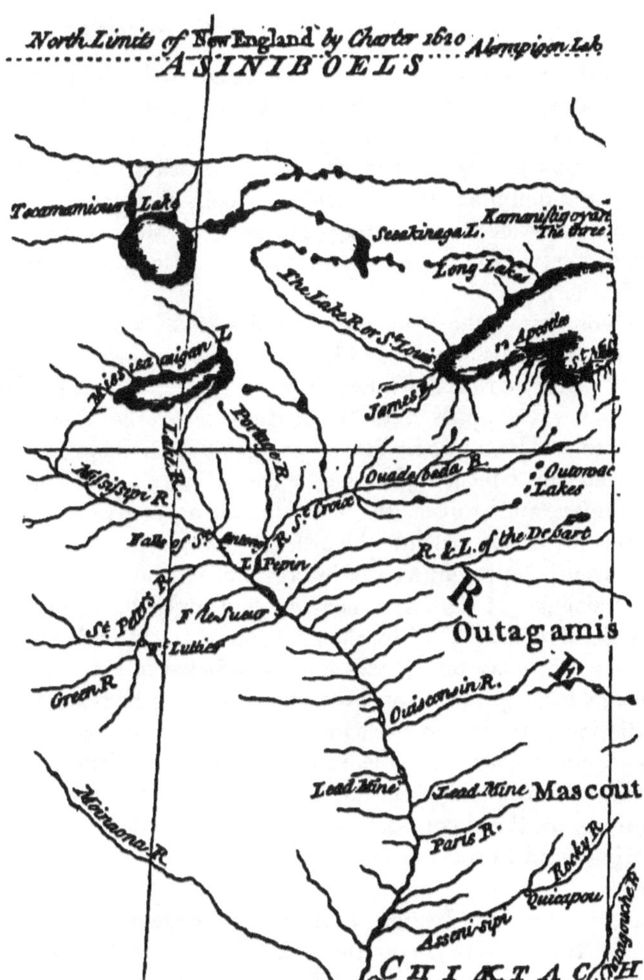

[From Sayer and Jefferys' reproduction of Danville's *North America* (London), showing the position of Lake Pepin and the upper Mississippi, as then understood.]

Mississippi to the line of the Missouri, and in 1728 he stopped it at a point below the Ohio. His "Pays des Ilinois" lies north of this, between the northern parts of New Mexico and the Iroquois country. He places the designation "Pays de Iroquois" so indefinitely that it does not help to settle the vexed question whether the hunting-grounds of that confederacy stopped westwardly at the Scioto or the Miami, or extended even farther.

Bounds of the Illinois.

The country of the Illinois had been added, as we have seen, to Louisiana in 1717, but it was uncertain whether this carried the jurisdiction of its dependent governor beyond the Kickapoos and Mascoutins, or to the line of the Wisconsin. Homann, in his maps, ran the division line due west from the Chicago portage to the Mississippi. Moll, the Englishman, and Jaillot, the Frenchman, agreed in stretching it across the country below the Illinois River.

Vaudreuil, representing the interests of Canada, claimed that the Louisiana of Crozat's charter had only been increased under the decree of 1717 by the addition of the Illinois country, whatever that may be. It was a dispute between him and Boisbriant, as local governor at Fort Chartres, whether the latter's jurisdiction extended to the sources of all the affluents of the Mississippi or not. Some European geographers, like Homann and Jaillot, even made the Illinois include the basin of Lake Winnipeg, on the theory of the continuous connection of it and the Mississippi in one system of water-ways.

The Ohio country.

The territory in dispute between the French and English traders was along the Wabash and up the Ohio and its lateral valleys. Charlevoix speaks of the region north of the Ohio as likely to become the granary of Louisiana. Senex, the English cartographer, made it appear that through this region "of one hundred and twenty leagues the Illinois hunt cows," and he magnified the reports of the trade in buffalo peltries. The waning power of the Iroquois and the coming of the Delawares and Shawnees into the Ohio valley had permitted the French to conduct more extensive explorations, and they had found themselves liable to confront all along the valley the equally adventurous English.

The Mississippi Company had urged (September 15, 1720)

the building of a fort on the Wabash as a safeguard against the English, and the need of it had attracted the attention of Charlevoix. Some such precaution, indeed, was quite as necessary to overawe the savages, for now that the Maumee-Wabash portage was coming into favor, the Indians had lately been prowling about it and murdering the passers. La Harpe, in 1724, feared the danger of delay. In 1725, the necessity for some such protection alarmed Boisbriant early in the year. The Carolina traders had put up two booths on the Wabash, and rumors reached Kaskaskia of other stations which they had established farther up the Ohio valley. These last intruders were probably Pennsylvanians, — at least, it is so assumed in the treaty made at Albany in 1754. The language of such treaties is rarely the best authority; but it is certain that Vaudreuil, in Quebec, believed it at the time. He reported to his home government that the English were haunting the upper waters of the Wabash and trading among the Miamis. As a result, we find the Company of the Indies (December, 1725) instructing Boisbriant to beware of the English, and to let M. Vincennes, then among the Miamis, know that these rivals were moving in that direction. The next year the company informed Périer (September 30, 1726) of their determination to be prepared, and authorized him, in concert with Vincennes, to repel the English if they approached. Vincennes had already been reconnoitring up the Ohio valley, to see if any English were there.

The Wabash country.

The English on the Ohio.

Here, on the Ohio, the claims of authority between the New Orleans and Quebec governments again clashed. The region which Vaudreuil wished to protect on the upper Wabash was held by him to be within Canada. But there was a very uncertain line separating it from the lower regions on the same river which Vincennes was urging the government of Louisiana to strengthen. This lower post, later called Vincennes, after the name of that pioneer, did not take the shape of permanence till about 1734, when some families began to gather about the spot; but all the while its chief communications seem to have been with Canada by the Maumee portage beyond the post of Ouiatanon.

Regions in dispute between Canada and Louisiana.

Vincennes.

The French always had a certain advantage over the English on the Ohio. Their approach to it from below was assured as long as they held the lower valley of the Mississippi. The Lake Erie portages offered ready communication with Canada. Their possession of Niagara enabled them to watch the approaches from New York and Pennsylvania. Along the Alleghany River Joncaire was most active in his intrigues with the Shawnees, now scattered upon these upper waters of the valley. He succeeded at times in bringing them into treaty relations with Montreal. To strengthen their obligations to the French, he took care that smiths were kept among them to repair their guns.

The French on the upper Ohio.

Once more to return to Charlevoix.

He passed Fort Chartres in company with a young officer, St. Ange by name, who was destined, forty years and more later, to haul down its flag, then the last banner of France floating east of the Mississippi. Charlevoix remarked how the increasing settlements between the fort and Kaskaskia were beginning to look like a continuous village. He spent about a month at Kaskaskia (October–November, 1721), noting much of what has already been recounted as to the condition of the country and of the neighboring regions. From Kaskaskia he started, November 10, to descend the Mississippi. Passing the mouth of the Ohio, — he called it the Wabash, — he thought it the finest place in Louisiana for a settlement, the country up the river consisting, as he says, of "vast meadows with many streams, and covered with herds of buffaloes, and affording the shortest route to Canada." He felt that an armed post at the mouth of the Ohio could best keep in awe the Cherokees, "the biggest tribe of the continent."

Fort Chartres and Kaskaskia. 1721.

Reaching the bluffs at Natchez, he comments on what he calls Iberville's fascination with the spot, and the laying out of a settlement there, which had been called Rosalie, after Madame the Duchess of Pontchartrain. "But this project," says Charlevoix, "is not likely soon to be carried out, though our geographers choose still to set down such a town on their maps." He found a storehouse, but little trade.

Natchez. 1721.

Farther down the river, the Jesuit stopped and inspected the concessions recently awarded in furtherance of the financial movements in France, and on January 5, 1722, he reached

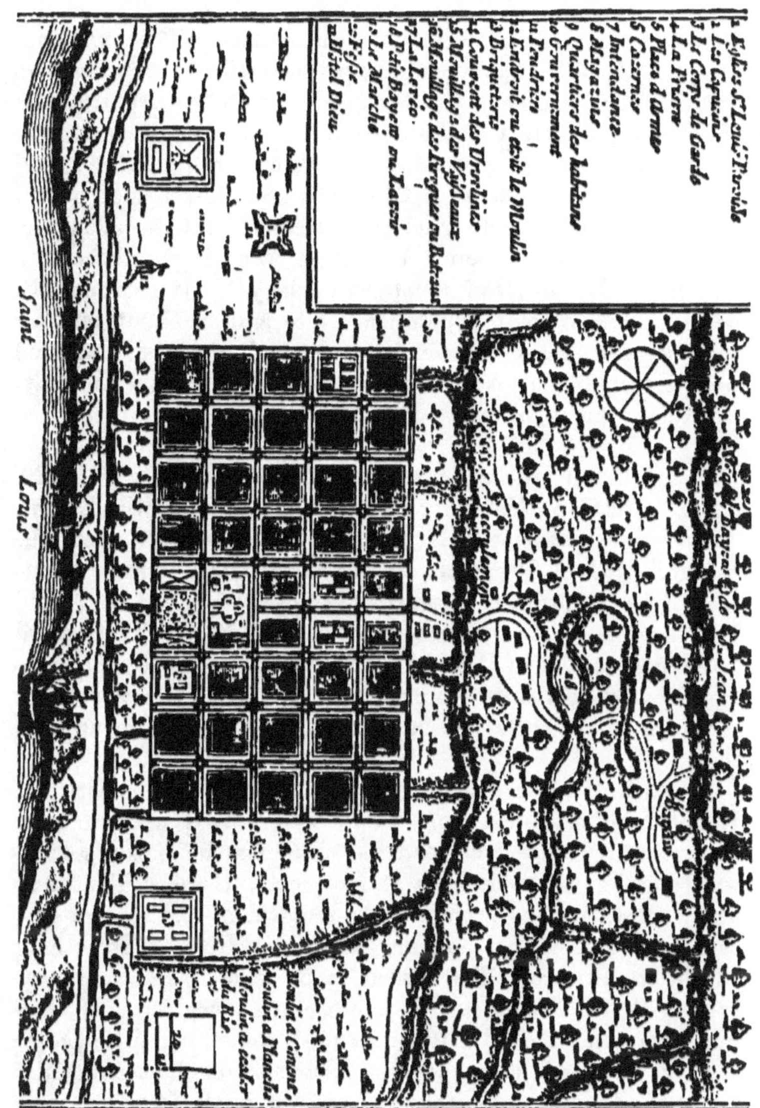

DUMONT'S PLAN OF NEW ORLEANS, 1718–1720.

New Orleans. Five days later he writes thus: "The eight hundred fine houses and five parishes which the newspapers two years ago [in the time of Law's frenzy] said were here are reduced to a hundred cabins for the troops, irregularly placed, a storehouse of wood, two or three mean dwellings, and an unfinished warehouse. This wild and desert spot is still nearly all covered with reeds and trees." But, he adds prophetically, "the day cannot be distant when it may become a rich town, the capital of an opulent colony." At this time the province had a total population, white and black, of not far from five thousand five hundred, of which about six hundred were slaves. Charlevoix remained in New Orleans till July, and then went to Biloxi.

New Orleans. 1722.

Peace, which had been made with Spain, February 17, 1720, had now lasted for two years, and France, with Spain's acquiescence, held the Gulf shore westward from the neighborhood of Pensacola as far as she could venture to occupy. In the previous August (1721) Bienville had instructed La Harpe to take possession of the coveted Bay of St. Bernard (Matagorda), but in October it had been abandoned. The savages who dwelt about it had not softened in their ferocity since the days of La Salle, and it was found impossible to appease them.

France on the Gulf.

To control this coast and to keep communications with the Illinois, neither Biloxi nor Mobile had proved well situated. Now that the peace had rendered them less important as bulwarks against the Spaniards at Pensacola, it was evident that many considerations prompted the removal of the seat of government to some position on the Great River. Something within her own capability needed to be done if Louisiana was to flourish, for France had of late been very neglectful of colonial interests. Unless matters mended, something little better than an independent freebooting existence must be occasionally dreamed of. The colonists could at least in this way get some of the products of enterprise, now checked by monopolies and other exactions. Added to this vacillating and neglectful policy

NOTE. The opposite map is from Bowen and Gibson's *North America*, London, 1763, showing the basin of the Red River and the Spanish frontiers; and, east of the Mississippi, the country of the Chickasaws, Choctaws, Creeks, and Alibamons.

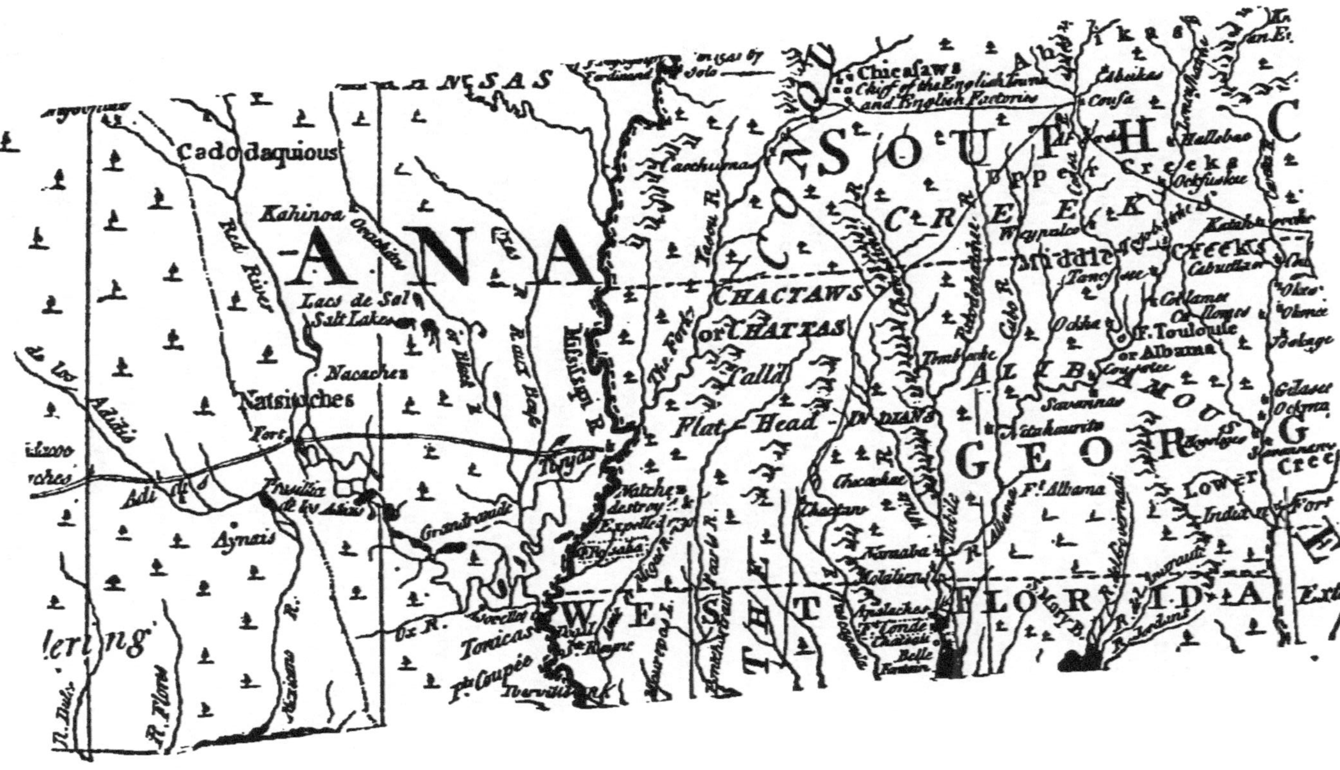

Cadodaquious
Kahinoa
Red River
A N A
Lacs de Sal
Salt Lakes
Nacaches
Natsitoches
Fort
Aynais
Mississipi R.
CHACTAWS
or CHATTAS
Flat Head
INDIANS
The Forks
Yasou R.
Chicasaws
Chief of the English Towns
and English Factories
SOUTH
CREEK
Upper
Creeks
Middle
CREEKS
Coosa
Abeikas
Hallebao
Ockfuskee
F. Toulouse
or Albama
Savannas
GEOR
Ft. Albama
Mobile
Chactaw
Lower
Fort
W E S T
FLORIDA
Tonicas
Pte. Coupée
R. Flores
Grand Ecraille
Pearls R.
R. aux Boefs

of the home government, the unpopularity of Bienville and his quarrels with Hubert, the commissary, had not served to make prospects better. Charlevoix came at a time to see this, and exercised his powers as a peacemaker to some effect.

For a year or two, the governor had been advocating the removal of the capital, and in 1720 he had sent Le Blond de la Tour to choose a site on the Mississippi. A town was staked out, as we have seen, and records of baptisms were begun there as early as September 10, 1720. These early days, as Charlevoix found, were dismal ones. Some Swiss who had come for garrison duty had been scattered among the neighboring tribes, the better to feed them. They brought disease with them and found more of it. Out of one lot of Germans who sailed from France, not a quarter survived the voyage. The negroes who were brought from Guinea fared better, but not much. Hurricanes swept along the coast in the autumn of 1721, and leveled the huts both at New Orleans and Biloxi.

New Orleans laid out. 1720.

In the spring of 1722, while Charlevoix was looking on, commissioners arrived with orders to transfer the government to New Orleans. In June the removal of stores began, and by August Bienville had taken up his residence in the new capital. A fort was soon built at the Balize, in a position which, as Charlevoix describes it, was on the edge of the Gulf, but which is to-day nine miles up the pass.

New Orleans the capital. 1722.

Charlevoix was on the ground in time to understand the perplexities which environed the poor governor on all sides. The news from the Red River was discouraging, and Bienville resolved to increase the fifty men who constituted the garrison at Natchitoches Island. This was rendered necessary, for the Spaniards had made good their position among the Adayes. Here they had converted a mission into an armed post, bringing up their supplies from the Gulf, and Bienville looked upon it as a distinct threat to the French. He wrote (December 10, 1721) to protest against it, as an unfriendly interjection of alien power between two French posts. The Spaniards maintained at this new post, which was

The Red River country.

NOTE. The opposite section of Mitchell's great map of 1755 shows the country of the Cenis, and the positions of the Adayes.

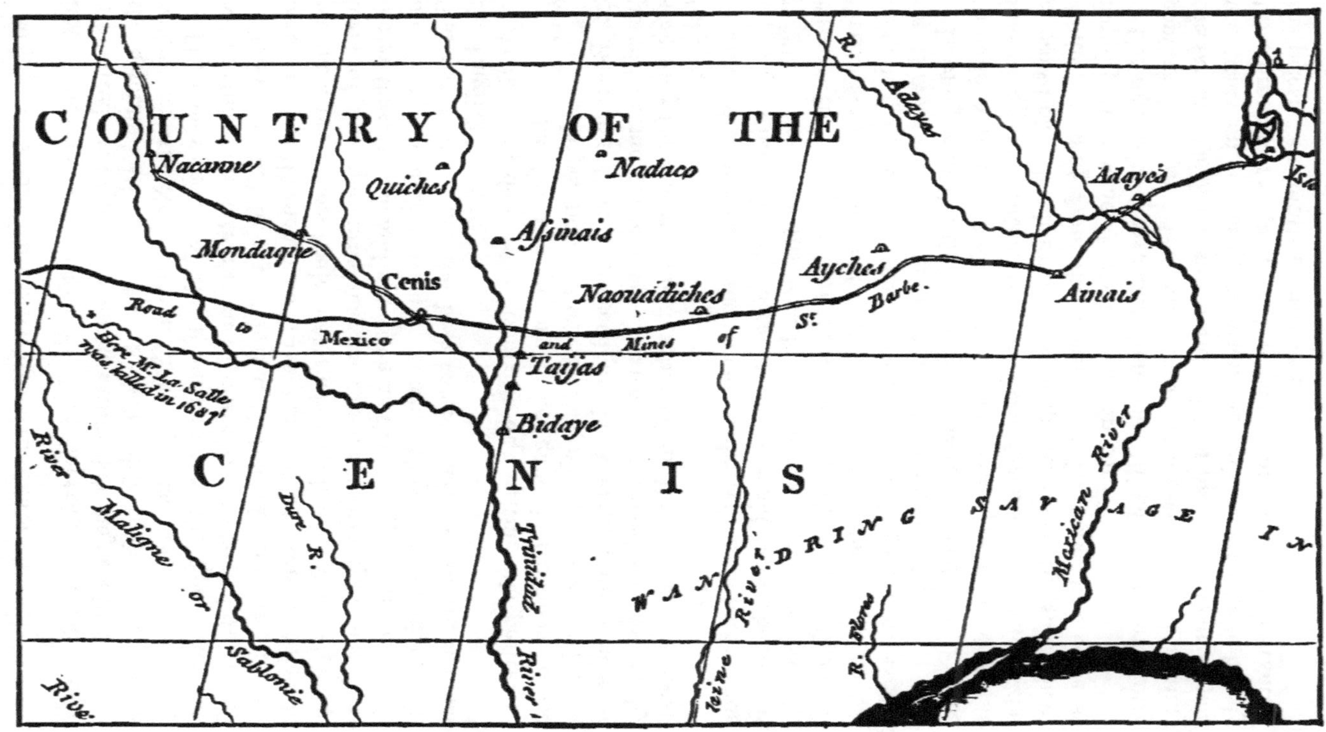
COUNTRY OF THE
CENIS
Nacanne
Quiches
Nadaco
Assinais
Mondaque
Cenis
Naouadiches
Ayches
Ainais
Adayes
R. Adayes
Road to Mexico and Mines of St. Barbe.
Here Mr. La Salle was killed in 1687
Taijas
Bidaye
River Maligne or Sablonie
Dure R.
Trinidad River
WANDRING SAVAGE IN
Mexican River
R. Flores

but seven leagues from Fort St. Jean Baptiste at Natchitoches, a hundred men and six cannon, with which they could threaten the communications of the French with their more distant post among the Nassonites at Cadadaquions.

These movements of the French toward the Spaniards met with scant appreciation from Charlevoix. "The neighborhood of the Spanish," he says, "had at all times been a fatal allurement to the French, who leave the best of lands untilled to pursue a precarious trade with such neighbors. The neighborhood of the Spaniards may have some advantages, but it is better that they should approach us than we go to them. It is not their interest to drive us away. They understand, or will find out, that we are the best barrier they can desire against the English."

La Harpe.

At the very date when Bienville was writing his protest to the Spanish governor, he gave instructions to La Harpe, now returned from his fruitless mission to St. Bernard's Bay, to proceed up the Arkansas, and secure, if possible, some cattle from Mexico. He varied his mission by searching for emeralds, and returned in May, 1722, unsuccessful again.

The Arkansas River.

Charlevoix speaks of the ascent of the Arkansas being made with difficulty because of its rapids and shoals. It was near the mouth of the river that he saw the "sorrowful ruins of Mr. Law's grant, where nine thousand Germans were to be sent. It is a great pity they never came," he adds, "for there is not, perhaps, in Louisiana, if we except the Illinois, a country more fit for tillage and cattle."

It was just at this time that orders were received from France to build a fort at the mouth of the Arkansas to protect the line of communication between New Orleans and Kaskaskia. A crowd of palisaded cabins soon sprang up on the spot where Joutel, escaping from the assassins of La Salle, had come so happily upon some of Tonty's men in 1687.

Convoys with provisions from the Illinois were constantly coming down the river, and it was necessary to guard against the famine which too successful raids of prowling savages upon the boats might easily occasion, for this country had hardly been brought, except at a few points, under the subjection of the priests' meliorating influences.

Charlevoix, in 1721, did not find a Christian brother to greet him anywhere on the lower Mississippi, except at Yazoo and New Orleans. "It is five years," he says, "since a priest said mass at the Natchez," and he mentions that he was called upon while there to give the sanction of the church to sundry couples who had already joined themselves in marriage.

Priests on the Mississippi. 1722.

The next year, by orders issued in France in May, 1722, more active missionary agencies were at work, and the river became the great highway of the church. The Jesuits had brought the tribes of the Illinois almost to a man over to the faith. "They are almost all Christians," says Charlevoix, "mild in temper and often loving towards the French."

To the Jesuits the future ecclesiastical control of all the country north of the Ohio was now assigned, and in the following year we find their recruits frequently passing up the river. The lower regions of the valley were divided between the Carmelites and the Capuchins, but before long all fell under the control of the Capuchins, who were recognized from the Alabama to the Red River, and up the Great Valley as far as the Natchez.

It was upon the Natchez that all eyes were soon to turn. They were restless, and had never been quite reconciled to the presence of the French. In October, 1723, Bienville led seven hundred men against them and devastated two of their villages. The time for a more fearful outbreak was only put off.

The Natchez.

Meanwhile, Bienville's enemies had brought about his recall to France, and Boisbriant came down from Fort Chartres to take temporary command. On reaching France, Bienville pressed his defense, and La Harpe, who supports him, says that he had laid up no more than sixty thousand livres during his long control in Louisiana, and defies the traducers of the governor to point out a more honest record. Bienville, however, failed of reinstatement. There was some talk of making La Noüe his successor, but the choice fell on Boucher de la Perrière (or Périer), who received the appointment August 9, 1726, and started to his province. Louisiana was now supposed to have a population of eight thousand, of whom three thousand were blacks.

Bienville in France.

Périer. 1776.

Before Périer started, the Company of the Indies (September 30, 1726) revealed to him their anxiety about the English encroachments on the Wabash, and the Regent expressed a hope for peace, not disguising his fear that it might become impossible to maintain it. At the same time there were apprehensions on the part of the English. We have an apt expression of them in the *Memoirs of John Ker of Kersland* (London, 1726). The grounds of this fear were certainly exaggerated, when Ker declares that France had sent over ten thousand troops to Louisiana, but not perhaps so much so when he argued that France intended the conquest of the whole continent. If the Great Valley was what Ker represented it, "of vast extent, with such a temperate, wholesome climate and wonderful, fruitful soil to produce everything useful as good if not better than any other country," England might well fight for her sea-to-sea charters. The Jesuits who were now settled on a grant at New Orleans were beginning to show the capabilities of the soil in their plantations of oranges, figs, and sugar cane. It is very likely that the country owed the indigo plant also to them. The influx of vagabonds, which the holders of concessions under the Law régime had been sending over, was almost stopped, and new social amenities were appearing.

English and French encroachments.

The Jesuits as planters.

The miry ground, with its stray growths of palmetto, willow, and brake, the slab sides, bark roofs, and clay chimneys of the cabins, scattered along streets which bore the high-sounding names of the French nobility, made up the new capital, now becoming a more salubrious town since Périer had completed his levee along the river. The chief evils in life within it came doubtless from the lack of personal loyalty to the crown and country, which a commercial despotism had done so much to destroy.

New Orleans.

The salutary effects of domesticity were increasing. The company had agreed with some Ursuline nuns to undertake hospital service and maintain a school, and in July, 1727, they arrived, — a body destined to become one of the wealthiest of the religious corporations of the future commonwealth. A few years later they built a new convent, which is still standing as the residence of the archbishop, and is

The Ursulines. 1727.

perhaps the oldest building in the valley. The king sent over a body of worthy, marriageable girls, fitting each out with a small chest of clothing. The Ursulines took the charge of them, saw that they were established in virtuous homes, and to these "filles à la cassette," it is said, some of the best creole blood of to-day traces back its origin. Filles à la cassette.

CHAPTER VIII.

ALONG THE APPALACHIANS.

1720–1727.

Treaty of Utrecht. 1713.

THE concessions of the French under the treaty of Utrecht (1713), or what the English claimed to be their concessions, often came back to plague those Gallic rivals. The great gate of the Mississippi valley at the northeast was in the English opinion securely gained for them when they preëmpted the rights of the Iroquois. To offset the pretensions of the sea-to-sea charters of the English, the French simply made a sweeping pretension that the New World in this northern half of it belonged to France and Spain alone, and that England had no claim beyond what France had ceded by treaty. Consequently, in the extreme French view, their cession of Acadia gave the English their sole legal possession, while the protection granted to the English at Utrecht over the Iroquois carried no territorial rights. When it came to a test, the English cared for little but the right of might, as the French found out and could have anticipated. In the appendix of his *Half Century of Conflict*, Parkman prints two documents which represent these French views. One is a *Mémoire* by that Father Bobé already mentioned as the prompter of Delisle (1720), and the other is an official representation (1723) of much the same purport. The priest contends that the English in the treaty of St. Germain (1632) restored their American conquests to France. Even if the English did not intend it, this restoration, he argues, in consideration of the French claim arising from the voyage of Verrazano, covered all America not Spanish, and so included the entire range of English colonies along the Atlantic coast. It was a part of this restored territory called Acadia, from the Kennebec eastward, which

English and French claims.

Bobé's views.

had been wrested by England from France under the treaty of 1713, and that only constituted the proper and legal possessions of England. Bobé now makes a liberal proposition which was not new, — for Lahontan had expressed it in his map of 1709, — that by French sufferance merely the bounds of the English should run due west from the mouth of the Kennebec, thus throwing Lake Champlain into Canada. The line was then to turn south so as to follow the crest of the Alleghanies to Florida. This being accepted by England, France, says our complacent priest, being generous, will live in peace with her neighbor, provided as a recompense England restores what lies east of the Kennebec, being "Acadia with its ancient limits," to the French crown. If the English, not knowing their honorable duty, refuse this, then the terrible power of Law's Mississippi Company is to be brought to bear upon them for their temerity! It never occurred to the docile priest that England had an equally powerful South Sea Company to offset the other, just now in as high a feather. Unfortunately for Bobé and the English, before a few months had passed both speculations were to be classed among the world's great failures. The English, however, were in no mood to abate any pretensions. They only accepted the bounds of the Appalachians as a temporary necessity. Moll, in his maps, was expressing the English assumptions for the time being. He stretched the western line of the colonies along the Alleghanies northward, but bearing enough to the west to strike the Great Lakes at the eastern end of Erie, and so to include the entire region of the Iroquois tribal occupation. Thus all rights were denied the French along the southern shore of Ontario and at Niagara. The Lords of Trade appreciated the situation and memorialized the throne to prevent the weak posts of the French beyond the mountains growing defiantly strong.

The English view of their bounds.

Byrd of Westover in Virginia looked with wonder on the content of the colonies to be hemmed in by the mountains. "Our country," he says, "has now been inhabited more than a hundred and thirty years, and still we hardly know anything of the Appalachian Mountains, which are nowhere above two hundred and fifty miles from the sea."

This English people, whom Colonel Byrd thought so negligent of their opportunities, now numbered, with their foreign admixtures, half a million of souls. It was a population tolerably well compacted in New England, where the current increase was now become the least, and where the spirit which prefigured the coming independence was most ardent. The New England charters were already threatened by the king, but they found a strenuous defender in Jeremy Dummer, then the Massachusetts agent in London. He claimed that these charters were contracts which the throne was bound to respect. Though the monarch had formally granted the territory, it had really been won by the pioneers, who had defended it from the French. The bill before Parliament, to which these arguments were an answer, was one introduced by the Board of Trade for the express purpose of making the colonies better able to confront the French. The plan was to confederate them under a captain-general, and at one time there was a purpose to send over the Earl of Stair to fill that office. Various other plans of union were advanced now and later by Coxe, Bladen, and others, — all for the same end. The youthful Turgot in France comprehended the drift of sentiment when he spoke of the "colonies like fruit clinging to the tree only till ripe." Dummer, too, forecast the future when he warned the government in London that to unite the colonies in a vice-royalty was the best way to fit them for future independence. The bill was withdrawn and the scheme slumbered; and when, in 1723, Massachusetts sought to unite with the neighboring colonies in a struggle with the Indians, the Board of Trade thought the project mutinous!

The English colonies.

Proposals for union.

But New England was on the outskirts of the great arena. Berkeley had written his verses on the westward course of empire, and had come to Newport with the ultimate hope of founding a college for savages. Franklin was making an influence to surpass the pulpit by fashioning public opinion through the *New England Courant.* When Jacob Wendell placed the first settlement in the Berkshire hills, in 1725, and Fort Dummer was built at the modern Brattleboro in Vermont (1724), New England had reached the western limits of her home-country, and must wait a half century and more for her later developments on the Ohio. Not since the days, forty years earlier, when La Salle took some vagrant Mohegans down the Mississippi, had the New England savages passed beyond Albany and the Mohawks.

Berkeley and Franklin.

Settlements which the Dutch had formed on the Hudson, and the intercourse which that people had wisely regulated with the neighboring Indians, had come by the transition of power into the hands of those who fully comprehended the nature of their inheritance. No one among the supplanting English knew it better than Cadwallader Colden. He spoke of New York as "the only province that can rival and I believe outdo the French" in the Indian trade; and trade was on the whole the most important influence now at work in the struggle for a continent. In a pamphlet which Colden had published in 1724, on the encouragement of the Indian trade, he had urged the occupation of the country south of the Great Lakes. It was partly to aid such encouragement, and at the same time to make manifest how the Five Nations could be helpful in such schemes, that he set about preparing a history of those tribes. He hoped by this publication (New York, 1727) to instruct those English statesmen who had shown supreme ignorance of American geography, in contrast to the enlightened apprehensions of their French rivals. The difference between them was naturally much the same as that which Delisle with his care, and Senex and Moll with their wild conjectures, had made manifest in their respective maps. There seemed sometimes in this application of intellectual discernment in American matters a predetermined purpose on the part of the insular English to go wrong if possible. When they reprinted Colden's book, in London, in 1747 and in 1750, the text was so perverted as to convey on some points little conception of what the author had written.

Colden and the Indian trade.

English lack of discernment.

The influence of Joncaire among the Onondagas and Senecas has frequently been mentioned. It might have led to a revulsion among the confederated Iroquois, if they had not been brought to a treaty at Conestoga in 1721. But far more important for the English interest was the flocking of English traders to Oswego. That little post in the busy season was redolent with the smell of furs, and confused with a Babel of tongues. Nothing could disturb the merchants of Montreal more than this intercepting at Oswego of the annual flotillas from the distant waters. The next year (1722),

Oswego.

the southern governors, Spotswood of Virginia, and Keith of Pennsylvania, sought to settle with the Iroquois their more immediate grievances. The confederates agreed not to extend their southern raids beyond the Potomac, and even then to carry their warpaths on the western slope of the Alleghanies only.

At this time the Palatines were pushing farther west and were settling at German Flats (1723), near the portage to Oswego. The air was no longer wild with the savage whoop along the western route, and the Albany traders began to take courage and to respond to the invitations of the Indians on the Wabash to bring their packs among them. The confidence was reciprocal, and presently a band of Mackinac Indians appeared at Albany. Along a route of twelve hundred miles they had resisted the efforts of the French to turn them back.

The English and the western tribes.

A sharp clash was near at hand. Vaudreuil and Burnet were exchanging diplomatic notes over Oswego. Words were equal in the contest; but behind argument there was great disparity. The Canadian governor had a population of less than thirty thousand at his back. The English governor stood for the rights of twelve or fifteen times as many, who were scattered along the Atlantic seaboard. It was this vast preponderance in the Britons' favor which made Pontchartrain think the time was not far distant — and it was not — when Canada could be pushed to the wall.

Vaudreuil and Burnet.

The post which Joncaire had established at Niagara as a counterfoil to Oswego was become stronger and more threatening to the English, and to draw the attention of the English from it, Vaudreuil kept up the bewildering attacks along the New England frontiers. These were the orders of the government in Paris, which thought it less a risk than a direct attempt to drive the English from Oswego, as the Canadian governor persistently urged. Vaudreuil was firm in the conviction that the onset upon Oswego should not be longer delayed. He was not suffered to attempt it. He died, October 10, 1725, an octogenarian, with a head still clear, and with the zeal of youth. He had been the front of the Quebec government for twenty-one years. He had seen the devastating raids of the Iroquois along the St.

Oswego and New England.

Vaudreuil died. 1725.

Lawrence. He had made such reprisals as his hopes to win over the confederates indicated, and the New Englanders wondered why they and not the New Yorkers were the victims of his activity. It was he who proposed that Niagara should be strengthened with a stone fort, and this was hardly done when Beauharnois launched two vessels on Ontario.

Meanwhile the English had brought the Senecas, Cayugas, and Onondagas to a new treaty at Albany, in September, 1726. These tribes had endeavored to prevent the French strengthening Niagara, but failing in that they were the more ready to play into the hands of the English. By this pact they confirmed what was claimed to be an earlier cession of the land north of Lake Erie. They also granted a strip sixty miles wide along the southern bank of Ontario, including the post at Oswego, and extending to the modern Cleveland on Lake Erie. They acknowledged their lands to be "protected and defended for the use of us" by the English king. It may be a question if the Indian consciousness quite comprehended the interpretation which the English intended by those words. This done, Burnet strengthened the fort at Oswego, and sent eighty soldiers to defend the workmen, while two hundred armed traders assembled there.

Treaty of 1726.

Oswego strengthened. 1727.

In August, 1727, Begon, the Canadian intendant, demanded its evacuation, on the ground that the treaty of Utrecht did not allow either party to encroach upon disputed territory until commissioners had established the bounds between them. The French, however, were not prepared to go farther than to protest; nor did Burnet, in denying the rights of the French to Niagara, act more boldly. The English governor disavowed any other purpose than trade, and in defending his position at Oswego fell back on the provision of the treaty, which allowed each to trade with the Indians, and either to go to the native villages, or to have the savages come to established posts.

To be prepared for the worst, it was not long before a large force was put into the Oswego fort. The advantage which Burnet, largely through the expenditure of his own fortune, had thus secured was soon in some degree neutralized by the intrigue of the Albany merchants, who obtained from the crown a reversal of the governor's order which had prohibited their trade with Montreal. This

Trade of Albany with Montreal.

change opened the way to further intrigues of the French with the Iroquois.

The Scotch-Irish element had now begun to strengthen rapidly throughout the English colonies. Emigration from Ulster was become a habit, "spreading like a contagious distemper." It is said that, for several years after the second quarter of the century began, something like twelve thousand of this people were landed yearly at the Atlantic seaports. They all possessed a tendency to push inland after arriving. In Pennsylvania, they drifted towards those regions where the boundary controversies with Maryland and Virginia were still unsettled, and in these disputes they were to become important agents. In 1724–25, three thousand of them are said to have landed in Philadelphia. It was computed that in the single year 1729 five thousand of them entered Pennsylvania. This great influx put the Quaker element of the province in a decided minority, but it was many years later before the Society of Friends ceased to have a predominant power in the political machinery of the province. Already James Logan, representing the conservative Quakers, was looking to Parliament for relief from what seemed an impending inundation of this hardy stock.

The Scotch-Irish.

This stream of new-comers forced the settlements farther and farther west; and the pioneers were opening the way to the mountain gaps and toward the valley of Virginia. Earlier, in 1723, the Palatines, who had been settled on the Mohawk, were seeking freer service in Pennsylvania. One famous among the directors of the western progress in later years, Conrad Weiser, now a vigorous man of thirty-three, proficient in the Maqua tongue, and knowing the Indian character well, had cast in his lot among them in 1729. Mixed in this human drift toward the upper Susquehanna, and making head toward the mountain gaps, were a few New Englanders. They were representatives of Connecticut come to possess themselves of lands claimed in opposition to the charter of Penn. These lands were held to be within the sea-to-sea rights as established by the Connecticut charter of 1662, and beyond the interjected claim of the Duke of York along the Hudson, granted by his royal brother in

The Palatines and Conrad Weiser.

Settlers from Connecticut.

1664 and 1674. These interlopers, as Penn's people thought them, were a sturdy race, later to be heard from.

The Delawares, once the savage denizens of this region, had already begun to follow the flying game over the mountains, and had found new hunting-grounds on the Ohio. The Pennsylvania packmen were not far behind, and they soon encountered on the Alleghany the French traders. The two rivals were each anxious to discover the other's routes and purposes, and the secretary of Pennsylvania, in his reports to the Lords of Trade, was complaining that the French were pressing even within the limits of the province's charter.

The Delaware and the Pennsylvania traders.

As to the more remote regions beyond the forks of the Ohio, New York was already pressing her claims derived from the Iroquois, in order to keep out the traders of the other colonies. She held that the parliamentary acts of 1624, 1664, and 1681, which made this region crown lands, were enough, even without her Iroquois claim, to bar them out. But the urgent question, after all, was whether the activity of the French was not of itself enough to keep the English out. Coxe was expressing the fear that the better knowledge which the French possessed of the mountain passes might, "in conjunction with the French of the Meschacebe," enable them to "insult and harass these colonies." There was one favorable condition, however, — favorable, as he thought, to the British, in that the Chicazas (Chickasaws) were "good friends of the English." Their country extended to the Mississippi, and took in the valley of the Tennessee, which, as we have seen, was often marked in contemporary maps as the traders' route.

The Ohio region.

It was ten years since, from one of the passes of the Blue Ridge, Spotswood, with his Knights of the Golden Horseshoe, had looked down into the valley of the Shenandoah. If we may safely accept the story, the first settler on the river-bank of that leafy basin came in 1726, when a Welshman, Morgan by name, built a house beyond the Blue Ridge. It is possible that, about the same time, some Germans from Germanna, in the lower country of Virginia, where Spotswood had seated a colony of that people, had also made an entrance into the valley. Two adventurers, Mackey

First settlers on the Shenandoah. 1726.

and Salling, are reported to have wandered before this through the valley. Salling was captured by the Cherokees, and was held by them for some years as a prisoner. Experiencing a variety of vicissitudes, he was passed from them to Kaskaskia, thence to the Spaniards, and again to the French in Canada. After an absence of six years, he joined the English once more in New York.

Mackey and Salling.

The Cherokees, the cause of such trials, dominated all this western region south of the Iroquois and west of the mountains. They had, in 1721, ceded to the Carolinians a tract lying east of the Alleghanies and between the Edisto and Congaree rivers, — the earliest English acquisition from them, stretching up the Carolina streams. The paths of the traders who sought the Cherokee villages from Virginia and the Carolinas united in what is now the extreme northwest of South Carolina among the broken hills of the southern end of the Alleghanies. The Virginians already, in 1728, had a considerable pack-horse traffic with the Cherokees along this path, and there had been an intermittent trade with them carried on by the Carolinians for three quarters of a century. Coxe, in 1722, speaks of their centre of trade being only sixty miles distant from the Carolina outposts, and says that the English are "always very kindly entertained by them." But the French were not altogether deficient in influence among them, and both the Cherokees and Creeks were at times objects of solicitude in Carolina.

The Cherokees and the traders.

The trail from Virginia was a circuitous one. William Byrd of Westover speaks of its five hundred miles as most likely almost double the necessary distance if the Assembly would but order surveys to see if it could be shortened. Byrd's *History of the Dividing Line* is one of the few readable accounts which have come down to us of the life and sights of this period. He expresses the inquisitiveness of an active mind when he says, "It is strange that our woodsmen have not had curiosity enough to inform themselves more exactly of [this region]; and it is stranger still that the government has never thought it worth while [to incur] the expense of making an accurate survey of the mountains, that we might be masters of that natural fortification before the French, who in some places have settlements not very distant from it." It

The Virginia trail and Byrd of Westover.

was rather striking how, in all such statements, what was known to the traders entered so little into the sum of the common knowledge pertaining to the mountains and to what they shut off.

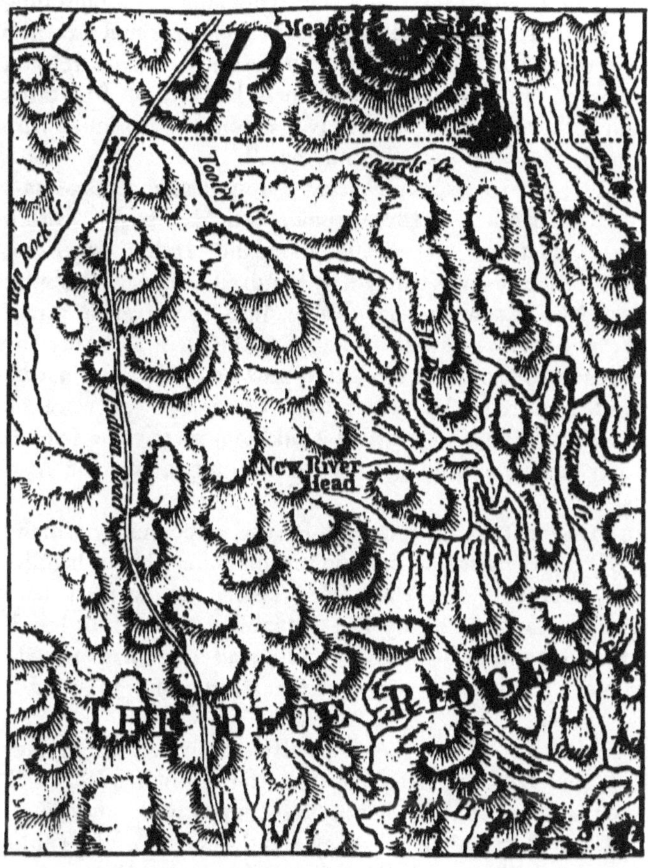

[From Jefferys' *American Atlas*, showing the Indian trail from the Shenandoah country to the Cherokee country. Tooley's Creek is the head of the Holston River.]

Joshua Gee on Carolina.

Joshua Gee, in his tract on the English trade, speaks of Carolina as "a noble colony, the most improvable of any of our colonies;" but he regards it as "liable to be overrun by the French and Spaniards for want of a sufficient protection." Referring to the French encroachments beyond the mountains, he adds: "If we have any sense of the value of that commodious tract of land, it ought to put us upon securing to ourselves such excellent colonies which may, if properly improved, bring this nation a very great treasure; and at least build some forts on the Appalachian Mountains, to secure us the rights of the mines contained in them; to protect the Indian and skin trade; and to preserve the navigation to ourselves of those great rivers which have their fountains in the said hills, and empty themselves through Carolina, Virginia, Maryland, etc., into the Virginia Sea."

In 1721, it was estimated that lying between Carolina and the French on the Alabama and Mississippi there were something over nine thousand Indian warriors, of whom nearly thirty-five hundred formerly traded with the English, but were now drawn into the French interests. The French were likewise thought to be in a fair way to win over about two thousand who were now neutral. Against about fifty-four hundred who either were at present or were likely to become hostile, the English could count on the friendship of nearly four thousand Cherokees dwelling along the Appalachians.

The southern Indians.

The danger to Carolina lay in the opportunity which the rivers east of the mountains offered for hostile descents if the Cherokees ceased to form a barrier. The greater danger was by the Altamaha. This risk had been represented to the Board of Trade, and they had urged the government to dispatch troops to Charleston and to build forts on the rivers.

Dangers of Carolina.

After Pensacola had been finally confirmed to Spain, in 1721, it was held in Carolina that the French could find an easy route from Mobile north till they struck and then descended the Altamaha. If they should do this, "it would be the most fatal blow yet to his Majesty's interests."

CHAPTER IX.

THE RIVALRIES OF FRANCE, ENGLAND, AND SPAIN.

1730–1740.

IN 1730, Montesquieu had predicted that England would be the earliest of the western nations to be abandoned by her colonies. He little anticipated that France would in reality be the first to be bereft of hers. Just at a time when France had determined to restrict the English to the seaward slope of the Appalachians, in the hope of sharing the greater spaces of the New World with Spain, his Catholic majesty and the English king were formulating policies which were to deprive those monarchs of their American dependencies. It was the production of sugar which was to be used in these magisterial ways. Joshua Gee, a contemporary English economist, was in 1731 urging upon his government to follow the French practice of sending vagrants to the colonies, since by the "incredible numbers" of them which France had sent to the Mississippi she had established a successful rivalry in the exportation of sugar. "If once the French can bring their settlements," he adds, "to bear upon the back of ours, along that most fertile valley which is watered with the river Overbachee [Wabash] and the great river Ohio, we may expect they will gain a great part of the tobacco trade also."

European colonies in America.

The sugar trade.

It was observed in London that the non-resident planters of the British Sugar Islands in the West Indies were accustomed to spend money lavishly. The inference was natural that to foster the production of that staple would bring more money still to the mother country. The result was the passage of parliamentary measures which, in aiding the sugar planters, bore hard on the Atlantic colonies, since the West Indies trade of Boston and Philadelphia was thereby forced to make a circuit through the British islands for the benefit of the English merchants. The colonial merchants were too active and the Atlantic coast too long to insure an exact or even general compliance with such restrictive measures, but any coercive attempt was an irritation. The Viscount Bury and other apologists have asserted that imperial orders, the subject of colonial jeers, and with difficulty enforced, could not have been oppressive; but they forget that vexatious and inoperative legislation is sometimes the most irritating.

The English Parliment restricts colonial commerce.

The liquor question in our recent sociological days is one mainly of domestic concern; but in the eighteenth century on this continent it affected the destiny of peoples. In the rival designs for the possession of the Great Valley, rum — and largely New England rum — played an important part. It was more than a calumet in the intercourse of white and savage. Western progress as tracked by successive purchases of lands was a chronicle of rum. "Plenty of wine and punch was given to the Indians," is the usual accompaniment of a deed. Not a victory but the pale-face and his red ally quaffed a glass. "You tell us you have beat the French," said a sachem. "If so you must have taken a great deal of rum from them, and can better spare us some of that hot liquor to make us rejoice with you in the victory." The record reads: "The governor and commissioners ordered a dram of rum to be given to each, in a small dram-glass, which the governor called a French glass." The record of a later day says that the Indians found the French glasses "unfortunate," referring to their diminutive size. "We now desire you will give us some in English glasses," said the unsated savage. The governor turned it to good account: "We are glad to hear you have such a dislike for what is French. They cheat you in your glasses as well as in everything else." The entry closes with the statement that they all had some rum "in some middle-sized glasses."

The influence of rum.

A French Jesuit complained that an Indian would be baptized ten times a day for a pint of brandy. "All the unhappiness that befalls you," said the governor of Pennsylvania at an Indian council, "is generally owing to the abuse of that destructive liquor, rum, of which you are so fond;" but there was very little beyond futile injunctions to prevent the mischievous trader carrying it to the Indian villages. Even in their councils, when the chiefs reprehended the traffic and its effect upon their wayward youngsters, and solemnly vowed to break every cask brought over the mountains, they were seldom averse to being refreshed at the trading-house. Indeed, there were laws of trade that no righteous indignation of white or savage could stay, for by such laws the Indian got more rum for his skins from the English than he could get of brandy from the French. Conrad Weiser at one time told the Indians on the Ohio, who were complaining that the English traders brought rum to their villages, that they themselves "sent down their skins by the traders to buy rum. You go yourselves down and bring back horse-loads of strong liquor. Beside this you never agree about it. One will have it; the other won't have it, — though there are very few of these last; and a third says, We will have it cheaper. This last we believe speaks out of his heart," and the recorder adds, "Here they laughed." Rum, in fact, was the main prop of the English trade, and the distilleries of New England got their full share of the profit. It mattered little whether the Yankee product passed up the Hudson to Albany, and so clandestinely reached the merchants of Montreal and competed with French brandy; or by an alternative channel found its way to the Delaware and Chesapeake Bay, and the pack-horse of the trader bore it over the Alleghanies. There were passages farther south perhaps more effective. "A great part of the molasses from the Dutch and French islands," says a contemporary tract, "imported into Rhode Island, Massachusetts Bay, etc., is distilled into rum and afterwards shipped by them into Virginia, Carolina," etc. In this traffic the distillers of New England were using yearly some twenty thousand hogsheads of molasses. To conform to the law passed in the interests of the Sugar Islands, and ship it through English ports, with increased cost of duties and transportation, was a burden, when not shirked, well calculated to make the merchants of Boston and Newport uneasy. The fact was that besides being a primary cause of western progress, rum was likely to prove a contingent influence for American independence. The more rum the more beaver, and when the British Parliament listened to Old-Country felt-makers and made

The beaver trade.

it punishable for the colonists to wear any covering but those furnished by the English furriers, we find hats and rum working out the great problem together. Parliament was making these two products lawful commodities only by their going through England. It would have been hard to patrol the Alleghanies with excisemen; and skins and rum passed and repassed, and there was free trade across the mountain barrier, while it was embarrassed on the coast.

Oswego and Fort Frederick. 1731.

Nothing at the north was shaping this traffic in the colonial interests more than the English post at Oswego, and nothing angered the French more than the maintenance of that station. In order to checkmate the English, and to place themselves in the line of communication between Albany and Montreal, the French now advanced along Lake Champlain. We have seen that under the French claims the southern bounds of Canada ran west from the mouth of the Kennebec, and this threw Champlain almost entirely within their limits. Crown Point, or, as the French termed it, Scalp Point, thus became for the first time a prize in the rival contentions of French and English, when the Canadians began here, in 1731, the erection of Fort Frederick. This post, accordingly, was a direct threat against the Iroquois, who laid claim to the region of the lake, and a danger to the English, who saw in it a possible movement which hazarded the connection of New England and New York. Late in the summer of 1731, two Dutchmen came to Albany from Canada, and reported the progress of the fort. They added that in the spring the French intended to take possession of Irondequoit Bay, on the southern side of Ontario, and so flank Oswego on the west as Fort Frederick did on the east.

French grants on Lake Champlain.

Nothing had of late occurred to arouse the English more. Logan sent from Pennsylvania his signal of alarm to Parliament. Rip van Dam in New York appealed for support on the one hand to Belcher of Massachusetts, and on the other to Gordon of Pennsylvania. Protests were made in Paris by the British ambassador. Nevertheless, the work at Crown Point went on. There was planted at the same time through the adjacent country by manorial grants a feudal spirit, contrary to English habit. The region was laid out in seigneuries, parceled out without recompense in a country that the Iroquois called their own, while the English claimed it under the treaty of Utrecht, as being within their jurisdiction. These surveys laid the foundations of disputes of title which it fell to New York to settle in vindication of her own right after the treaty of Paris in 1763.

The alarm at the English agitation threw Canada into solicitude lest the occupation of Crown Point should incite new attacks upon the St. Lawrence. The English, however, had enough to do elsewhere, and the French were suffered to go on strengthening their post, and finally (1737) to put an armed sloop on the lake. It was nearly ten years from the date of the first occupation of Crown Point before Fort Frederick was pronounced complete.

The Shawnees.

The disposition of the Shawnees had become a growing factor in the problem of western progress for the English. These Indians — or such of them as were not nomadic — had lived for some time, while their villages were on the Susquehanna, in a sort of subjection to the Iroquois. During this period the confederates watched their wards from Shamokin, at the forks of that river, where they kept a representative chieftain to control them. The Shawnees later claimed that they were forced across the Alleghanies because they would not join the confederates in war against the English. They were certainly restless in being what was termed "petticoated" by the Iroquois, and so sought friendly relations with some Delawares whom they found living on the waters of the Alleghany. This took place in 1732, a period of peace flecked with a cloud of danger on Lake Champlain.

The French, meanwhile, were assuring the Shawnees in their new Ohio home that the hatchet was buried. In May, 1732, Edmund Cartlidge wrote from the Alleghany valley to Governor Gordon of Pennsylvania: "The French seem very kind and courteous for the present; but how long it may hold I know not. The French coming to settle here, there is more necessity for the better regulation of the Indian trade, for the French will take all advantages against us to insinuate with the Indians in order to lessen their esteem for us." When the Shawnees, in September, 1732, sent a deputation to Philadelphia, and its members were asked why their tribe had crossed the mountains, and why their chief went so often to Montreal, they protested it was with no evil intent towards the English.

That the Shawnees did go to the French, the Pennsylvania traders were sure. These mongrel packmen made the most of the peaceful times, and were now swarming over the barrier ridges to pursue a trade always more or less nefarious. It was their custom to give the savages large credit in the autumn. When they exacted payment in the spring, a winter of rum-drinking had brought the poor debtors nigh unto destitution. This "trusting" process was so common hereabouts that, according to a memorial of some traders who had suffered by French blandishments interfering with the spring payments, it was termed "Alleghanying" the poor Indians.

The Pennsylvania traders.

These traders were at this day reporting that the French were building a log fort near the Ohio, and a certain Canadian, Cavelier by name, was said to come year after year among the tribes on the Alleghany to entice them to trade with Montreal.

The Iroquois, through that portion of them dwelling on the Ohio, and known as Mingoes, were another source of trouble to the English, who trusted the Shawnees. The Mingoes had a full share of the Iroquois longing for room, and were determined to push the Shawnees south of the Ohio. The Shawnees had long been wanderers, and they were not much averse to getting beyond the scrutiny of their quondam masters.

The Mingoes.

The French met the Mingoes, as they had met the Shawnees, with fair speeches; but the Iroquois were little inclined to brook the presence of the French as far east as the Alleghany, and the French saw in this Mingo aversion the instigation of the English. The ultimate question for the rival whites, as well as for the intermediary natives, was: Who should supply the rum to the distant Ottawas and Miamis? — and the better bargains at Oswego were sure to tell.

It was not long after this that Hocquart, the intendant of Canada, in a memoir which he prepared on the state of that country, acknowledged that this trading advantage of the English was beyond question. Oswego, he said, was getting the lion's share of the furs from Lake Su-

The French and the Indians.

perior, Mackinac, and Green Bay. The Sioux country, which was now become the principal source of supply, was also a tributary of the English post. There was nothing for the French to do but to outwit their rivals, as they had often done in more artful diplomacy with the Indians. English folly could certainly be counted on in the match, when such iniquities as "The Walking Purchase" of the Pennsylvanians were gloried in. The French were already benefiting themselves by their diplomatic skill. Beauharnois had a conference in 1734 with the Onondagas from the heart of the Iroquois Confederacy. The Wabash Indians were welcoming the French among them. Vincennes was becoming a settled post, with Louis St. Ange in command of its garrison. This was something to compensate the decadence of the French allies farther west, for the Illinois, from a powerful tribe as the French first found them, had been reduced to scarce six hundred fighting men.

Thomas Salmon, in his *Observations*, accounted the French wise in the quiet which they kept "before their designs are ripe for execution." The French threat of flanking Oswego at Irondequoit, though for a long time impending, had never been put in action, and by 1737, the English asked the Senecas, living adjacent thereto, for permission to possess and fortify the same bay. To this end the New York legislature made an appropriation to buy the site of the fort, and later it was thus acquired. The Indians on the Alleghany, meanwhile, were as quiet as Salmon thought the French to be, and when some stragglers were reported among them, showing white scalps, they hastened to relieve themselves of the imputation of hostility by telling the governor of Pennsylvania that the mischief-makers were wicked vagrants from the far Mississippi.

Irondequoit Bay.

For fifteen or twenty years the valley of Virginia had been looked into from the gaps of the Blue Ridge. Occasionally, hunter or trader had descended from the passes and found the fords of the Shenandoah. But no settlement up to 1730 had, beyond question, been made along its meadows, nor a single tract of its umbrageous paradise been cleared. This year, Governor Gooch issued a warrant for forty thousand acres in the lower parts of the valley to John

The valley of Virginia. 1730, etc.

and Isaac Vanmeter. The next year (1731), they sold their rights to one Joist Hite of Pennsylvania, and in 1732 Hite settled near the site of the future Winchester (founded in 1752). If the claims of Morgan, already mentioned in the preceding chapter, be rejected, Hite is thought to have been the first white settler in the valley of the Shenandoah, and he was instrumental in leading thither sixteen families from Pennsylvania.

Scotch-Irish and Germans.

The early immigrants of the valley were a mixed concourse of hardy people. Among them was a part of that Scotch-Irish influx which was animating the colonial blood in Jersey, and indeed all along the Atlantic coast it brought in the martial spirit of Bothwell Bridge. There were also many of those Rhinelanders and Palatines who had flocked into New York, Pennsylvania, and Carolina, fugitives from the horrors which the Thirty Years' War had visited upon the Germans. They had fled from sumptuary laws and official extortions, — symptoms of that same despotism which, nearly a half century later, sent regiments of Hessians and Brunswickers to these same American wilds, when finally those of them who abided here became the stanchest adherents of the Federal Constitution. These Germans were in their own way a merry, hearty people, calculated to make the life of a pioneer as buoyant as a certain sluggishness would permit. Some among them, particularly those lingering by the Potomac, were Catholic, tributary to the only organization in America before the Revolution which publicly celebrated mass, — the isolated Roman Church in Philadelphia, — and they were never quite free from the suspicion of their neighbors lest their religious sympathies might too easily affiliate them with the French.

Huguenots.

The French Huguenots, as a part of the un-English population, had no such doubts cast upon their sincerity. They had long ago weakened France, and had been denied the chance of strengthening Canada. From Boston to Charleston they were giving a rich strain to the conglomerate races of the seaboard. Some of them were among the first settlers of what is now Augusta, and they did their full share in creating a race of valiant first-goers in the wilderness.

The modern local antiquaries of this region are not in full accord as to dates and details of these first comers in the valley of Virginia; but it seems certain that all or nearly all came up the valley from Pennsylvania, after crossing the Potomac. It was later when others from the tidewaters of Virginia crossed the Blue Ridge. In the absence of surveys, the lands were occupied in large part at a venture,— a slight cabin, a few hills of corn, or trees blazed along a supposed boundary, constituting all the act of possession. The settlement at the modern Woodstock (1734) was in the same year in which all the country west of the Blue Ridge was set up as the county of Orange, extending west "to the utmost bounds of Virginia," according to her sea-to-sea charter. During the next few years (1735–1740), the tide moved up the valley to where the sources of the Roanoke and James interlace with those of the Kanawha. It was a region where a single rain-cloud might in a few hours feed, on the one hand, the fountains of the Atlantic streams, and on the other those of the Great Valley.

First comers in the valley of Virginia.

In 1735–36, Colonel James Patton, one of the North of Ireland stock, received a grant of 120,000 acres not far from where Staunton now is. John Salling, whom we have already mentioned as a captive of the Cherokees, borne through the Cumberland Gap, after six years of wandering had returned to Virginia, and in 1736 he had settled at the forks of the James west of the Blue Ridge. In September of the same year, Governor Gooch, in pursuance of an Order in Council and in the royal name, created the manor of Beverly on the Sherando (Shenandoah). Its precise limits of 118,491 acres signify a supposably careful acquaintance with the country. Indeed, the local names of landmarks defining the bounds of this grant indicate that the region had become more or less familiar. There were, apparently, squatters here and there throughout its extent. The chief patentee was William Beverly, a son of that historian of the name who had been a sharer in the adventurous merriments of Spotswood a score of years before. This manor lay in the upper valley, where Staunton now stands. Beverly soon bought out his copartners and began settling families. Gooch, in the same year (1736), made a grant of land higher up the valley to one Benjamin Borden.

Patton and Salling.

Manor of Beverly.

In 1736, Colonel William Mayo and a party of surveyors followed the Potomac up to one of its springs, and discovered other waters not far off flowing westward into the Monongahela. The search for river sources fell in with the habit of making grants between rivers, and these grants were limited, up their valleys, by lines connecting their springs. It was a custom that gave rise to many disputes in these early apportionments of land, arising from a difference of claim as to what constituted a source, particularly in case of alternative forks. In this way the grant made to Lord Fairfax of a territory between the Rappahannock and the Potomac, with bounds at the west defined by the shortest distance between their respective fountains, helped materially the settlement of the Beverly manor. His lordship claimed that such a western line for his grant threw the lower parts of the Shenandoah valley within his domain; but the running of that line depended on which was taken as the source of the Potomac, the fountain of the north or of the south of its upper branches. Fairfax and those who disputed his claim naturally stood respectively for that interpretation which increased their lands. The dispute was a long one, and for fifty years served to render the titles in the lower parts of the valley uncertain, and this drove settlers farther south, where no such rival claimants contended. The decision was ultimately against the Fairfaxes (1786). In much the same way, north of the Potomac, the boundary disputes between Maryland, Virginia, and Pennsylvania, complicating the service of writs, had a tendency to prevent settlers lingering on their way to the valley of Virginia.

Colonel Mayo at the forks of the Potomac. 1736.

The Fairfax grant.

The valley had been for years the stamping-ground of the Cherokees and Catawbas going north, and of the Delawares and Iroquois ranging south in counter raids, with a fearful energy that the English, who counted all as allies against the French, often endeavored to assuage. Washington speaks of encountering such war parties when he was surveying for Lord Fairfax in the valley. The Iroquois, in some of these incursions, thinking to secure immunity from English molestation farther south, sometimes tried to get from the frontier officers of Virginia a certificate of the confederates' good intentions toward the whites. The practice did not serve to soften the southern Indians, and it became necessary to break up this hostile habit. To hold the valley free from such conflicts fell in large part to the Scotch-Irish, who had been for some years

The valley a warpath.

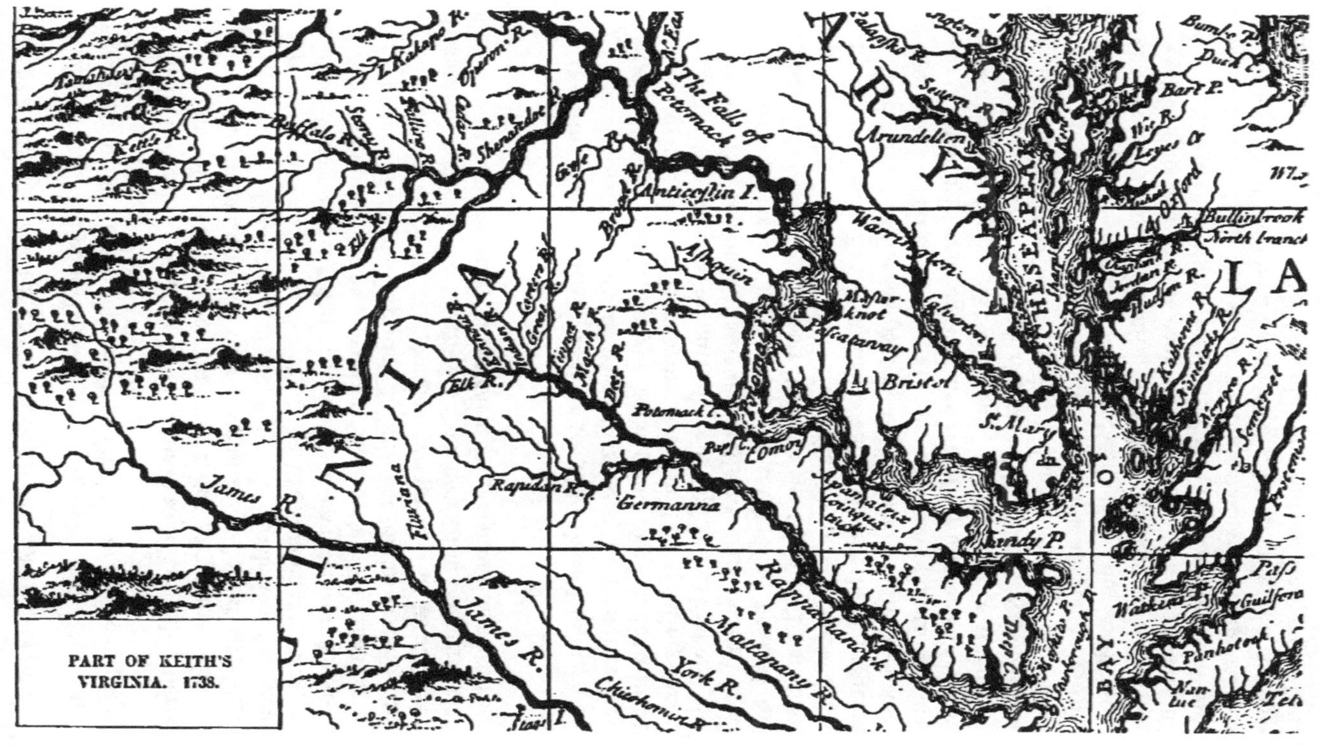

PART OF KEITH'S VIRGINIA. 1738.

coming in from Pennsylvania, and proving themselves the virile race which later represented Virginia in the campaign of Braddock and at Point Pleasant.

Western extent of Virginia.

When Governor Gooch, in 1738, assured to this people liberty of conscience, a new incentive was given to their immigration, and the valley began to be dotted with hamlets. This increase needed new legislation for local government, and all the territory of the Virginia charter west of the Blue Ridge was divided into the two counties of Augusta and Frederick, the latter covering the northerly extension to "the utmost limits of Virginia." This act, under the existing pretensions of Virginia, carried her jurisdiction at least to the Mississippi, while to the northwest it included the western parts of Pennsylvania, and gave cause for a long contention with that province.

Early English on the Ohio.

It is quite possible that previous to 1740 there had been an occasional straggler who had crossed the western range of the Appalachians in some other pursuit than trade or the chase. Surveyors and men "prospecting" may have gone this way in an adventurous spirit. Mitchell, the geographer of a somewhat later day, tells us that he had seen the journals of some Virginia surveyors who had crossed the gaps and followed down Wood River to the Ohio, and had then passed down to New Orleans. He professes to have made from these itineraries a draft of the country which these pioneers had traversed; but the supporters of England's claim to priority over the French in Mitchell's time are often open to the suspicion of making a case against her rivals by all sorts of possibilities stated as facts. At all events, the knowledge which the English had at this time of the trans-Alleghany region must have been very defective. Thomas Salmon, who was now supplying (1736) the popular demand in England for geographical knowledge, seemed to comprehend that the headwaters of the York, Potomac, James, and Rappahannock, as he expressed it, "locked within each other, as are also the heads of several other rivers, that rise in the same mountains and run toward the west." But when he undertakes to describe this distant region of western-flowing rivers, he manifests a surprising ignorance of what the French geographers had published.

"On the west side of the mountains," he says, "are a great many lakes of which the French are in possession, as 't is said, but these have not a communication with each other or with the river St. Lawrence, as is commonly reported." Even the great English map of Popple in 1732 displays little knowledge of any development beyond that represented by Delisle some fifteen years earlier.

Farther south, the Cherokees were still the bulwark of Carolina. In 1729, word had reached England that the French had succeeded in detaching these Indians from the British interests, and that with the Creeks they were rendering trade beyond the mountains insecure. It needed a bold stroke to break this savage pact, and bring the Cherokees back to the English allegiance. The man for it was found. A Scotch baronet, Sir Alexander Cuming, now a man of about forty, who had been interested in Berkeley's scheme of an Indian college at Bermuda, was sent hither to prepare the way for a revival of this over-hill trade. With a train which he gathered at Charleston he started on his perilous mission. The account of his journey which we have was brought to light by the late Samuel G. Drake in 1872, and presents a picture of the undaunted Scotchman moving through the hostile country like a potentate, overawing village after village by his daring, and forcing the recalcitrant savages to bend the knee in acknowledgment of the sovereignty of the British king. This, day after day, is the story of his progress between March 13, 1730, when he set out, and his return to Charleston, April 20, when he had accomplished a circuitous tour of five hundred miles. He brought back with him several headmen of the Cherokee villages, and took them to England to verify by a treaty at Whitehall, on September 7, 1730, an agreement which he had made with the tribe.

The Cherokees and the Carolinians.

Sir Alexander Cuming.

Treaty with the Cherokees. 1730.

"The chain of friendship," says this London document, "between King George and the Cherokee Indians is like the sun, which shines both here and also upon the great mountains where they live, and equally warms the hearts of the English and the Indians." This warmth induced them to grant to the whites the right to build habitations and forts among them. They promised also not to trade and not to have other intercourse with any but the English.

Of the condition of the Cherokees at this time we have an extended statement by James Adair, a trader for many years among them. He is, however, an unsatisfactory guide for the sequence of events, as he gives few dates, and those confused. When he began to trade among the Cherokees, about 1735, he reckoned that they had nearly six thousand warriors. His wanderings took him as well among the Creeks and Choctaws, and he saw everywhere the evidence of their descent from the lost tribes of Israel!

The condition of the Cherokees.

Two years after Cuning's expedition over the mountains, the English government reënforced their sea-to-sea claims by the Georgia charter of June 9, 1732. This document was a distinct threat to the French, or at least they considered it such, since it was but the beginning of a push westward around the southernmost edge of the Alleghanies. By this, it was seen, the English might hope to reach the Mississippi and sever Louisiana from Canada. It was quite as distinct a challenge to the Spaniards, when the trustees of the new province sought to push against the Floridian frontier fresh settlements of whatever persecuted people they could drag from the debtors' jails in England or gather in the mountains of the Tyrol.

The charter of Georgia. 1732.

The bounds of Georgia were the Savannah River on the one hand and the Altamaha on the other, and from their respective sources the lines were to run due west to the Pacific or "South Seas," cutting athwart the French on the Mississippi. It was apparent that, in parting with something of her territory to the new proprietors, South Carolina had secured a bulwark against the Spaniards, as well as against any hostile Indians coming round the southern verge of the Appalachians. Her dangers were now to be expected solely through the gaps toward the modern State of Tennessee from the Indians in the French alliance. It was the object of Oglethorpe, at the head of the Georgian settlements, to bring these tribes into friendly relations with the new province. The next year (1733) we find him compacting with the Creeks, Cherokees, Chickasaws, and Choctaws, enlarging the English sovereignty and placating the savage nature.

This movement by Oglethorpe was easily an affront to the French, and for some years it was a varying struggle between the English and these rivals on the Mississippi to secure the Indian sympathy. It was a trial of English pluck and French blandishments. Adair says that it was about this time (1736) that the French seriously began to think of walling the English in by the Appalachians. Along this southern stretch of those mountains, the help of the Cherokees was essential to that end. The English saw, as the French did, that this tribe held with the Catawbas the key to the situation. To make them allies in fullest sympathy, it was necessary to force them into harmony with their old foes, the Iroquois. In 1737, Conrad Weiser was bending his skillful energies to bring about the reconciliation of the northern confederates and the Catawbas.

Oglethorpe and the French.

Cherokees, Catawbas, and Iroquois.

It is to be feared there was quite as much need of a similar spirit of concord among the whites of the Atlantic colonies, for intercolonial forbearance had little steadiness. The Carolina traders complained that the Georgian authorities taxed them for a passage across the Savannah on their way to the Cherokees, and in other respects the people of one province or another found their neighbors a burden.

Intercolonial jealousies.

We find the average English notion of these Carolina barrier hills in what Salmon was writing at this time in his efforts to enhance their glories in the eyes of stay-at-home Britons. He speaks of "glittering sands being frequently washed down," while acknowledging scant acquaintance with a region where there are no towns or settlements, and no inhabitants, as he says, but wild beasts. "Our people only pass over the mountains when they go to traffic with the Indians near the banks of the Mississippi." Counting little on the intervention of the French, he supposes that there may come a rupture with the Spaniards. If this should happen, he sees nothing "to prevent our passing the mountains and possessing ourselves of the mines of St. Barbe, if we make the Indians of those countries our friends, who are frequently at war with the Spaniards. . . . If we suffer [he adds] the French to build forts and fix themselves on the Mississippi or in the neighborhood of the Appalachian Mountains, they will not only be in a con-

Salmon's views.

dition to invade and harass our plantations from north to south, but will possess themselves of the mines there, . . . which will render that nation more formidable even in Europe than it is at present. . . . It is to be wished, therefore, that Spain and England would in turn understand their mutual interest, and enter into a defensive alliance in America, at least since the French can only be defeated in their ambitious and covetous views by the united forces of Great Britain and Spain." This was a welcome complement to the pet scheme of France to unite with Spain and drive the English from the continent.

England and Spain.

Neither scheme looked promising. The English merchants fretted under the vigilance of Spain in thwarting their smuggling trade with the Spanish islands. Spain saw the same contraband trade successful enough to lessen her commerce, and she was stirred to greater vigilance. This increased the British discontent, and Pope and Johnson made the most they could of it in indignant verse, aimed to overthrow an inert ministry. In January, 1739, Walpole made a convention with Spain, and commissioners were named to settle the boundary disputes of Georgia and Florida. All this simply delayed, but did not prevent war, and on June 15, 1739, Newcastle notified the colonial governors that hostilities with Spain were renewed, and authorized them to seize Spanish property and issue letters of marque.

War of England and Spain.

It was not till September that Oglethorpe heard of the actual declaration of war. He strove at once to make the Creeks as good a barrier against the Spaniards as the Cherokees were towards the French. He agreed with the Creeks for cessions of their lands on the Savannah as far as the Ogeechee and along the coast to the St. John's River, and so inland as far as the tides went. The savages further agreed to bar out the Spanish.

In June, 1740, the English had pushed well into Florida, and were before St. Augustine. Here Oglethorpe suffered from the defection of some of his followers, and was obliged to withdraw. The Moravians whom he had called from Germany, and who had begun to set up missions among the Creeks, revolted at the war, and rather than take part in it turned north to confront later conflicts in Pennsylvania. The campaign closed with the Spaniards likely to hold their own on their side of the Great Valley.

Of the tribes to the east of the lower Mississippi, the Chickasaws were accounted — if Charlevoix reflects the general view — the "bravest of the Louisiana Indians." Allied with the English, they had provoked in many ways the enmity of the French; but their allegiance was somewhat inconstant, and their attacks occasionally were directed against the English. Whichever way their hostile frenzy turned them, those who felt the weight of their resentment, whether English or French, charged the mischief on the instigation of the other, and very likely with entire justice.

The Chickasaws.

Lying two hundred miles west of their main country were the Chickasaws' friends, the Natchez, bordering on the Mississippi. This inter-tribal friendship had for a long time rendered the situation of Fort Rosalie a source of anxiety to the French. It ought to have opened the eyes of its commandant to the precarious peace of the little colony clustered about the fort; but he was an imperious and heedless man, and his character hastened the crisis.

The Natchez.

The Choctaws, a treacherous people, ostensibly friendly to the French, had secretly agreed with the Natchez and Yazoos to rise upon the French and destroy them. It was the part assigned to the Choctaws to attack New Orleans. The Natchez, being impatient, anticipated the appointed day, and so the plot failed of its full effect. They fell, November 28, 1729, on the defenseless colonists in and near Fort Rosalie, and massacred nearly all. A single fugitive reached New Orleans, and his bewildered story created the utmost consternation.

The Natchez war. 1729-1731.

The Choctaws had recently made warm protestation of fidelity, and this had blinded the people in that town to the danger which their insecurity invited. The precipitancy of the attack at Fort Rosalie proved their protection, for by it they were forewarned and escaped like horrors. Excepting a small commotion occasioned by the Yazoos on the Washita, beyond the Mississippi, the sudden outburst of the Natchez failed of support elsewhere.

The French showed their energy in moving toward the Natchez to avenge the massacre. The Choctaws, still professing friendship, were the first on the spot; but were soon joined by a force from New Orleans. The Natchez yielded their ground, and, leaving some white prisoners behind, fled across the Mississippi. They were pursued, but only their women fell into the hands of the French. A kind of guerrilla war lasted for a year, and when Périer brought it to a close (January 1, 1731) he found himself possessed of nearly five hundred captive Indians, who were sold as slaves in the San Domingo market. There is some question as to the place where the Natchez made their last stand, supposed to be about forty miles northwest of Fort Rosalie. Some contend that it was near the modern Lake Lovelace.

New Orleans fortified.

The outbreak had shown the necessity of improving the defenses of New Orleans, and Périer began to dig a moat around the town, and to plan forts at several points on the river. There was great need of it, for the remnant of the Natchez were active, now falling upon the friendly Tonicas, and now attacking French barges as they struggled up the river, carrying supplies to the upper settlements. A part of the tribe sought refuge among the Chickasaws, and there nurtured their revengeful spirit.

Servile rising in New Orleans.

This Natchez war was the first serious hostile encounter which the Louisianians had had. The depletion of New Orleans, by sending its available adults to man the new posts, exposed the town to the dangers of a servile insurrection. Nothing but good luck and prompt action, whereby a dozen of black ringleaders were hanged, prevented other scenes of horror in a colony where out of seven thousand souls nearly a third were black and in bondage.

The Company of the Indies gives up its charter. 1731.

The cost of the war and the uncertainty attending it had discouraged the Company of the Indies. Other schemes for profit in Asia and Africa were by contrast far more promising for the company's capital. For this cause their interest slackened, and Louisiana got less and less of their attention. The discontent culminated, January 33, 1731, in a surrender of the company's charter to the king. Louisiana, thus freed from a depressing monopoly and become a royal province, could not be worse off than she had been, and might be better. So the colonists waited developments.

The king, May 7, 1732, organized a council of government, and

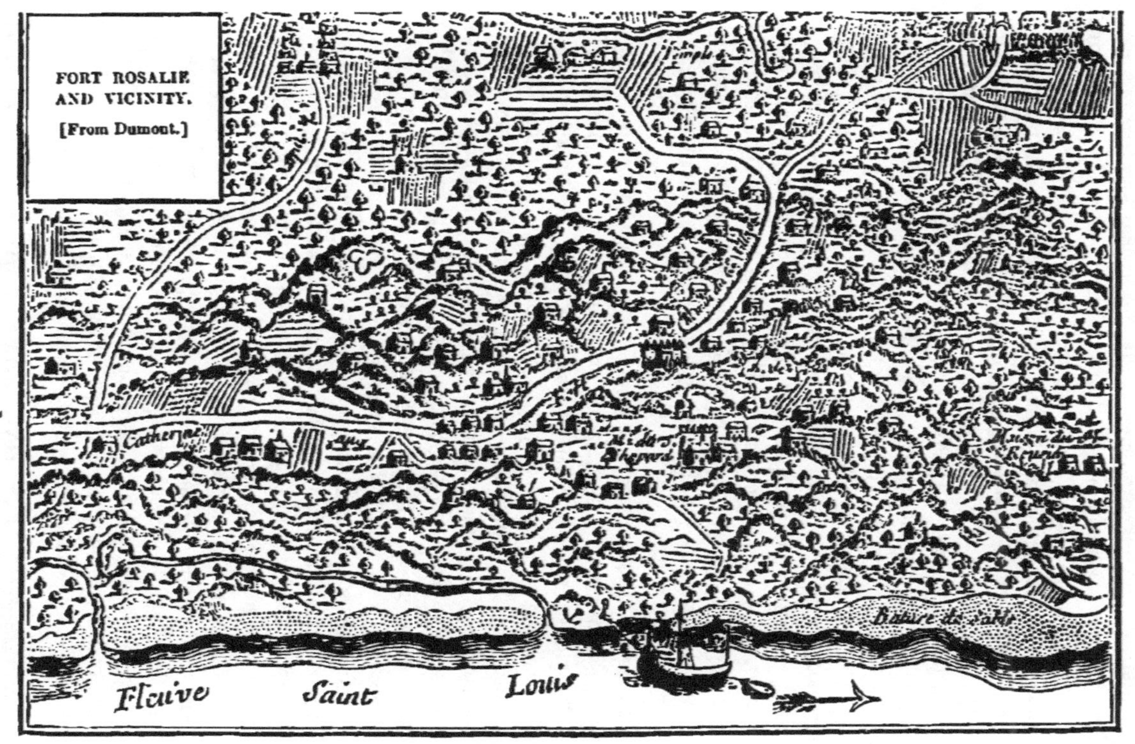

FORT ROSALIE
AND VICINITY.
[From Dumont.]

recalling Périer for promotion, sent back Bienville to his old post. Unfortunately, little was done to improve the character of the emigration which followed, and New Orleans received a fresh accession of the lazy and vicious, — poor material with which to recuperate its energies.

Bienville governor of Louisiana. 1732.

All this was not promising for the serious work which Bienville soon took in hand. This was to demand of the Chickasaws the surrender of the Natchez fugitives. The governor by gifts sought to gain over the Choctaws for a united campaign against these harborers of the enemy. As the trading-path went, the Chickasaw country was a hundred and sixty miles to the north of the Choctaw villages, between the upper forks of the Mobile River. The march thither was a more laborious one for the French than for their savage allies; but there was the prospect of plundering the English traders domesticated among the Chickasaws, and this was lure enough for both. The Chickasaws were known to belong to the savage league which was imperiling the passage of the Mississippi, and Bienville saw no alternative but the trial of war.

War with the Chickasaws.

The Choctaws were not quick to respond to the French entreaties, though they at last yielded. It took time to lay such plans of coöperation that a supporting army could be brought from the Illinois country for a simultaneous attack. Meanwhile, it was determined that Bienville should advance from the south by way of the Mobile and Tombigbee rivers.

On April 1, 1736, Bienville's army left Mobile Fort in thirty piraguas and as many bateaux. In three weeks, they were at Tombigbee, where a fort had already been built, and where the Choctaws, coming across the country, joined them. In a month more, they had gone as far as their boats would carry them; and at this point, seven leagues from the nearest Chickasaw village, they built a palisade to protect their boats, and moved on by land. On reaching the Chickasaw village, they saw the English flag flying above the defenses, and recognized some Carolina traders on the ramparts.

The attack which was made on May 26 was vigorously repelled by the Chickasaws. Firing from pits, they reserved their volleys till the French were close upon them. This method of defense may have given rise to stories, later common, that the Chickasaws lived in holes like weasels, as we sometimes find it stated on legends in contemporary maps.

Fifty of the assailants are said to have fallen at the first discharge from the fort, and thirty at the second. The Choctaws who accompanied the French are variously stated to have been from six hundred to twice as many in number, and, like all savages, they lost heart rapidly under the steady repulse. So the French, numbering perhaps five hundred, were soon left to themselves, in a condition not much more sanguine than the Choctaw fugitives. All the French plans, indeed, had miscarried. The attack had been set down for May 10, when it was supposed the forces from the Illinois would be in position to assault simultaneously on the north. Bienville had been delayed by rain, and had been obliged to tarry at intervals to build ovens and bake bread. He was accordingly a fortnight and more behind time. He had heard rumors which led him to suspect that D'Artaguette, commanding this northern party, was in position; but he does not seem to have had confirmation of the story before he himself was obliged to retreat.

D'Artaguette's attack.

The fact was that D'Artaguette, leading some four hundred French and Indians, was not pleased with Bienville's orders to make haste slowly, so as not to be ahead of the attack on the south. When he came upon the northern villages of the Chickasaws, he unadvisedly rushed to an attack. The onset was a failure. The commander was captured, and his Indians fled. The victor secured a supply of powder, and captured some of Bienville's orders, which the English traders deciphered. So the movements on the south were anticipated, and the governor more easily foiled in his attack.

Bienville prepares for a new campaign.

Bienville returned to New Orleans with his bedraggled and downcast followers as best he could. He was as determined, however, as before to punish the foe; but it took three years to complete his new preparations. Meanwhile, he kept parties of Choctaws and Illinois skirring along the trails of the English traders to intercept their supplies. Other parties were sent to explore different paths of approach to the Chickasaws, so as to find the best. It was finally determined to try that which followed the Mississippi and the Yazoo. Making a new treaty with the Choctaws, to get what help he could from their four thousand warriors, he established a base near the modern Memphis. He built here Fort Assumption, and waited the accumulation of supplies from the Illinois country, as well as the coming of troops from France. These, to the number of seven hundred, arrived in 1739. Delays brought the usual embarrassments. Horses and cattle strayed off. Provisions were lavishly consumed. The Indians deserted. It took at last three months to open the roads necessary for the march back from the river.

A peace follows. 1740.

The Illinois colonists had responded generously, and Buissonnière and Longueil had come with a good following from Fort Chartres. So Bienville found he was ready to start, in March, 1740, with about twelve hundred whites and twice as many Indians. Céloron, come from Canada, was sent ahead with a force fitted to try the temper of the enemy. The Chickasaws took alarm, and were induced to send their chiefs to Fort Assumption. A peace followed, and by April 1, 1740, Bienville was able to boast of success, and returned to New Orleans.

The prospects of New France.

It seemed for a while as if France was assured of a future in the Great Valley, and England and Spain were to be kept afar. St. Denis had already confronted and warned the Spaniards on the Red River, and England had nowhere got a footing beyond the Alleghanies. Signs of material prosperity were soon apparent in the French capital on the Mississippi. The rice and tobacco of Louisiana began to find a market in Europe, and timber was sent to the West Indies.

But provisions came mostly from the Illinois, and the peace with the Chickasaws was not so effective but that courage was requisite to defend the barges passing up and down with their burdens. It was not a satisfactory sign, for it meant that the English were still stirring the Chickasaws to break their peace with the French, and to offer a bar at every point to any intercourse by land as well as by water from the Gulf to the Ohio.

CHAPTER X.

THE SEARCH FOR THE SEA OF THE WEST.

1727–1753.

Pierre Gaultier de Varennes, Sieur de Vérendrye, was a man approaching fifty years of age when he attracted notice as a discoverer. He was the son of the governor of Three Rivers, and was born in that town. His career had been somewhat varied. He had done his part in ravaging the New England frontiers, and he had campaigned as a soldier-of-fortune in Flanders, where once he had been left for dead on the battlefield. Vérendrye.

Vérendrye had been placed in charge of a fort on Lake Nipigon, north of Lake Superior, in 1727, where he heard the Indians tell their stock stories of a westward-running river, with its ebb and flow, and a great salt lake at its mouth. These tales soon gave him an ambition to lay open the secrets of the continent which lay hidden toward the setting sun. He left his post to go east, in order to bring his plans before the government at Quebec. He sought to represent the danger of allowing the English — as old rivals of the French for the Indian trade — to take the lead in the possession of this remote region. At Lake Nipigon. 1727.

It was in the spring of 1728, when going east, that he met Father Guignas at Mackinac, and found him fully believing in a discoverable way to the western ocean. He also fell in with Father Degonnor. This priest had been for a while at Lake Pepin, as the spiritual head of a post established by Beauharnois. It was a part of a project of that governor to capture the trade and sympathies of the Sioux, in the hope of securing their assistance in a westward movement from that point. To this end a fort had been lately built on that lake. It was one of the most exposed positions on the Lake Pepin.

frontiers, and ever since the French had known its neighborhood, they had had strange vicissitudes in all their efforts to make it a trading-post. Floods and attacks had incessantly followed its founding. For the next ten years, the post was to be the centre of intermittent activity against hostile Indians, who came in the main from the region of Green Bay. The danger became eventually (1737) so great that Legardeur de St. Pierre, then in command, had found it prudent to fire the fort and escape. We shall see that at a later day it was to devolve upon St. Pierre to be the successor of the discoverer whose career we have now entered upon.

Vérendrye's new acquaintance, the priest from Lake Pepin, was ambitious of further duty in even more exposed positions, and the two determined to ask the French government to found a post and maintain a mission among the Assiniboines. This northern tribe, denizens of what is now Manitoba, is supposed to have been an offshoot of the Dacotah stock. Their name as just given is in accordance with the designation bestowed by the French rather than the English, and this diversity of ear has supplied a great variety of forms to their tribal appellation.

It was Vérendrye's belief, and Beauharnois shared it, that the chances of finding a good route towards the west were better here than from Lake Pepin. They counted, not very wisely, on finding these northern Indians more placable than the treacherous Sioux.

The rovers of the remotest frontiers had never ceased to be animated by a hope of discovering the great western sea. While at Lake Nipigon, Vérendrye had often questioned the Indians, and Pako, a chief, had told him of a great lake toward the declining day, which poured its waters in three different directions, — one outlet being to Hudson's Bay, another toward the Mississippi, and the last westward, with an ebb and flow of the stream in the direction of a great salt sea, where there were villages of a dwarfish race. In confirmation of all which Vérendrye produced a map of an Indian guide, Otchaga, which, in the interpretation of Danville a few years later, was a premonition of the Lake of the Woods, with a western-flowing outlet.

Stories of a western way.

These stories of an ocean-side folk far to the west were of

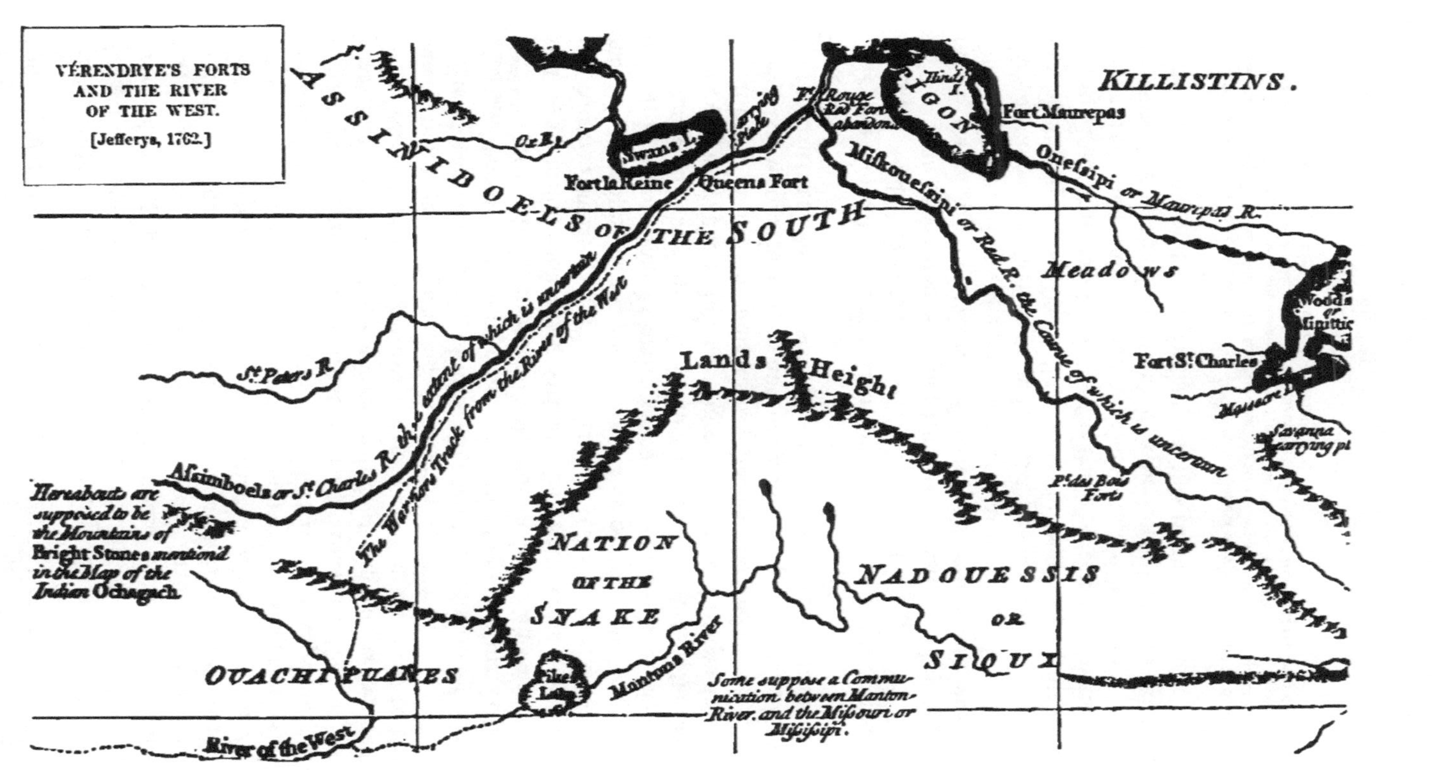
VÉRENDRYE'S FORTS
AND THE RIVER
OF THE WEST.
[Jefferys, 1762.]
KILLISTINS.
ASSINIBOELS OF THE SOUTH
Ox R.
Swans L.
Fort la Reine
Queens Fort
Fort Maurepas
Onesipi or Maurepas R.
Miskouesipi or Red R. the Course of which is uncertain
Meadows
Fort St. Charles
Savanna
Assimboels or St. Charles R. the extent of which is uncertain
The Warriors Track from the River of the West
St. Peters R.
Lands Height
Pt. des Bois Forts
Hereabouts are supposed to be the Mountains of Bright Stones mention'd in the Map of the Indian Ochagach
NATION OF THE SNAKE
NADOUESSIS OR SIOUX
OUACHIPUANES
Pike Lake
Mantons River
Some suppose a Communication between Manton River and the Missouri or Missisipi.
River of the West

course nothing but rehabilitations of many old fables, such as Sagard, a hundred years before, had repeated. The English were being regaled with them at this same time on Hudson's Bay. La France, a half-breed Indian, told Arthur Dobbs, now in that region, that in 1726 he had gone with a party to the western sea, where he had seen large black fish sporting in the waves. It was here that he and his companions had attacked a town, and none of the assailers but himself had escaped to tell the story. Ellis, another frequenter of Hudson's Bay, a few years later, reports it a common belief among the tribes that there were rivers flowing west to a great ocean far away to the sunsetting, where ships sailed, and men wore beards.

A mid-continental sea.

Such were among the stories that in the autumn of 1729 could be cited in proof of water-ways to this distant sea. It is curious to note how a belief in some central water basin, connecting with all the great oceans surrounding North America, afforded a leading feature of the experimental geography of the continent. Two centuries before, such a faith had encouraged Cartier to leave the salt tide of the St. Lawrence in the hope of finding a central fresh-water sea. Modern geographers find that like physical conditions are impossible in normal circumstances; but in the eighteenth century, they were relied upon and exemplified by Bellin and the leading cartographers, to solve the riddle of a trans-continental water-way.

Vérendrye's views.

It was Vérendrye's belief that this lake of multiple outpours could be reached in twenty days from Nipigon, and that an expedition starting from Montreal in May might arrive there in September. Vérendrye's representations at Quebec, and, through the governor, at Paris, were not received with confidence sufficient to induce the government to embark any capital in the scheme. The king, however, was quite willing to grant a monopoly of the fur trade in this wild region, if Vérendrye could induce some merchants to aid him in an outfit. The result was the formation of a new company for trading with the Sioux and other Indians of this region.

NOTE. The opposite map is from Bowen and Gibson's *North America*, published by Sayer and Bennett, London, 1763. It shows the Sioux country and the upper waters of the Mississippi River, and the portage connecting Lake Superior and the Lake of the Woods, which was later forgotten. The dotted line "settled by Commissaries" is that of the southern bounds of the Hudson Bay Company, "after the treaty of Utrecht."

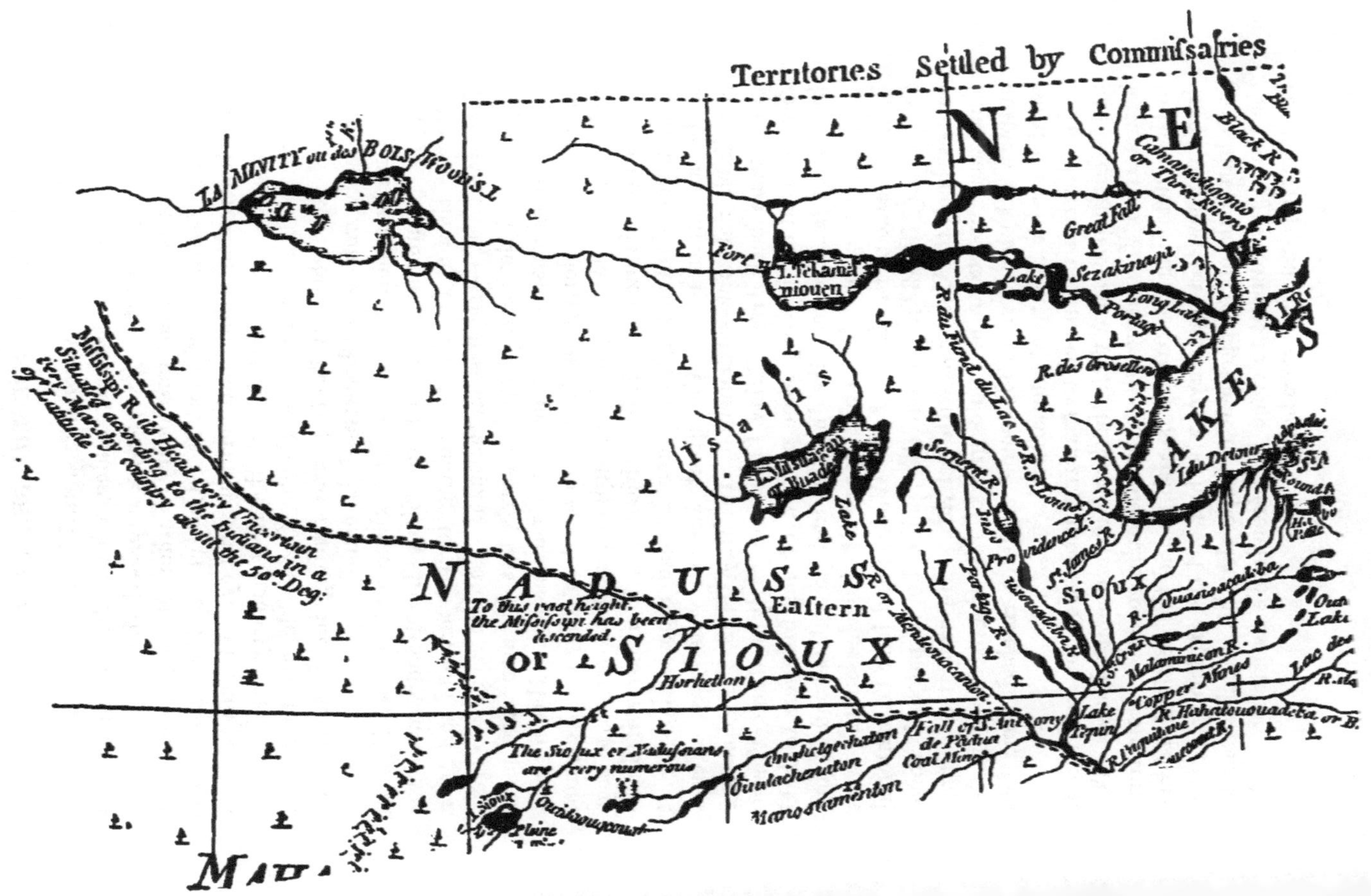

Territories Settled by Commissaries
LA MINITY ou des BOIS WOODS L.
Fort
L. Tekama nioüen
Lake
Sezakinaga
Great Fall
Long Lake
Portage
R. des Groseillers
R. du Fond du Lac or R. S. Louis
Black R.
Camanestigouia or Three Rivers
LAKE
L. du Detour
Missisipi R. its Head very Uncertain Situated according to the Indians in a very Marshy country about the 50th Deg. of Latitude.
NADUSSI
Eastern
To this vast height the Misissipi has been ascended.
OR SIOUX
L. Mississagan or Buade
Lake
S. or Menkonoacanton.
Serpent R.
Isles
Providence L.
Portage R.
S. James R.
SIOUX
Ouasisacadeba
Malamincan R.
Copper Mines
R. Hahatououadeba or B.
Lake Pepin
Fall of S. Antony de Padua
Coal Mine
Horhetton
The Sioux or Nadusians are very numerous
Oushelgecitation
Oüulachenuton
Manostamenton
Sioux
Plaine

On May 19, 1731, Vérendrye signed an agreement with some Montreal traders, under which they furnished his equipment. His party comprised the leader's three sons, a Jesuit missionary, Father Messager, and some Canadian boatmen and hunters. On June 8, 1731, the canoes left Montreal on a long and perilous journey. Vérendrye's purpose was to take possession of the new country for his royal master, to find a way to the Pacific if possible, and to support himself meanwhile by hunting and trading for furs, while he afforded a profit to his backers if he could.

Vérendrye's equipment and departure. 1731.

By midsummer, he was on Lake Superior. He avoided all communication with the Sieur La Ronde, who was then at La Pointe, seeking for copper, and sailing a forty-ton bark, — the first on the lake. Late in August, Vérendrye crossed the portage farther north, but his men were more or less mutinous, and hampered his movements. Having sent forward an exploring party, he wintered on Pigeon River, and built a stockade to guard his supplies and to afford a base for future advances. His first object was to discover if Lake Ouinipigon (Winnipeg), of which he had reports showing it to be an expansion of the great western water-way, offered a suitable field for settlements. In May, 1732, the exploring party came back from Rainy Lake, and early in June, Vérendrye started on, leaving some portion of his followers to hold his fort of St. Pierre. By July, he had passed beyond Rainy Lake, and had built Fort St. Charles on the west side of the Lake of the Woods; and here he wintered (1732–33). From this point he dispatched some canoes back to Montreal, with peltries. He sent at the same time such reports as he could give of his progress, and in the autumn (September, 1733) some supplies reached him, forwarded by his Montreal supporters.

On Lake Superior.

At the Lake of the Woods. 1732-33.

Beauharnois continued to manifest interest in the expedition, as his correspondence with the home government shows. The letters from Vérendrye which reached the governor from time to time, detailing the party's hardships and the death of Vérendrye's nephew, La Jemeraye, who had led the exploring party, gave him little encouragement to hope that his solicitations to the Paris government to come to Vérendrye's assistance would be effective; and they were not.

In the spring of 1734, Vérendrye sent one of his sons to build Fort Maurepas just where the river, flowing west from the Lake of the Woods, entered the larger Lake Winnipeg. It was another of the various stockades which Vérendrye within a few years scattered about the country to secure better possession and to increase the trade. Lake Winnipeg.

In August, 1734, Vérendrye and one of his sons returned to Montreal, to give his personal influence to the business side of his undertaking. His stay was not long, and in June, 1735, we find him again turning to the west, and by September he had reached Fort St. Charles (Lake of the Woods), to find its garrison almost prostrate from famine. The perils of the undertaking were increasing, and for many months it is a story of disheartenment and misery, including the loss of a son in an attack by the Sioux upon one of his roving parties. The disasters of 1737, both in the loss of men and stores, so discouraged the adventurer that we find him in October advising the minister that he must abandon his whole project. At the Lake of the Woods. 1735. Disasters. 1737.

The next year (1738), his spirits recovered, and he was eagerly questioning the Assiniboines and Cristineaux, another tribe of the neighborhood, as to more distant parts. He heard stories of walled towns farther down this supposable westward flowing river, with white inhabitants; but they were without firearms. These peoples were said to work in iron, however, and an Indian said he had killed one of them, who was cased in iron. Stories. 1738.

These savage informants all told of a people upon the Missouri, known as the Mandans, who lived on the path to the distant sea, and who could probably show the way thither. The Mandans, then, must be found.

In the summer of 1738, Vérendrye left Fort Maurepas, and passing up the Red River at the southern end of Lake Winnipeg, turned into the Assiniboine. Here he built a new stockade, calling it Fort De La Reine (October, 1738), at a point where a portage led to Lake Manitoba. Some days later (October 18), with a party of twenty hired men and thirty others, including some Indians, he began his march toward the valley of the Missouri, reaching, after a journey of about twenty-six leagues, his first obstacle in what was proba- Fort De La Reine. 1738.

bly Turtle Mountain. From the time when Joliet and Marquette, nearly seventy years before, remarked upon the great volume of water which fed the Mississippi from this turbid northwestern affluent, the hope had not been abandoned that the Missouri might prove the chief channel to the western sea. It came to be believed that it could be followed toward the west a distance corresponding to the practicable ascent of the Ohio toward the east. Mitchell, on his map, records this as a current opinion. The French had from time to time explored it, led by reports of silver mines, and by stories of the access thereto which the Spaniards got by some of its southern branches. While Vérendrye was traversing its upper reaches, other French were now exploring from its main stream toward New Mexico. Two Frenchmen, Mallet by name, and one, at least, a priest, in 1739 followed up the Platte, and by its southern fork reached the plains of Colorado. Passing the upper Arkansas, they were at Santa Fé in July, and tarried through the winter. In the spring (May, 1740), their party divided, and while some went across the plains to the Panis (Pawnees), others coursed down the Arkansas to the Mississippi. Their reports induced Bienville to suspect that the regions they had traversed were parts of China, — a curious survival of the old Asiatic theory of the continent, — and accordingly he sent an exploring party up the Canadian fork of the Arkansas. It accomplished nothing.

The Missouri.

French exploration toward the Spaniards. 1739.

Meanwhile, Vérendrye was having startling experiences among a people whose unwonted customs observed by later explorers gave rise to a theory, welcomed by the Welsh, that in the Mandans were to be found some of the descendants of the hapless companions of Prince Madoc. Vérendrye first encountered this people on November 28, 1738, and on December 3 he entered their village. His narrative shows that he was struck among his hosts with a physiognomy which was not Indian, and with a mixture of light and dark in their complexions, the women particularly having in many cases almost flaxen hair. He observed, too, that their method of fortifying their village was not one which he had seen among other tribes.

The Mandans. 1738.

These Mandans told the new-comers that a day's journey off there were white men who were habitual horsemen, and who were incased in metal when they fought, — and he naturally thought of Spaniards from New Mexico.

Vérendrye's sojourn among this interesting people was but short, but he lost no time in taking formal possession of their country in the king's name. He left two men among them to learn their language, and to discover, if possible, who these workers in metal were. After having suffered, as he says, more fatigue and wretchedness throughout his journey than he had ever before experienced, he reached La Reine on his return in February, 1739. The men whom he had left behind joined him at La Reine in September, and had a new story to tell him. While they were in the Mandan village, some of a tribe farther west had come to trade there. These strangers reported that white and bearded men lived near their home. They called them pale faces, and said that they built forts of brick and stone and mounted cannon on them. They prayed with books, worshiped the cross, cultivated gardens, and garnered grain, used oxen and horses, wore clothes of cotton, and strapped soles to their feet. Their habitations stood by a large sea, which rose and fell, and whose waters could not be drunk. It was wondered if they were Spaniards upon the Gulf of California.

The documents printed by Margry give but scant knowledge of the experiences of these two years; but Brymner has well supplied the want in the journal, kept by Vérendrye, which is printed in the *Report of the Dominion Archives* for 1889. The fatigues of the expedition had told upon the leader, and he spent a part of the winter and spring of 1739 at La Reine, exhausted in body and troubled in mind. In April, he sent his son to explore the portage toward Lake Manitoba, and upon that water the younger Vérendrye constructed Fort Dauphin, and then pushed on to explore the Saskatchewan region.

Lake Manitoba and the Saskatchewan. 1739.

This period of activity was followed by one of doubt and exhaustion. In October, 1739, some supplies reached La Reine, but Vérendrye found it necessary to go back to Montreal to secure what merchandise was needed for traffic. Reaching the settlements, he found his affairs in a rueful condition: he was 40,000 livres in debt, and a defendant in the courts. His commercial backers were exacting, and his business rivals in the peltry trade harassed him. Beauharnois was almost alone active in his behalf.

Afterwards, in 1741, Vérendrye joined his companions at the west. In the spring of 1742, he sent his two surviving sons to renew the western search. They left La Reine on April 20, and proceeding up the Assiniboine and Souris rivers, passed on (July 23) in a west-southwest course over a rolling prairie to the Mandan towns, seeing no one for twenty days. On August 11, they reached some hills. It is now supposed that these elevations were the Powder River range separating the forks of the Little Missouri, a southern affluent of the greater river. To inquiries after the sea, the wanderers got the same answer, which led them on from one tribe to another, each referring them to the one beyond. None had seen this great water; but later they found a tribe who had captured some Snake Indians, and these prisoners reported it lying still farther west. A war party, preparing for an attack on these same Snakes, opened the way for a further advance, and the brothers went on.

Vérendrye's sons go westward. 1742.

It was the 1st of January, 1743, when these two sons of Vérendrye saw what was perhaps the Big Horn Range, an outlying buttress of the Rocky Mountains, running athwart the sources of the Yellowstone, and lying a hundred miles or more east of the Yellowstone Park. Their narrative does not indicate that the sight was in any way a striking one, and there has been doubt expressed as to the identification of the actual summits which were seen. One of the brothers went with the advancing war party to the foot of these mountains, which were "well wooded and very high," as he describes them (January 8). He little dreamed that beyond them, and beyond the Snakes, lay eight hundred miles or more of mountain and declivity, stretching to the coveted sea.

They see mountains, January 1. 1743.

The conclusion reached by Professor Whitney in his study of the problem is that the explorers "may have been within one or two hundred miles of Snake River. Here they heard accounts of the missions of the Spaniard in California, which contained enough of truthful items to prove beyond doubt that there had been communication across the country between the Pacific coast and the upper Missouri region." Parkman's study of their route gives much the same conclusions as reached by the present writer, but he thinks it not unlikely that the explorers may also have pushed somewhat beyond this mountain barrier of the Big Horn. Their narrative tells us that they reached, at all events, the Snake village which they searched for, but found it abandoned. Thus balked in their purpose, the party, with their white companions, turned back, and left the great barrier of the Rockies unscaled.

In the spring of 1743, the young Vérendryes were back on the banks of the Missouri, and here, amid a tribe — very likely one of the bands of the Sioux — they buried a leaden plate, engraved with the royal arms. Turning up the Missouri, by the middle of May they were again among the Mandans. Here they found a party of Assiniboines traveling east, and falling in with their train on July 2, 1743, they later reached La Reine, having been absent about fifteen months.

Spring. 1743.

This period of venturesome exploration stands out amid the dreary monotony of Vérendrye's misfortunes. Five or six years of life remained to him, but they were barren in results and harassing in incidents. He tried to get the minister to listen to tales of what he had done. He recounted to him the story of the posts he had established, and outlined the promise of further discoveries, but it was the appeal of a wearied and poverty-stricken adventurer, and made little impression. At one time he was relieved of command, and then later sent back to try once more; but nothing came of it. His sons went to Quebec, seeking to gain the attention of the government, or to incite the cupidity of the merchants, but in vain.

Vérendrye's later years. 1743-1749.

Kalm, the Swedish traveler, met Vérendrye in his last year, and records something of what he learned from him. The retired leader told him that he had in some places observed furrows in the soil which indicated that a people advanced enough to use ploughs had once been in occupation. He had found, he said, monumental stones, generally without inscriptions, but in one case there were "Tartar characters," but no one could tell their origin. Kalm makes no mention of any mountains, as figuring in Vérendrye's story. This is the more singular, because Vérendrye knew the Indian map by Otchago, which often figures in contemporary accounts, and which designates what we now know as the Rocky Mountains, as the "Mountains of Bright Stones."

Vérendrye dies. Succeeded by Legardeur de St. Pierre.

The elder Vérendrye died at Three Rivers on December 6, 1749, and on February 27 following, La Jonquière, who was now governor of Canada, wrote to the minister at Paris that Legardeur de St. Pierre had been selected to follow up the discoveries of the dead hero.

La Jonquière and the western search.

It was evident that La Jonquière was determined to institute a new control of this western search, for the younger Vérendrye had in vain sought to be appointed to carry on the work which his father had enjoined upon him. By the influence of Galissonnière, the cross of St. Louis had been indeed bestowed on the elder discoverer, but this availed little. The new governor had his own plans, and it has been suspected that they involved commercial interests to be shared in common with Bigot, the new intendant, and St. Pierre himself. The governor was by no means sure that Vérendrye's search had been in the best direction. He accordingly instructed the Sieur Marin, commanding at Green Bay, to go to the source of the Mississippi, and discover if there was not over the divide "rivers flowing into the western sea." La Jonquière reported these orders to the minister in October, 1750.

The source of the Mississippi.

The region of many lakes, margined by the birch, maple, and pine, with wild rice plentiful in the glades, which is now known to gather the multiplied waters that unite to form the Great River, had once been the home of the Dacotahs, but now for twenty years these savages had been scattered before the Chippeways. It was many years yet before the hydrographical relations of the region were to be all understood. Vaugondy was at this very time (1750) making these fountains of the Mississippi the same with those that supplied the smaller affluent of Lake Winnipeg. Bellin, another leading French cartographer, from the period he made the maps for Charlevoix's journal, had advocated various notions, wild to us, of the hydrography of this interior region. He had contended that the "Mer de l'Ouest" lay not more than three hundred leagues west of Lake Superior, and thought it highly probable that there were connecting waters, rendering easy a passage from one to the other. With this propensity to find interlinking natural canals, Bellin now curiously complicates the question of the source of the Mississippi. In his map of 1755, he connects Lake Winnipeg by a continuous

Various conjectures.

channel with the Mississippi, through an intervening link which he calls the "Rivière Rouge," saying that "the course of it is little known." He places the springs of the Mississippi not in Winnipeg or beyond, but on a lateral affluent of this same mysterious river. This "Rivière Rouge" is made one with the "Assiniboils" just before it reaches "Lac Ouinipigon," and the

[From Vaugondy's *Amérique Septentrionale*, 1750, showing the Mississippi rising in the "L. Assinipoils."]

"Rivière des Assiniboils" is supposed to be the stream "by which one is believed to go to the sea of the west." Any one, therefore, could at that day appeal to *Le Neptune François*, in which Bellin's map appeared, as authority for a supposed passage from the Gulf of Mexico, through the Mississippi and connecting streams, to Lake Winnipeg, from which there were water-ways to the Pacific and to Hudson's Bay, — a fair exposition of the geographical delusion clinging about an imagined interior basin, with its multiplied outlets.

Mitchell, the leading British geographer of the day, is less imaginative in saying that the Mississippi had been ascended to about 45° north latitude, and that its source was supposed to be in 50° of latitude, while in its longitude it lay about midway across the continent. Jefferys, the rival of Mitchell, places the source more nearly in 45°, while Danville, in France, puts it at 46°.

There is no record of what Marin discovered, but it was given out that his purpose was ultimately to unite with St. Pierre at some point on the Pacific.

The movement under St. Pierre began in June, 1750. We are enabled to follow him by a journal which he drew up, and which is printed both by Margry and Brymner. The expedition was absent three years, but accomplished little, though its leader had had many years' experience in wood-ranging, and came of a forest-loving race, for he was a great-grandson of that Jean Nicollet who had got the first intimations of the Mississippi. St. Pierre lost time at the start by trying without avail to compose a peace between the Rainy Lake Indians and the Sioux. He was later impeded by the hardships of his travel and by the treachery of the Assiniboines. He proceeded himself no farther than Fort La Reine on the Assiniboine. He had determined, on any northern march, to avoid Hudson's Bay by turning to the west, and thereby to find, as he thought, the sources of the Missouri, so that its current might be made use of in transporting his supplies. It was Vérendrye's mistake, he contended, in not clinging to that river "by which some settled peoples could be reached, and no other than the Spaniards."

St. Pierre. 1750.

It was in this direction that St. Pierre did all that was remarkable in his three years' absence. He sent his lieutenant, the Chevalier de Niverville, to command a party starting (May 29, 1751) for the Saskatchewan. Some portion of it ascended that river — called by them Paskoya — "aux montagnes des Roches, — the earliest use, in Kingsford's opinion, of the appellation Rocky to any part of the great range. They built Fort La Jonquière, three hundred

The Saskatchewan explored. 1751.

miles above the river's mouth, but only to abandon it and fall back to La Reine. St. Pierre, finding further progress in this direction deranged by continued inter-tribal hostilities among

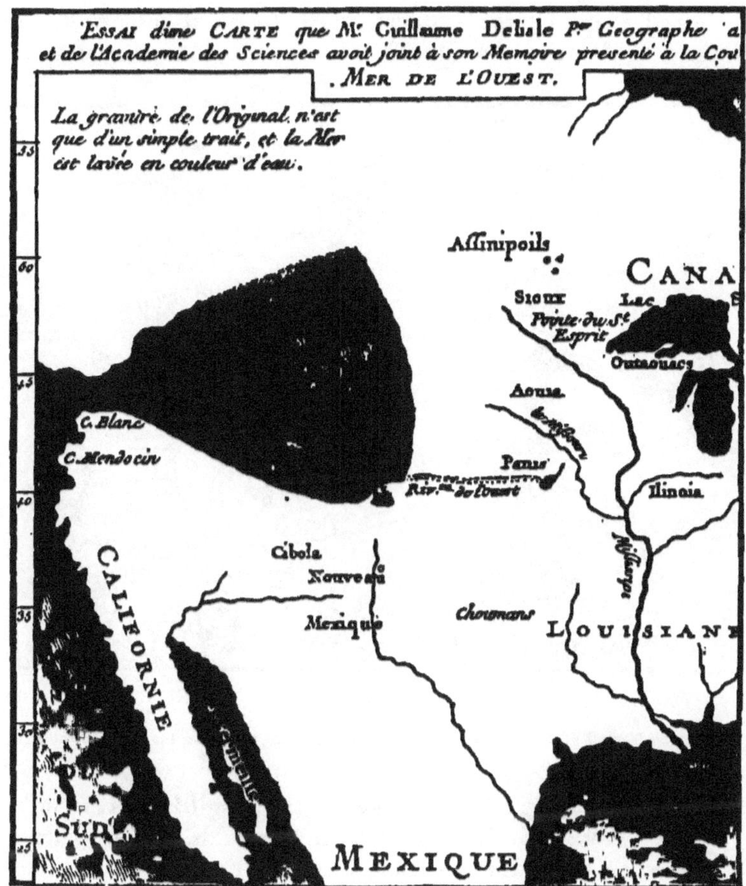

[Taken from the *Mémoire* presented to the Academy of Sciences at Paris by Buache, August 9, 1752.]

the savages, — the most perfidious, as he claimed, which he had ever encountered, — lingered on at La Reine, seeking in one way and another to prevent his expedition being an absolute failure. In his talks with the Indians, one old man told him of people, "not quite so white as the French," living in the west, "where the sun sets in the month of June," which he considered to be in a west-northwest direction. "It is certain," he says, "that there are civilized people, not unknown to the English, in this distant region, and I have myself seen the horses and saddles obtained there by the Indians." He found it impossible to induce the natives to furnish an escort thither, because, as

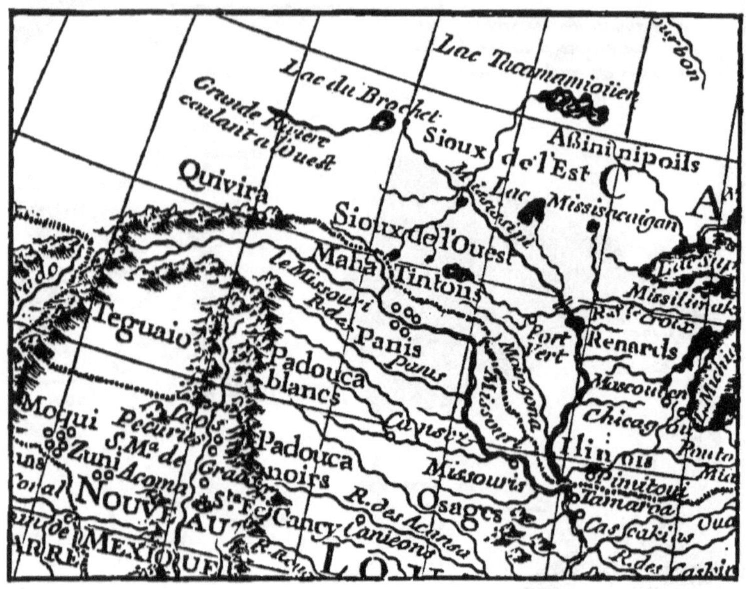

DELISLE, 1722.

[From his *Carte d'Amérique* (Paris), showing a river running west, near the source of the Mississippi.]

he says, they feared the revenge of the English at Hudson's Bay. "It is evident, then," he adds, "that so long as these Indians trade with the English, there is no hope of succeeding in finding a western sea. If there were no English settlements at Hudson's Bay, all would be easy."

The English at Hudson's Bay.

He finally dispatched a body of Indians, without any French in company, to this western settlement, and gave them a letter to its commandant; but he never heard more of the party, — a disappearance which he again laid to dread of the English.

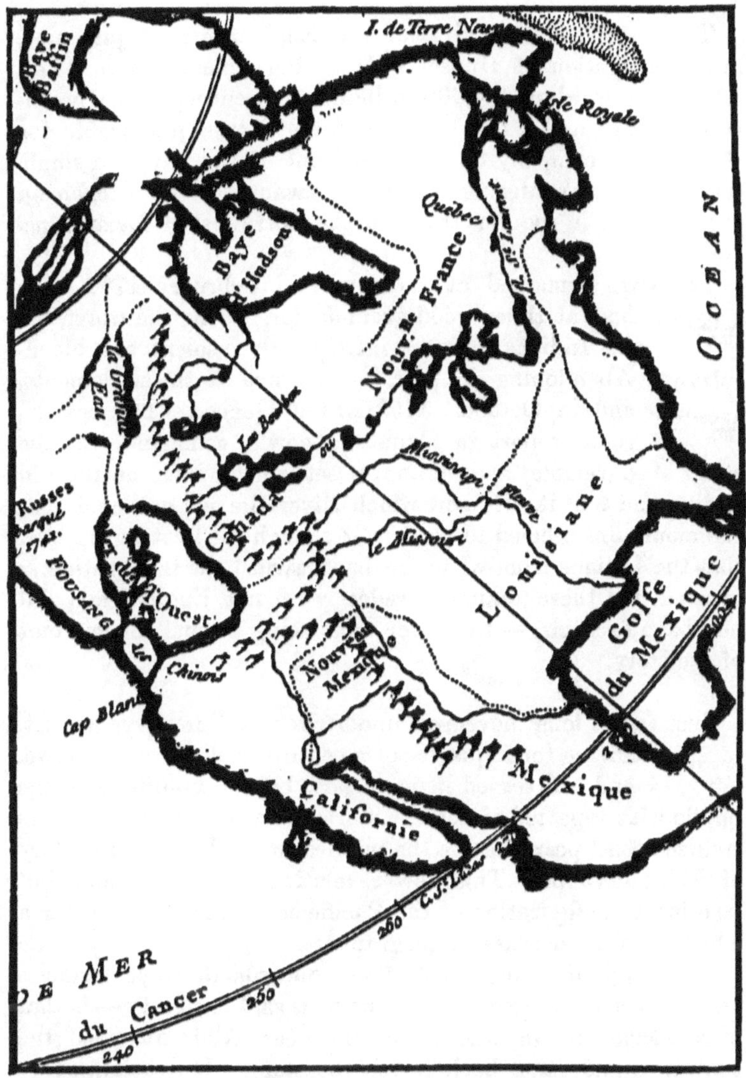

[Philippe Buache's idea of the Sea of the West, with approaches from the Mississippi and the Great Lakes, in a map presented to the Acad. des Sciences, August, 1752, and given in *Exposé des découvertes au nord de la grand mer*, par Philippe Buache, September 2, 1755.

There was a fresh revival of the English interest just now, in the navigation of Hudson's Bay. Parliament had, in 1745, offered a reward of £20,000 to induce a discovery of the northwest passage, and it had been found that it was practicable for ships of the company to go in and out of the bay in a single season without wintering. This all meant for the French an eager rivalry in the fur trade to the northwest of Lake Superior.

St. Pierre remained at La Reine till February, 1752. He

At La Reine. 1752.

had at times good grounds for fearing the worst, for the Indians were not infrequently insolent and bloodthirsty. Abandoning the post, he returned to the settlements,

At Quebec. 1753.

and in October, 1753, was at Quebec. The best he could report to Duquesne, now in command, was the story of a remote and unknown settlement, such as the old Indian had told it. Rumors which Niverville had gathered near the mountains seemed to confirm it, though the lieutenant added that the Indians from whom he had learned the tale distinctly averred that these unknown traders were not English, and did not have firearms, — the latter want being a usual concomitant of the story.

Just as the long movement undertaken by Vérendrye and St.

Moncacht-Apé.

Pierre for a quarter of a century had proved abortive, and had served little purpose beyond familiarizing the public with repeated if not idle stories of a western sea and its civilized coast people, came the publication in Paris of the story of Moncacht-Apé. This new revelation of a supposable but imaginary configuration of the Pacific coast line unsettled for a while the soberer sense of geographers.

The story of Moncacht-Apé — "one who destroys obstacles and overcomes fatigues," as the name is said to signify — is that of a Yazoo Indian, who, about the year 1700, traversed the continent, and came back to tell the story. His recital, as we have it, was made about the year 1725, when he was old and garrulous; and Le Page du Pratz, then a French settler near the Natchez, listened to it. It ran thus: —

Impelled to travel in search of information about the origin of his race, and easily severing home ties because he had lost wife and children, Moncacht-Apé went among the Chickasaws, making his inquiries. Getting no satisfaction here, and possessed of a vague notion that the east must be the cradle of his people, he started toward the sunrise. In the story of his experiences in this direction we recognize some knowledge, by hearsay at least, of the Falls of Niagara, and some apprehension of the extraordinary tides of the Bay of Fundy. Not finding his question answered at the east, Moncacht-Apé determined to try the west.

The narrative now carries him north to the Ohio River, which he crossed. Tracking a prairie land, he passed the Mississippi near the mouth of the Missouri, and gives a recognizable description of the commingling of the waters of the two great rivers. He followed up the Missouri to a tribe of that name, where he wintered and learned their language. He speaks of finding large herds of buffalo. In the spring, he started up the river again, and among the Canzés (Kansas) he first learned of a divide, beyond which a river would be found flowing west. The Missouri Indians had told him to follow up their river for a single moon, and then to diverge to the north, where, after several days' journeying, he would reach a western-flowing river. It happened that he was not forced to find his way alone. He chanced upon a camp of Otters, as the tribe was called, who took him up to a place whence a nine days' march carried the party to a turning-point. Here bending their course north, after five days they reached the river that flowed west, upon which, farther down, these Otters lived. In descending this river, our wanderer had the company of some Otters for eighteen days. After this he proceeded alone in a dug-out to a village, where he tarried for the winter to learn the language spoken by a people farther on, which these new friends could teach him. In the following spring, he went on to a tribe who wore long hair. A blind old chief among them, Big Roebuck, was kind to him and promised him an equally good reception from the tribes beyond, if he would only say that Big Roebuck was his friend.

If one confidently seeks to identify his landmarks, he was now well down the Columbia River. When about a day's journey from the sea, he began to hear stories of a strange people who annually came to the coast in ships. They were represented as white, bearded, and clothed. Their sole purpose of coming was to secure yellow dye-wood, which had a disagreeable odor. Though they had guns which made a great noise, they withdrew if confronted by Indians more numerous than they were. The natives had sometimes struggled with these visitors, and the strangers had occasionally carried off some of the Indian women, but had never captured any men, — so one form of the narrative says. The Indians had never succeeded in taking any of these strange comers either dead or alive.

The identification of localities fails here, for there are no such dye-woods on the Oregon coast, nor is any tree of a single kind so universally prevalent in that region that, if entirely destroyed, the country would be treeless, — as is one of the statements of the story.

Moncacht-Apé arrived on the coast at a time when the neighboring Indians were gathering for a concerted attack on these strangers, who were soon expected to make their annual appearance. When the ship appeared, its people occupied three days in filling water-casks "similar to those in which the French put fire-water." After this they scattered to fell the dye-wood trees. The savages now attacked them, and killed eleven before they reëmbarked. This gave the narrator an opportunity to examine the slain. On two only did he find guns with powder and ball. Their bodies were thick and short; their skin white; their heads heavy, and wound with cloth; their hair cropped except on the middle of the crown; their garments of a soft stuff, and their leggings and shoes one piece, and too small for Moncacht-Apé to wear. It was the evident intention of the story-teller to convey the impression that the visitors were an Oriental people.

After this conflict, the rover went north along the coast till he found the days were growing longer. When he had learned that still farther on the land was "cut through from north to south," he only expressed what European geographers had figured ever since Bering, in 1741, had finally proved the proximity of the American and Asiatic shores.

Of Moncacht-Apé's return to the Mississippi valley we have no particulars, but he is reported as saying that though he had been absent five years, he could go over the same route again in thirty-two moons.

We have the story in two forms, — first as published by

Dumont in his *Mémoires de la Louisiane* (Paris, 1753), in which he professes to have known the Indian, whose ordinary name among his people was "The Interpreter," in recognition of his mastery of tongues. Dumont acknowledges that he got the story from Le Page du Pratz, who published it later, also at Paris, in 1758, in his *Histoire de la Louisiane*. Le Page, then, is the source of the story. He had come to Louisiana in 1718, and remained there, chiefly near the Natchez, till 1734. He had been a wanderer, was of an inquisitive turn of mind, and a theorist by impulse. He was, moreover, interested in discussing the origin of the American Indians. This led him to much converse with those among the savages who were intelligent, and he seemed to think that the Yazoos were particularly noteworthy in those habits in which they showed a difference from their neighbors. This readily accounts for the special intercourse with one of that tribe, who had, or was represented as having, similar tastes. Such was the reputation of Moncacht-Apé.

Le Page du Pratz.

At the time when Dumont got the story from Le Page, if we can rely upon the way in which Dumont tells it, Le Page made it in the ending quite different from the shape in which he later published it himself. Le Page must have been in France when Dumont printed his version as professedly derived from Le Page, and yet we have no protest from the original narrator that his recital had been changed.

The difference in the two texts is that Dumont omits some part of the details of the bearded men, and makes Moncacht-Apé learn of the other details only by hearsay, since a hostile tribe had prevented his actually getting to the coast.

Differences in the texts of the story.

So far as the story had influence in later years, the ending as given by Le Page seems to have prevailed. It was made to enter into the considerations affecting the probability of a northwest passage, and Samuel Engle, a few years later, in 1765, discusses it and marks the supposed course of the Indians in a map. In 1777, Moncacht's farthest point is put down on a map published in a French encyclopædia. In 1829, the tale was translated in the *Proceedings* of the Literary and Historical Society of Quebec, and during the discussion of the Oregon dispute between England

Transmission of the story to later times.

and the United States, Greenhow refers to the story, not without an inclination to believe it. It got for the first time what may be called a scientific treatment when Quatrefages, in the *Revue d'Anthropologie*, in 1881, attracted by its ethnological interest, unwaveringly accepted it as an honest recital. Still later, Mr. Hubert Howe Bancroft, in repeating the story, is much inclined to accept the same conclusion. A weightier judgment on its credibility seems, however, to have been reached by Mr. Andrew McFarland Davis in his reëxamination of it after Quatrefages's essay. This critic, on various grounds, pronounces it to be of the class of fictions of which Defoe's *Apparition of Mrs. Veal* is a conspicuous example. He judges that the change in the termination which Le Page finally gave to the tale arose from a necessity to save it from the discredit into which, in its original form, it would have fallen at a time when the new notions of Delisle and Buache respecting a sea of the west were displacing the earlier drafts of the western coast lines. Dumont had given his adhesion to the newer views.

A. M. Davis's views.

The sea of the west.

There is no occasion in the present chapter to go into the details of the stories, now discredited, of Admiral Fonté and Maldonado, who were said to have made inland discoveries by water on the northwest coast in the region where we now know the basin of the Columbia to be in part. These stories showed the coast hereabouts to have been intersected by large inland seas opening on the west to the Pacific, and affording passages on the east to Hudson's Bay and other waters of the Atlantic system. The wish to find such a transverse passage, beginning with the supposable Straits of Anian in the sixteenth century, had never ceased to guide cartographers to point out the way in which it might exist, if they could not say that it did exist. Bellin had, as we have seen, in these middle days of the eighteenth century (1743), connected Lake Superior — which he was inclined to put too far north by ten degrees — by a water-way with the Pacific, and a little later (1755), when the new views were overtopping the old, he conjectured that over the mountains there might be a possible nearly landlocked sea of the west. Le Rouge, another French mapmaker, made a similar westward connection for the Great Lakes in 1746.

Supposable cartography.

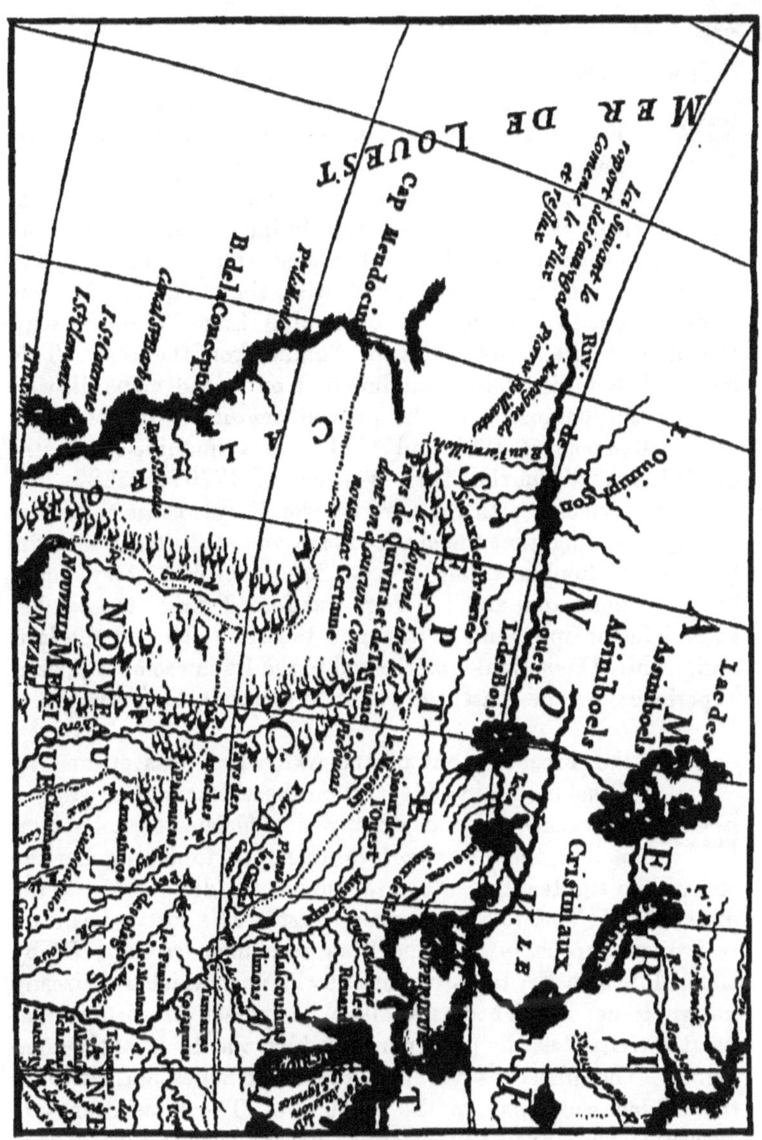

RIVER OF THE WEST.

[From *L'Amérique, par le Sieur le Rouge, suivant le R. P. Charlevoix*, etc., Paris, 1746.]

It was shortly after 1750 that the theory of these great inland seas and the story of De Fonté captured the leading French geographer, Delisle, whose maps gained currency over central Europe by the republications of Covens and Mortier at Amsterdam. The most ardent advocate of these views, however, was Philippe Buache, and some of his maps are a marvel of reticulated waters. The English geographer Jefferys was tainted with the rest, but he was more content to connect in his own mind Lake Winnipeg with the alleged inland discoveries of Aguilar from the west. This erratic belief died hard, and lingered on in the maps till well toward the beginning of the present century. In the Paris *Atlas Moderne* of 1762 and 1771 it was simplified but still existed, as it did in the *Atlas Nouveau* of 1779 and 1782.

Delisle, Buache, Jefferys, etc.

It was evident, with the view of the Pacific coast then prevailing, that the simple north and south trend and the Columbia valley of the Moneacht-Apé story could not stand, and Le Page was forced either to abandon it, or join the opponents of the new theories. He did the last, and, as Mr. Davis thinks, attributed to the Indian some supposed experiences on the coast, the better to maintain his narrative.

Their effect on Le Page and his story.

With the breaking out of the war, which was opened by Washington in 1754, and on the withdrawal of western garrisons beyond what was sufficient to hold vital points, there was no favorable opportunity during the rest of the eighteenth century to pursue the discoveries in the direction of Vérendrye's farther quest. The last scheme on record was probably an expedition recommended in 1753 by Colonel Joshua Fry to Governor Dinwiddie, in which one already known to us, Dr. Thomas Walker, "a person of fortune and great activity," as the governor calls him, was to have the command. The plan was to cross the Alleghanies and discover the hidden water-way to the great sea. The impending war prevented the expedition starting, but the chances of success as they lay in the popular mind are well expressed in a letter of the Huguenot, James Maury, written in Virginia in 1756: "When it is considered how far the eastern branches of that immense river, Mississippi, extend eastward, and how near they come to the navigable, or rather canoeable parts of the rivers

Ceasing of the westward search.

which empty themselves into the sea that washes our shores to the east, it seems highly probably that its western branches reach as far the other way, and make as near approaches to rivers emptying themselves into the ocean west of us, the Pacific Ocean, across which [approaches] a short and easy communication, short in comparison with the present route thither, opens itself to the navigator from that shore of the continent with the Eastern Indies." He then goes on to show how the stories which Coxe had published thirty years before, of early English adventurers, in the upper Mississippi basin, were having their influence in confusing the common belief. "One of the branches of the Mississippi, Coxe followed through its various meanders for seven hundred miles (which I believe is called Missouri by the natives, or Red River from the color of its waters), and then received intelligence from the natives that its head-springs interlocked on a neighboring mountain with the head-springs of another river to the westward of these same mountains, discharging itself into a large lake called Thoyago, which pours its waters through a large navigable river into a boundless sea, where they told him they had seen prodigious large canoes, with three masts and men almost as fair as himself." Then making a palpable reference to the Moncacht-Apé story, he adds: "As I have read a history of the travels of an Indian towards those regions, as well as those of Mr. Coxe, the reports of the natives to both of them as to the large canoes are so similar that I perhaps may confound one with the other." Maury next says that the only copy of Coxe's "very scarce" book which he has heard of in Virginia was seen by him at Colonel Fry's house, and this leads him to suspect that Coxe's stories had incited Fry's scheme of western exploration, to which reference has just been made. Maury tells us further that preparations had been attentively made by Walker, so as to reach an estimate of the expense, when the outbreak of hostilities occurred. There were some reasons, even after the project had been abandoned, for concealing the purpose from the French, and Maury informs his correspondent that "in case the ship I write by should be taken, the person to whom I have recommended this packet has instruction to throw it overboard in time."

CHAPTER XI.

WAR AND TRUCE.

1741–1748.

In the war with Spain, England had suffered in America more than her foes. Vernon's unfortunate attack on Cartagena (1741) had carried to the grave nine out of ten of the contingent which the colonies had added to the attacking force. The loss was not great in a population now approaching a million; but it was discouraging. The eleven colonial newspapers published along the Atlantic seaboard kept the mishaps from being forgotten. Shirley had been made governor of Massachusetts Bay, — a popular man, at a time when popularity was to count much. He was destined to become conspicuous, and though not greatly more than respectable in ability, he had some qualities which the colonies were to prize in the near future.

War of England and Spain.

Governor Shirley.

Parliament had at last recognized the necessity of amalgamating the vast alien population which had doubled the numbers on the seaboard in a little more than a score of years. It provided in 1740 that Protestants who had been seven years in the colonies could be naturalized, but in New England the law had little effect. The religious distinction was significant. France and Spain as Catholic powers were pressing hard on the colonial frontiers. Local legislation in New England had long nurtured Protestant antipathies, and there was a gleesome joy among the Boston people when Fleet the printer printed — as the story goes — some popular ballads on the blank side of a bull of Pope Urban, of which a bale had been captured in a Spanish prize. The New England metropolis was now in her proudest days, if the pinnacle to which commerce may lift a town determines that comparative preëminence. In 1741, there were forty top-

Protestant and Catholic.

Boston and New England.

sail vessels on the stocks in Boston shipyards, and this meant an active leadership in all places where there was trade by sea. There was no enemy of England in the Gulf of St. Lawrence or on the Spanish main which the privateers of New England did not reach. The forests of New Hampshire afforded the best masts that a royal frigate could have. In every eligible harbor about the gulf of Maine they were building ships for the British navy and barkentines for the English merchants.

It was in New England that the crown had its best compacted body of subjects. They constituted perhaps two fifths of all that were living on the Atlantic slope, and rarely had a people developed in a more self-contained way. They had long been in the habit of setting up pretensions that ill became dependent colonies. They were conscious, too, of a certain sympathy for these aspirations which were now and then manifested in the advanced sentiments of wary Englishmen. Murray the lawyer, later to be famous as Lord Mansfield, was becoming known in his opinions upon an ominous constitutional question. He held that the king, and not Parliament, could compel a colony to tax itself for the benefit of the whole. Samuel Adams, prefiguring the colonial claim, was selecting for his graduating thesis at Harvard: "Whether it be lawful to resist superior magistrates, if the Commonwealth cannot be otherwise preserved."

The spirit of independence.

Kalm, the German traveler, shows us how, a little later, he was conscious that this feeling, which Samuel Adams's youthful ebullitions indicated, so pervaded the colonies that he felt it was only the necessity of combining against the French which could insure continued dependence on the mother country. Joshua Gee had already thought it worth his while to array the risks in order to disprove them. "Some gentlemen," he had said, "assert that if we encourage the plantations they will grow rich and set up for themselves and cast off the English government." But he looked to the diverse interests and jealousies of the several colonies to preserve their dependence on the mother country. It was these disunited interests which made the Indians liken the colonies to a chain of sand, and Gee spoke of these mutual antipathies as making the colonies "like a bold and rapid river, which, though resistless when inclosed in one channel, is yet easily resistible when subdivided into several inferior streams." This disagreement among the several colonial governments had indeed become notorious. It was in fact almost if not quite impossible to induce the southern colonies to share the cost borne by New York and New England in confronting, for the benefit of all, the French from Canada. No one perceived this lack of adhesion more clearly than the Indians, and there was a touch of satire in the Iroquois when they advised the English to act in such concert as their confederacy was accustomed to do.

Lack of cohesion in the English colonies.

This was the condition of the British colonies, when a turn in European politics disclosed a new drama both in the Old World and the New. The English colonies, with all their repellent forces mutually exerted, had become prosperous in trade, and perhaps the more so because of an ill-concealed zest in thwarting the restraints of the navigation laws imposed upon them. This was in their enterprises by sea; those by land were making the French believe that the English activity threatened the complete absorption of the western fur trade.

War declared. 1744.

Colden, in preparing a new edition (1742) of his *History of the Five Nations*, had the distinct purpose "of drawing the attention of the ministry and Parliament to the interests of North America in respect to the fur trade, and the encroachments which the French are daily making on our trade and settlements." At the same time Clinton was urging the occupation of Irondequoit Bay and Crown Point. All this had thrown the French into a sort of desperation, when their antagonism was intensified by the declaration of war in Europe.

Henry Pelham was now the prime minister of England. Dettingen had been fought in June, 1743. There was no knowing what the Pretender might attempt. It was necessary to keep faith with Austria and the other supporters of the Pragmatic Sanction, and this brought England into opposition to France. The French promptly declared war, March 15, 1744, and England accepted the challenge on April 11. Beauharnois, the Canadian governor, anticipating war, had already reinforced Crown Point, Fort Frontenac, and Niagara. He had for the coming struggle perhaps six hundred regulars and some fifteen thousand Canadian militia all told. Such a force could be successfully met only by some concert of action among the

English, and Governor Clinton was urging, with little chance of success, a union of the colonies.

The word that hostilities were determined upon reached Canada in the spring of 1744; but it was not till June 1 that they knew it in Boston. This priority of information gave the French some advantage, and they profited by it in Acadia. They were hardly prepared to spring upon Oswego in this same interval, though the English later wondered they had not, after it began to be feared that the war was going to jeopardize the trade at that post. The stockade there had been suffered to decay, and two years before it was pronounced defenseless. Governor Clarke, in 1743, had feared for it even before war was declared, and in urging the home government to protect it better, he had pictured to them the disaster which would follow its fall, and particularly the alienation of the Iroquois. Now upon the French being earlier informed than the English of the declaration of war, the confederates had been promptly notified by messengers from Quebec, who told the Indians to expect a sharp contest and an easy victory for the French. Before the summer was far advanced, the English traders at Oswego became alarmed and abandoned it in a body. Governor Clinton, when he heard of this rapid desertion, dreaded its effect upon the western Indians, who had been so securely held by the opportunities of trade which Oswego offered. Both French and English hastened to send emissaries among the confederates, the one to use the flight of the traders, "cowards as they are," as signs of the failing fortunes of the English, and the other to try, but unsuccessfully, to induce these Indians to hold that post against the French, till a garrison could be sent there. So the summer and autumn (1744) passed, and the hostile forces had not confronted one another in the field. Meanwhile, there was far from confidence in the authorities at Quebec, who were anxiously looking for Boston privateers in the St. Lawrence.

Tidings of hostilities reach America. 1744.

Oswego abandoned by traders.

The next year, 1745, the New England militia under Pepperrell, aided by some royal ships under Sir Peter Warren, made a lucky stroke at Louisbourg. Shirley, whose energy and luck had conduced to this yeoman victory, wrote to the Earl of Newcastle that the capture of Louisbourg had secured the Newfoundland fisheries and estab-

Shirley and Louisbourg. 1745.

lished a nursery for seamen. These things, he contended, made the way easy to master the northern parts of America, if their success were promptly followed up by an invasion of Canada. The conquest of the west was to be made by fighting a battle in the north.

Proposed invasion of Canada.

New England and New York took the campaign in hand, and troops were raised. Newcastle promised to support them with a fleet. While these preparations were making, there were vexatious raids all along the New England frontiers, and Fort Massachusetts was taken. The main energy of suffering New England was directed to reinforcing Clinton for an advance on Crown Point and Montreal. The New York governor had sore need of all the comfort which New England could give him. His assembly were stubborn in their opposition to his plans. The province had a chief justice in De Lancey who, in efforts to embarrass the chief magistrate, knew how to smirch his robes with a politician's touch. These intestine quarrels demoralized the militia and disconcerted the neighboring confederates. It gave the French new opportunities, and as Franklin, a looker-on, said of the Indians, the English could afford "to spare no artifice, pains, or expense to gain them."

New York politics.

Boston alarmed. 1746.

To add to the discouragement, the English fleet, expected at Boston, never appeared. Instead of the stir of warlike preparation which Boston had hoped for in her harbor, the town was thrown into consternation from an expected attack. Shirley, in September, 1746, learned that a French fleet under Admiral D'Anville was at sea with orders to attack Boston and recover Louisbourg. The troops sent to Clinton were hurriedly returned to defend the coast. D'Anville's ships were happily scattered in a storm, and Boston breathed freer.

Both sides had failed of their purpose, and the western question had not been helped to a solution. There was a suspicion that the backwardness of the home government in not sending a fleet was due to an apprehension that another success like Louisbourg might bring the colonies to an inordinate sense of their importance. Those who wished to keep the friendship of the Iroquois and the more distant tribes had more pressing apprehensions in that, as Conrad Weiser expressed it, the failure of the expedition to Canada "had done a great deal of hurt, since no man is able to excuse it to the Indians." Weiser had never doubted the Iroquois neutrality, but he had all along maintained that they could not be urged to active hostilities against the French, and the untoward campaign had rendered, to some, even their neutrality uncertain. One thing, however, had happened on which the English had reason to depend. A band of Chickasaws had come north eager to wreak vengeance on the French for some affront which had been put upon their tribe. This opportunity for the English had influenced the Senecas, usually much inclined to the French, to hold back from aiding them.

Neutral Iroquois.

With all this inaction, the trans-Alleghany question grew more and more complicated for the English, when a new embarrassment unexpectedly occurred in the luckless phrasing of the title of a new edition of Colden's book on the Five Nations, which was again reprinted in London in 1747. This was a statement that the "Six Nations lived in Canada," which the French eagerly seized upon as an acknowledgment that the Iroquois country, south of Ontario, was within the bounds of Canada.

Colden's *Five Nations*, ed. 1747.

There came a vigorous spirit to the French at Quebec, in the person of their new governor, Galissonnière, who arrived there September 19, 1747, to assume command over the fifty thousand people of the St. Lawrence valley. He was not attractive in person; in fact, he was deformed. His mind, however, was as alert, and his impulses were as steady, as was befitting a commander facing great odds. He had a firm purpose to check the English wherever he could find them throughout either the St. Lawrence or the Mississippi valley. He felt equal to the task everywhere except by sea, and he was anxious lest Quebec should be attacked by an English fleet. So, when he learned of Shirley's hope to make a winter attack on Crown Point, it caused him little apprehension, for he knew New York had no desire to undertake the task. He was not quite prepared to plunge upon Oswego, now reoccupied by the English, but he sought to intercept its trade by founding Fort Rouillé at the modern Toronto.

Galissonnière in Canada. 1747.

The spring and summer of 1748 were rife with rumors of peace, and William Johnson was exerting himself among the Onondagas to foil the persistent efforts of the French to gain them over in a body. The confederates were, in July, brought to a council at Albany and urged to expel the French emissaries among them, and to desist from their incursions against the western tribes. Weiser was sent among these Ohio Indians to warn them against too much confidence in any peace which the French promised. "A French peace is a very uncertain one," he told them. "They keep it no longer than their interest permits. The French king's people have been almost starved in Old France, and our wise people are of the opinion that after their belly is full again, they will once more quarrel and raise a war." It was a weighty prophecy.

Johnson and the Iroquois. 1748.

Weiser and the Ohio Indians.

The French had among them in Canada another person who was quite as vigilant and far-seeing as Galissonnière, and this was the Abbé Piquet, now a man of forty. The governor had already asked (October, 1747) the minister to give him a pension for the zeal with which he had planned and instigated more than one hostile raid upon the English borders. The main object of this wary man was to break the alliance of the Iroquois with the English. Already, at Caughnawaga, near Montreal, about three hundred Mohawks and Oneidas had been drawn away from their own country to form a settlement. To make similar drafts upon the Onondagas, Cayugas, and Senecas was Piquet's immediate purpose, and in September, 1748, he set out from Quebec with the intention of selecting the fittest site for a mission. Not long after, Galissonnière succeeded in drawing deputies from the confederates to Quebec, and put to them the crucial question of their fealty to the English. "We hold our lands of Heaven," they said, "and have never ceded any." The French had longed for just such an asseveration to meet the claims of the Iroquois subjection, now constantly advanced by the English.

Abbé Piquet.

But this and all other questions in dispute between the two crowns were studiously ignored by the diplomats who had just succeeded in patching up a truce in which neither party had any confidence. This truce, called

Treaty of Aix-la-Chapelle. 1748.

the treaty of Aix-la-Chapelle, consummated October 7, 1748, was proclaimed in Montreal July 27, 1749, but it had been known in Boston in the previous May, — a new instance of the disadvantage to Canada, during a large part of the year, in being shut off from communication with France by an ice-locked river.

The peace broke up the alliance of England and Austria. It secured for England a renewal of her profits in the West India slave trade. It restored to France all that she had lost at Louisbourg and elsewhere. The claims of the French against the pretensions of the English sea-to-sea charters were left untouched, and the dispute over the barrier of the Appalachians remained unsettled.

No one understood this dubious outcome of the war better than the little humpbacked governor at Quebec. He knew that it gave to his countrymen a breathing-time, so that they might the better prepare for the final struggle in the Great Valley. He began now, with a finer appreciation of the true colonizing spirit than any of his predecessors, except, perhaps, Champlain, had had, to urge upon the ministers the sending of sturdy peasants to occupy the Ohio valley. But he asked in vain, while in the same hour the flower of France, in her Huguenots, were being hunted down and allowed no asylum even in her colonies.

Galissonière and the Ohio valley.

Piquet's aims were, in some sense, the complement of those of Galissonnière, and he had now selected a spot for his mission at La Présentation, near the site of the future Ogdensburg on the St. Lawrence. The position was well chosen, since it covered the Indian trails both north and south of Lake Ontario. It was further well placed in being at the mouth of a stream which had its source near the Mohawks, and which was a ready route for their canoes to the St. Lawrence. The Mohawks, being perhaps the most persistent in the English interest of all the confederates, soon fell upon the little post (November, 1749). This led to a reinforcement, and the missionary was aided by the Quebec government to construct a palisade, mount a few guns, and build magazines and a mill. In a year or two, Piquet saw a colony of eager converts clustered around him. The civil authorities found in this mission of the church a new help to divert the Indian trade from Oswego, since it added another station on the way to Montreal.

Piquet and La Présentation.

London Mag: for Decr 1747.

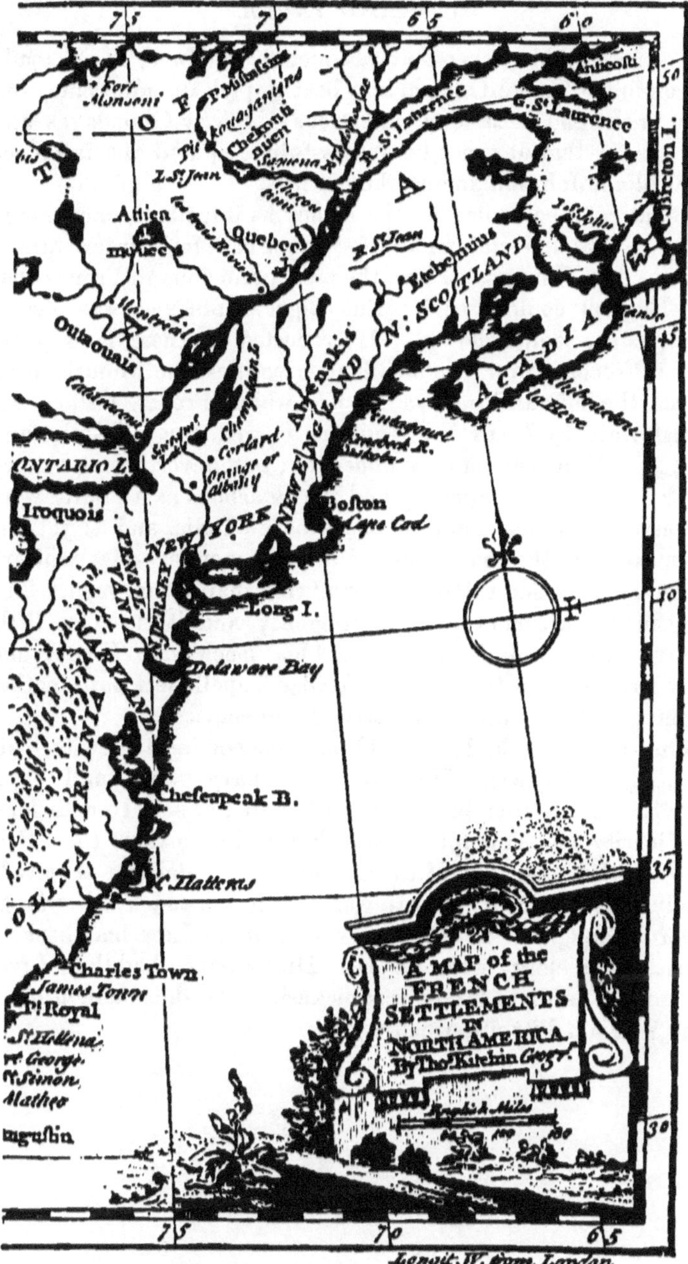

A MAP of the FRENCH SETTLEMENTS IN NORTH AMERICA By Thos. Kitchin Geogr.
Anticosti
G. St. Laurence
R. St. Laurence
Quebec
Montreal
Outaouais
ONTARIO L.
Iroquois
Champlain L.
Abenakis
Etechemins
N: SCOTLAND
ACADIA
NEW ENGLAND
NEW YORK
N. JERSEY
PENSILVANIA
MARYLAND
VIRGINIA
Boston
Cape Cod
Long I.
Delaware Bay
Chesepeak B.
C. Hattens
Charles Town
James Town
Pt. Royal
Longit. W. from London

To increase his dependents, Piquet later (June, 1751) made the circuit of Lake Ontario in a boat to pick up adherents, and they in the end became so numerous — chiefly Onondagas and Cayugas — that at times he successfully disputed the influence of William Johnson among those tribes.

Bigot. Bigot, who had come to the colony as intendant, encouraged the undertaking as affording a base for a future attack on Oswego, "a post the most pernicious to France that the English could erect." But Bigot's influence was one of peril, as the sequel showed. He reflected, in these later years of the French power, the brilliant frivolities, the whimsical caprices, the mischief and vanity into which French history was transformed by Louis XV. and the Pompadour. Voltaire and Montesquieu were unheeded; but, nevertheless, France was still imposing, and the Bourbons as a family were powerful. France could lay one hand on India, and as yet the other covered the major part of North America. Her military prowess had failed rather in her officers than in her men. The king made bureaucracy a potent agency, and it cared as little for the nobles as it did for the rabble. Such were France and New France when the peace of Aix-la-Chapelle left both mother country and province with a struggle to come.

Power of France.

Condition of England. On the whole, England could face this coming trial with little confidence. Her army and navy gave small hope. There was but scant virility in her social conditions. Mediocrity and corruption were hardly less patent than they were on the other side of the Channel. Scandal and turpitude easily made heroes. Gossip was deadly. Beau Nash was as baleful, though in a different way, as John Law had been in Paris. The clergy were menial. Highwaymen had their Lives written. The royal family was bickering like the common herd. But William Pitt was ripening.

CHAPTER XII.

THE PORTALS OF THE OHIO VALLEY.

1740–1749.

ALREADY, by 1740, in the valley of Virginia, in addition to the patents of Beverly and Borden, various small grants had been made by Governor Blair. Log dwellings were springing up here and there as the Scotch-Irish and Germans spread along the banks of the Shenandoah. The valley was spotted with tomahawk claims, as squatters' rights were termed, traceable for years by the lighter color of the wound made by the woodsman's hatchet on the boundary trees. There were no wagon roads as yet, but bridle paths went from house to house, and led up to the eastern passes, where the buffalo had once made their traces. Hither, on court days, the frontiersmen went to the more civilized centres toward the rivers which flowed into the Chesapeake, where along their banks an Anglican governing clan held the country. The best traveled trail came from the north, and crossing the Fluvanna, a headstream of the James, found its way by the defile of the Staunton River, and then turned south. It next passed the Dan, and came to the Yadkin, a river which, rising in North Carolina, joins the Pedee and then seeks the ocean.

Valley of Virginia. 1740.

Colonel Abraham Wood had led an expedition up the Dan, a branch of the Roanoke, in 1744. Passing the Blue Ridge by what came to be known as Wood's Gap, he followed on the other side a stream which flowed into the New River, and thus opened one of the upper routes to the Kanawha, an affluent of the Ohio. It was twenty years before this that Joshua Gee had urged the planting of colonies beyond these mountains, but only now, in 1748, was a way opened to induce the earliest English settlement, with domestic life, beyond the Alleghanies.

Colonel Abraham Wood on the Kanawha. 1744.

The Lords of Trade had urged the Privy Council to authorize the governor of Virginia to make grants of land in this direction. Virginia had at this time about eighty-two thousand inhabitants; but only a few hundred had as yet made a movement into the Shenandoah valley, and there was just now a purpose shown to cross the inner chain of the Appalachians. There had already been grants of land made beyond the mountains to Dr. Thomas Walker, Colonel James Wood, Colonel James Patton, and others; and Walker organized a party to make explorations thitherward. They entered Powell's valley near Laurel Ridge, and pushed westward beyond the sources of the Clinch River. They were mindful enough of the proud duke who had crushed the Scots' rebellion, to place the name of Cumberland on the gap and river, which they were the first to find. They turned northeast and reached the springs of the Big Sandy River, passed on to the Louisa Fork, and then wended their way eastward to New River. Walker was enabled thus to be of assistance to Evans in the mapping of this region at a later day. The result of this movement was the incorporation of the Loyal Land Company in June, 1749, which had a grant of eight hundred thousand acres above the North Carolina line and west of the mountains. In the November following, Governor Lee of Virginia informed Governor Harrison of Pennsylvania of these and other grants, and of his purpose to assist the pioneers in establishing a settlement and building a fort. He at the same time complained of the traders of Pennsylvania, who incited the Indians to mischief. He added that in view of the threatening attitude of France, it behooved both provinces to stand united in making this western progress.

Settlers in the valley of Virginia.

Grants and explorations.

Loyal Land Company. 1749.

On the divide between the upper waters of the Roanoke and New River was a beautiful intervale, the pasturing ground of large game, known as Draper's Meadows. The local antiquaries hold that shortly after the return of Walker's party, the Inglis family and others passed over to the New River side of the divide and formed a settlement. It was here, in 1749, that the house of Adam Harmon was attacked by the Indians, the earliest instance of such devastation west of the mountains. The Draper's Meadows settlement lay to the

Draper's Meadows.

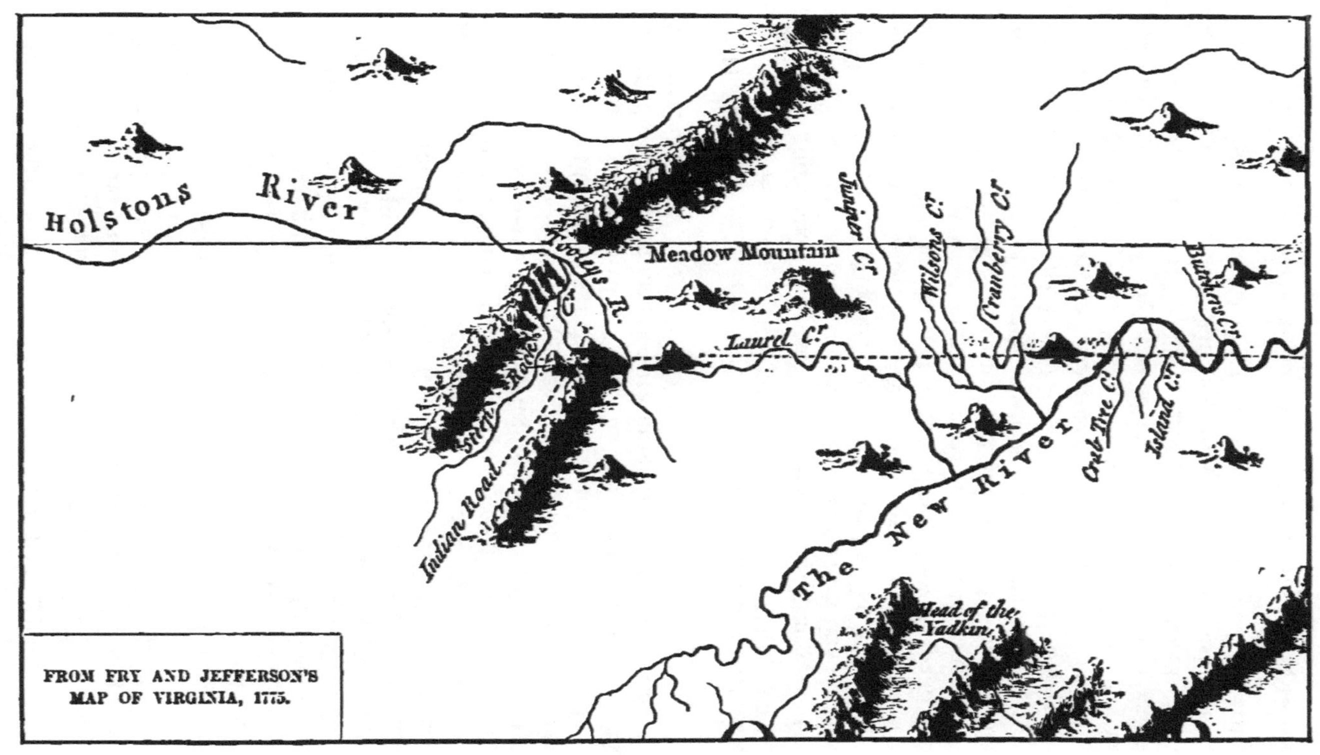

FROM FRY AND JEFFERSON'S
MAP OF VIRGINIA, 1775.

north of the line run in 1749 by Colonel Joshua Fry and Peter Jefferson, — father of Thomas, — which separated Virginia from Carolina, and was not yet carried farther west, athwart the sources of the Tennessee.

More to the north, and well within the valley of Virginia, there were at the same time other and unknown wanderers, pushing along beyond the springs of the James and crossing the height of land which brought them upon the river later known as the Greenbrier, — opening still another route to the Kanawha and the Ohio. We have seen that farther down the Shenandoah and beyond a transverse line which connected the sources of the Rappahannock and the Potomac, the manor of Lord Fairfax stretched across the valley. While these pioneers farther south were working westward, the young George Washington, dragging a surveyor's chain, was wandering over the five or six million acres which constituted this nobleman's estate. The youthful surveyor says he was struck "with the trees and richness of the land," during his summer's work in marking out the spaces of this vast domain.

The Greenbrier River.

Fairfax manor.

The English claim toward the west, based on their sea-to-sea charters, was at best illusory, but in New York, in Virginia, and in the colonies farther south, it nevertheless was of constant interest as the warrant for this western progress. Massachusetts was to find a like interest before the century closed, — as Connecticut was finding one even now, — but in this earlier half of the century New England was thinking more of what might come from a western trade than from jurisdiction which she could not enforce. It is noticeable that Dr. Douglass of Boston, when he wrote on the subject, was quite content with the line of the Appalachians, if the trade with the Chickasaws and Cherokees could only be assured. Another Bostonian, Dr. Franklin, now became prominent in Pennsylvania politics, and a resident of a province which had a definite western limit by charter had much less difficulty than a Virginian would have felt in coming to the conclusion that, after all, these sea-to-sea charters were awkward, and the Alle-

The English sea-to-sea charters and western trade.

NOTE. The opposite map is from Fry and Jefferson's *Map of Virginia*, 1751. It shows the lower Shenandoah, the Fairfax residence, and the wagon road from Philadelphia.

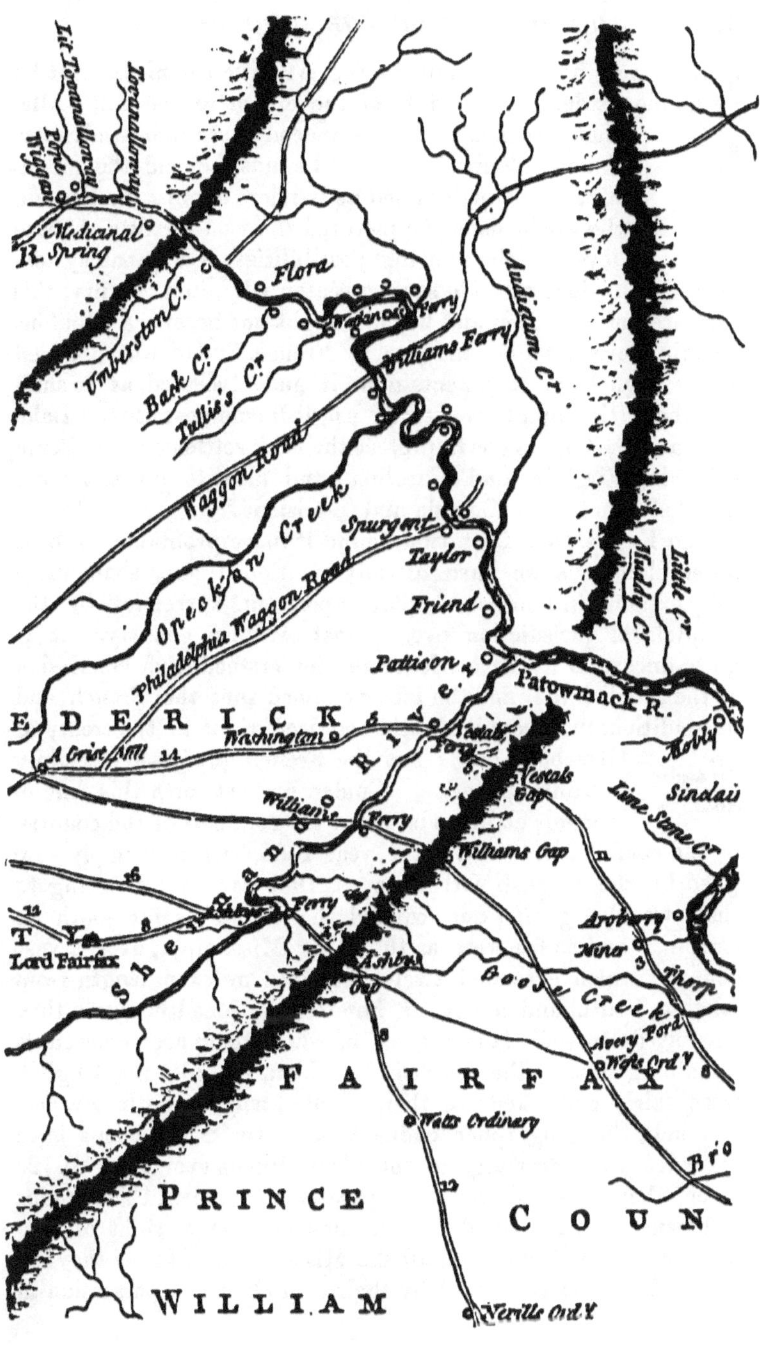

Lit Tonanalloway
Tonanalloway
Pope
Wiggan
Medicinal
R. Spring
Flora
Umberston Cr
Back Cr
Tullis's Cr
Watkins Ferry
Williams Ferry
Waggon Road
Opeckon Creek
Spurgent
Taylor
Friend
Philadelphia Waggon Road
Pattison
Antietum Cr
Muddy Cr
Little Cr
Patowmack R.
EDERICK
Washington
A Grist Mill
Vestals Ferry
Vestals Gap
Mobly
Sindair
Lime Stone Cr
Williams
Ferry
Williams Gap
Shenandoah River
Ashbys Ferry
Lord Fairfax
Ashbys Gap
Aroberry
Miner
Thorp
Goose Creek
Avery Ford
West's Ord'y
FAIRFAX
Watts Ordinary
PRINCE
WILLIAM
COUN
Nevills Ord'y

ghanies were a natural limit to the Atlantic colonies. But he by no means denied the right of the crown to the trans-Allegheny region. He was indeed a strenuous advocate of new colonies, with new bounds, beyond the mountains, to be maintained as barriers against the French. To those who would listen, he pictured the vast fertility of these distant valleys and the alluring possibilities of a great system of inland navigation. He saw no reason why, in a century, this vast area of the Ohio and beyond might not become a populous domain "either to England or to France." He was alarmed at the French encroachments upon it, and advocated, as we shall see, the setting up of two strong English colonies between Lake Erie and the Ohio, so as to protect the back settlements of Pennsylvania, Virginia, and Carolina, and also to prevent "the dreaded junction of Canada and Louisiana."

Franklin's views on the west.

The English had for a time found it more profitable to base other claims, as we have already mentioned and shall more fully explain in another chapter, upon the surrender by the Iroquois of jurisdiction over a vast western country. It is quite uncertain if the confederates understood this concession as the English did, and the latter claimed that the French had unconditionally recognized this acquired right in the treaty of Utrecht (1713); but the French professed certainly to think otherwise. Colden had set forth this Anglo-Iroquois claim as based on the conquest of the country by the confederates "about the year 1666," when, "amply supplied by the English with firearms, they gave a full swing to their warlike genius and carried their arms as far south as Carolina, and as far west as the river Mississippi, over a vast country, which extended twelve hundred miles in length from north to south, and about six hundred in breadth, where they entirely destroyed whole nations, of whom there are no accounts remaining among the English." When, in 1755, the English were fairly embarked in their final struggle with France, Mitchell, the geographer, claimed that "the Six Nations have extended their territory to the river Illinois ever since 1672, when they subdued and incorporated the ancient Chaouanons [Shawnees]. . . . Beside which they exercise a right of conquest over the Illinois and all the Mississippi, as far as they extend. This was confirmed by their own claims to possession in

The Anglo-Iroquois claim.

1742 [at the treaty in Philadelphia], and none have ever thought fit to dispute them. . . . The Ohio Indians are a mixed tribe of the several Indians of our colonies, settled here under the Six Nations, who have always been in alliance and subject to the English."

There was an unfortunate encounter of the Virginia militia with the Iroquois in the valley of the Shenandoah in 1742, which for a while boded mischief. The confederates claimed a reserved right to a passage south for their war parties against the Catawbas, along the most westerly wall of the mountains, and had demanded that the English refrain from settling along that trail. This had been agreed to by Spotswood, in consideration of their warriors not attempting to follow their older path on the eastern side of the valley. The promise had not been kept, and a skirmish occurred. The Virginians claimed that the Iroquois had agreed (1741) not to molest the Catawbas, and but for their failure to keep their promise, there would have been no difficulty. The confederates replied that the Catawbas had not come to them to confirm the peace, as the English had promised they would, but had sent taunting messages. The encounter destroyed confidence on both sides, and the Indians sent messengers to the Ottawas asking them to join in resisting the English if they sought to avenge their loss. The Virginians, however, preferred to allay the feeling by giving some presents.

Virginians and the Iroquois. 1742.

Underlying it all, however, was a deeper question, which pertained to the rights of the Iroquois to be compensated by the English for the occupation of these mountainous regions. The confederates had already been thinking of the French as a resort in case of need. Governor Clarke was reporting how "complacent these Indians now were to the French, but only through fear, knowing them to be a treacherous and enterprising people."

To settle this question of compensation, and to elicit further confirmation of the savages' friendship and land cessions, the English had determined upon a new conference. All the confederated tribes, except the Mohawks, met at Lancaster, Pennsylvania, with the commissioners from Pennsylvania, Maryland, and Virginia. The meetings began on

Treaty at Lancaster. 1744.

June 22, and were continued to July 4, 1744. Conrad Weiser was present as the principal interpreter for the English, but the Indians had a witness in Madam Montour, the half-breed captive of the Indians, who was now a woman of sixty. Her usual attendant, her son Andrew, was now absent, on the warpath against the Catawbas, by whom his father had been killed a few years before.

The Montours.

The commissioners from Virginia professed to the Indians that these western lands were without occupants when they first knew them. They added that the English king "held Virginia by right of conquest, and the bounds of that conquest to the westward is the great sea." The Iroquois's answer had the dignity of truth and good manners: "Though great things are well remembered among us, yet we don't remember that we were ever conquered by the great king [of England], or that we have been employed by that great king to conquer others. If it was so, it was beyond our memory." It is safe to say it is beyond the cognizance of the historian, who knows that truth is not necessarily an essential of a treaty-speech. "All the world knows," exclaimed a chief, "that we conquered these lands, and if ever the Virginians get a good title to them they must get it through us."

The Indian answers to the English claims.

When the Maryland commissioners claimed that they had owned their lands a hundred years, an Iroquois chief laughed, and said his people had owned them for much longer than a hundred years, and it was these Potomac lands which they asked pay for.

The conference ended in the payment of £400 by the English, and the deeds were passed for an indefinite extent of territory west of the Alleghanies. Both savage and white knew perfectly well that the title they passed and received was a dubious one, for it was contested by other tribes of Indians, as well as by the French. It answered, however, the English purpose to have their right substantiated against their rivals by documentary records of some sort.

Deed given by Indians.

NOTE. The map on the opposite page is from Fry and Jefferson's *Map of Virginia*, showing Beverly manor and the upper valley of the Shenandoah. To the right of the dotted "Boundary Line" is Lord Fairfax's manor, embracing the lower valley of the Shenandoah. The river sources near the "Calf-pasture" are those of the upper affluents of the James River, beyond the Blue Ridge. The road allowed by the Indians at the treaty of Lancaster in 1744, beginning in Virginia, followed down the Shenandoah valley and passed on to Philadelphia.

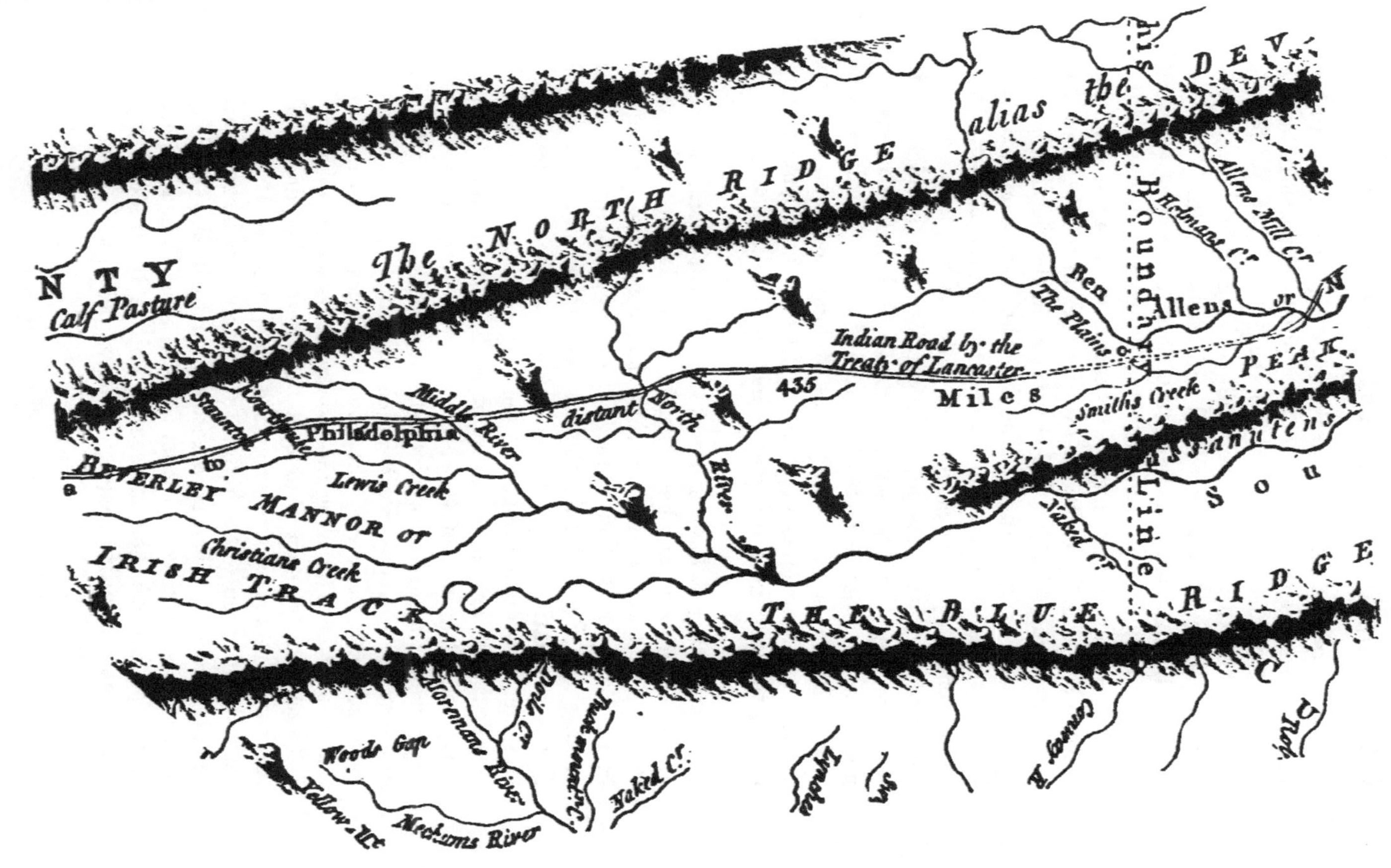

The NORTH RIDGE alias the DEV
NTY
Calf Pasture
Boundary Line
Allens Mill Cr.
Holmans Cr.
Ben
Allens
The Plains
Indian Road by the Treaty of Lancaster
435
Miles
distant
Philadelphia
Smiths Creek
PEAK
Middle River
North River
Staunton
Courthouse
BEVERLEY MANNOR or
IRISH TRACK
Lewis Creek
Christians Creek
Naked Cr.
SOU
THE BLUE RIDGE
Moremans River
Doils Cr.
Woods Gap
Yellow Mt.
Mechums River
Conway R.
Lynches
Rob

The treaty also confirmed to them the right to a great wagon road, starting from Philadelphia, and passing through Lancaster and York to the Potomac at Williams's Ferry. Thence it ran up the valley of Virginia to Winchester, and then followed an Indian trail still farther south.

Road and trail.

The Virginia commissioners, in presenting their case, traced back their alliance with the Indians to treaties fifty-eight and seventy years earlier, "when we and you became brethren." There are two passages in the speeches that were interchanged which are significant in the English mouth, and pathetic in the savage. The commissioners reminded them that the tribes had agreed, in a treaty with Governor Spotswood, not to come east of the mountains, while the Virginians on their part pledged themselves not to let these tidewater Indians pass the other way; but the commissioners added that this could be no bar to the English themselves passing west. The Indians in reply referred to their concessions of land, and said, with an emotion easily understood: "What little we have gained from selling the land goes soon away; but the land which you gain lasts forever!"

The Virginia demands.

This meeting at Lancaster was the first considerable conference that had been held in Pennsylvania. It showed how the Quaker province had come into prominence in its rivalry with New York. The over-mountain trade was making the Pennsylvania settlements prosperous. Lancaster had a population busy in the making of pack-saddles. The Germans now far outnumbered the original English stock, and they had been largely recruited, as we have seen, from the discontented Palatines of the Mohawk. A pamphleteer of the day reflected a current opinion when he spoke of this accession of aliens as "a happy event, which no nation except England ever met with, in having the power to raise a great empire in America without draining the country of its useful subjects."

Pennsylvania.

These Pennsylvania Dutch, as they were colloquially called, had come from countries where the roads were good. They had accordingly given to the highways of their new home a part of the excellence they had been accustomed to in the Old World. These roads all converged from the west upon Philadelphia, now a town of thirteen thousand souls. Thither the traders' wagons came from the Indian country, bringing peltry and news.

The most important position in this country for communicating with the distant tribes was at the forks of the Susquehanna, whence the Ohio trail ran up the west branch, and crossing the mountains reached Kittanning on the Alleghany. Here at Shamokin, as the forks were called, lived Shikellimy, an Oneida chief, — father of Logan, later celebrated, — who, in the name of the Iroquois, exercised a sort of lordship over the tribes hereabouts tributary to the Iroquois. He had acquired a good name with the English as a gracious mediator, and when he died, December 17, 1748, Zeisberger and his Moravians tenderly buried him.

Shamokin, — the forks of the Susquehanna.

A scandalous act of Thomas Penn some years back (1737) had asserted inordinate claims to land by virtue of what was known as the "Walking Purchase." The extent of the concession was dependent on the distance a man could walk in a day and a half by an honest tramp. By trick and sly advantages practiced by Penn's agents, the Delawares' favorite haunts were brought within this English acquisition. The poor creatures persisted in retaining occupancy of their own, and Penn called upon the Iroquois to eject them, which in subserviency they did. A part of this distressed people then scattered into the Wyoming valley, whence they drove out some ubiquitous Shawnees, who happened to be there. They were in turn pushed out by the English, and in 1740 they had resolved to cross the mountains and join the Wyandots on the Muskingum. Other portions of the Delawares lingered upon the Juniata, among some other Shawnees who were seated there as tributaries of the Iroquois; but it was not long before the confederates complained to the governor of Pennsylvania that English settlers were crowding these dependents, and that the English agents who were sent to dislodge the settlers had become so enchanted with the country as to become settlers there themselves.

The Walking Purchase.

The Delawares.

The Juniata.

The increasing trade by which Pennsylvania was profiting carried with it all the demoralizing influences of a traffic beyond the reach of law. Many of the traders

The traders.

NOTE. The map on the following pages is a part of *A Map of Pensilvania, New Jersey, New York, and the Three Delaware Counties, by Lewis Evans, MDCCXLIX.*

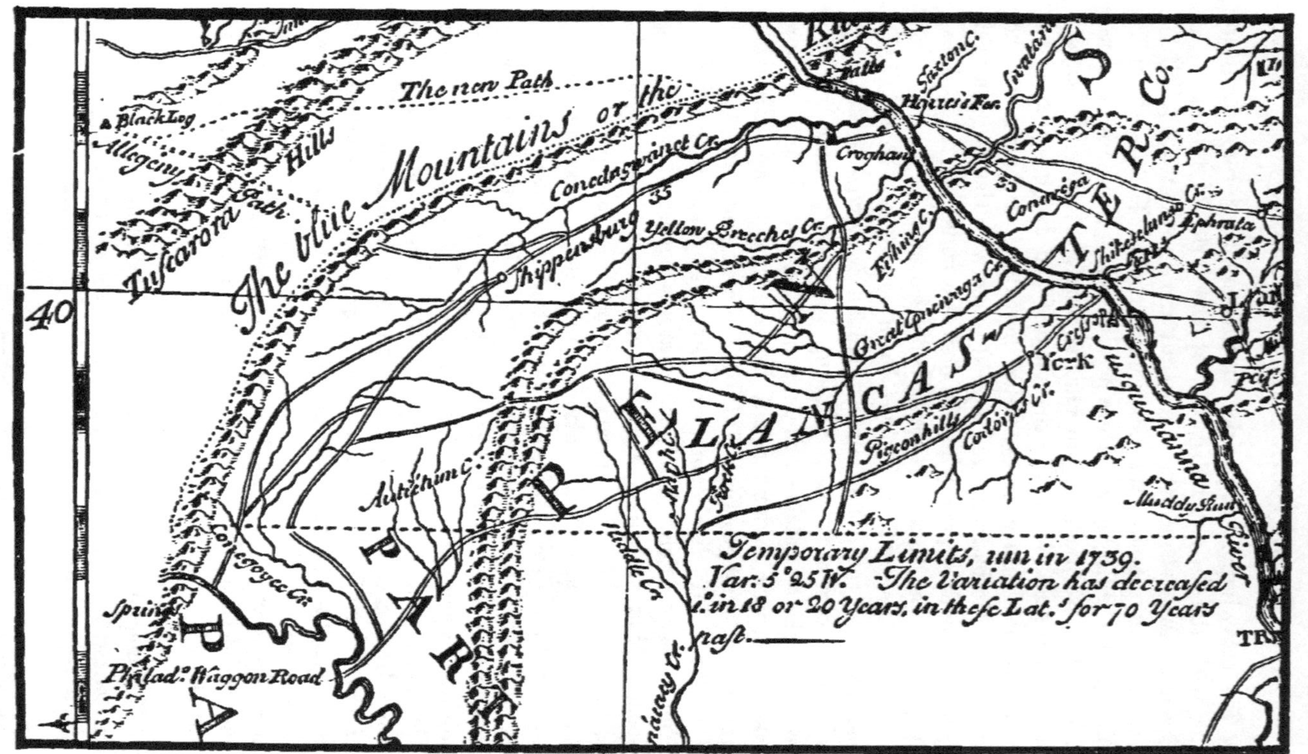

The new Path
Black Log
Allegeny Hills
Tuscarora Path
The blue Mountains or the
Conedagwainet Cr.
Shippensburg
Yellow Breeches Cr.
Croghan
Harris's Fer.
Saxton C.
Swatara
Conewaga
Shikeslungo Cr.
Ephrata
Fishing C.
Great Conewaga Cr.
York
Codorus Cr.
Pigeon hills
Susquehanna
Muddy Run
River
LANCASTER Co.
Antietam C.
Conegocheague Cr.
Springs
Philad. Waggon Road
Temporary Limits, run in 1739.
Var: 5°25 W. The Variation has decreased 1° in 18 or 20 Years, in these Lat.s for 70 Years past.
40

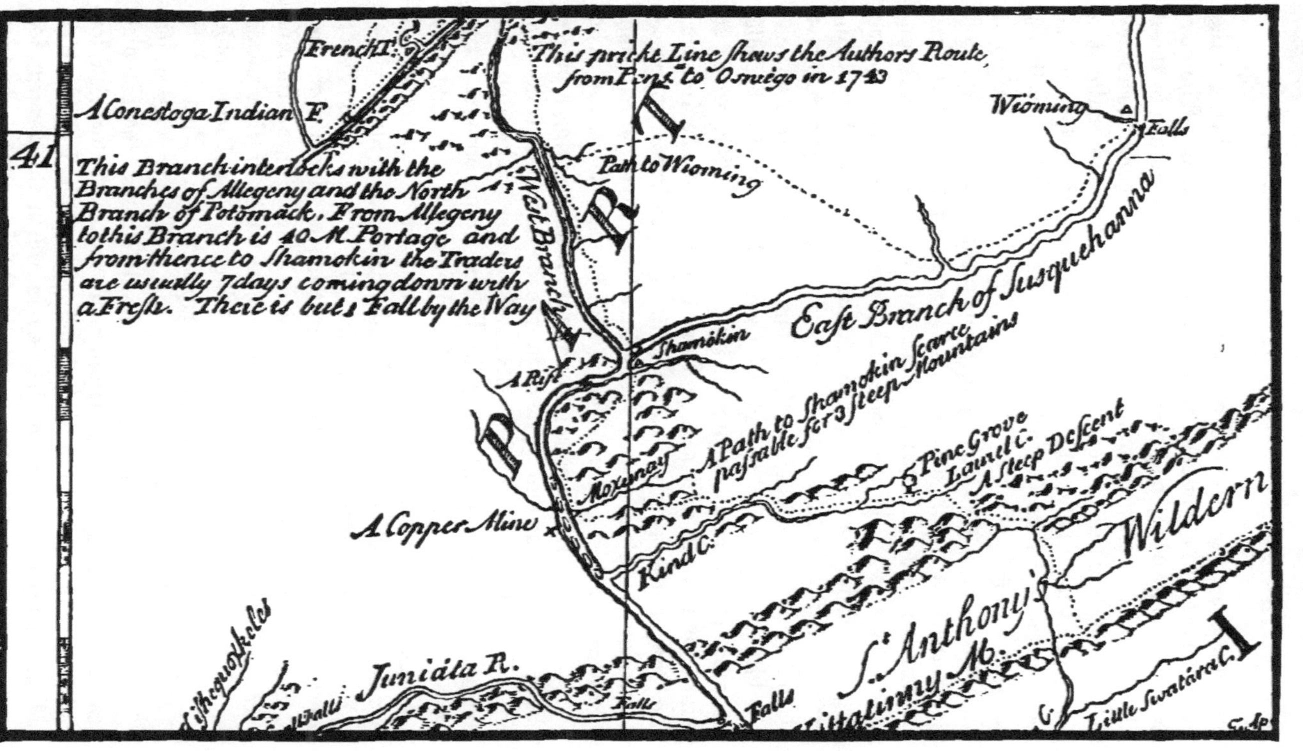
41
French T.
A Conestoga Indian F.
This prickt Line shews the Authors Route, from Pens to Oswego in 1743
Wioming
Falls
This Branch interlocks with the Branches of Allegeny and the North Branch of Potomack. From Allegeny to this Branch is 40 M. Portage and from thence to Shamokin the Traders are usually 7 days coming down with a Fresh. There is but 1 Fall by the Way
Path to Wioming
West Branch
PART
East Branch of Susquehanna
Shamokin
A Rift
A Path to Shamokin scarce passable for 3 steep Mountains
Moxinay
Pine Grove
Laurel C.
A steep Descent
A Copper Mine
Kind C.
Wildern
St. Anthony's
Tittatimy M.
Juniata R.
Falls
Little Swatara C.

deserved the name which Franklin gave them, of being "the most vicious and abandoned wretches of our nation." The governor of the province had more than once, in reference to these fellows, warned the assembly that it might become necessary to prohibit individual ventures in this traffic and make it a government monopoly. The savages had come to believe, under the pernicious habits prevailing, that the white man's religion was rum and debauchery. When the New Englander, Sargeant of Stockbridge, had come among them, the Indians had scorned the instruction which he offered. It was apt to be thus that the English trader blasted the hopes of the Protestant missionary. It was as a rule otherwise with the influence of the French

and the priests.

trader on the mission of the Jesuit and Capuchin. Still, Catholicism as well as Protestantism was not without trial in the presence of the bushrangers of either nation. Franklin recognized this difficulty when he proposed to hold the tribes in the English interest by a trained militia, so as to protect both white and savage from the evils of the frontier. The Quaker assembly of Pennsylvania had persistently opposed all military legislation, and Franklin effectively answered their arguments in his *Plain Truth* (1746). The Germans, who

The defense of Pennsylvania.

had no aversion to powder, were fast becoming a power in the assembly, and in the dozen years following, and under renewed stress of danger, something like fifty stockades were built along the Pennsylvania borders. But dread of danger had long called for vigilance in a community that could perpetrate a "Walking Purchase." The story of that disgraceful deceit was spread easily among indignant tribes, and was known beyond the mountains. In November, 1747, an attempt was made to soothe a deputation of chiefs from the Ohio tribes, in a conference at Philadelphia. These Indians were bold enough to tell the commissioners that if they pitted the tribes against the French on the Ohio, the least they could

The English and the Indians.

do was to aid them in the imposed task. This failure of the English to support the Indians in wars which the savages undertook for the defense of the colonies was nothing new. The constancy of support which, under similar circumstances, the French afforded their Indian allies had not a little to do with the way in which the French for many years combated so successfully the far more numerous

English. "The several governments of the English colonies," writes Colonel Stoddard at this time (1747) to Governor Shirley, had for three years been persuading the Iroquois "into a war wherein they had not any concern but to serve their friends, and they have left their hunting and other means of living and exposed themselves and families for our sakes," only to be left in the lurch. It was scarcely better for the colonial soldiers, in the neglect they suffered from the provincial assemblies. Stoddard adds: Colonel Johnson and his friends "waste their substance" in paying for the equipments of their warriors. The Indians did not fail to observe this selfishness of the colonial legislatures. Joshua Gee had offered some very good advice when he said, "If our people cannot come up to the engaging ways the French use with the Indians, at least good manners should be shown to them."

There was, in some respects, a surprising sense of forgiveness in the Indian for all such slights, and the English knew the soothing efficacy of rum and strouds. The colonists brought about a new conference at Lancaster in July, 1748, when the Twightwees — as the Miamis were called by the English — committed themselves to an English alliance for the first time. This, as we shall see, effectually established the English traders on the Wabash, where they had had a precarious traffic since 1723.

The Twightwees, or Miamis, 1748.

The packmen of Pennsylvania and Virginia now pushed boldly into the Ohio valley. Those from the Quaker province had some advantage over their rivals in a better route, for, leaving Philadelphia, there was a wagon road through Lancaster to Harris's Ferry (Harrisburg), and a bridle path thence to Will's Creek on the Potomac, from which the path was continued by an Indian trail to the forks of the Ohio (Pittsburgh). From this point there was another Indian path to the Miamis' towns. On the west branch of the Susquehanna, from a point known as the Great Island, Indian paths ran also in different directions, and one crossed the mountains to the Alleghany. A late writer has said that, at many places in the mountains, these beaten tracks can still be seen.

The Pennsylvania route to the Ohio.

NOTE. The opposite maps on the succeeding pages are parts of Lewis Evans's *Middle British Colonies* as reissued in London by Jefferys in 1758, "with some improvements by I. Gibson." It shows the traders' routes north of the Ohio and the position of the Indian settlements.

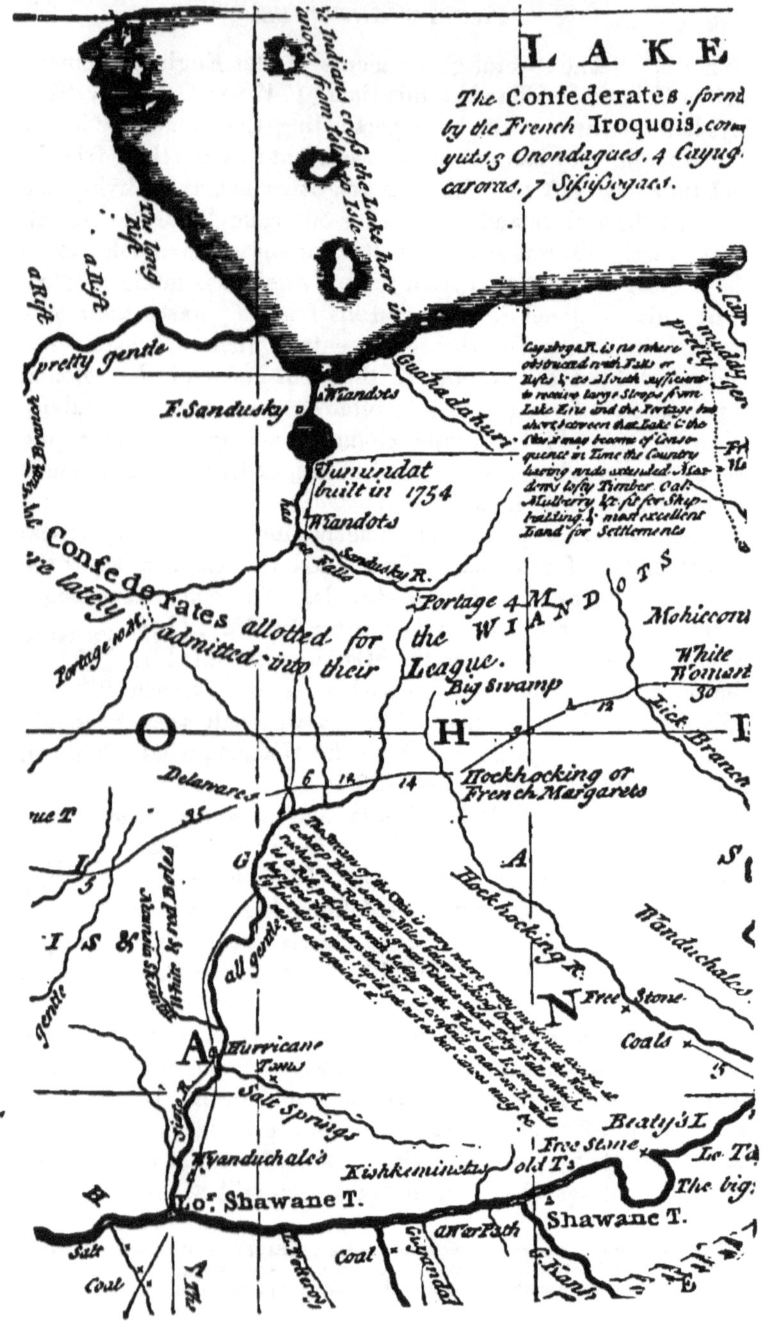

LAKE
The Confederates formd by the French Iroquois
F. Sandusky
Wiandots
Junundat built in 1754
Wandots
Sandusky R.
Confederates allotted for the admitted into their League.
Portage 4 M.
WIANDOTS
Mohiccons
White Woman
Big Swamp
Lick Branch
O
H
I
Delawares
Hockhocking or French Margarets
Hockhocking R.
Wanduchales
Free Stone
Coals
Hurricane Tom
Salt Springs
Wanduchale's
Kishkeminetas
old T's
Beaty's I.
Free Stone
Lor. Shawane T.
Shawane T.
a War Path
Coal
Salt
pretty gentle
all gentle
Guahadahuri
Cayahoga R. is no where obstructed with Falls or Rifts & at its Mouth sufficient to receive large Sloops from Lake Erie and the Portage but short between that Lake & the Ohio it may become of Consequence in Time the Country having wide extended Meadows lofty Timber Oak Mulberry &c. fit for Ship-building & most excellent Land for Settlements

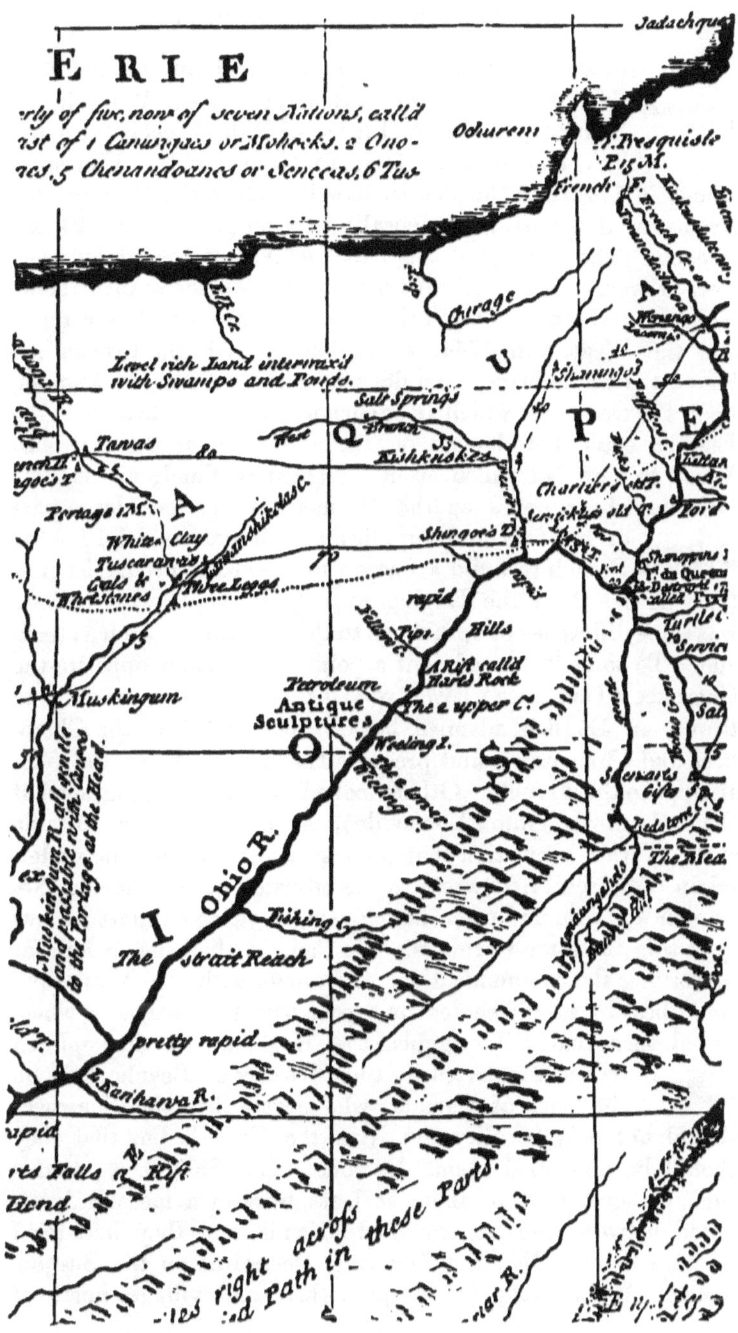
E R I E
rly of five, now of seven Nations, call'd
rist of 1 Canungaes or Mohocks. 2 Ono-
res, 5 Chenandoanes or Senecas, 6 Tus-
Odurem
F. Presquisle
P. & M.
French
Curage
Level rich Land intermixt with Swamps and Ponds.
Salt Springs
West Branch
Kishkuske
Tawas
Portage
White Clay
Tuscarawas
Coals & Whetstones
Three Leggs
Shingoe's T.
Charliers
F. du Quesne
Turtle C.
rapid
Hills
A Rift call'd Harts Rock
Petroleum
Antique Sculptures
The 2 upper C.
Weeling I.
The 2 lower Weeling C.
Muskingum
Muskingum R. all gentle and passable with Canoes to the Portage at the Head.
Ohio R.
Fishing C.
The strait Reach
pretty rapid
L. Kanhawa R.
Stewarts
Gists
Redstone C.
Falls
Rift
Bend
right across
Path in these Parts.

This treaty of 1748 was a substantial triumph for the English, as this western confederacy on the Wabash had been playing fast and loose with the French for many years. They had granted land to them for the Vincennes colony in 1742, and the Piankashaw branch of the Miamis, who lived near that post, had generally kept on good terms with the French. The feelings of this tribal section of the confederacy were, however, an exception to the general aversion to the French, which was shared by the Miamis proper, the Eel River tribe, and the Weas. In 1744, it had looked as if the French had bound the whole league to a devastating war upon the English, upon the assurance which Beauharnois had given them that the English could not depend on the assistance of the Iroquois. When this project failed, it had seemed to Vaudreuil at New Orleans, who counted on the Miamis' country for a large part of his furs and supplies, that it was essential for the French to build a fort on the Wabash fifteen leagues from its mouth, if the English were to be kept away. There was some difference of opinion as to the best site for such a stockade. To some it seemed as if a point on the Ohio opposite the Cherokee (Tennessee) River was the better place, not only to thwart an English advance, but to hold back both the Cherokees and Chickasaws, and preserve the navigation of the Mississippi to the French. Others looked upon the neighborhood of the falls of the Ohio (Louisville), as being the more suitable spot. With a conviction that some such defense must be undertaken, Vaudreuil first wrote to the minister of the marine, November 4, 1745, and often later during a year and more he was repeating the same warnings. He thought that such a fort for preserving the communications of Canada with the Mississippi could best be supplemented by a pact with the Shawnees, which would turn that tribe against the English. In this opinion he was supported by the advocacy of Beauharnois on the part of Canada, who urged that the Shawnees should not only be alienated from the English, but that they should be domiciled about Detroit. The Shawnees, at this time, or some part of them at least, were in a measure interposed between the Senecas and Miamis, and they had tried to draw to the Ohio the lingering Delawares on the Susquehanna. Bellin's map (1744) puts their main villages north of

The Wabash Indians.

The French on the Ohio.

The Shawnees.

THE INDIAN PATHS IN OHIO.

[From Andrews's *New Map of the United States*, London, 1783.]

the Ohio and above the mouth of the Kanawha. Just after this, they began to move west into the Scioto country, and some of them pushed as far as the valley of the Wabash. Here they came more within the control of the French, and could be better played off against the English influence, which by this time was likely to be increased with the neighboring Miamis.

Adair tells us that a Frenchman, Shartel, as he calls him, was the agent to carry the Shawnees finally over to the French, in the year before the Lancaster agreement of 1748. That chronicler adds that this negotiator was helped in the matter by "the supine conduct of the Pennsylvania government."

The French had need of the Shawnee alliance. In 1745, English traders were at Sandusky Bay erecting houses for their goods, perhaps the first English structures in the present State of Ohio. Some Hurons had wandered thither the year before (1744) from the vicinity of Detroit, and were not averse to receiving the flatteries of the English. Not one of them was more disposed to the English than Nicholas, a chief among them.

Sandusky Bay. 1745.

In June, 1747, some French who happened to come into the neighborhood were killed. When the commander at Detroit heard of it, he demanded the murderers, and insisted that the English traders should be driven away. It was the opportunity of Nicholas. He had of late been urging upon his neighbors, the Ottawas, to unite in a plot of his people, in which the Miamis should join, in order to attack Detroit and pillage its storehouses. The conspiracy grew, and all but the Illinois tribes were finally brought to promise assistance, when a squaw, overhearing the councils, revealed the scheme to a priest, and Longueil heard of it in the summer of 1747. The Hurons cabined about Detroit fled, and the plot lost impetus. There was a murder here and there, and Nicholas seized Fort Miami at the confluence of the St. Joseph and St. Mary rivers. The pact was loosened, and the seventeen tribes which had conspired together began to fall off. By September (1747), reinforcements had reached Detroit from Montreal, and Nicholas lost heart. During the winter, the French rebuilt (February, 1748) the fort on the Miami, and ordered the English out of the valley. Shortly after, Nicholas disappeared from Sandusky, and Conrad Weiser later learned at

The plot of Nicholas. 1747.

Logstown that a hundred fighting Hurons (Wyandots) were coming to put themselves under English protection. By June, the members of the league were nearly all restored to the favor of the French. But the danger was not passed. In October (1748), the commandant at Detroit was again counseled to be wary and prevent the English getting a lodgment in the Ohio country. He was told to exert force if need be, though peace ostensibly existed.

This hostile combination having failed, the Miamis alone threw themselves into the English interest, and the treaty of Lancaster (July, 1745), as already mentioned, was brought about. The subsequent active disaffection of the Miamis, and the new intrusion of the English packmen, was the subject of Sieur Raymond's reports the following year (1749). The Pennsylvania and Virginia people were now founding their most advanced post (1748) at Pickawillany on the Big Miami, one hundred and fifty miles up the stream from the Ohio. It was estimated at this time that during a single season some three hundred English traders were leading their pack-horses and dragging their bateaux over the mountain passes into the Ohio valley.

The Miamis.

Pickawillany. 1748.

No man was so conspicuous among them as George Croghan. He was an Irishman, who had been for several years trading along the shores of Lake Erie, learning the Indian tongue and becoming acquainted with the geography of the region. The southern shore of Lake Erie was the last of any of the borders of the Great Lakes to come to the knowledge of the map-makers. Bellin, who made Charlevoix's maps, knew nothing of it, nor was it comprehended by Céloron, whose expedition we shall soon follow.

George Croghan.

Southern shore of Lake Erie.

When Conrad Weiser recommended the Pennsylvania government to employ Croghan as an official almoner to the tribes of this lake-shore region, he was the best available man to counteract the French slyness in "speaking underground." An honest man, as Weiser termed him, Croghan recognized certain tricks in the French methods of trade, which he felt the English might well learn to copy. He held the opinion that in this as in other intercourse with the savages, the French, better than the English, knew how to manage their peculiarities. Equally conspicuous with Croghan, if indeed not more so, from his constant employment as a public interpreter, was Croghan's sponsor, Weiser himself. The government of Pennsylvania in particular largely depended on him to gather tidings of what was going on among the Indians; and his correspondence with Peters, the secretary of that province, shows how vigilant in this respect he was. No one knew better than he how the Six Nations held the balance of power, not only among the savages farther west, who waited their motions, but also in the counter movements of the French and English. When New York began to convert its temporary structure at Oswego into a stone fort, it was the French distrust of the Iroquois which restrained the Canadians from attacking it. When the English sought to occupy Irondequoit Bay, it was an intimation from the confederates that Oswego and Niagara were near enough together for rivals, that made the New Yorkers desist. These mutual distrusts were no doubt complicated by the clandestine trade between Albany and the St. Lawrence, which neither party wished to put to a hazard. Peter Kalm, who had some experience with these sly hucksters on the Hudson, felt they were sharp enough to ruin a Jew; and John Reinhold Forster, his English editor, would soften the charge by thinking it arose from the ancient sympathy of the Swedes for the French. Despite this mutual wariness, Beauharnois succeeded in drawing the confederates to a conference in the summer of 1745; but it did not prevent retaliatory raids, stirred up by Piquet on one side, and conducted by the Mohawks on the other.

Conrad Weiser.

The Iroquois as mediators.

The Albany traders.

But the struggle was soon to be transferred to the Ohio. The English made the first movement in 1748 south of that river; the French followed the next year north of it.

The Ohio country.

The projection of the Ohio Company in 1748 was in the interests of Virginia, whose traders hoped by the facilities of water carriage between the Potomac and eastern branches of the Ohio to attain an advantage over the Pennsylvanians. The movement was supported by the leaders of the tidewater gentry, and an application for a grant of five hundred thousand acres south of the Ohio, and between the Monongahela and the Kanawha, was made by their London agent, John Hanbury. His petition was supported by the Board

The Ohio Company. 1748.

of Trade on the ground that such a grant would consolidate trade for the English, and give them advantages over the French, —arguments that prevailed with them at this period, but were not much thought of when, twenty years later, these western settlements might, in the board's judgment, prove to be independent of the manufactures of the mother country.

On May 19, 1749, a royal order awarded two hundred thousand acres of those asked for, with a ten years' freedom from rent, on condition that a hundred families were settled upon them within seven years, and a fort built and maintained. This complied with, the full grant of half a million acres would be made. Accordingly, the orders were delivered to Governor Nelson on July 12, 1749.

Some years before this, in 1742–43, a vagrant Yorkshireman, Colonel Thomas Cresap, then near forty years old, had built "a hunting and trading cabin" near the uppermost fork of the Potomac,—the earliest permanent settler in western Maryland. His abode was near an old Shawnee town, and its position is shown in Mitchell's map (1755). Previous to this he had lived on the Pennsylvania side of the line, and Evans in his map indicates the spot. Cresap was a man not unsuited to the rough and boisterous phases of a frontier life, and had joined in the somewhat hazardous border difficulties between these provinces so conspicuously that he had become well known, and was turned to in any troublesome venture. He was therefore just the man for the company to employ to open a way to their new domain, and it was through his rude surveying efforts that a track was run across the divide and into the company's grant, pretty much in the same direction as later developed in Braddock's road.

Thomas Cresap.

The company had relied in part upon the Pennsylvania Germans to make up the quota of a hundred families. The proprietors, however, held to their ancient ways, and fastened Episcopal tithes upon the soil. The Germans loathed such a vassalage and held back. It seemed then, for the present at least, that the scheme was to fail. It had certainly gone far enough to arouse the French, who saw in it a new assertion of the old doctrine of the sea-to-sea charters, and Dumas in a *Mémoire* expressed the government's anxiety: "Every man of sense who is conversant with the

The French and the Ohio Company.

manner in which war can be carried on in that country will agree with me that all the resources of the state will never preserve Canada, if the English are once settled at the heads of these western rivers."

Galissonière and Céloron's expedition. 1749.

No one saw this better than Galissonière, and he determined on a movement to the Ohio. His purpose was soon divined at Albany, and Johnson sent messengers to the tribes along that river warning them of a French inroad. Clinton, in June, 1749, sent word to the governor of Pennsylvania that some New Englanders, coming from Canada, reported a force of a thousand men preparing to go to the Ohio. Croghan was at once instructed to send out scouts to discover the truth. The fact was that on June 15, 1749, Bienville de Céloron had left Montreal, under instructions from Galissonière, to traverse the Ohio region, take formal possession at points, discover the temper of the natives, and drive off the English traders. Joncaire, the son of a French officer by a Seneca mother, who was to the French what William Johnson was to the English, — the best man they had to guide the Indian will, — was put in the van. As one of the incised plates, recording the French occupation, and intended for burial along the route, fell into Johnson's hands, he was possessed very soon of the object of the expedition; and it has been surmised, and was believed by Johnson, that this plate was stolen from Joncaire while among the Senecas.

Joncaire.

Céloron's route.

Céloron did not have anything like the force which the New England men had reported, for beside his officers he had only twenty French soldiers, a hundred and more voyageurs, and thirty Indians, Iroquois and Abenakis. The party turned in from Lake Erie at the portage which rises a thousand feet in eight miles to Lake Chautauqua. This was the most difficult of all the Erie portages, and was found so wearisome that it was usually neglected for that of Presqu' Isle, by the modern city of Erie. At the end of July, the expedition was fairly embarked on the Alleghany, and passed down the Ohio. What Céloron in his itinerary calls "the finest place on the river" was a Delaware village, probably at the forks of the Ohio, where the historic Fort Duquesne later stood. At Logstown, somewhat farther down the main stream, Céloron had an interview with the Indians, and told them that they might make the most of this year's hunting, in order to pay their English debts, for it was the last year the English would be allowed on the river, — a speech received with contempt according to the English report.

The French commander says he was struck with the way in

L'AN 1749 DV REGNE DE LOVIS XV ROY DE
FRANCE NOVS CELORON COMMANDANT D'VN
DETACHEMENT ENVOIÉ PAR MONSIEVR LE M.IS
DE LA GALISSONIERE COMMANDANT GENERAL DE
LA NOUVELLE FRANCE POVR RETABLIR LA
TRANQVILLITÉ DANS QVELQVES VILLAGES SAUVAGES
DE CES CANTONS AVONS ENTERRÉ CETTE PLAQVE
AU CONFLUENT DE LOHIO ET DE TCHADAKOIN CE 29 IVILLET
PRES DE LA RIVIERE OYO AUTREMENT BELLE
RIVIERE POUR MONUMENT DU RENOUVELLEMENT DE
POSSESSION QUE NOUS AVONS PRIS DE LA DITTE
RIVIERE OYO ET DE TOUTES CELLES QUI Y
TOMBENT ET DE TOUTES LES TERRES DES DEUX
CÔTES JUSQVE AUX SOURCES DES DITTES RIVIERES
AINSI QVEN ONT JOVY OV DÛ JOVIR LES
PRECEDENTS ROIS DE FRANCE ET QVILS S'Y
SONT MAINTENVS PAR LES ARMES ET PAR LES
TRAITTES SPECIALEMENT PAR CEVX DE RISWICK
D'VTRECHT ET D'AIX LA CHAPELLE

ONE OF CELORON'S PLATES.
[Taken from the *Pennsylvania Archives*.]

which the savages were mixed in their villages, — Iroquois, Shawnees, Loups, Delawares, Miamis being often domiciled together; and all, as he was troubled to find, much more inclined to the English than to his own people. He found traces of English packmen everywhere. Some of them had entered the valley, as he found, by the Kanawha,

English traders.

which was mainly the route for the Carolina traders. He makes the usual observation that the cheapness of the English goods made the greater attraction of their traffickers, and he intimates a belief that they purposely sold at a loss, in order to gain the Indians' allegiance, while the English government made good the deficiency.

His buried plates.

Here and there, generally at river mouths, Céloron buried his incised plates. Their inscriptions were much the same: "We have placed this plate here as a memorial of the establishment of our power in the territory which is claimed by us on the river Ohio and throughout its tributaries to their sources, and confirmed to us by the treaties of Ryswick, Utrecht, and Aix-la-Chapelle." One or two of these plates have since been unearthed. That which was buried near the mouth of the Muskingum was found by some boys in the early years of this century. It was protruding from a bank which had been washed by the current. The youngsters melted a part of it to make bullets, and the remaining fragment is now preserved in the collection of the American Antiquarian Society at Worcester, Massachusetts. Another was discovered near the mouth of the Kanawha in 1846.

English traders warned.

In August, as Céloron tells us, the party met a band of six English, who had fifty horses and one hundred and fifty bales of fur. They were returning from a successful trafficking tour, and were bound for Philadelphia. The French leader warned them, in writing, to withdraw from the valley and not to return. They replied, either "through fear or otherwise," that they would not come back. He sent by them, writing the letter among the Shawnees, August 16, a message to Governor Harrison, asking him to prohibit such trespasses in the future, as the French would be compelled to expel them by force if necessary, should they encounter them. He had soon an occasion to dispatch a like missive to the governor of Carolina by some traders from that province.

Burying his last plate at the mouth of the Great Miami (Rivière à la Roche), Céloron turned up that stream at the end of August. Here, as elsewhere, he found that the Indians kept aloof, and the Miamis even rejected his offer of powder and ball. There were English traders close by, but being warned, they kept out of sight. By September 20 the French had ascended the river so far that there was no longer sufficient water for the canoes. They accordingly burned them, with all else that was too burdensome for a land journey, and, procuring horses from the Indians, struck across the country one hundred and twenty-five miles to the Maumee, reaching it on September 25. Here Céloron found a French fort, with a small garrison commanded by Raymond.

Fortunately we are aided all along Céloron's route by documents, pointing out landmarks. The leader's journal is preserved in the Archives of the Marine at Paris, and has been printed by Margry. It was first brought to the notice of American students in an essay, with an abstract, by the late O. H. Marshall of Buffalo, and is now included in his *Historical Writings*. A fuller translation has been printed in the *Catholic Historical Researches*, 1885–86. Father Bonnecamps, a Jesuit, was a professor of mathematics and hydrography at the College of Quebec, and accompanied the expedition. He made a map and kept a journal, also preserved in the Marine, and first brought to our attention by Marshall. These three documents make an all-sufficient account of what was done.

Céloron's journal and Bonnecamps's map.

The remainder of Céloron's journey has little to interest us. He kept in the van with his Frenchmen, and reached Detroit on October 6, and there waited for his Indians to come up. On November 9, he was again in Montreal, having lost on the way but a single man, who was drowned.

Hendrick the Mohawk soon learned from the St. Lawrence settlements enough to make him believe that the expedition was looked upon as a failure, and so he reported to Colonel Johnson. Céloron himself does not disguise his disappointment: "All I need say is that these Indian nations are not kindly disposed to the French, and are wholly friends of the English," and he believed the secret of it lay in their better inducements for trade. He had seen it conspicuously on the Big Miami at the mouth of Loraine Creek, where the new English post of Pickawillany stood. It was much the same everywhere, as he believed, along the twelve hundred leagues of his travel, — much the same among the Delawares on the Muskingum, among the Shawnees on the Scioto, and among the Wyandots on the Sandusky.

The expedition a failure.

The news of the failure spread rapidly among the English, and in October Governor Harrison was assured of it by rumors from over the mountains, and communicated them to Clinton of New York. Scouts which the Pennsylvania governor sent along the Frenchman's track made the same report.

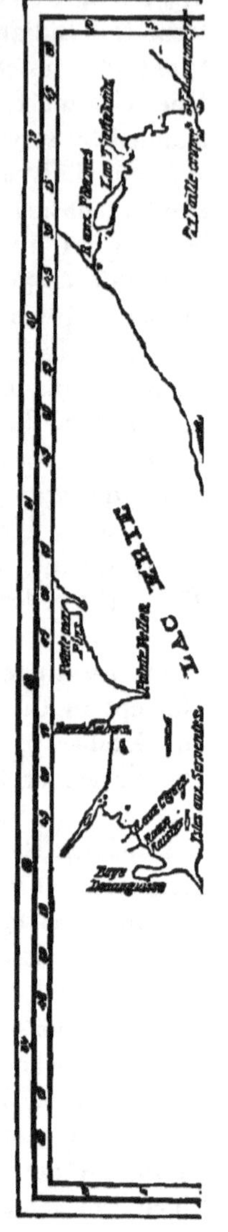

Galissonnière recalled, September, 1749.

Galissonnière, who had hoped so much from the undertaking, was no longer in Quebec to feel the discouragement. He had been summoned home to take part in the diplomatic conferences, and left Quebec in September, 1749. He had felt from the first that there was little chance of averting a protracted war with the English. It had, indeed, only been delayed by the peace of 1748, as already signified in the preceding chapter. He was succeeded by Admiral Jonquière, who had had rather rough experiences in reaching his post. He had been in D'Anville's fleet, which the storms had scattered so fortunately for the Bostonians. He was again at sea bound for Quebec in 1747, when he was captured by the English. Liberated by the peace of Aix-la-Chapelle, he had at last succeeded, in August, 1749, in reaching his government, and it was to him that Céloron now made his report.

Jonquière succeeds, 1749.

But while English influence was found by Céloron to be everywhere active along the Ohio, there was one of the approaches to the Ohio valley where English pioneers were provoking discontent. This was in the valley of the Juniata, which the Iroquois had reserved as a hunting-ground for their dependents. The Senecas objected to the squatters, who were marking their "tomahawk claims" well up the valley and even over the passes. "The Indians," wrote Conrad Weiser, who never

The Juniata valley.

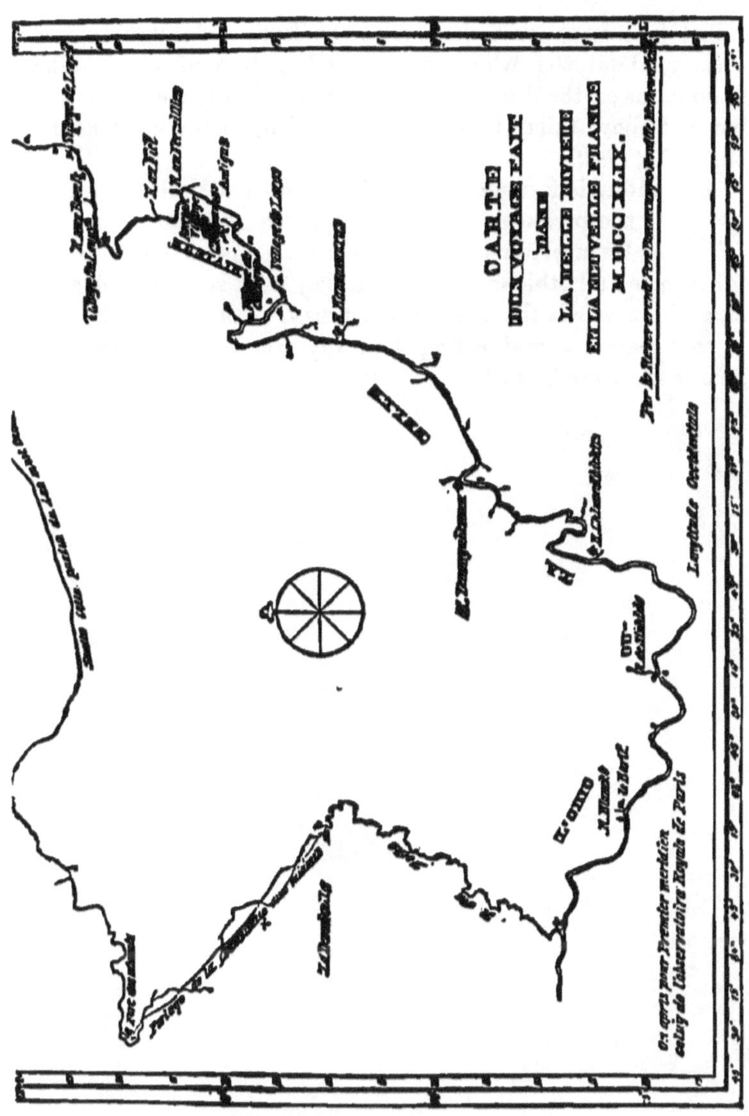

CÉLORON'S MARCH.

[Taken from King's *Ohio.*]

failed in honest convictions as to the Indian rights, "are very uneasy about the white people settling beyond the Endless Mountains on the Juniata, on Sherman's Creek, etc. They tell me that above thirty families are settled upon Indian lands this spring" (1749).

Moravians.

The Moravians under Zinzendorf, who had left Georgia on the breaking out of the Spanish war, had come into Pennsylvania some years before this, and set up their tabernacle at Bethlehem. Thence they were sending their missionaries towards the Wyoming country, — the first whites seen in that region, — and feeling their way even over the mountains, nearer the New York line.

CHAPTER XIII.

LOUISIANA AND ITS INDIANS.

1743–1757.

It was in 1743 that Bienville, now a man of sixty-two, wearied with buffeting events and enemies, and not well satisfied with all that fortune had bestowed upon him, resigned his command in Louisiana. In May, he was succeeded by the Marquis de Vaudreuil. The province then contained, it was reckoned, about six thousand inhabitants not of native stock, — two thirds of these were French, the rest mainly negroes. There was some political corruption in the government, and New Orleans was far from having become the place which Bienville had figured in his dreams. Still, there was a growing air of briskness about it, and its commerce outward to Europe and the West Indies, and within toward the Indian country and up the river, was beginning to be considerable. The territory immediately dependent on the lower Mississippi hardly afforded as yet adequate supplies of food, and Vaudreuil notified his home government, in 1744, that if an importation of flour had not arrived, he could not have controlled his famished garrison. The fact was that, for a while, Louisiana existed only because the Illinois country could send down the necessary food.

Bienville succeeded by Vaudreuil. 1743.

New Orleans.

There were at this time two thousand, possibly nearer three thousand, whites in the Illinois settlements of Kaskaskia, St. Philippe, Cahokia, and Prairie du Rocher. Life in these communities was certainly picturesque, and the poetic temperament might consider it Arcadian. It was to a certain extent contented, for ignorance and self-indulgence are not wholly hostile to a life of complacency. They got a sufficient support from the soil, and cared very little for the mines which had

The Illinois colony.

earlier attracted attention. We see in their church registers how they were baptized and married, and the Jesuit mission gave them something to which they could cling. They had, to share their labor, a number of horses secured from a Spanish stock which had been passed beyond New Mexico from tribe to tribe. Traders came and went among them, and gave their women the opportunity to buy the gewgaws which both pleased them and doubtless lightened the burdens of life. The men built barges. Filled with flour and pork, one could see, in the proper season, no inconsiderable flotillas push out into the stream, perhaps uniting from the different settlements in one compact body. They carried life and merriment as they started down to New Orleans. Such a combining of boats was far more necessary than mere companionship required, for they sometimes encountered predatory bands of savages along the lower country. Starting in December, as was usual, their lading was disposed of by February. The adventurers then filled their bateaux with cotton, rice, sugar, and tobacco, and entered upon the tedious ascent. Carrying ropes ahead to be tied to trees on the bank, and pulling their boats against the current by relay after relay, and sometimes poling in the shallows, they made the wearisome homeward voyage.

Trade with New Orleans.

Vaudreuil, at New Orleans, had begun with somewhat lordly social aims. He wished the official circle which surrounded him to have some of the splendors and pleasures of a little court. He did not see as well as others saw the rather incongruous exhibition which the manners of Paris made in the swampy little town. The commerce of the place enlivened the humble life, and an occasional arrival of "casket girls" stirred the domestic passions. With it all, Vaudreuil had his share of anxieties. There was always the fear of the interruption of his supplies from the up-country; if not by Indian interference, it might come from the inevitable, ubiquitous English. To maintain his communications with Canada by the portages of the St. Lawrence valley was an incessant solicitude. At one time, while Berthelot was command-

The social and political life of New Orleans.

NOTE. The opposite map is from *The Middle States*, by James Russell, which appeared in Winterbotham's *America*, and shows the portages.

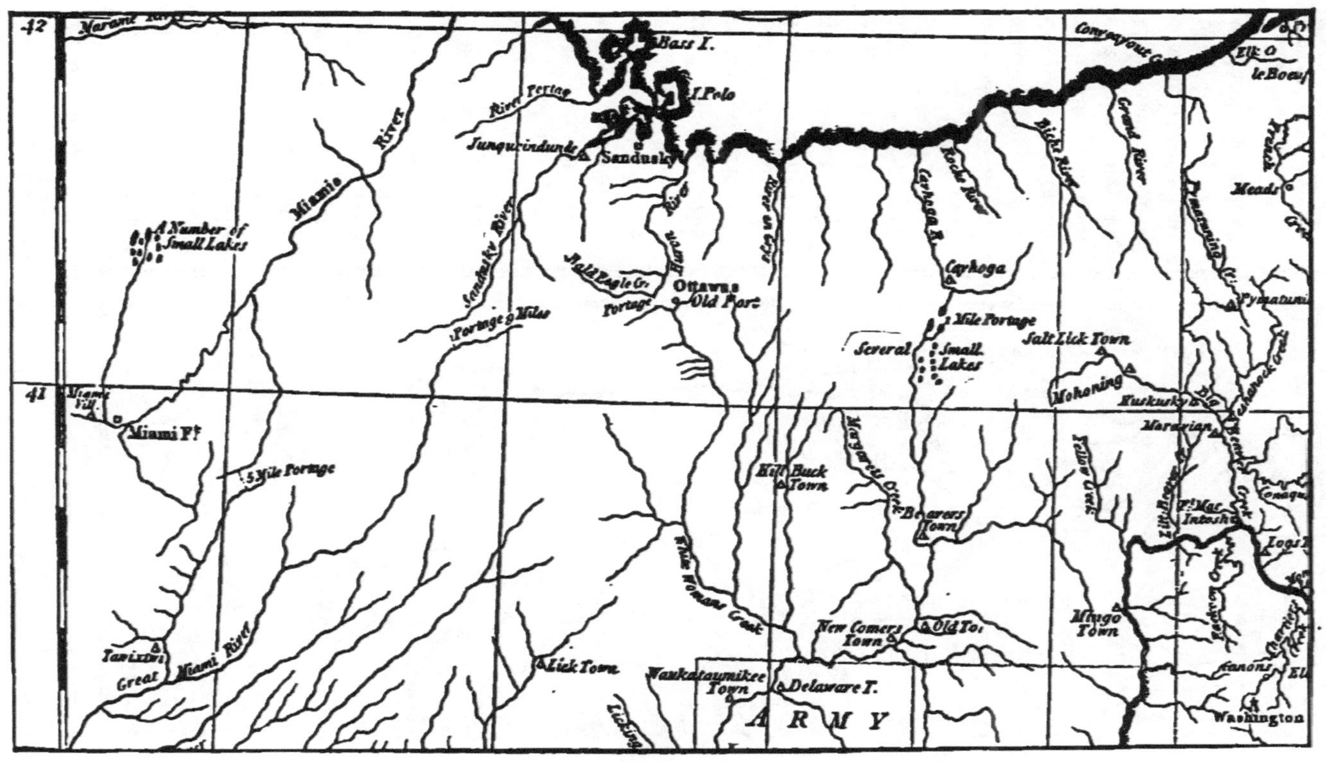
42
41
Bass I.
I. Pelo
River Portag
Sandusky
Miamis River
A Number of Small Lakes
Sandusky River
Portage 9 Miles
Ottawas Old Fort
Huron River
Portage
Cayhoga
1 Mile Portage
Several Small Lakes
Salt Lick Town
Mohoning
Grand River
Miami Vill.
Miami Ft
5 Mile Portage
Kill Buck Town
Bearers Town
Moravian
Tawixtwi
Great Miami River
Lick Town
White Womans Creek
New Comers Town
Old To
Waukataumikee Town
Delaware T.
ARMY
Mingo Town
Yellow Creek
Washington
le Boeuf
Meads

ing on the Illinois, that officer was wholly cut off from tidings from New Orleans. Ignorant of political conditions and reduced in stores, Berthelot had been forced to draw in his little force and concentrate it at Kaskaskia.

Native tribes.

The Indian natives throughout the province were a constant perplexity. The tribes of the Illinois, which, at the time of the treaty of Utrecht, had been steadfastly French in sympathy and a foil to the Foxes, always the foe of the French, had of late years been moving south and east. They were even opening trade with the English, and welcoming the Carolinian packmen coming by the Cherokee River. This rendered the upper

Foxes, Sioux, Sauks.

NOTE. The annexed map is from James Adair's *History of the American Indians*, London, 1775, showing the positions of the tribes.

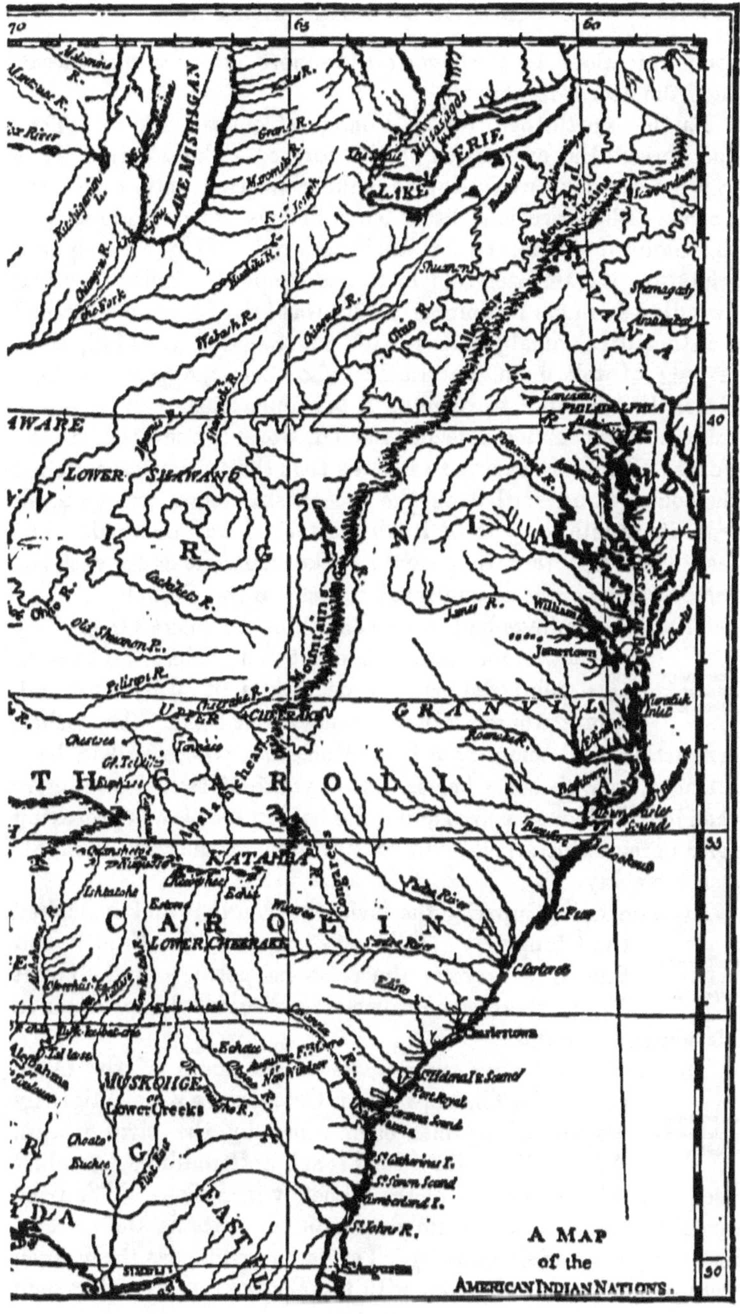

A MAP
of the
AMERICAN INDIAN NATIONS.
LAKE MISHIGAN
LAKE ERIE
PHILADELPHIA
LOWER SHAWANO
VIRGINIA
UPPER CHEERAKE
CAROLINA
KATAHBA
LOWER CHEERAKE
MUSKOHGE or Lower Creeks
GEORGIA
EAST
Charlestown
Port Royal
Jamestown
Williamsburg
Wabash R.
Ohio R.
James R.
Congarees
St. Augustine
St. Johns R.
Cumberland I.
Savanna
Old Shawanon R.
Allegeny
70
65
60
40
35
30

communications by the river all the more insecure, and threatened the access to Detroit.

Farther north there was still danger from the Sioux. They had forced the evacuation of the fort on Lake Pepin. They were constantly threatening to make concerted action with the Foxes. This ferocious little band always stood ready to join the Sioux if forced to flee their country. They were equally ready to give themselves over to the Iroquois. Since they had dwindled so much in numbers, what was left of them maintained a rather fitful amalgamation with the Sauks. In 1746, their levying of toll upon the traders who took the portage from Green Bay became so onerous a tax upon this body that the traders united under a leader named Morand and attacked the Foxes. Their onset was so furious that the Indians abandoned the country and settled on the Wisconsin, about twenty miles from its mouth, only to be further attacked and pursued. The fear after this that they would make common cause with the Sioux was a source of continual anxiety to the French.

The Langlades at Green Bay.

These proceedings had done something to make Green Bay attractive for settlers, and the Langlades, who were at this point the earliest occupants of Wisconsin soil, soon gathered a little colony about them. The father, Augustine, had come there from Mackinac, where he had been a trader, and his son Charles, now a youth of twenty-two, more than half Indian in spirit, and quite half in blood, was preparing for a career which made him conspicuous in the great struggle at a later day.

Chippeways on Lake Superior.

Even on Lake Superior the insidious English had inspirited the Chippeways (Ojibways) against the French, and thus from beyond the remotest portage of the Great Valley there came reports to disquiet the governor in his southern capital.

Choctaws, Chickasaws, Creeks.

The most perplexing rumors were from south of the Ohio, where the Choctaws and Chickasaws were diligently played off against each other by the rival whites. Adair tells us that the French at Tumbikpe (Tombigbee) were the instigators of the Choctaw irruptions. This tribe made the most extortionate demands for gifts as the price of immunity from their hostility. The same writer says the French were penurious as compared with the English in bestowing such gratuities. The English were at intervals successful in sowing dissensions among the Choctaws, and then it would happen that for a while some portions of that tribe would espouse the English interests, and even make hostile demonstration against those who adhered to the French. This at one period went so far that there was apprehension at New Orleans that an Anglo-Choctaw invasion was in store for them.

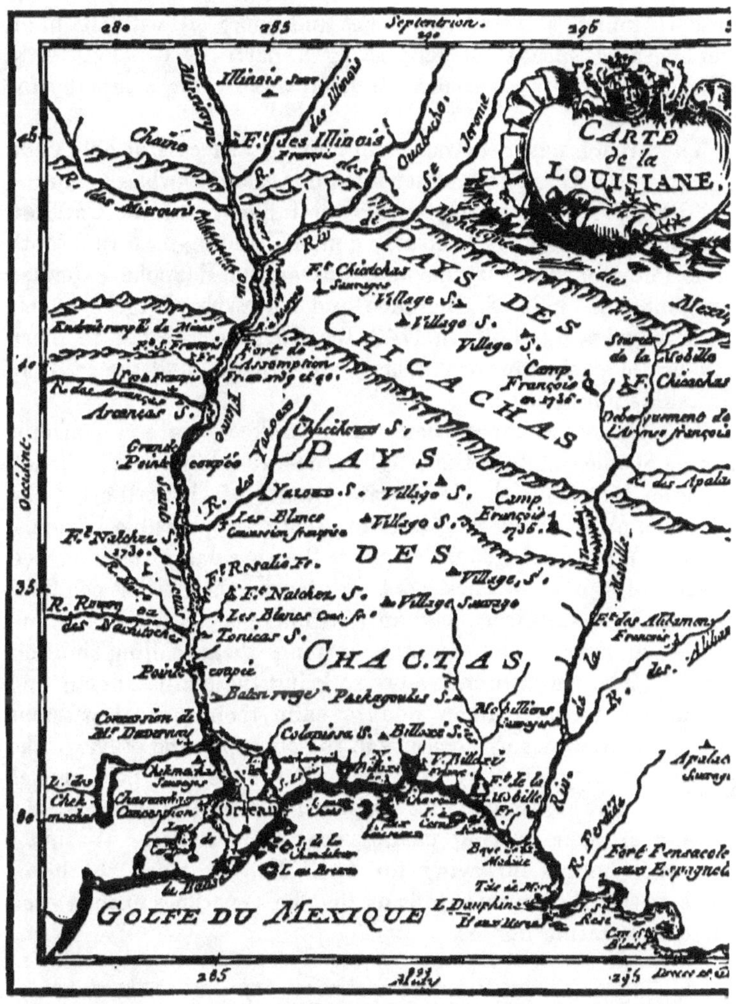

DUMONT'S MAP OF THE CHICKASAW AND CHOCTAW COUNTRY.

Adair had opened trade with the Chickasaws in 1744, and at this time he encountered French emissaries seeking to arouse them against the English, on the plea that the Carolinians would overrun their country in their progress toward the Mississippi.

The Chickasaws and Creeks were usually proof against French persuasions, and we find them making raids upon the French villages wherever exposed beyond support. In retaliation, such Indians as the French could control were sent to storm the traders' houses among those tribes and make off with the plunder. Adair speaks of conducting a party of Chickasaws to Charleston, on one occasion, to keep alive their sympathy for the English.

Cherokees, Catawbas.

The French never succeeded in getting a successful hold upon the Cherokees, much less upon the Catawbas, who were more completely within the influence of the Carolinians and Virginians. A clearly defined trading-path ran south from Petersburg in Virginia and, crossing the Roanoke, extended well into the circle of Cherokee and Catawba villages. After Fort Augusta was built in 1740, the Cherokees began to mark out bridle paths toward it from their villages, and the trade in deerskins flourished.

Hostilities with the Iroquois.

The Catawbas, more than the Cherokees, were a constant source of uneasiness to the English, not from any fear of French intrigue, but from the inveterate enmity of this tribe for the northern allies of the English, the equally irrepressible Iroquois. Conrad Weiser, who could compare the singularly well-balanced checks of the New York confederates in their tribal councils, speaks of the Catawbas as "an irregular people, with no council,—the richest and greatest among them calling himself king." The English endeavors to bring these allies, north and south, into friendly union and to calm their mutual passions were met by accusation, the one upon the other. The valley of Virginia, long after a certain permanence was secured for its settlements, was disturbed by the passing of their warring parties, bent on mischief. Washington, when he was surveying for Lord Fairfax along the lower parts of the Shenandoah, tells us that he sometimes encountered these devastating hordes.

NOTE. The map on the opposite page is from Sayer and Jefferys' reproduction of Danville's *North America* (London), showing the positions of the southern Indians.

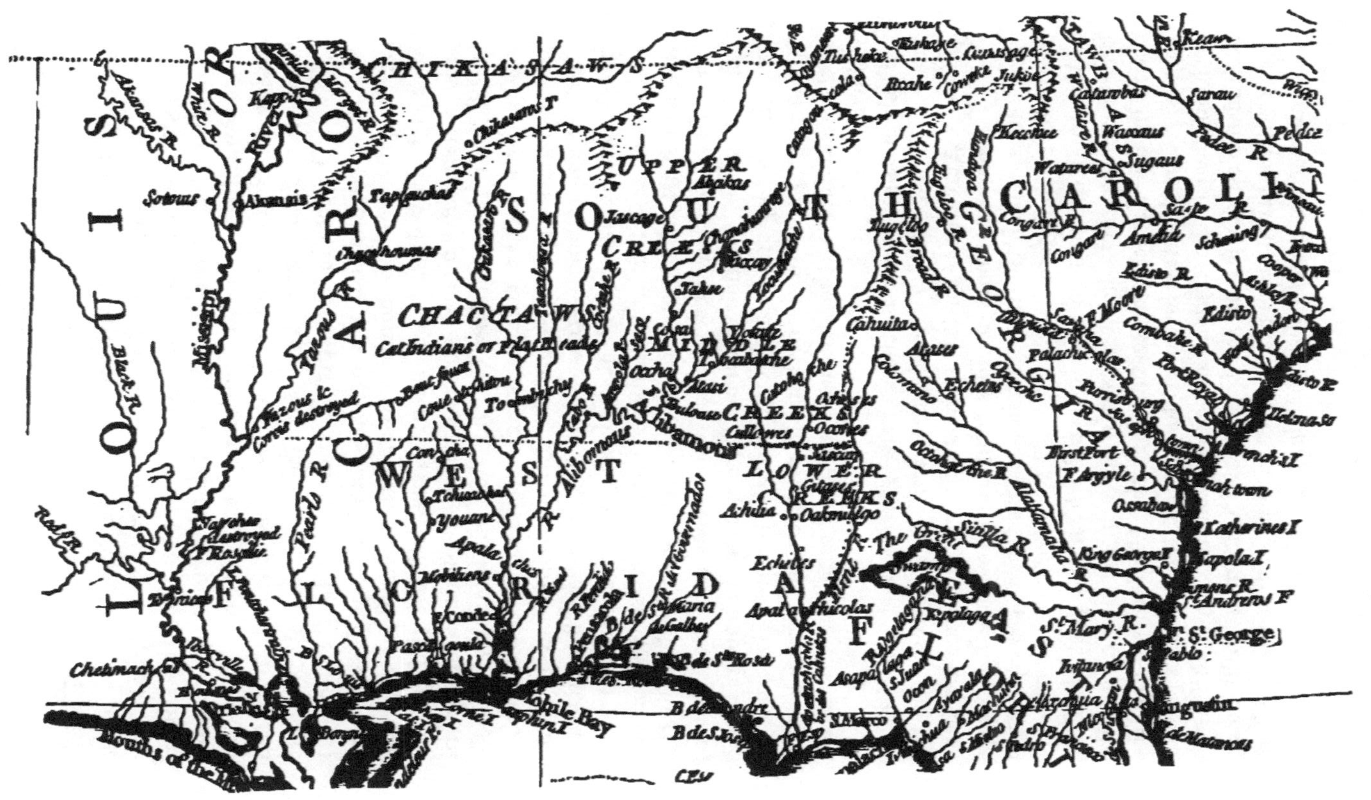

LOUIS
CHIKASAWS
SOUTH CAROLI
GEORGIA
UPPER CREEKS
MIDDLE CREEKS
LOWER CREEKS
CHACTAWS
WEST FLORIDA
Misisipi
Arkansas R.
White R.
Black R.
Red R.
Pearls R.
Mobile Bay
Alibamous
Tuscalooza R.
Chikasaws T.
Cat Indians or Flat Heads
Toocambachy
Edisto R.
Combahe R.
Port Royal
St. Mary R.
St. Katherines I.
Sapola I.
King George F.
St. Andrews F.
St. George
Apalachicolas
Ocmulgee
Cahuita
Echetes
Oakmulgo
Congaree R.
Santee
Sugaus
Waxaus
Catawbas
Keowee
Pedee
Jukise
Pascagoula
Natchez destroyed
Yazous & Coroas destroyed
Chetimachas
Alkansas
Sotous
Edisto
Amelia
Apalaga
S. Juan
Ocon
Palachuclas
Purrisburg
Kaskaskia
Ockmulgee
Tugeloo
Broad R.
Jascage
Tahse
Allabama

By the middle of the century (1750) the French in Louisiana were well intrenched outside New Orleans, in at least eight districts. Not far from the capital they had a post and settlement at Point Coupée on the Mississippi, below the Red River. They maintained a post at Natchitoches toward the Spanish frontier in New Mexico. They had another at Natchez, and still another near the mouth of the Arkansas. There were also settlements dependent on Fort Chartres in the Illinois country, the best compacted of all the occupied regions, numbering at this time, as was computed, eleven hundred whites, three hundred negroes, and about sixty Indian bondmen. This estimate did not include those settlements above Peoria accounted a part of Canada, nor those settlers on the Wabash similarly classed. Beside three native villages near Fort Chartres, with about three hundred warriors, — for the Illinois tribes had been reduced by migrations, — there were, not far away, five distinct French communities: that at Kahokia, below the modern St. Louis; one at St. Philippe, above Fort Chartres; the parent village at Kaskaskia; and another gathering at Prairie du Rocher. Still another, but west of the Mississippi, was that at Ste. Geneviève. A new commander was soon to appear at the fort, Macarty by name; and with him was to come Saussier, an engineer, prepared to strengthen the ramparts of Fort Chartres in the near future, the last hold of the French in the Great Valley.

Districts of Louisiana.

Illinois country.

Besides these centres there were garrisons at Mobile, at Tombeckbé (Tombigbee), and at Alibamons on the Alabama. In this enumeration no reference has been made to more or less temporary and shifting groups of shanties, which the traders had scattered near the centres of the Indian population.

Various garrisons, Mobile, etc.

Vaudreuil counted on the influence which the post at Tombeckbé among the Choctaws would have in keeping that tribe active in the French interest against the Chickasaws and the English. In this way he hoped to preserve the communications of Mobile with the regions dependent on it. From the Tombeckbé mixed parties of the French and Choctaws could go by canoe within seven or eight leagues of the Chickasaws. There were also trails practicable for light guns toward the region

LE PAGE DU PRATZ'S MAP, 1757.

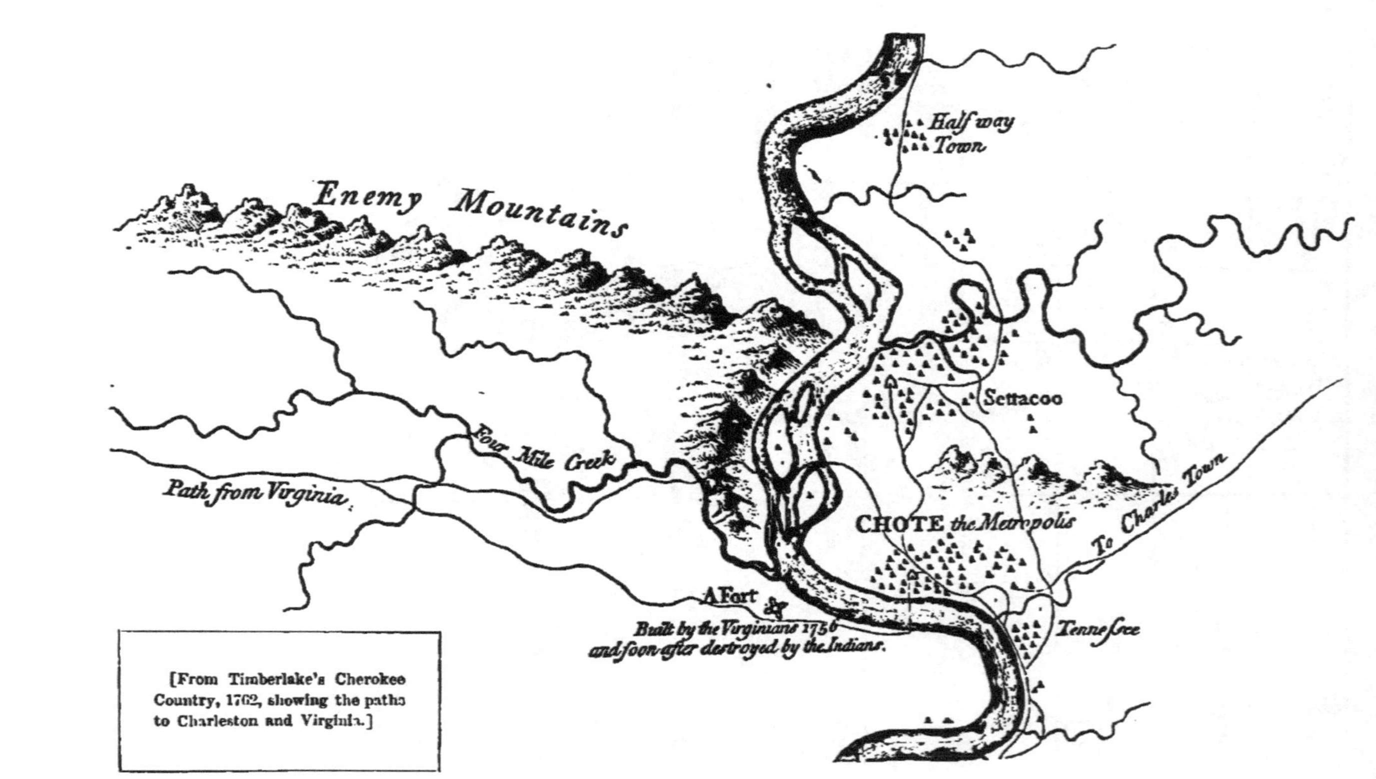

[From Timberlake's Cherokee Country, 1762, showing the paths to Charleston and Virginia.]

frequented by the Carolinians. Nevertheless, a French and Indian invasion of the Atlantic slope beyond the Carolina frontier was hardly yet thought of. It followed a year or two later, in 1753, when the English and Irish — for large numbers of Ulstermen had been settling in Carolina — were pressing the Chickasaws upon the French.

The community at New Orleans was indebted to the Jesuits for the first introduction (1751) of the sugar cane from San Domingo, though it was to be a dozen years or more before the cultivation increased enough for exportation. The growth of tobacco and rice was fostered, and cotton was becoming a productive crop, owing to a rude kind of gin of native origin, used in separating the seeds.

Agricultural products of Louisiana.

In February, 1753, Kerlerec, a naval officer, succeeded Vaudreuil as governor. His policy soon manifested itself. He reduced expenses by cutting down the armed service, and made up for it by paying court to the Choctaws, to induce them to fight his battles.

Kerlerec succeeds Vaudreuil. 1753.

The Carolinians were improving their position. In a treaty at Albany, in 1751, the differences which their immediate neighbors, the Catawbas, had had with the Iroquois were composed. This allied tribe was thus freed for service with the English. The governor of Carolina now pushed his jurisdiction quite up to the mountains, and bargained with the native owners for land between the Savannah and Wateree rivers. This carried the English settlers well up to the sources of the Congaree, which ran midway between the bounding rivers. The governor of North Carolina was not to extend his government for some years yet beyond the Catawba River and the mountains north of it. But he was urging upon the Lords of Trade the seizure of the Alleghany gaps as the only measure to prevent further invasion by the French (1754). The commissioners of this province, with Peter Randolph and William Byrd, sent by Virginia, had, in February, 1756,

Carolina.

NOTE. The map on the two following pages is from the *London Magazine*, Feb. 1760. It was engraved by T. Kitchin "from an Indian draught." The river called the "Missisipi" is really the Ohio,and its two affluents are the Tennessee ("a branch of the Missisipi") and the Cumberland ("Cherokees or Hegohegee R."). It illustrates an account of Gov. Littleton's expedition brought "by the last ship from South Carolina."

Misisipi River
Hogohegee R.
Tallassee
Cherokees or
Coo Saw
Jelleco
Chotee
Tunnasee
Joko
Savanna Hill
Savannas
Great Teriquo
Open Land for Corn fields
Little Teriq
Cunnu
Iwassee
A Branch of Misisipi R.
Gt. Uporsee
Quanuasee
NB, Col. Pawley wrote in 1746, That there was
a Fall ¼ Mile long 12 Miles below Uporsee to
which the French Boats Might come & from
thence transport what they please to any Town
over the Hills. Mr. Kelly a Trader Said the French
Boats came up formerly to great Uporsee.
A New MAP
of the
CHEROKEE NATION
with the Names of the Towns &
Rivers They are Situated on
No. Lat. from 34 to 36

For the London Mag:

d. from an Indian Draught, by T. Kitchin.

brought the Cherokees and Catawbas into new treaty relations, and as a result Fort Loudoun was built at the junction of the Tellico and Tennessee rivers. In June, a force from Virginia was marching to erect a stockade and to take the earliest military possession for the English of what is now the State of Tennessee. As this fort would relieve the Cherokees from maintaining a force at home to hold the French in check, these Indians had agreed to furnish five hundred warriors to aid the English in the war, which we shall later see was now raging at the north. Thus the new fort was thought to be able to counteract any French attempt upon the constancy of the Cherokees. In fact, it gave the English a strong intrenchment, one hundred and fifty miles beyond their most advanced settlement. It was not long before Dinwiddie was complaining that the Indians had not furnished their promised quota. The war had already been begun in Virginia. As a result, at the extreme east the treacherous Acadians, rebelling at an enforced subjection, and having been the first at Chiegnecto to shed blood, had at last been forcibly ejected from their country. The English had borne for ten years the risks of the ill-concealed enmity of this priest-ridden people. As early as 1746, Knowles, the governor of Louisbourg, had foreseen the inevitable necessity of some drastic measure to subdue their treachery. The French Neutrals — as these Acadians were called — had now, since 1755, been deported and scattered along the Atlantic coast of the English colonies. While some who were landed at southern ports had tried to work their way inland to the French flag at Duquesne, others had coasted back to the north in hopes to reach their old homes. Still others had sought the cover of the old banner at New Orleans, and, settling along the Mississippi above that town, had established their new villages on what is known to this day as the Acadian coast.

Fort Loudoun. 1756.

Acadians.

Conrad Weiser, in 1755, was reporting from the Chickasaws that the French were generally hated by the southern tribes, and the Chickasaws knew enough of the French and Choctaw hostility to make their testimony emphatic; but it was always too much to expect constancy of any Indian, and the Creeks were at intervals won over to the Choc-

The French and the southern tribes.

taws' side and against the English. Pownall at this day (1756) pictures the Creeks as debauched by the enemy and alienated beyond recovery, and in 1757 Colonel Bouquet was put in command of some two thousand hastily armed militia to de-

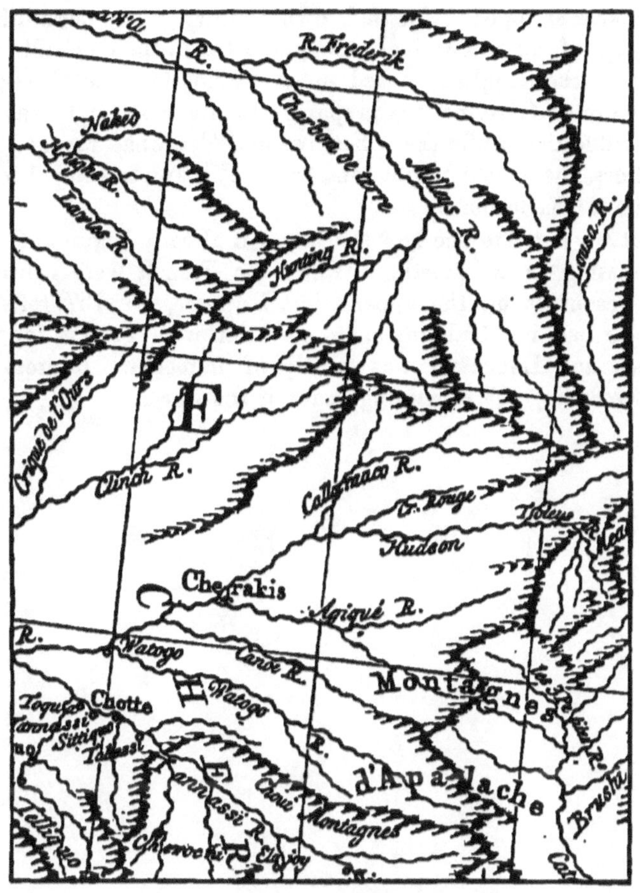

THE CHEROKEE COUNTRY.
[From a *Carte de la Louisiane*, etc., Coveus et Mortier, 1758.]

fend the frontiers. In July we find him, from his headquarters at Charleston, urging the commander at Fort Loudoun to send Indian scouts toward the French settlements, and in August he reports that one of his own scouts had brought in word that the

French were building a new fort on the Ohio. Similar intelligence reached Fort Cumberland at the same time, where the Cherokee contingent sent to help the English was quartered. Hearing also that the French had succeeded in turning the Catawbas against their tribe, and fearing for their villages, these Cherokees stampeded for their own country. The possibilities of an inter-tribal struggle between these old allies of the English caused much trepidation, and Governor Lyttleton of Carolina was preparing for the worst. It was not impossible that while the Choctaws and Catawbas ravaged his frontiers, the enemy might send from Hispaniola a naval force to attack Charleston by sea.

The English anxious.

But we need to see how the war had already begun and was progressing in the north. While the French were centring their resources on the upper Ohio, Kerlerec, in 1757, tells us that he had not had any communication with France for two years; and Louisiana was hardly of immediate interest to France during the remaining years of the war.

CHAPTER XIV.

UNDECLARED WAR.

1750–1754.

The expedition of Céloron had been a distinct enunciation of the French purpose to maintain — war or no war — their hold upon the Ohio valley. The burying of plates at the mouths of the tributaries of the river had evinced a claim to the side valleys as well as the main stream, as indeed the inscriptions on the plates asserted. The English were no longer in doubt of this purpose after they had secured one of the plates, which was obtained "by some artifice." Johnson, as we have seen, notified the Ohio tribes of this French movement, and his own Indians promised to send a belt "through all the nations as far as the Ohio River, that they may immediately know the vile designs of the French." We have seen how the English interests profited, and the French prospects waned, as the result of this warning.

Céloron's expedition. 1749.

It has been said that in the previous year the Ohio Company had received their grant. Now, while Céloron was on his march, the Virginia council, on July 12, 1749, authorized the Loyal Company to survey their eight hundred thousand acres, preparatory to seating families in these western parts. The bounds were to be north of the Fry and Jefferson line, and Dr. Thomas Walker, whom we have already encountered on an earlier exploration, was sent with a squad of surveyors to define the metes. In March, 1750, he passed into the Shenandoah valley. Crossing the site of the modern Staunton, he went over the Alleghanies, and striking New River, followed it to Walker's Creek, now so-called. Taking this stream on his way, he next crossed to the head of Clinch River and entered Cumberland Gap. The region which he now entered was hardly yet alive with the

English surveys made in the Ohio country. 1750.

Walker's expedition.

variegated blooms of the full spring, but its stately trees and blue-grass meadows, the haunts of the buffalo and the deer, were already basking in the promise of the new year. The wandering pioneers followed up the Cumberland River, and finding a spot to their liking, they cleared the ground and built a house, finishing it on April 25. This was in all likelihood the earliest structure for man's use in what is now Kentucky, though it is possible that the French may have earlier erected a cabin opposite the mouth of the Scioto. Walker's journal of this expedition remained in manuscript till 1888, when it was printed at Boston under the editing of William Cabell Rives. This settlement long remained a solitary post, and is found laid down in the maps shortly after it was occupied.

First house in Kentucky.

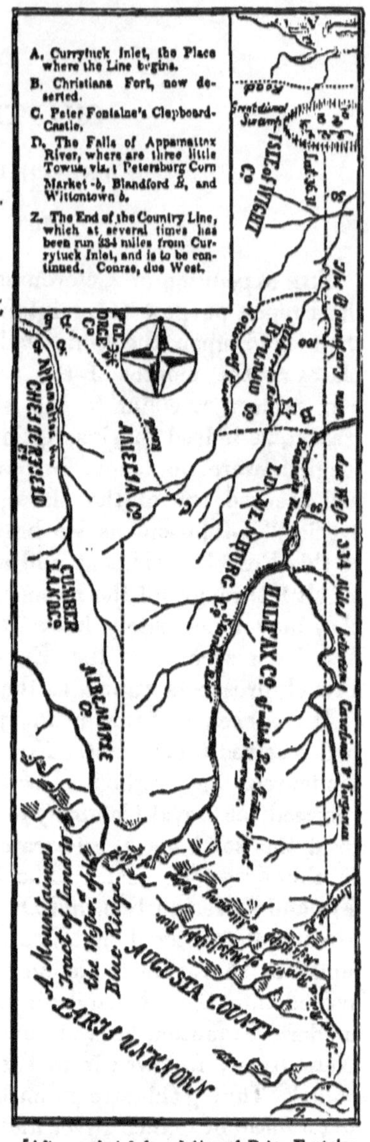

[After a sketch in a letter of Peter Fontaine, July 9, 1752, given in *The Memoirs of a Huguenot Family*, p. 356.]

Traders' routes in the Ohio country.

The traders' routes in the Ohio valley, at this time or shortly after, were farther north. A wagon road from Philadelphia reached the upper Potomac at Watkins's Ferry, and a trail proceeded thence to one of the tributary valleys of the Ohio, beyond the divide. The Ohio Company opened in 1753 a trail from Will's Creek on the Potomac, where its factor had established a storehouse in 1749. This path — later to be made a wagon road by Washington — passed the head of the south branch of the Potomac, and descended on the other side of the gap to the forks of the Youghiogheny, and so on to the mouth of the Monongahela. These routes took the passers away from the haunts of the French till they struck the Ohio itself. It was not so with the trails still farther north, which, after passing the mountains, came to the Alleghany or one of its eastern branches, where the English packmen were likely to fall in with the French coming from Lake Erie or the Seneca country.

The objective point of all these routes, English and French, was the forks of the Ohio, where the Alleghany and Monongahela met. The site of the modern Pittsburgh, occupied at this time by an Indian village of twenty wigwams, with fifty or more people living there, was thus a position vital to whomsoever possessed the Ohio valley, and the predestined scene of an obstinate but wavering conflict.

The forks of the Ohio.

The conditions of this coming struggle were in geographical connections favorable to the English; but not so in all other respects. An unfortunate dispute between Virginia and Pennsylvania as to their bounds did much to dispirit settlers and sow dissensions among them. Pennsylvania claimed that the charter given to Penn carried her limits beyond the forks, much as the modern State is bounded, though a longitudinal five degrees west of the Delaware River was not easily computed in view of the crooked course of that river. But Virginia, then and long afterward grasping in her territorial claims, denied it. She pressed a vague demand to an indefinite northwestern extension, which stretched her newly created county of Augusta to the Mississippi and even beyond, "up into the land throughout west and northwest." She was quite ready to call all settlers inhabiting this bountiful domain and up to 40° north latitude her loyal people. By another claim, Virginia was equally at variance with Maryland, and she would restrict both that province and Pennsylvania by a meridian which cut the source of the Potomac. Since this river had two upper branches, meridian lines cutting the springs of each gave a considerable triangle of

Boundary disputes of Virginia, Maryland, and Pennsylvania.

intermediate territory, which the rival provinces disputed about, each naturally standing by that meridian which increased its own limits of jurisdiction.

All such disputes embarrass settlements, and the country toward the forks of the Ohio had not failed to suffer from this cause. In time it became further apparent that it was the interest of leading Virginians to give a personal advocacy to the claim of their province because it improved the rights of the Ohio Company, and Pennsylvanians thought that something of the undue precipitancy of Virginia in pressing her demands even to the verge of actual war betokened such selfish and individual interests. So matters of this kind served to alienate these neighboring provinces from a common object, while their rivals, the French, in their movements toward the Ohio, were certain to act with a single purpose. The other colonies saw this, and Governor Glen of South Carolina had not hesitated to offer a warning rebuke.

George Croghan and Pennsylvania.

Pennsylvania, in her contest with the French, had an active guardian of her interests in George Croghan, whose services in behalf of the province were long and dutiful. He claimed at a later day that he had never asked from the province any remuneration for his time, in all that he did to keep the Indians fast to the English policy, beyond being recompensed for the hire of horses used in running expresses. Croghan and Colonel William Trent were brothers-in-law, and had recently formed a partnership in the fur trade. They clearly saw that the protection of that trade required the English to fortify themselves at the forks of the Ohio. To this end they gained the consent of the Indians, and asked the Pennsylvania Assembly to order a stockade built there. The project, though backed by the Proprietary, failed of support in that Quaker body, and nothing was done, though the assembly had organized two counties in this western region which had claims to be defended, — York County, organized in the southwestern part of the province in 1749; and Cumberland County, taking all lands within her bounds west and north of York County and west of the Susquehanna, which had just been set up (1750).

Colonel William Trent.

NOTE. The opposite map is from Mitchell's *Map of the British Colonies* (1775). It shows Walker's and other frontier English settlements, and the traders' routes in eastern Kentucky and Tennessee.

Walkers
Extent of the English Settlements 1750.
Bear Grass Cr.
Clinch's R.
Pelisipi River
Hogohegee or Callamaco
Cherakee
Watogo O.T.
River
Canoe R.
Watogo R
Upper
Toqua
Tellico
Settiquo
Gr.Telliquo
an English Factory
Chatuga
Euphasee
Euphasee R.
Telliquo
Tomatly
Nontealy
Chewochee
Elejoy
Coweechee
Hyoree
Watoga
Ivassee
Quanessee English Factory
Noyowee
Lit.Telliquo
Naquassee
Kewochee
Midd
Tasache
Cuttagochee
Cholee
Nanquchee
Desert Country by all Accounts
Estowee
Tugeloo
Lower
Cherakee
Chatuga R.
Settlements
H
K
E
A
R

Virginia, as represented in the Ohio Company, moved promptly. On September 16, 1750, Christopher Gist received his instructions from the company's agents. By these orders he was to go as far as the falls of the Ohio, observe all passes, make note of the tribes on the way and compute their numbers, and look out for good level lands fit to be selected under their grant. Gist started from Colonel Cresap's on October 31, 1750. His journal has been preserved, as published by Governor Pownall in his *Topographical Description of North America* (London, 1776), and his route is pricked on the English maps of Mitchell and Evans. Gist was at Logstown on November 25, where he learned that George Croghan and Andrew Montour, sent out by Pennsylvania, had a little earlier passed that way.

Gist sent out by the Ohio Company. 1750.

His journal.

The exact position of this trading-post, Logstown, is in some dispute. It was seventeen or eighteen miles below the forks, near the modern town of Economy, but whether on the north or south side of the river is in doubt. It was very likely on both sides, or at least some of its buildings may have been on each bank. The principal settlement was perhaps on the north side, where it is placed by Mitchell, Evans, Kalm, Christian Post, and Hutchins. Croghan, in 1765, places it on the south side; and Arthur Lee, in 1784, speaks of it as "formerly a settlement on both sides of the river."

Logstown.

Gist reached the Muskingum River on December 14, and saw an English flag flying above Croghan's house. Here he found some Wyandots, divided in their interests between the English and French, perhaps a hundred families of them, a fragment of the ancient Hurons. They had been recently admitted to the Miami confederacy, and were now scattered in their villages along the southern shore of Lake Erie, between points marked by the modern Cleveland and Toledo. They were centred about Sandusky Bay, and this region, judging from a legend on Mitchell's map, was regarded by the English as the chief point of Indian interest.

Gist at the Muskingum, December, 1750.

Sandusky Bay.

Gist had no reason to complain of his reception. Here he overtook Croghan, the idol of the Scotch-Irish traders, and saw a companion whom Croghan had, almost as conspicuous as Croghan himself in this wilderness life, and

Croghan and Montour.

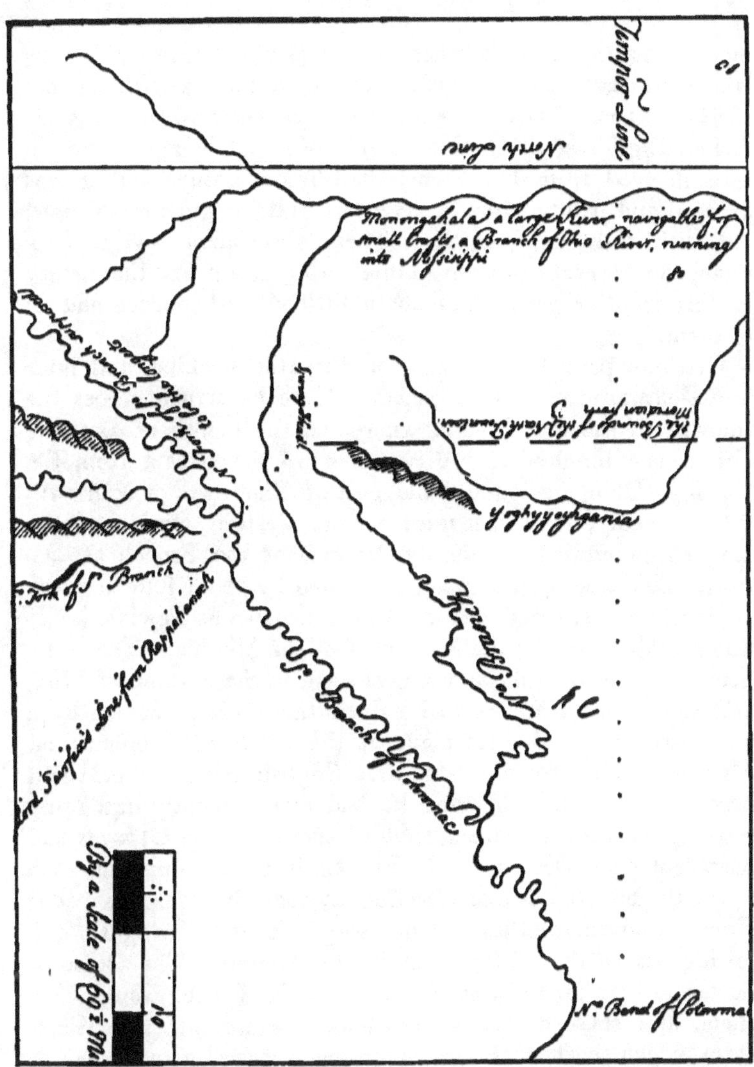

[Colonel Thomas Cresap's manuscript map of the sources of the Potomac, following a sketch in *Sharpe's Correspondence*, vol. i. p. 72 (in *Maryland Archives*, vol. vi.). It shows the divide between the Potomac and the Monongabela and the line of Fairfax manor, running from the source of the North Branch.]

more picturesque. This brisk personage was Andrew Montour, whom we have already spoken of as on the warpath against the Catawbas. These Indians, some years before, had slain his father, Big Tree, an Oneida chief. Montour had a European face, derived from his French half-breed mother, but it was greased and painted like a savage's; and his garb was decked out with tinkling spangles. These three men — Gist, Croghan, and Montour — were an interesting group, and the history of this frontier period was not a little shaped by each and all of them.

Gist now passed to a village on the Hockhocking, and later to a Delaware town on the Scioto. Here he struck across the country to the Big Miami, where, at the mouth of Loramie Creek, one hundred and fifty miles up the stream from the Ohio, he founded the post of Picktown, or Pickawillany, then the most remote western station of the English, maintained in hardy defiance of the French at Detroit. This trading-post was surrounded by about four hundred Indian families, forming a settlement known as Tawixtwi. It was presided over by the head chief of the Miamis. The storehouses had been built, as we have seen, in the autumn of 1750, and the Pennsylvanians had gained the Indians' assent by a free distribution of gifts made at the hands of Croghan and Montour. Gist found about fifty English packmen gathered here, and with their backing he had little difficulty in making a treaty with the Indians assembled there. Some Ottawas had been sent from Detroit in the French interest, to prevent such a treaty, but the Miamis scoffed at their interference. The French and their allies did not forget it, and during the following winter they killed fifty of the Miamis. The Ottawas, however, were far from as constant as the French would have them, and these deserters occasionally came into the Miami town, which the French always approached with great risks.

Pickawillany.

Galissonnière, as we have seen, felt, before he was recalled, that the situation in this Ohio region was becoming grave, and the home government had evinced little interest in his scheme of settling French peasants thereabouts. In December, 1750, he had warned the ministry that the communications of Canada and Louisiana were in danger. To Champigny it seemed as if the dominance of

Galissonnière and the Ohio region.

trade over agriculture was sure to lead to evil, and Galissonnière forebodingly pointed to the farming and home life of the English and the growth which it prompted, as likely in the end to wrest the western country from the control of the French. If the English could only make and keep a gap in the chain of the French posts southward to the Mississippi, they would, as he thought, have every advantage in alienating the Indians still adhering to the French. In this manner, these rivals would open their way to Louisiana and ultimately to Mexico. Such were the views which Galissonnière was now urging in Paris, and he had the sympathy of his successor, Jonquière, in Quebec.

There were two places in the western country the possession of which was necessary to the French cause: one was Detroit, the other was Niagara.

Detroit and Niagara.

Céloron had been put in command at the straits in 1750. Here the Bourbon flag was flying from a palisaded town, and on either hand, up and down the Detroit River, for seven or eight miles, numerous Indian villages were scattered. The fixed population of the post was, perhaps, five hundred, but including the dependent tribes, the whole number of souls under French control was about twenty-five hundred. The savage part of this motley assemblage was essentially nomadic. Some bands of the Hurons still left there were soon to follow their brothers to the southern shore of Lake Erie, to be better known there as Wyandots. Here they were to become neighbors to the Ottawas already cabined in that region.

The French of the straits were making the best of a rather dull life. A few families had come there to get the bounties which were promised; but on the whole, young men predominated, and there were few girls to make them wives. Such was the place held, now by the French and later by the English, in the hope of controlling the destinies of the Ohio valley. Forbes at Duquesne in 1758, and Wayne at the Fallen Timbers in 1794, were at a still later day to change its masters, with the downfall successively of the French and English flags.

The main channel of communication from Detroit southward was by Fort Miami at the confluence of the St. Joseph and the Maumee rivers, and thence to the Shawnee town at the mouth of the Scioto, the modern Ports-

Communications of Detroit.

month. A second trail ran from Fort Miami to Fort Ouiatanon on the Wabash. In this direction the French government had strengthened their position by grants of land, the titles to which were not all extinguished till a century and more later.

The Niagara route.

The more direct route into the Ohio valley from Montreal was of course from the Niagara post, and so on to the more easterly portages of Lake Erie. We have seen that Céloron in 1749 had gone by Lake Chautauqua. A better route was now recognized as passing by Presqu' Isle. The safety of these passages depended upon the temper of the Iroquois, and both English and French had efficient and wily agents to employ among them, in William Johnson and Joncaire. The Irish squire of the Mohawk was quite the equal of the Frenchman in the arts which allured the savage. Johnson had been made a member of the New York council in May, 1750, and he told his associates that declared hostilities would be more tolerable than the uncertainties of the game of bribery, which both French and English were now playing. "I can at any time get an Indian to kill any man by paying him a small matter," he said. "Going on in this manner is worse than open war." The fact was that what one side did the other must do, and there seemed no remedy as long as peace ostensibly lasted.

William Johnson and Joncaire.

The Iroquois.

Jonquière was not only sending warning letters to Governor Clinton, while the English government was entering counter protests in Paris, but the Canadian governor was instructing his emissaries to win over the Cayugas. As the season went on, Conrad Weiser discovered through his spies that the Senecas were in the same way being roused to attack the English on the Ohio. The French priests were doing their part, and it was reported they were making converts by the hundred among the Onondagas. The results of all these agencies were enough to make Jonquière confident. "The English interests among the Six Nations can be of no consideration any longer," he said. "The Indians speak with contempt of the New York and Albany people, and much the same of the rest of the English colonies."

Oswego.

Amid all this supposed defection of the Iroquois, the English still held fast to Oswego, and its increasing trade showed that the French traffic was proportionately decreasing, and that the founding of Fort Rouillé (Toronto) had not done what was hoped for.

It was evident that Oswego must fall, or at least its capture be attempted by the French, as a first act of declared hostilities. Galissonnière, in Paris, was urging preparations for it. So Jonquière was instructed to stir up the Iroquois to attempt its destruction. He was cautioned to be polite in all his intercourse with the English, so as not to disclose his purpose.

No business could better suit Piquet, the Jesuit master of La Présentation (Ogdensburg). The government at Quebec had for some time supplied him with clothing, arms, and ammunition, to win the confederates and to get their consent to build a fort at Irondequoit. This priest, saint or rascal as he was to one and another, was a man of energetic purpose, fertile in devices, and he had completely won the admiration of both the civil and ecclesiastical rulers at Quebec. He is said to have boasted that his services did more for France than troops or money. His ardor was sometimes questionable, at least, when his garb as a priest became the cloak of a skulking enemy.

Piquet.

It was he who was now to do service in reconnoitring Oswego. He discovered that there were hills on all sides to command it, — a fact not lost upon Montcalm a few years later. He was aware that the secret of Oswego as a trading-post depended upon the fact that two beaver-skins would buy as good a bracelet at Oswego as ten at Niagara.

There was cause for alarm at Albany, when it was learned that the French had really secured command of Lake Ontario by launching a three-masted vessel at Fort Frontenac. This ugly fact was one of the points which came up in July, 1751, at a conference which Clinton had called at Albany. The purpose of the meeting was to form some alliance among the colonies, if possible, and a league with the Six Nations. The only colonies which responded were Massachusetts and South Carolina, — the latter for the first time brought to an acknowledgment of her joint interests with New York. The southern province's present object was to mediate between the Catawbas and the Iroquois. The reconciliation of these tribes had long been desired, and often attempted, as their enmity was awkward

The French on Lake Ontario.

Albany conference. 1751.

Iroquois and Catawbas.

for the colonies north and south, considering that both were friendly to their immediate English neighbors. The contests of these foes usually taking place in Virginia, the government of that province had an almost equal interest in the pacification of the combatants. Colonel Lee of Virginia had already tried within a year or two to see what effect a bestowal of gifts on each would do. Governor Glen of Carolina had only recently been complaining that the Senecas, on pretense of warring on the Catawbas, were plundering the whites of his province. The Senecas had replied that if the Catawbas would send some chief men to Albany, they would confirm a peace. This brought about the meeting at Albany under consideration, when the grounds of reconciliation were accepted by both tribes, the Catawbas agreeing to restore their Iroquois prisoners.

Farther than this, Clinton got little satisfaction out of the conference, and he grew to feel that nothing but compulsory legislation on the part of Parliament could ever bring the colonies into a pact for common defense.

Jonquière and Clinton.

Jonquière, at Quebec, was hardly less uneasy than his antagonist at Albany. He felt that the government at Paris, in requiring him to drive the English from the Ohio, was putting a task upon him difficult, if not impossible, to accomplish, unless he could be reinforced by royal troops; and he could get no promise of these. He therefore asked to be recalled.

Affairs on the Ohio.

Meanwhile, the news from the Ohio was disquieting. Smallpox had broken out among the French, and there was great scarcity in their supplies. Longueil reported that if the disease would only seize the rebel tribes about them, it would be "fully as good as an army." Lingeris at Ouiatanon sent word that the best he could do with the Kickapoos and Mascoutins was to keep them neutral. "They were nourishing vipers," as Vaudreuil sent word from New Orleans, if they persisted in harboring the English traders.

Jonquière dies. 1752.

It looked as if everything was going so far wrong that it is no wonder that Jonquière desired a quieter life. Besides, he was now a man of seventy-seven, and could ill bear the strain. It happened that before he could be relieved, he suddenly died in the spring of 1752 (March 6), not in the best of humor with a people that believed stories of his corruption and saw evidence of his nepotism. He sank amid the last solemnities of his religion, but his detractors said that with all his riches he died amid the smoking glare of tallow dips, his parsimony even in that hour forbidding the cost of wax. Longueil, who was in authority at Montreal, hastened to Quebec to take the reins of power during the interregnum.

We left Gist at Pickawillany, and need to follow him farther. He was impressed with what he deemed the power of the Miamis or Twightwees, as, following the English habit, he called them. "They are accounted the most powerful people to the westward of the English settlements," he says; "at present very well affected toward the English and fond of their alliance with them." They had sought this connection by breaking with the French and passing over the Wabash.

Gist at Pickawillany with the Twightwees.

Gist's course from this point would, according to his instructions, have taken him to the falls of the Ohio, but rumors reached him of parties of French lingering in that region, and he thought it prudent to retrace his steps in part, so as to descend the Scioto. At its mouth he found a colony of Shawnees, living in what was usually called the Lower Shawnee town. This village had not been long established, but it had already become a station for traders. It was about two hundred and seventy miles from Philadelphia as the Pennsylvania packmen commonly went. The Shawnees at this time were partly at least reclaimed from the French interests, which they had embraced in the last war.

Shawnees of the Scioto.

Gist had now in his circuitous route come in contact with all the great divisions of the Ohio tribes, and for the most part he felt that the English could depend upon them in the coming struggle. Governor Hamilton of Pennsylvania had already, through his scouts, come to this conclusion, and had communicated it to Clinton in May, 1750. Later in the year, Croghan was on the Ohio, reporting that the French were trying to persuade the Indians to let them build a fort. The Indians on their part were warning the English that war must come, and that they should be prepared for it by building a fort themselves. Croghan's plan was to induce the Shawnees and Twightwees to move farther up the Ohio, so as to

The Ohio tribes.

be nearer English support. He was confident the Wyandots toward Lake Erie would stand firm. In the following April (1751), the Indians in a conference with Croghan prepared a distinct request to the Pennsylvania authorities to fortify the forks of the Ohio for the protection of them and the English traders. A few weeks later, Croghan and Montour confronted the French agents at Logstown, each distributing presents to the Indians. There was such decided success on the part of the English in this rivalry that Joncaire apologized to Croghan for the necessity, in obedience to his orders, of attempting to diminish the English influence. Croghan speaks highly of Montour's aid in this work: "He is very capable of doing business, and is looked upon by all the Indians as one of their chiefs."

The Delawares and Iroquois.

Unfortunately for the English, the Delawares and Iroquois — who occupied the eastern and southeastern parts of what is now the State of Ohio, and were thus interposed between the Wyandots, Miamis, and Shawnees, and the English frontiers — were the least to be trusted in the coming emergency. The Delawares were nowhere gathered in compact settlements, and had not forgotten the treatment which they had received from the Pennsylvanians in being ejected from the Susquehanna regions. Gist says that the Delaware town on the east side of the Scioto was the farthest west of these wandering people. They had about five hundred warriors, and in Gist's judgment could be depended upon. By this time more of the Iroquois were living on the upper Ohio than were left in their original country in New York, and in Weiser's opinion it was quite uncertain how they would turn when pressed to take sides, — especially the Mingoes, a branch of the Senecas, who were prominent in this region.

The Lower Shawnee town.

This Lower Shawnee town, where Gist now crossed the Ohio, is described a few years later by Mitchell as having "an English factory, and being by water four hundred miles from the forks of the Ohio." It was on March 13, 1751, that Gist thus entered upon the Kentucky territory. With the aid of a compass, he records his courses carefully, and we easily follow his further progress. He went

NOTE. The opposite map is from Mitchell's *Map of the British Colonies* (1775), showing Gist's route south of the Ohio River.

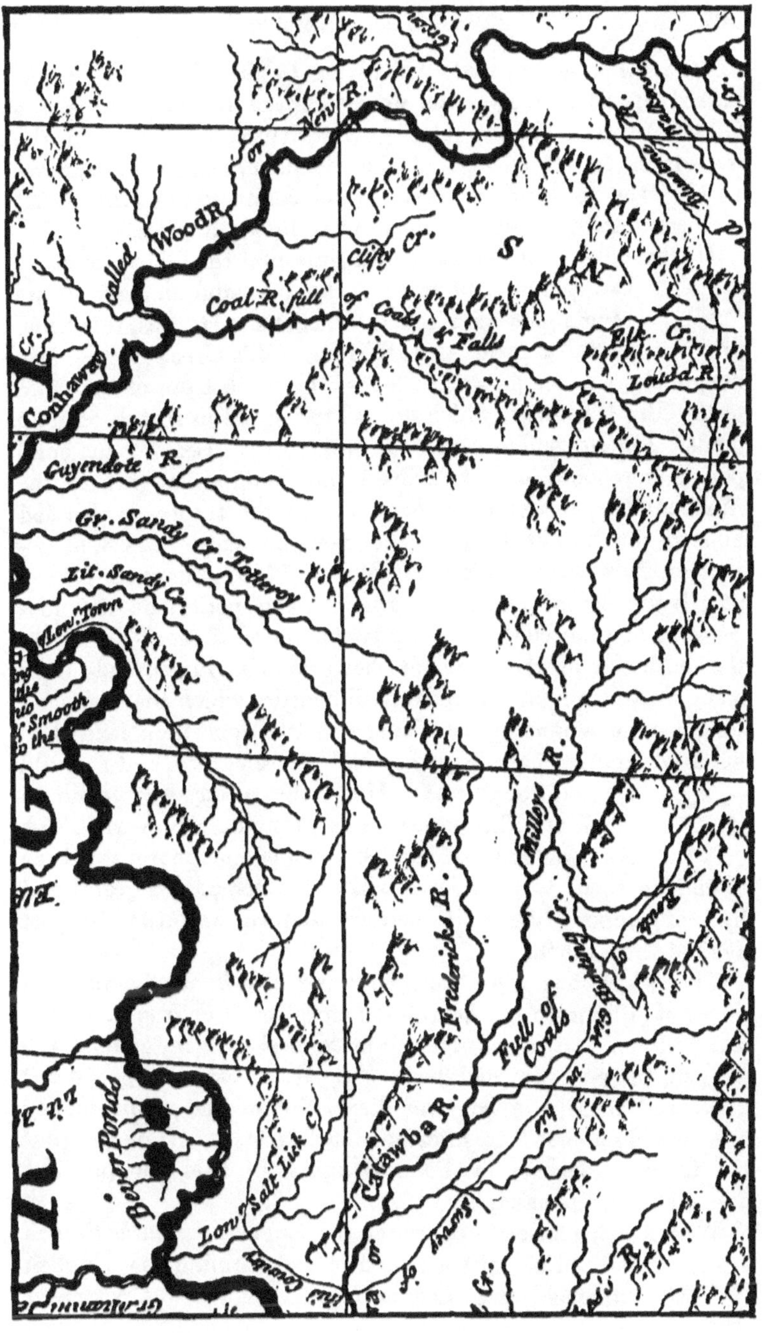

or New R.
called WoodR.
Clifty Cr.
S
Coal R. full of Coals & Falls
Elk Cr.
Louisa R.
Conhaway
Guyendote R.
Gr. Sandy Cr. Totteroy
Lit. Sandy Cr.
Smooth
Milleys R.
Fredericks R.
Full of Coals
Catawba R.
Lower Salt Lick C.
Bever Ponds

up the Licking, crossed the divide to the Kentucky River, passed up that stream, and went eastward to the head of the Clinch River. Thence passing New River, he went over the mountains to the springs of the Roanoke, — thus in part reversing the route of Walker, — and completed in May, 1751, his protracted journey of about twelve hundred miles.

Gist's second expedition. 1751-52.

He found on his return to Virginia that the Ohio Company had planned other work for him, and on July 16, its agents gave him new instructions. He was, this time, to find a good passage from Will's Creek to the Monongahela, whence he was to course the south bank of the Ohio to the Big Kanawha, which he was to ascend in search of good lands. On November 4, he was on his way. Leaving the company's storehouse at Will's Creek, he found a new gap to the Monongahela, nearer than that used by the traders, which led him to the middle fork of the Youghiogheny. He was absent on this second quest till March, 1752, and upon his report being made, the company in October petitioned the governor to be allowed to take up two hundred thousand acres on the south side of the Ohio. Other grants having already been made in this region, there were difficulties which the company sought to surmount by promising to settle upon their lands two hundred families more than they had before agreed, and to build an additional fort. Upon this a way was found to yield, and the petition was granted. In April, 1752, Gist was sent among the Indians once more, this time to induce them to take land within the company's grant, and by living among the white settlers to form a mutual support against the French.

The Ohio Company and the Indians.

The Virginians were thus outdoing the Pennsylvanians in offers of alliance, for when, just before this (February, 1752), the Indians had asked Hamilton to assist them against the French, the governor had been obliged to acknowledge (April 24) that "those who have the disposition of the public money are entirely averse" to affording such help. This meant that the Quaker element in Pennsylvania still held the political ascendency in its assembly.

The French despondent.

With all this lack of concert on the English part, the French had not as yet succeeded in undermining the English influence; and when in April Longueil was possessed of Jonquière's power, he complained that he was invested with the government "under very unfortunate circumstances." "The English," he adds, "look with longing eyes both on the lands of the Beautiful River [Ohio] and generally on all that vast country." Joncaire's reports had disheartened him. The Piankashaws had declared against the French, he learned, and nothing could save the Ohio country but to throw into it a sufficient force.

As the summer came on, the Virginians were again astir. Gist, with Colonel Trent and others, met the Indians at Logstown in the latter part of May, and the meeting was prolonged till toward the middle of June (1752). It was the object of the Ohio Company to get the tribes to confirm the cessions which the Indians had made at Lancaster in 1744. They soon encountered opposition from the Shawnees and Mingoes, but with the assistance of Croghan and Montour, representing the interests of Pennsylvania, the disaffected tribes yielded, and between June 9 and 13 difficulties were composed, and a deed was finally passed. The Indians at the same time agreed not to molest the Virginia settlers on the south side of the Ohio. They also, recounting the neglect by Pennsylvania of their request, repeated to the Virginia government their wish to have an English fort at the forks of the Ohio.

Conference at Logstown. 1752.

The way was now opened for settlers to push down the Monongahela, and twelve families were soon picking out their home lots along its banks. Gist was instructed to lay out a town and fort at the mouth of Chartier's Creek, four miles below the forks, while Trent, laden with messages and gifts, was sent forward to the Miamis' country to confirm the alliance of these western tribes. He found the conditions here far from as satisfactory as he had left them near the forks.

Settlers on the Monongahela.

A season of disquietude among the French, when their traders had been pushed back toward Detroit, had been followed in the early summer of 1752 by an organized attack on the English post at Pickawillany. The act was simply necessary, if the French were to maintain their position at Detroit. The half-breed, Charles Langlade, had come from Mackinac with a following of Ottawas and Chippeways, and he

Pickawillany attacked. 1752.

was equal to the emergency. Céloron found in him an active lieutenant, and with a force of about two hundred and forty French and Indians, Langlade fell upon the Miami town, and savage and English trader fled before him. By this attack, the valleys of the Maumee and Miami were delivered from the presence of the pestilent English. The legend on Evans's later map says that it was this success which prompted the French to undertake their ambitious scheme of establishing armed posts throughout the Ohio valley, and so finally provoked the armed outbreak under Washington.

Meanwhile the movements of the rival powers in Europe were bringing the conflict nearer. Charles Townshend was urging (1752) warlike measures in the English Commons. Bigot, the Canadian intendant, was pressing like measures on the Paris ministry. In July, the Marquis Duquesne de Menneville had reached Quebec, relieving Longueil of his temporary command. His instructions recapitulated the old story of La Salle's discovery of the Mississippi, as a warrant for the French claims, and in the main he was authorized to carry out the projects which Galissonnière had advocated. The government fairly acknowledged that their past policy of inciting one tribe against another had failed, and there was no resort now but to exert a direct force themselves. Canada, at this time, could muster about thirteen thousand militia, and Duquesne ordered stated drills among them. He also put in as good condition as possible the small body of regular troops which were scattered in the various garrisons.

Portents in Europe. 1752.

Duquesne in Quebec.

The strategic point seemed for the present to be among the Miamis. In the spring of 1753, Joncaire was at work among them, and they soon sued for peace. The assemblies of Pennsylvania and Virginia, anticipating this defection, had bestirred themselves, and had ordered Trent and Montour to carry gratuities to these western tribes. It was too late, however, to regain them. The French had accomplished their purpose.

The Miamis support the French. 1753.

NOTE. The map on the opposite page is from Sayer and Jefferys' reproduction of Danville's *North America* (London), showing the geography of the Ohio valley as understood in the middle of the eighteenth century.

TWIGTWEES
ILINOIS
MIYAMIS
of Virginia & New England by Charter
Buffalo R
F. Orleans
Missouri
Rock
Missouri R.
Osage R
Burning Hills
Pimitoui L.
Ilinois R
Miamis
le Rocher or the Rock
Pecuarias or Pimitoui
Emicouen R.
Kahokias & Tamaroas Fort
Matchigamis
Ft Chartres
Kaskakias
Grand L.
Cave in a Rock
C. St. Antony
French Fort ruined
Ft a la Course
Wabash or St. Jerom R.
Slackado Fort Fr.
Fr Fort
Eng Fort
Miyamis R.
Miyamis
Lower Shanan's
Ohio or Allegany R
Gr. Sandy
Guyandot
Little Kunhaway
Kunhaway
Falls
The Little Canaway R
Walker's Settlement 1750
Cumberland or Shannowens R
Coles R
Cherakees R
Holstons R
Bounds of Virginia and Carolina
GRANVILLES
R. St. Francis
Chikasaw R
Cherakees
Valoga
Chestoue
Tomase
Charna
ROKEES
Tamate
Keowee
Congart
Roanoke
PROPE.
Shanopin
F. du Quesne built by French 1754
Potomack
North Ridge
James R
Pig Cr
Logs T.
Alligany
Elks Eye
NORTH CAROLINA
VIRGINIA

It was now evident that the English must direct their close attention upon the forks of the Ohio. Dinwiddie had already, in December, 1752, appealed to the Board of Trade for aid in establishing some forts on the Ohio. He had

Forks of the Ohio.

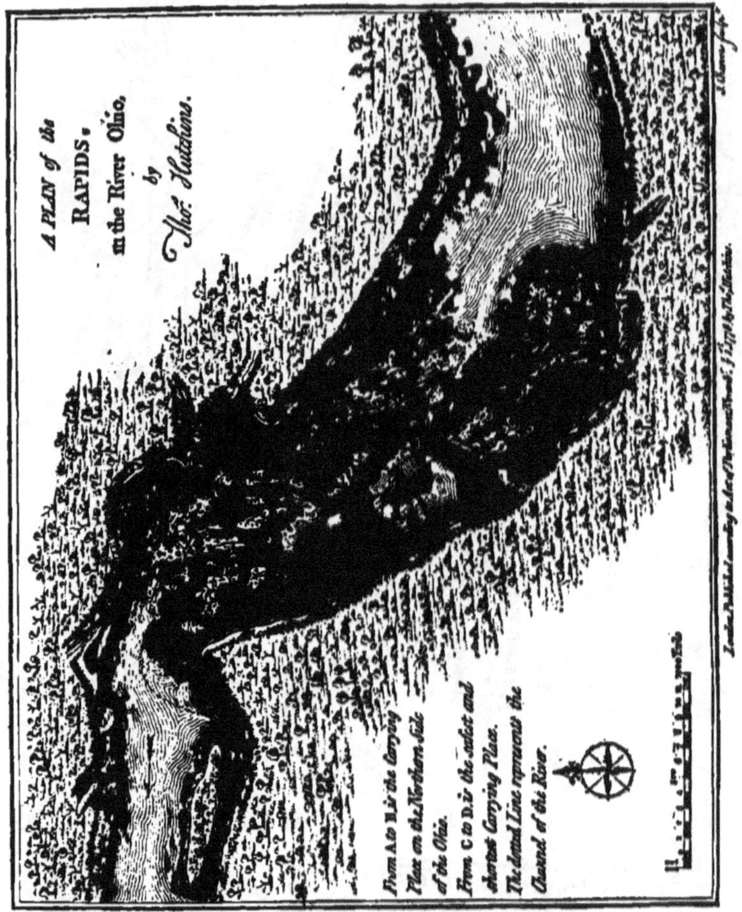

[From Hutchins's *Topographical Description of Virginia*, London, 1778.]

also asked for twenty or thirty small cannon. He informed the board that a practicable road, made by the Indians, already existed, by which with only eighty miles of land-carriage such guns could be carried from the head of the Potomac to a branch

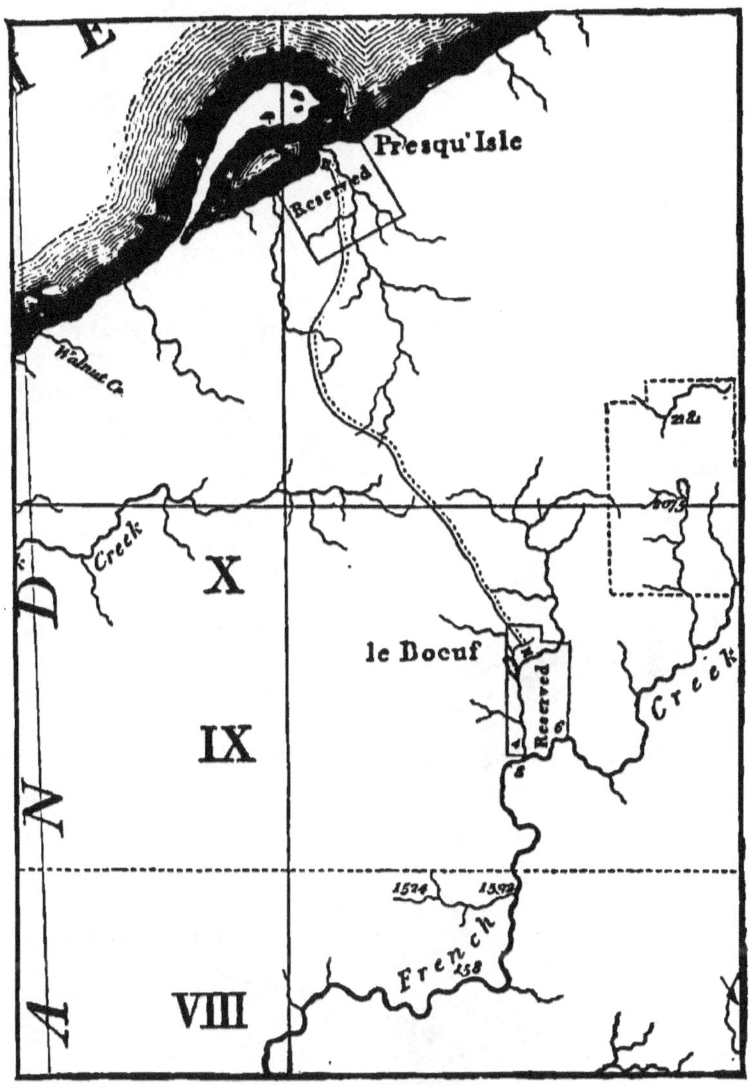

THE FRENCH CREEK ROUTE.

[From Howell's *Map of Pennsylvania*, 1791.]

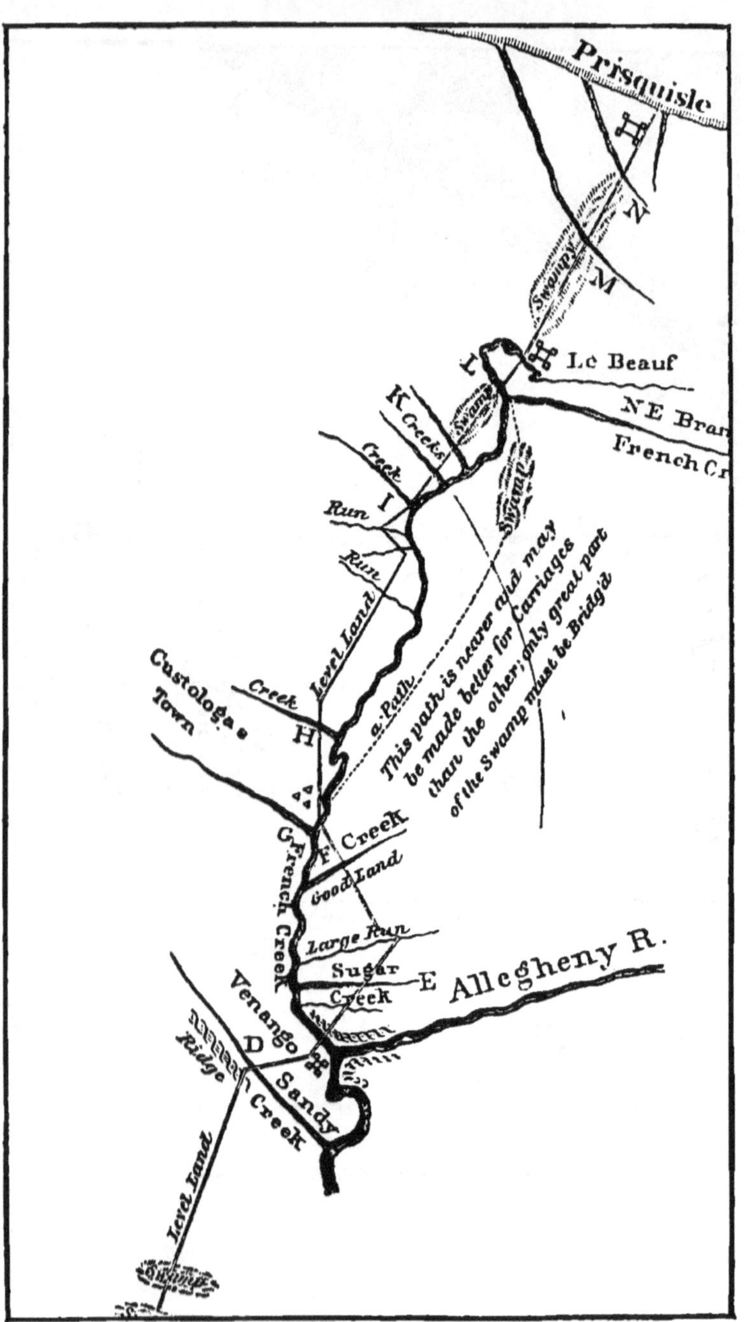

Prisquisle
N
M
Swampy
Le Beauf
NE Bran
French Cr
L
K
Creeks
Swamp
Creek
I
Run
Run
Swamp
Level Land
a Path
This path is nearer and may be made better for Carriages than the other; only great part of the Swamp must be Bridg'd
Custologa's Town
Creek
H
G
F Creek
Good Land
French Creek
Large Run
Sugar Creek
E
Allegheny R.
Venango
D
Ridge
Sandy Creek
Level Land
Swamp

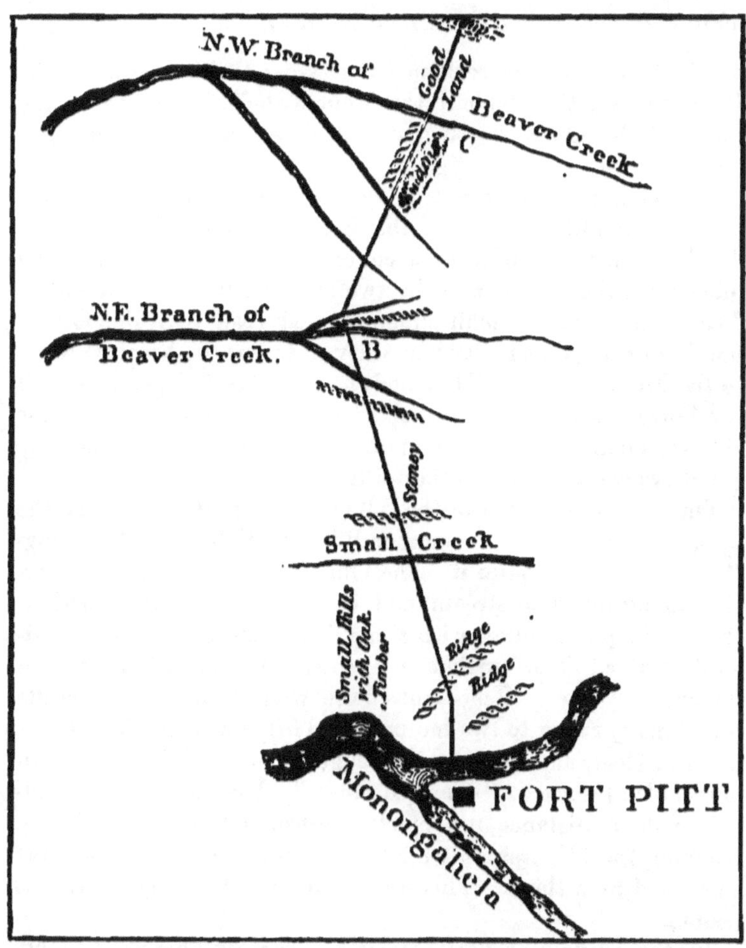

NOTE. This and the opposite map (continuing this one at the top) are from an original contemporary sketch, reproduced in the Aspinwall Papers, in 4 *Mass. Hist. Coll.*, vol. ix. p. 302. It shows the usual route from Fort Pitt to Venango, Le Bœuf, and Presqu' Isle. The capital letters are explained in a key giving the width of the various streams, to which the letters are attached. The key adds: "Opposite Venango the river is 200 yards wide; the mouth of French Creek 100 yards wide; a wagon road may be made over any of the hills."

of the Ohio. It was reckoned that from Will's Creek on the Potomac, over the divide to the Monongahela, and so on to the forks of the Ohio, was a distance of one hundred and eight miles.

It was a pressing question whether the French or English would first get to the forks in force. The English must reach it by a course of more than a hundred miles from the Potomac, or by two hundred from Philadelphia. The Pennsylvanians maintained a good road to Will's Creek, but from this point it was necessary to follow the Virginia route to the Monongahela. They had, however, an independent trail for horses, which followed up the Susquehanna and ran for sixty-seven miles over the mountains, and reached the Alleghany about twelve miles above the forks.

Routes to the forks.

Once at the junction of the Alleghany and Monongahela, the position was a commanding one, well worth the struggle to acquire it. The Ohio lay in front, with a watershed along its main stream, and branches of over two hundred thousand square miles, with about five thousand miles of navigable water. The current moved at three miles an hour in its ordinary flow. The banks were well elevated, with bluffs occasionally rising to two hundred and fifty and sometimes to six hundred feet, and there was throughout most of its course an agreeable absence of "drowned lands." The meandering channel made a distance not much short of a thousand miles in reaching the Mississippi, while as the bird flies the distance was shortened by a third. This was the natural highway for a great people.

The Ohio valley.

In the autumn of 1752, Marin was sent by Duquesne to begin fortifiying the line of march which Céloron had followed in 1749. Leaving Niagara, the leading detachment of three hundred men began to build a fort at Chautauqua Creek, but when Marin himself came up with the main body, he disapproved the position and moved on to Presqu' Isle. Here he cut a road, twenty-one miles long, through a level tract of country to the Rivière aux Bœufs. This road is still in use, the local antiquaries say, for a distance of seven miles south of Erie; and as late as 1825, cannon-balls and other military relics were occasionally found along its route. Within the limits of the modern Waterford

Marin's expedition. 1752.

Fort Le Bœuf.

(Pa.) he built a stockade, and called it Fort Le Bœuf. It was on the west branch of French Creek, and was the first armed station of the French in the northeastern parts of the Great Valley.

Thus much had apparently been accomplished without the

[From the *Amérique Septentrionale, par Mitchel, Paris : par Le Rouge, 1777 ; corrigée en 1776 par M. Hawkins.* It shows the routes from Duquesne. The most westerly fort on Lake Erie is "Sandoski, bati par les Fran. en 1751."]

English getting any definite knowledge of the movement. In the following spring (April 20, 1753), Johnson learned by runners from Onondaga that there was a force gathering at Fort Frontenac, which he suspected was intended for the Ohio. It was in fact reinforcements which were to join Marin's advance already there. On May 14,

The French reinforced. 1753.

thirty-three canoes of this force were seen to pass Oswego, and on the next day Captain Stoddart notified Johnson of the event, but grossly exaggerated the numbers, when he represented that this hostile movement was carried on with six thousand men. He added that the Indians accompanying the French were taken as hunters, and had refused to be combatants against the English.

In May, Governor Hamilton was aroused, and urged the Pennsylvania Assembly to succor the Indians on the Alleghany, so as to prevent their being overcome by the French. Messengers conveying tidings of the danger were dispatched both to the Maryland authorities and to the Ohio Indians. Some of these had already made protests to the French commanders, but they got nothing but defiant answers. The Half-King, a local Mingo chief, sent messengers to the settlements for arms; while, on the other hand, Marin found no difficulty in getting the aid of Delawares, Shawnees, and Senecas, to furnish men and horses to carry his supplies over the portage.

Logstown.

The nearest English at this time, except wandering traders, were at Logstown on the Ohio, a score of miles below the forks. Croghan, foreseeing danger, had before this advised the Pennsylvania authorities to stockade this post, and to compel the traders to keep within it and not heedlessly wander about.

When the news of this threatening movement reached the English ministry, Holderness at once instructed the Pennsylvania governor to use force, if necessary, to expel the French from "the undoubted limits of his Majesty's dominions." But before this injunction was received, Franklin and others met a deputation of Ohio Indians in council (September, 1753) at Carlisle (Pa.).

Conference at Carlisle. September, 1753.

The representation of these Indian delegates was that their permission to the English to occupy the forks had drawn upon them the enmity of the French. They averred that they had already three times protested against their movements in French Creek, but they had got no satisfaction. The French had assured them that they intended in all events to fortify Venango, the Forks, Logstown, and Beaver Creek, and that nothing could prevent it. Upon this presentation of the French purpose, Croghan suggested, and the Indians urged, that the English at once develop and strengthen their trading-posts at Logstown, the mouth of the Kanawha, and at the forks. If the English would do so, the Indians promised to come to those posts for their trafficking.

Already, in August, Colonel Trent had been sent by the Virginia authorities to look over the ground at the forks, and select a site for the proposed stockade. While he was returning to tidewater to make report, the Mingo Half-King, who had been with him, went on to Le Bœuf, to renew the protest to Marin. This native chief later gave Washington an account of the stern way in which the French officer received him. "I *will* go down the river, and I *will* build upon it," was all the answer he got. Marin was doubtless satisfied from the Half-King's bearing that the French advance under himself would be resisted, but fate had determined that another leader should bear the brunt of the conflict. In October, Marin died at his post; but it was not till December that Legardeur de St. Pierre, who was just back from his search for the western sea, and appointed to succeed Marin, arrived at his post. He came to a diminished garrison, for a considerable part of the force had been sent back to Montreal, where they could be better supported during the winter. The appearance of these on their return convinced Duquesne that Marin had been wise in not pushing on too rapidly, for the fatigues of the campaign had borne heavily upon them. He wrote of them, that to have tried to reach the Mississippi would only have choked the river with their dead bodies. The return of this detachment had been observed from Oswego, and in ignorance of its meaning, Governor de Lancey was encouraged to think the danger was over.

The Half-King rebuffed by Marin.

Marin dies, October, 1753.

Legardeur de St. Pierre succeeds.

When Trent gave his report to Dinwiddie, that governor determined to make a formal demand upon the French to withdraw. He prepared the necessary letter, and selected Washington, then adjutant-general of the Virginia forces, to deliver it. His instructions, dated October 30, 1753, were to proceed to Logstown, and ask of the Half-King a safe-conduct to the French post. He was to deliver Dinwiddie's letter, and make all the observations he could respecting the numbers of the French and their communications with Canada.

Washington sent to Le Bœuf. 1753.

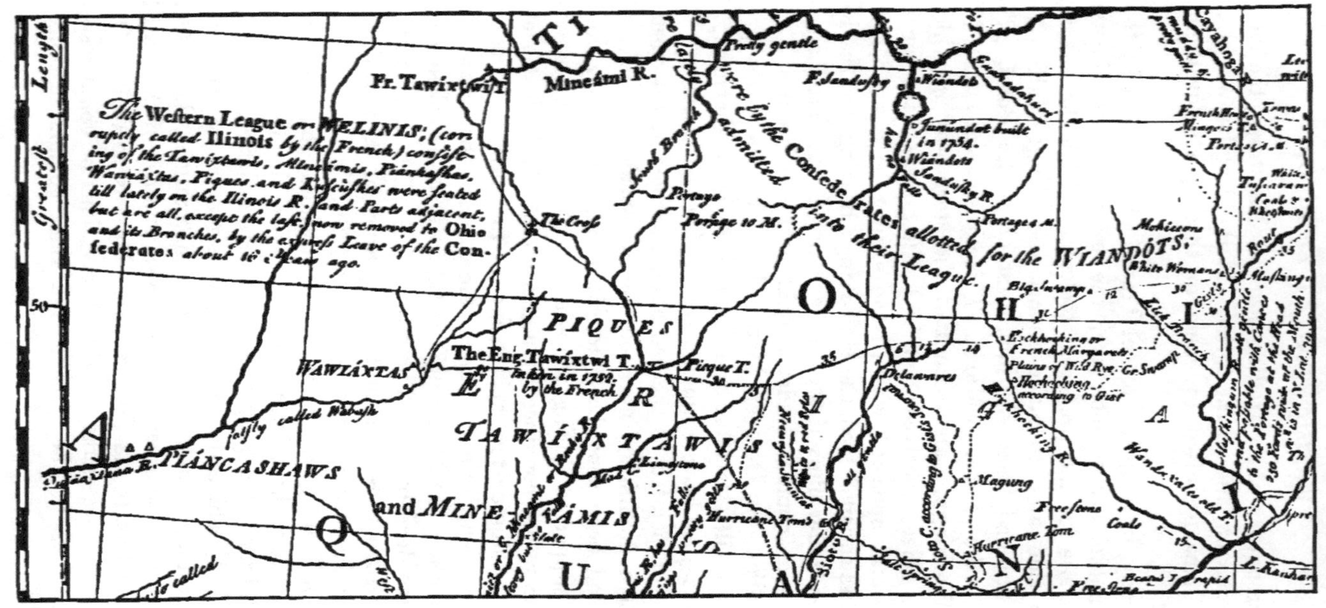

Greatest Length
50
The Western League or WELINIS; (corruptly called Ilinois by the French) consisting of the Tawixtawis, Mineamis, Piankashas, Wawiaxtas, Piques and Kuscushes were seated till lately on the Ilinois R. and Parts adjacent, but are all, except the last, now removed to Ohio and its Branches, by the express Leave of the Confederates about 16 Years ago.
Fr. Tawixtwi T.
Mineami R.
Pretty gentle
F. Sandusky
Wiandot
Junundat built in 1754.
Wiandots
Sandusky R.
were by the Confederates admitted into their League.
allotted for the WIANDOTS.
The Cross
Portage
Portage to M.
PIQUES
The Eng. Tawixtwi T. taken in 1752 by the French
Pique T.
WAWIAXTAS
falsly called Wabash
PIANCASHAWS
TAWIXTAWIS
and MINEAMIS
Delawares
Hockhocking R.
Plains of Wild Rye
Magung
Hurricane Tom
Free Stone
Coals
Mohicons
White Womans
Muskingum R.
L. Kanhawa
Cayahoga

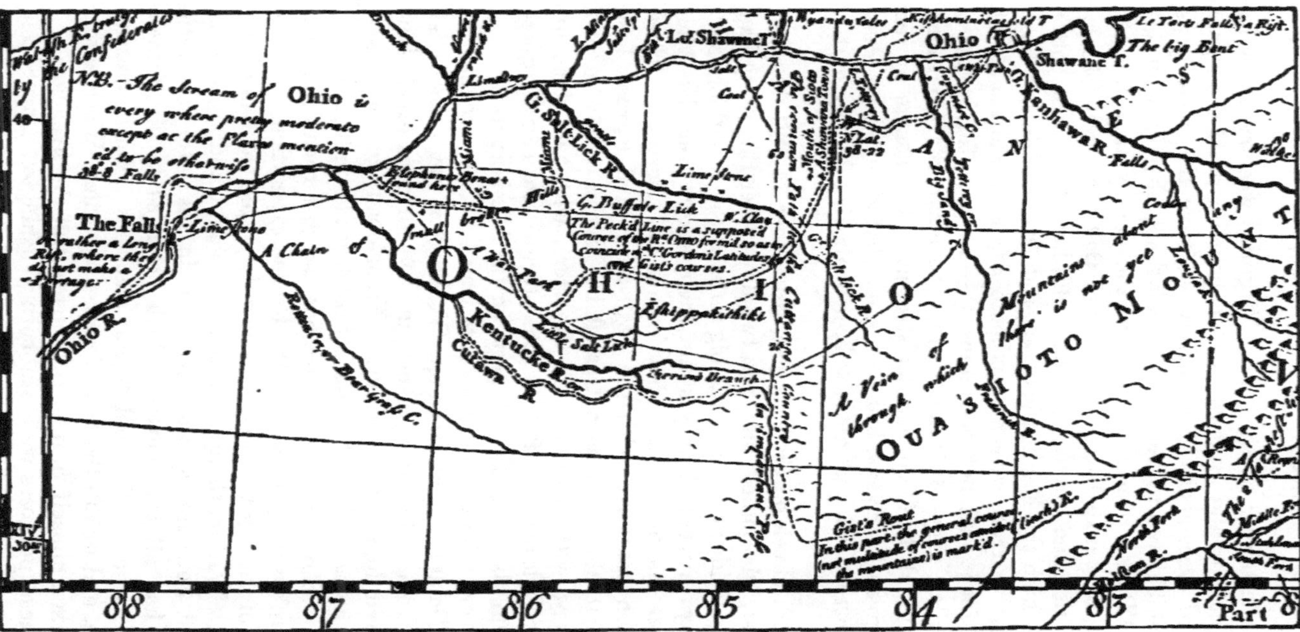

NOTE. This map (taking both pages) is a section of the *Middle British Colonies in North America*, first published by Mr. Lewis Evans of Philadelphia, since corrected and extended by T. Pownall, London, 1776. It shows in the dotted double line the course of the Ohio as supposed by Gist.

This undertaking of the young Virginian was trying in its nature, and promised to be exhausting amid the rigors of December. Fortunately, we have the messenger's journal, which was printed at Williamsburg shortly after his return. When reprinted in London, the next year, it was accompanied by a map, based upon that of Bellin, given in Charlevoix, at this time nearly ten years old, but still much better than any which the English had yet produced. Bellin had been the earliest to trace with approximate accuracy the course of "L'Oio," for it had not been unusual — as seen, for instance, in the Dutch maps of Vander Aa — to make the Ouabache (Wabash) and the Ohio parallel streams. The course of the Ohio, as given by Evans, had been somewhat changed by Gist, but his corrections had not yet been embodied in any of the maps.

His journal and map.

At Will's Creek on the Potomac, November 14, Washington found Gist, who joined him, and two days later the party had passed the divide and was at the big forks of the Youghiogheny. A few days afterward, they swam their horses over the Alleghany near its mouth, and hurried on to Logstown. Here Washington conferred with the Half-King, and learned how roughly that chief had been treated by Marin. He also had an interview with some French deserters, who had come up from New Orleans on a flotilla with stores. He eagerly questioned them about the French posts on the Mississippi.

There were a hundred miles yet to travel before reaching Le Bœuf; but at Venango Washington got some relief from an irksome journey, in the courtesies which Joncaire offered him. This assiduous Frenchman was now occupying the house of John Frazier, a Scotch trader and gunsmith, who had lived here for some years, but had just been driven off by Joncaire's party, the van of the French expedition. Above the cabin of the fugitive, Joncaire now displayed the flag of the Bourbons. Within, there was a comfortable fire and a generous board, and Joncaire, as we have seen in his interview with Croghan, had all the courtesy which belonged to his French half-breed nature. This and liberal potations induced mutual confidence, and before the hour for parting came, Washington had possessed himself fully of the purposes of the French.

Venango.

That these purposes were stubborn Washington learned on

the 11th, when he reached the fort at Le Bœuf. Gist records that they were received "with a great deal of complaisance," for St. Pierre had all the politeness of his race. Washington presented Dinwiddie's letter, and three days later the French commander placed in the young adjutant's hands a reply as uncompromising as a determined purpose could make it. A journey back more perilous than the coming was before the little embassy. By the middle of January, 1754, Washington was again in Williamsburg.

Le Bœuf.

Washington's report convinced Dinwiddie that there was no resort left but force. The instructions of Holderness were timely. Following up the minister's advice, the Lords of Trade had, on September 18, 1753, counseled the colonies to aim at concerted action, and in December Johnson told the authorities of New York that the Indians were right in predicting French success unless the English bestirred themselves. Dinwiddie acknowledged that if the French succeeded for a while in holding the Ohio valley, they could introduce settlers to make their hold effective, for a much more attractive climate and soil than Canada possessed would invite them to the valley.

Force become necessary.

The Dinwiddie correspondence shows how expresses were speeding up and down the Atlantic coast carrying urgent appeals to the other governors to come to his assistance. The several assemblies, however, were little inclined to commit themselves to an unknown task, particularly as the feeling was growing that Dinwiddie's aims were rather political and personal than patriotic. It was thought that to advance the interests of the Ohio Company was not worth the risk of a harrowing border war. Contrecœur, a little later, when he summoned the paltry band of English at the forks, was not unaware of this feeling. "Your schemes," he says to the representatives of Virginia, "are contrived only by a company which hath the interests of trade more in view than to maintain the union and harmony existing between the crowns of Great Britain and France,"—and there was truth in his words.

The Ohio Company.

The Indians drew their conclusions from the way in which Virginia was pushing ahead. Croghan discovered that it was believed among them that the apathy of Pennsylvania was likely to leave France and Virginia alone

The urgency of the Virginia leaders.

to divide the Indian country between them, and he warned the colonial powers that if they suffered the Shawnees to want for ammunition, the French would surely gain them.

To Dinwiddie's mind, it was little short of treason for a Virginian to defend, as some were doing, the French interpretation of the rights of discovery. When his House of Burgesses, a little later, proved obdurate, and would not grant him subsidies, but professed much loyalty, he bitterly told them that their "ardent zeal was only an unavailing flourish of words."

New York's apathy.

Either a like defection or indifference prevailed outside of Virginia. New York was seldom as vigilant as she might be. When matters looked badly a year and more before, Hendrick, the Mohawk chief, taunted her people for sitting in peace at Albany, while their Indian neighbors were pressing a common foe. It took all of Johnson's adroitness to heal these sores of the Indians. "You may rest contented," they finally said, "that we will protect the tree which you have replanted, from the high winds of Canada." Now, when De Lancey was urging his assembly to stand by Virginia, it agreed to double the garrison at Oswego, and even do something more, but in no wise to give an adequate assistance. It even doubted whether the French occupation on the Alleghany was any encroachment on his majesty's territory.

The feeling in Carolina and Pennsylvania.

Governor Glen of South Carolina was indifferent enough to pooh-pooh at the indignant activity of the Virginia governor, but Dinwiddie rejoiced that the Cherokees and Catawbas were not disinclined to defend their Ohio hunting-grounds. The governor of Pennsylvania was not without sympathy; but his assembly could hardly be depended upon. The Proprietary stood ready to assist Virginia in fortifying the forks, but he cautiously wished it to be understood that he did not acknowledge thereby any territorial rights of that province about the forks.

Dinwiddie's war measures.

It seemed, therefore, if there were to be war, that it rested with Dinwiddie to begin it; and he determined to take the risk. It was evident from Washington's report that the French intended with the spring to advance upon the forks, and had gathered a large number of canoes for the purpose. There were also rumors that a great body of Chippeways and Ottawas were on the way to assist them.

Croghan heard from a Chickasaw that the French had a force of a thousand men gathered at the falls of the Ohio, and that they were prepared to give aid. French deserters reported that a large contingent of French troops had arrived in Quebec, and in January, 1754, Governor Hamilton of Pennsylvania was passing the story south. Dinwiddie felt that the time was come. The task before him was a burdensome one, and the home government looked to him in the emergency.

Dinwiddie and his assembly.

This Virginia governor once in a while hurt his prospects by an imperious air. He was occasionally unstable; but he had enthusiasm, persistency, and a hatred of the French. These latter qualities got some satisfaction at last, when he brought his assembly to the pitch of voting £10,000 for the emergency, and it was induced to offer bounties of land to those who would come forward in arms. Therefore Dinwiddie issued a proclamation, agreeing to divide two hundred thousand acres of this disputed territory among those who would defend it. This happened in February, 1754.

Stockade begun at the forks, February, 1754.

While this was taking place at Williamsburg, Trent, who had been sent with a fatigue party to the forks, placed the first post of a stockade on the spot on February 17. Rumors that the French were coming soon reached the little party, and a messenger was dispatched to Dinwiddie for help.

Washington advances toward the forks.

During March, Dinwiddie was busy organizing a regiment to be sent to occupy the fort. He placed it under the command of Colonel Fry, whom we have already encountered as a surveyor, and Washington was commissioned as the lieutenant-colonel. With such companies as were ready, Washington went forward to meet Trent's call for assistance.

Washington's French war letters.

We should have excellent material for following this first campaign of the great Virginian, and the later ones of the French war, in his letters and journals, if they had come down to us as he wrote them. Unfortunately, such of Washington's letters of these eventful years as are derived from his letter-books were revised by him at a later period, and in a way to obscure the ardor and change the natural expression of the young officer, since the wisdom and experience of riper years was made to overlay the spontaneity of youth. The care which Washington took of his papers showed his appreciation of documentary records, but his stilting of the unstudied effusions of his earlier days showed also his essential lack of the historical spirit. It is an added misfortune that some of Washington's editors have further diminished the representative value of his writings. It is a satisfaction that Dr. Toner and others have had a proper appreciation of the condition in print which should attach to a personal document, and so far as possible Washington's earlier journals are now readily accessible in a satisfactory shape. This cannot be true, however, of the itinerary which he kept during the venturesome experiences of the summer and autumn of 1754. This journal, falling into the enemy's hands, was published in Paris in a French version, and later re-Englished by another hand. It was thus subjected to changes, omissions, and insertions which, by Washington's own testimony, largely invalidate it as evidence. It is in these perverted forms only that we have it.

and early journals.

When Washington started out in March, 1754, Dinwiddie was urging the authorities of New York and Massachusetts to organize a counter movement against Canada, in order to prevent the sending of reinforcements to the Ohio. The appeal, however, was not heeded, though in April Dinwiddie was hopeful that a diversion would be made by way of the Kennebec. Thus Washington's party was left to its own devices.

Dinwiddie's hopes.

"It will be easier to prevent the French settling than to dislodge them when settled," wrote Dinwiddie to Sharpe of Maryland; and this was the task in hand. It was no small one if the stories of French deserters, which were being sent south from Philadelphia, were true. One such represented that there were twelve hundred in garrison at Presqu' Isle, and five hundred at Le Bœuf.

On April 9, Washington met an express from the forks, informing him that the force there was in hourly expectation of an attack from eight hundred French. Eleven days later, reports reached him (April 20) that the French had captured the unfinished fort. Washington was at Will's Creek on the 22d, when Ensign Ward, who had surrendered the works, appeared and told his story.

The forks captured by the French.

The French from Le Bœuf had passed Venango, where Washington had seen Joncaire, and where, near Frazier's house, the French had built a fort during the winter, which had been named Fort Machault, in honor of one of the favorites of the Pompadour. It was situated within the limits of the modern town of Franklin in Pennsylvania. Descending the Alleghany, Contrecœur, who commanded the detachment, had appeared before the English at the forks.

Fort Machault.

Trent, the commander of the post, in terror or bewilderment, had gone away, and his lieutenant had also left his post to see his family, living not far distant. This gave the command of the working party to Ensign Ward. When the French leader demanded his surrender, the ensign, at the Half-King's suggestion, pleaded his inferior rank, and asked that a reply might be delayed till the return of his superior officers. The plea was futile. Ward could but surrender, and now, five days later, — the surrender having been made on the 17th, — Washington was listening to the terms by which the fort and a score or two of men passed into Contrecœur's hands. The prisoners had been allowed by him to depart.

Ward's surrender, April 17, 1754.

There is no indisputable enumeration of the attacking force, except that they had eighteen small cannon. It was beyond question very greatly superior to Ward's. The hour was certainly passed for succor, but Washington knew that he was expected to prove his mettle. He sent forward a party to repair the road which Cresap had blazed over the mountains to the Red Stone Creek on the Monongahela, where the Ohio Company had recently erected a storehouse. Thus was made what was really the first wagon road into the Great Valley, from the Atlantic slope. It was later used in part by Braddock, and continued to be a thoroughfare till 1818, when the National Road was constructed in the same general direction. The line of the original highway can still be traced, or was to be traced, as late as 1877, when Lowdermilk, the local historian, followed it.

Washington advances.

On April 29, Washington started from Will's Creek with his main body of one hundred and fifty men. On May 9, he was at Little Meadows, on a tributary of the Yonghiogheny. This was well within the valley, and at a later day was part of a property which Washington acquired. Here he erected some slight protection for his supplies. Three days later, he met Gist, who told him he had seen tracks of a French force thereabouts. The Indian Half-King, who was hovering in the neighborhood, sent word to Washington that a French party lay concealed not far off, — a force under Jumonville, which Contrecœur had sent out three days before to patrol the country and warn off any English to be found. Washington and the Indian chief now met, and on consultation it was determined to attack the French. The Virginian commander had at this time no knowledge of the purpose of Jumonville, and after Washington's impetuosity the following day led him to an assault, in which the French leader was killed and most of his thirty-three followers were slain or captured, the English commander was put to some awkwardness in justifying his action. Jumonville had started out with a large force, but a part had been sent back to Duquesne, as Contrecœur now called the fort at the forks. It was the tracks of this returning force which Gist had observed. On Jumonville's person was found a summons which he was instructed to serve on any English he might meet. In this summons Contrecœur said to whoever should receive it that "the sale of lands on the Ohio River by the Indians has given you so weak a title that I shall be obliged to repel force by force." It proved that Washington in attacking had only anticipated an assault from Jumonville, who was simply waiting reinforcements. Two days later, Washington (May 30) dispatched his prisoners to Winchester, and fearing a retaliatory attack from Contrecœur, who is supposed to have had not far from a thousand men at his disposal, began to intrench. He was conscious that, in case of a parley, he was not well equipped in an interpreter, and in a few days wrote to Dinwiddie, asking that Andrew Montour might be sent to him. Armed supports began to reach him, and after a while he learned of the death of Colonel Fry, who was on his way to join the advance body. This gave the supreme command to Washington.

Jumonville attacked.

Washington takes supreme command.

NOTE. The map on the opposite page is from Fry and Jefferson's *Map of Virginia*, showing Lord Fairfax's manor, the dotted line running southeast from the "Springhead" of the North Fork of the Potomac giving the direction of the southern boundary of the manor, toward the Shenandoah valley. The "Springhead" is shown as contiguous to the source of the Monongahela. The road from Fort Necessity (on Red Stone Creek, a branch of the Monongahela) runs to the fort and storehouse at the mouth of Will's Creek. Farther down the Potomac, near the mouth of the South Fork, is Colonel Cresap's settlement. Christopher Gist's abode is in the northwest corner of the map, on the road from Will's Creek to the forks of the Ohio.

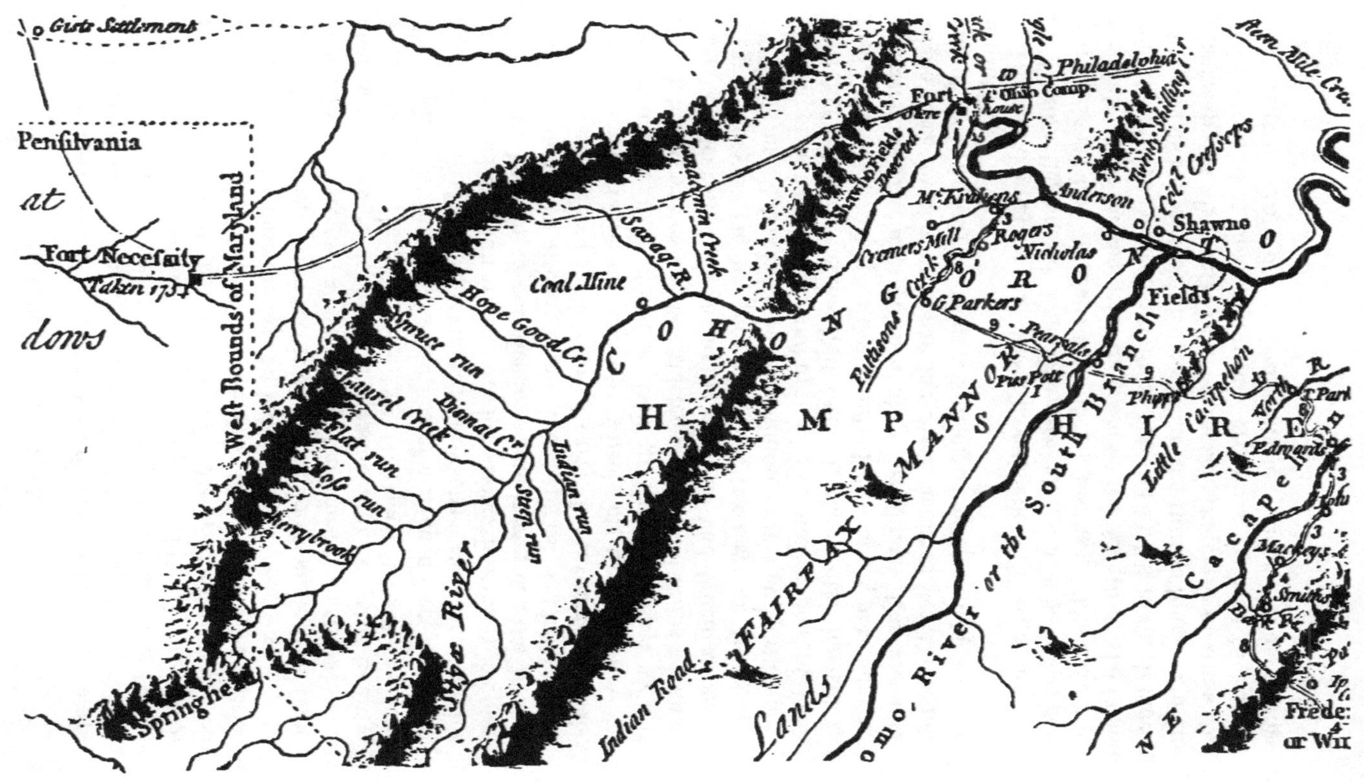
Gists Settlement
Pensilvania
Fort Necessity
Taken 1754
West Bounds of Maryland
Philadelphia
Ohio Comp.
Fort
Shawno Fields
Deserted
Savage R.
Coal Mine
Hope Good Cr.
Spruce run
Laurel Creek
Flat run
Mose run
Cherrybrook
Springhead
Indian run
Stony run
Indian Road
FAIRFAX MANNOR
Lands
River or the South Branch
COHONGORONTO
HAMPSHIRE
Cremers Mill
Rogers
Nicholas
M^c. Krakens
Anderson
Shawno
Col. Cresseps
Fields
G Parkers
Pattisons Creek
Pearsals
Little Cacapehon
Cacapehon
Edwards
Frede
or Win

While the intrenching was going on, rumors came of an approaching foe. At the same time about forty Indians gathered in the camp, including, beside some Iroquois, a number of Loups (Delawares) and Shawnees. Washington had every reason to believe that some of these were spies. He tried to deceive such in his representations, and on the 27th he made his last entries in the journal whose history we have traced.

In 1752, Gist, as the result of his explorations for the Ohio Company, had begun a settlement ten miles from the Monongahela, on what is now Mount Braddock, in Fayette County, Pennsylvania. Here, on June 28, Gist gave Washington the first explicit information he had had of a French force marching against him. The Virginian at first resolved to concentrate his men here and await an attack; but his second thoughts prompted him to fall back to Great Meadows and strengthen the breastwork which he had already begun at that place. He had but two wagons and a few pack-horses to carry his intrenching tools, but he could trundle on their own wheels his nine small swivel four-pounders. The distance back to Fort Necessity, as this intrenchment was called, was thirteen miles, and in his advance, clearing the road as he went, he had taken as many days. He now occupied but two days on the return march, but his men were almost overcome by the work. His supplies were scant, and even the expresses he sent back for relief made a welcome diminution of the mouths he had to feed. He had, perhaps, three hundred men in all, not counting a Carolina company which had joined him. Contrecœur's whole force by this time had increased to about two thousand, and of these a party of some six or eight hundred was now approaching.

Washington retreats to Fort Necessity.

The usual story is, that the Chevalier de Villiers, a brother of Jumonville, was at Fort Chartres, on the Mississippi, when word reached him of the death of his brother. The time was certainly scant for the news to traverse the length of the Ohio and the avenger of Jumonville to return; and it is much more likely, as better authorities say, that the tidings found him in Montreal. At all events, Villiers reached Duquesne on June 16, and learned that Contrecœur had organized a force to attack Washington. In a day or two it started under Villiers's command.

About eleven o'clock in the forenoon of July 3, 1754, Washington, at Fort Necessity, saw the enemy advancing through the mist, along the road which he had so laboriously made. The Virginians opened upon the foe at long range, with their little swivels, but without much effect. The Half-King, who was in the fort, was dissatisfied. He thought that Washington had not sufficiently intrenched himself, and that had he more effectively barricaded his force, he might have held out. The opposing force was certainly much larger than Washington's command, though perhaps not twelve hundred or even a thousand, as some testimony makes it. Adam Stephens's narrative gives Washington but two hundred and eighty-four men, and they were probably much less fresh than the French. The little fort is described as being "half leg deep of mud." Desultory firing was kept up the rest of the day, through a dismal rain, until in the evening Villiers sent an officer to demand a parley. The Virginians by this time had lost in killed and wounded about eighty. Washington now had sore need of an interpreter like Montour. There was in his force a German, Jacob van Braam, who knew little English and no more French. It had become evident that Washington could not successfully repel an assault, and he decided to obtain the best terms he could. By the light of a tallow candle in the misty rain, Van Braam and the French came to an agreement under Washington's directions. The terms secured for the vanquished the honors of war, the destruction instead of the surrender of the swivels, and the giving of hostages for the return of the prisoners taken in the fight with Jumonville, — a provision that Dinwiddie stubbornly refused to carry out.

Villiers's attack, July 3, 1754.

On July 4, 1754, Washington and his little army marched out of his breastworks, and five days later the Virginians were at Will's Creek. On the 24th, the news was known in Montreal. Thus were the northeastern tributaries of the Great Valley abandoned by the English.

Washington surrenders, July, 1754.

CHAPTER XV.

THE RIVAL CLAIMANTS FOR NORTH AMERICA.

1497–1755.

In considering the respective claims of the English and French to North America, it must be remembered that the conflict of rights is not only one on identical lines arising from discovery, but one also on opposed lines arising from different conceptions of the rights of discovery. The claims are also represented by contrary methods and purposes in enforcing them.

The French, in the time of Francis I. and later, claimed the new continent by reason of Verrazano's voyage along its Atlantic coast. The claim, however, was not made good by permanent occupation anywhere along the seaboard of the present United States.

Moreover, the English, under the Cabots, had sailed along this coast nearly thirty years before. Still, it was almost a century after those voyagers before the English government, urged by the spirit which Hakluyt and Dr. Dee were fostering, awoke to the opportunity, and began seriously to base rights upon the Cabot voyages. The French, at a later day, sought to discredit this English claim, on the ground that the Cabots were private adventurers and could establish no national pretensions. The English pointedly replied that their Henry VII. had given the Cabots patents which reserved to the crown dominion over any lands which were discovered. This reply was triumphant so far as it went, but it still left the question aside, whether coast discovery carried rights to the interior, particularly if such inland regions drained to another sea. The English attempt in the latter part of the sixteenth century, under Raleigh's influence, to occupy Roanoke Island and adjacent regions, but without definite extension westward,

The French and English claims.

was in due time followed by successive royal patents and charters, beginning in 1606 and ending in 1665, which appropriated the hospitable parts of the continent stretching from the Atlantic to the Pacific. For a north and south extension these grants almost exactly covered the whole length of the Mississippi, since the parallel of 48°, which formed the northern limit, and that of 29°, which made the southern, were respectively a little north of the source of the Great River and just seaward of its deltas.

The charter of Acadia, granted by the French king three years before the first of the English grants, covered the coast from latitude 40° to 46°, and was thus embraced in the pretensions of the English king, but his rival refrained from giving any westward extension, beyond what was implied in "the lands, shores, and countries of Acadia and other neighboring lands."

It is interesting to determine what, during this period of sixty years, mainly in the first half of the seventeenth century, were the notions, shared by the English king and his advisers, of the extent of this munificent domain, with which he and they were so free.

A few years before the first of these grants was made to the Plymouth Company in 1606, Hakluyt had laid before the world, in Molineaux's great mappemonde, the ripest English ideas of the New World, and these gave a breadth to North America not much different from what it was in reality. The Pacific coast line, however, was not carried above Drake's New Albion, our modern Upper California. This left the question still undetermined, if one could not travel on a higher parallel dryshod to Asia, as Thomas Morton, later a settler on Boston Bay, imagined he could.

Supposed width of North America.

Molineaux gives no conception of the physical distribution of mountain and valley in this vast area, further than to bulk the Great Lakes into a single inland sea. The notion of an immense interior valley, corresponding in some extent to our Mississippi basin, which Mercator forty years before had divined, had not yet impressed the British mind. Mercator, indeed, had misconceived it, in that he joined the Mississippi and St. Lawrence basins together by obliterating the divide between them. In this way he made his great continental river rise in Arizona and sweep northeast, and join the great current speeding to the Gulf of St. Lawrence. Here, then, in the adequate breadth of the continent, as Mercator and Molineaux drew it, is conclusive evidence that the royal giver of these vast areas had, or could have had, something like a proper notion of the extent of his munificent gifts. At the date of the last of these charters, in 1665, Cartier and his successors had for a hundred and thirty years been endeavoring to measure the breadth of the continent by the way of the St. Lawrence and the Great Lakes. They sought to prove by inland routes whether the estimated longitude of New Albion had been accurate or not. There had, it is true, been some vacillation of belief meanwhile. One thing had been accomplished to clarify the notions respecting these great interior spaces. The belief of Mercator had given way to the expectation of finding a large river, flowing in a southerly direction, whose springs were separated from those of the St. Lawrence by a dividing ridge. It was not yet determined where the outlet of this great river was. Was it on the Atlantic side of Florida, as a long stretch up the coast from the peninsula was at that time called? Was it in the Gulf of Mexico, identifying it with the stream in which De Soto had been buried? Was it in the Gulf of California, making it an extension of the Colorado River? Each of these views had its advocates among the French, who had already learned something of the upper reaches of both the Ohio and Mississippi. It was left for Joliet and Marquette, a few years later, not to discover the Mississippi, but to reach the truth of its flow, and for La Salle to confirm it.

These latter explorations of the priest and trader gave the French such rights as came from traversing throughout the water-ways which led with slight interruption from the water back of Newfoundland to the Mexican gulf. In due time this immense valley of the Mississippi was entered by the British traders, as they discovered pass after pass through the mountain barrier all the way from New York to Carolina. The French, indeed, had permanent settlements among the Illinois and on the lower Mississippi, but in other parts of the Great Valley there is little doubt that wandering Britons were quite as familiar to the Indians as the French trader or adventurer. If the evidence is not to be disputed, there was among

The Mississippi valley.

these hardy British adventurers a certain John Howard, who was, perhaps, the first, on the English part, to travel the whole course of one of the great ramifications of the valley. It was in 1742 that he passed from the upper waters of the James over the mountains to New River, by which he reached the Ohio. Descending this main affluent, he was floating down the Mississippi itself when he was captured by some French and Indians and conveyed to New Orleans. An air of circumstantiality is given to the expedition in the journal of John Peter Salley, who was one of Howard's companions. Fry, in his report to the Ohio Company at a later day, made something of this exploit as crediting the English with an early acquaintance with the Great Valley. The most western settlements of the Virginians are marked in Evans's map of 1755 as that of J. Keeney at the junction of Greenbrier and New rivers, and Stahlmaker's house on the middle fork of the Holston River. These isolated outposts of the English were an exception to their habit of making one settlement support another. The English alleged, as set forth by Mitchell, that the French planted their posts "straggling up and down in remote and uncultivated deserts, in order thereby to seem to occupy a greater extent of territory, while in effect they hardly occupy any at all."

The claims, then, of these rival contestants for the trans-Alleghany region, as they respectively advanced them at the time, may be thus put: —

The English pretended to have secured their rights by a westward extension from the regions of their coast occupation, and down to 1763 they stubbornly maintained this claim, though forced to strengthen it, first, by alleging certain sporadic, and sometimes doubtful and even disproved, wanderings of their people beyond the mountains; and second, by deriving an additional advantage from professed rights ceded to them by the Iroquois.

Grounds of the rival claims.

When the main grants to the Plymouth and London com-

Note. The following map is from the *Mémoires des Commissaires du Roi*, etc., Paris, 1757, and represents what the French understood to be the pretensions of the English sea-to-sea charters. The heavy black lines indicate the north and south limits of Virginia and New England (1620); the heavy dots the 1662 charter of Carolina; the lighter dots the extended Carolina charter of 1665; and the fine parallel lines the Georgia charter of 1732. The map also shows the supposed connection of the Mississippi and Lake Winnipeg.

CARTE
DES PRETENTIONS DES ANGLOIS DANS
L'AMERIQUE SEPTENTRIONALE
Suivant leurs Chartres
Tant sur les Possessions de la France que
sur celles de l'Espagne
Echelle de Deux Cent Lieues Marines de France
MER DE L OUEST Inconnue
N.° I.
N.° II
N.° III
Lac des Prairies
Fort la Reine
CALIFORNIE
Nouv.le NAVARRE
N O U
M E X I
E R
U
U D
140
135
130
125
120
115
110

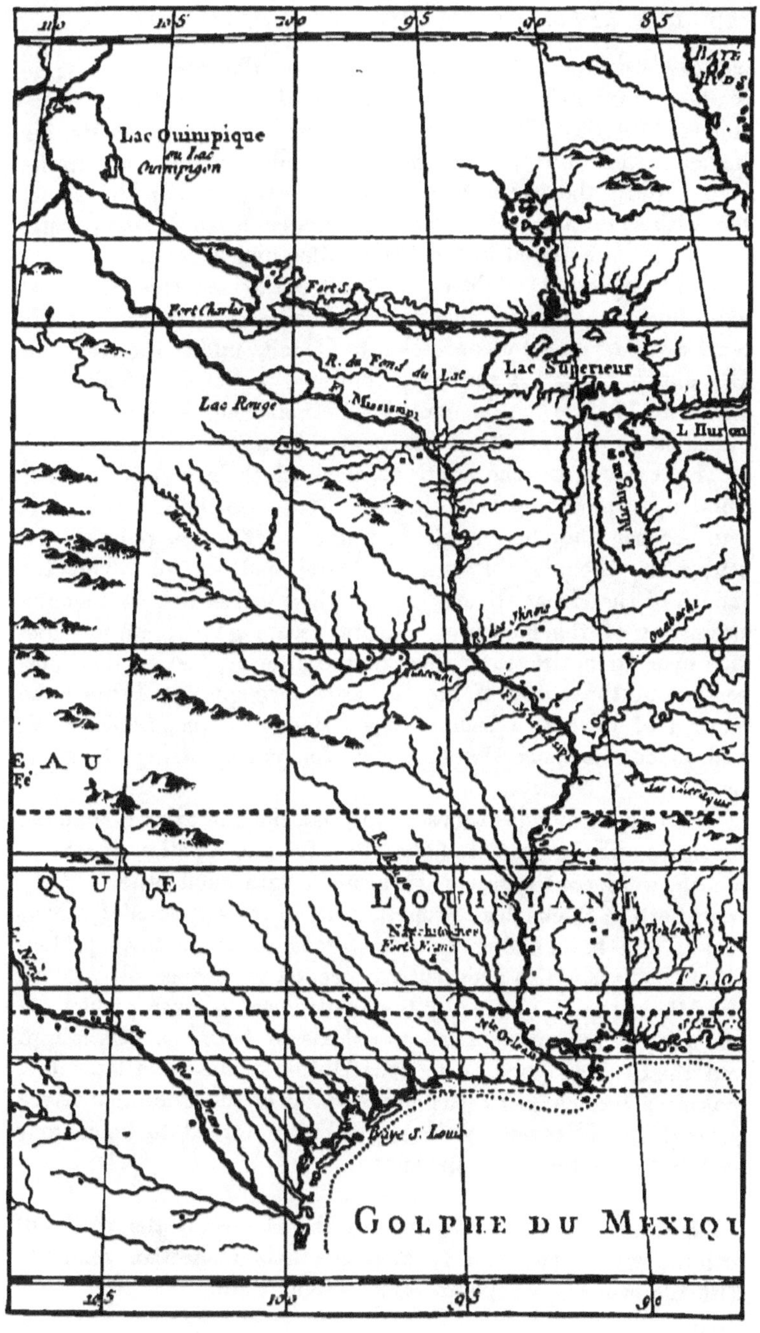

Lac Ouimpique
Fort Charles
R. du Fond du Lac
Lac Rouge
Lac Superieur
L. Huron
L. Michigan
LOUISIANE
Baye S. Louis
GOLPHE DU MEXIQU

panies were superseded by less extensive allotments, this same sea-to-sea extension was constantly reinforced as far as iteration could do it. The provincial charter of Massachusetts, for instance, in confirming the earlier bounds, carried her limits west toward the South Sea. That of Virginia did the same, but with so clumsy a definition that the claims of Massachusetts and Virginia collided in the Ohio valley and beyond.

The Congress at Albany, in 1754, reaffirmed this westward extension, but allowed that it had been modified north of the St. Lawrence only by concession to Canada under the treaty of Utrecht in 1713. A similar ground was assumed by Shirley at Paris, in 1755, when he met the French commissioners in an endeavor to reconcile their respective claims.

The French, on the contrary, derived their rights, in their opinion, from having been the first to traverse the Great Valley, and because they had made settlements at a few points; and still more because they possessed and had settled about the mouth of the Great River. It was their contention that such a possession of the mouth of a main stream gave them jurisdiction over its entire water-shed in the interior, just as their possession of the outlet of the St. Lawrence gave to France the control of its entire basin. Upon this principle, Louis XIV. had made his concession to Crozat for monopolizing the trade of the Great Valley.

These two grounds of national rights, the one arising from the possession of the coast and the other from occupation of a river mouth, were consequently at variance with each other. They were both in themselves preposterous, in the opinions of adversaries, and both claimants were forced to abate their pretensions. The English eventually conceded to France all west of the Mississippi. France by the arbitrament of war yielded, to one people or another, the water-sheds of both the Mississippi and the St. Lawrence, just as the United States at a later day, making a like claim for the entire valley of the Columbia River through the discovery of its mouth, were forced to be content with but a portion of their demand.

There was another difference in the claims of the two contestants which particularly affected their respective relations with the original occupants of the Great Valley.

The French asserted possession against the heathen, but cared little for the territory except to preserve it for the fur trade. They were not, consequently, despoilers of the savages' hunting-grounds. One to three square miles was estimated as each Indian's requirement for the chase. But, nevertheless, they seized such points as they wished, without thought of recompensing the savage owners. This prerogative of free appropriation the French persistently guarded. When, in 1751, La Jonquière told the tribes on the Ohio that the French would not occupy their lands without their permission, he was rebuked by his home government, and Duquesne, his successor, was enjoined to undo the impression which La Jonquière had conveyed to the savages.

Fee and jurisdiction.

On the other hand, the English pioneers, by their charters and patents, got a jurisdiction over, but not a fee in, the lands conveyed. In the practice which England established, or professed to establish, occupation could follow only upon the extinguishment by purchase or treaty of the native title.

Thus the Indian had exemplified to him, by these intruders, two diverse policies. He was inclined to the French policy because it did not disturb his life, and drive him away from his ancestral hunting-grounds. Duquesne was wont to tell the Indians that the French placing a fort on the tribe's lands did not mean the felling of forest and planting of fields, as it did with the English; but that the French fort became only a convenient hunting-lodge for the Indian, with undisturbed game about it.

The Indians and the rival policies.

The Indian was inclined to the English policy because it showed a recognition of his right to the soil, for which he could get cloth and trinkets and rum, if he chose to sell it. But he soon found that the clothes which he obtained wore out, the liquor was gone, and the baubles were worthless. The transaction, forced upon him quite as often as voluntarily assumed, was almost sure to leave him for a heritage a contiguous settlement of farmholders, who felled the forests and drove away his buffalo.

The savage was naturally much perplexed, between these rival methods, in determining which was most for his advantage. Accordingly, we find the aboriginal hordes over vast regions divided in allegiance, some preferring the French and others the English, and neither part by any means constant to one side or the other.

Moreover, these two diverse policies meant a good deal to such disputants in the trial of strength between them. The French knew they were greatly inferior in numbers, but they counted on a better organization and a single responsible head, which induced celerity of movement, and this went a great way in overcoming their rival's weight of numbers. Joncaire boasted of this to Washington, when as a Virginian messenger he went to carry the warning of Dinwiddie. Pownall understood it, when he said that Canada did not consist of farms and settlements, as the English colonies did, but of forts and soldiers. "The English cannot settle and fight too," he adds. "They can fight as well as the French, but they must give over settling." Thus the two people, seeking to make the New World tributary to the Old, sought to help their rival claims by gaining over these native arbiters. It was soon seen that success for the one side or the other depended largely on holding the Indians fast in allegiance.

The savage is always impressed by prowess. For many years, the French claimed his admiration through their military success, and the English often lost it by lack of such success. In personal dealing with the Indian, the French always had the advantage. They were better masters of wiles. They knew better how to mould the savage passions to their own purposes. With it all, they were always tactful, which the English were far from being. William Johnson, the astutest manager of the Indians the English ever had, knew this thoroughly, and persistently tried to teach his countrymen the virtue of tact. It was not unrecognized among his contemporaries that Johnson's alliance with a sister of Brant, a Mohawk chief, had much to do with his influence among the Iroquois.

"General Johnson's success," wrote Peter Fontaine, "was owing under God to his fidelity to the Indians and his generous conduct to his Indian wife, by whom he hath several hopeful sons, who are all war captains, the bulwark with him of the Five Nations, and loyal subjects to their mother country." This Huguenot, Fontaine, traced much of the misery of frontier life to the failure of the English to emulate the French in intermarrying with the natives, and he, curiously rather than accurately, refers the absence of the custom to an early incident in Virginia history; "for when our wise politicians heard that Rolfe had married Pocahontas, it was deliberated in council whether he had not committed high treason by marrying an Indian princess; and had not some troubles intervened which put a stop to the inquiry, the poor man might have been hanged up for doing the most just, the most natural, the most generous and politic action that ever was done this side of the water. This put an effectual stop to all intermarriages afterwards."

Both French and English were not slow in discovering that among the American tribes the Iroquois were the chief arbiters of savage destiny in North America. The struggle of each rival was to secure the help of these doughty confederates. In the early years of the European occupation, the Dutch propitiated the Iroquois and the French provoked them. The English succeeded to the policy of the Hollanders, and the French long felt the enmity which Champlain had engendered. The Dutch and English could give more and better merchandise for a beaver-skin, and this told in the rivalry, not only for the friendship of the Iroquois, but for that of other and more distant tribes. This was a decided gain to the English and as decided a loss to the French, and no one knew it better than the losing party.

The Iroquois.

Throughout the dire struggle, the English never ceased for any long period to keep substantial hold of the Iroquois. There were defections. Some portions of the Oneidas and Mohawks were gained by the Jesuits, who settled their neophytes near Montreal. The Senecas were much inclined to be independent, and the French possession of Niagara and the arts of Joncaire helped their uncertainty. Every tribe of the United Council at Onondaga had times of indecision. But, on the whole, the English were conspicuously helped by the Iroquois allegiance, and they early used it to give new force to their claim for a westward extension. The country which the Iroquois originally occupied was that portion of the State of New York south of its great lake, and their tribes were scattered through the valley of the Mohawk, along the water-shed of Ontario, and throughout the country holding the springs of the

Susquehanna and the Alleghany. From the days of John Smith, the Susquehanna had been an inviting entrance to the interior from the Chesapeake, and Champlain's deputy, in 1615, had found that it afforded a route to the sea from the Iroquois country.

It was a dispute between the French and the English which of the two peoples first penetrated this Iroquois country. La Jonquière, in 1751, claimed the priority for the French. There can be little question, however, that whatever right followed upon priority belonged to the Dutch, and by inheritance to the English. This was always the claim at Albany, and when the French seized upon Niagara, the English pronounced it an encroachment upon the Iroquois country, as, indeed, Charlevoix acknowledged it was. At the same time, the French contended that it was a part of the St. Lawrence valley, which was theirs by virtue of Cartier's and later discoveries. On this ground they also claimed the valley of Lake Champlain, and had advanced to Crown Point in occupying it, though the Iroquois considered it within their bounds.

So when the English seized Oswego, it was in the French view an usurpation of their rights, "the most flagrant and most pernicious to Canada." This sweeping assertion, transformed to a direct statement, meant that the possession of Oswego gave the English a superior hold on the Indians. It also offered them a chance to intercept the Indians in their trading journeys to Montreal. This advantage, as already indicated, was rendered greater by the English ability to give for two skins at Oswego as much as the French offered for ten at Niagara. De Lancey looked upon the English ability to do this as the strongest tie by which they retained the Indians in their alliance. "Oswego," said the French, "gives us all the evils, without the advantages of war." Duquesne, in August, 1755, confessed that it was nothing but a lack of pretext which prevented his attacking this English post.

The Iroquois conquests.

About the middle of the seventeenth century, the Iroquois by conquests had pushed a sort of feudal sway far beyond their ancestral homes. They had destroyed the Hurons in the country west of the Ottawa. They had exterminated the Eries south of the lake of that name, and had pushed their conquests at least as far as the Scioto, and held in vassalage the tribes still farther west. They even at times kept their enemies in terror well up to the Mississippi. Somewhat in the same way they had caused their primacy to be felt along the Susquehanna. Their war parties were known to keep the fruitful region south of the Ohio in almost absolute desolation.

The area included in these conquests is, perhaps, a moderate estimate of what the English meant by the Iroquois claim. As early as 1697, the Commissioners of Trade and Plantations, in formulating the English rights to sovereignty over the Iroquois, asserted something larger in saying that these confederates held "in tributary subjection all the neighboring Indians, and went sometimes as far as the South Sea, the Northwest Passage, and Florida, as well as over that part of the country now called Canada." Mitchell, in 1755, claimed that by the conquest of the Shawnees in 1672, the Iroquois acquired whatever title the original occupiers of the Ohio valley had, and that their conquest of the Illinois carried their rights beyond the Mississippi.

The English turned these Iroquois conquests to their advantage by assuming that the regions covered by this supremacy fell to their jurisdiction as one of the considerations of their alliance with the confederates. This pretension, in its most arrogant form, allowed there was no territory not under Iroquois control east of the Mississippi, unless it was the region of the south, where, with equal complacency, the English used their friendship with the Cherokees, Chickasaws, and Creeks to cover all the territory of the modern Gulf States, with a bordering region north of them. In Huske's English map of 1755, even this territory of the southern tribes is made tributary to the Iroquois, as well as all east of the Mississippi and the Illinois and Lake Michigan, and of a line thence to the upper waters of the Ottawa.

NOTE. The map on the following pages is from Bowen' and Gibson's *North America*, London, 1763. The upper section shows the country of the Illinois, Mascoutins, Miamis, Twightwees, all a part of the conquered country of the Iroquois, which is made to extend from the northern shore of Lake Huron to West Florida, its western limits being defined by the Mississippi as far north as the Illinois, along which the "pecked line" runs to Lake Michigan and then north, so as to include the "Messessagues" on the northern shore of Lake Huron. The under section shows the basin of the Ohio, and places the position of the Chickasaws and Catawbas. The present Tennessee River (called here Cherakee, etc.) was the route of the Cherokees from the mountains to the Mississippi, but the origin of placing on maps their country along its course was the desire to profit by an alleged claim for that tribe, pressed by their English allies, to strengthen the English claim to a westward extension.

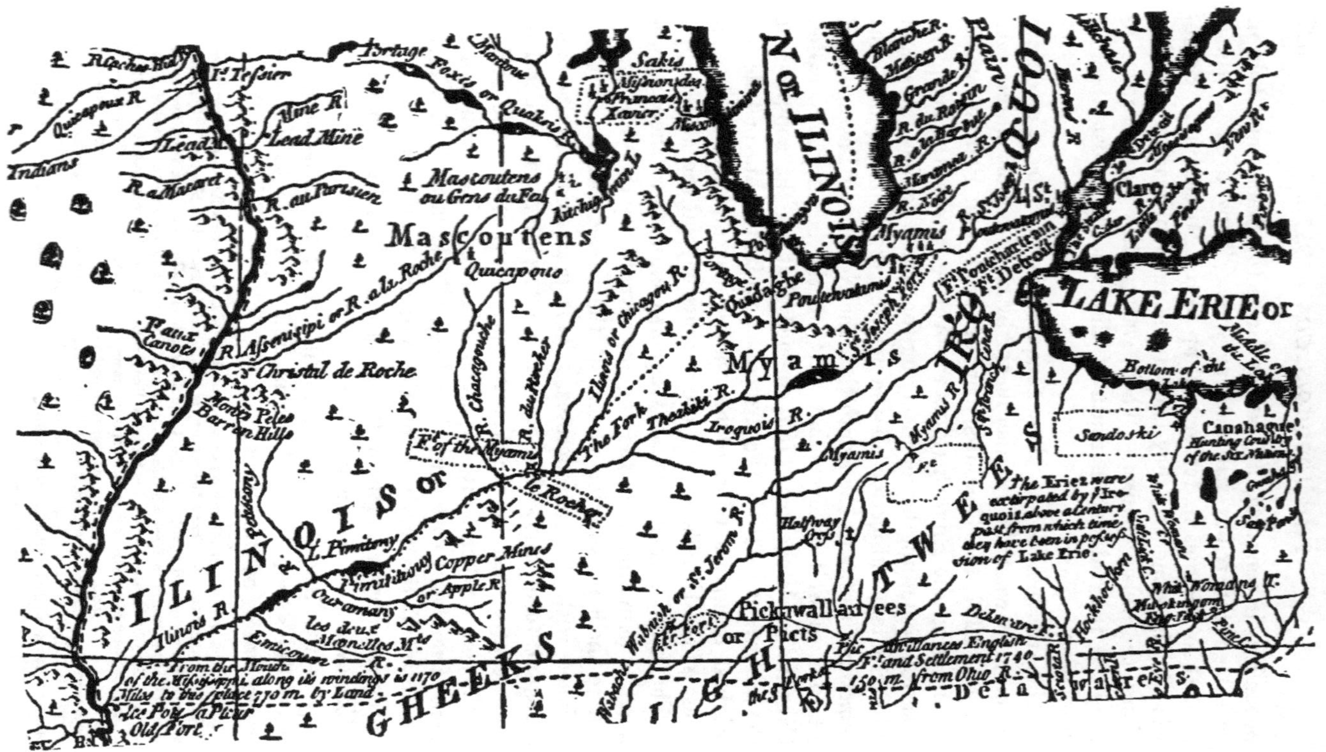
LAKE ERIE or
Bottom of the Lake
Sandoski
Canahague
Hunting Country of the Six Nations
The Eriez were extirpated by ye Iroquois above a century past from which time they have been in possession of Lake Erie.
Ft. Pontchartrain
Ft. Detroit
Myamis
Poutewatamis
Mascoutens
Mascoutens ou Gens du Feu
Quicapous
Portage
Foxes or Quakis R.
Sakis
Lead Mine
R. au Parisien
R. a Macart
Indians
Quicapoux R.
Assenisipi or R. a la Roche
Christal de Roche
Monts Peles
Barren Hills
Rauix Canots
Chacagouche R.
R. du Roches
Ilinois or Chicagou R.
The Fork
Theakiki R.
Iroquois R.
Ft. of the Myamis
le Roche
ILINOIS or
L. Pimitney
Pimiteoui
Copper Mines
or Apple R.
Ouramany
les deux Mamelles Mts
Ilinois R.
Emicouare R.
Wabach or St. Jerom R.
Pickawillanees
or Picts
Halfway Cross
Delaware R.
Hockhocking
White Womans R.
Muskingum
Salt Lick C.
Pine C.
Miami R.
Myamis R.
St. Joseph Fort
Plain
R. du Raisin
Grande R.
R. Noire
Myamis
Claro
Little Lake
GHEEKS
Dela
From the Mouth of the Missisippi along its windings is 1170 Miles to this place 770 m. by Land
Old Fort
Ft. and Settlement 1740
150 m. from Ohio R.

The Pecked Line extending by ye R. Illinois thro Quadoghe cross the Lakes Illinois & Huron: shews the bounds of the Territories of the Six Nations, which by deed of sale they surrender'd to ye Crown of Great Britain &c. in 1701 and renewed in 1726 and 1744.
CHIK'I
TW
BY
VIRGINIA
COUNTRY
NORTH CAROLINA
CHICASAWS
CATAWBAS
Ohio River
The Fork
One Mile
French Fr.
Charter
Cheraken
Broad
Cavern in a Rock
The Falls 6 Mi. long
Cumberland R.
1665
Walker's Settlemt. 1750
Hughs R.
Ponds R.
Hogohegee River
now Called
Hogohego
First Falls
Pelesipi
Second Fall
Chinches R.
Kallamak River
Holston's R.
Milley's R.
Fredericks R.
Salt lick R.
Catanba
Mines of Coal
Shannoah
Engl. Fact.
Shawnoe
Kishpupinloes
Harriskintom
Ohio R.
Lit. Conway R.
Fishing Cr.
Gr. Conway or Wood R.
Coal R.
Little Sandy
Remainder of ye Natchez allies of the English
Chikasaws R.
Tortoises I.
Hinds I.
Pt. a la Course
Pt. a la Sonde
Saline
Grand Ile
Cap St. Anthony
Metchigamy
Cap de la Croix
Watoga O.T.
Chotto
Sattiks R.
Catawba R.
Brushy Mt.
Sapona R.
Keowee O.T.
A Fit Place for a Factory
Uphasee
Here was the 1st Discovery

In pushing their conquests to the Illinois, the Iroquois claimed, as Pownall tells us, that they warred upon these distant savages because it was necessary to protect the beaver, which the Illinois were exterminating. There was little reason for so benign an excuse, for the ravages of the confederates were simply prompted by an inherent martial spirit. So distinguished a student of their career as Mr. Horatio Hale is inclined to give them a conspicuously beneficent character, which, however, hardly met the approval of a more famous student, the late Francis Parkman.

The English claim.

This Iroquois-English claim had distinguished advocates in Colden, Franklin, and Pownall, but there was some abatement at times in its pretensions. Sir William Johnson, in 1763, traced the line of this dependent country along the Blue Ridge, back of Virginia to the head of the Kentucky River; down that current to the Ohio above the falls; thence to the south end of Lake Michigan; along its eastern shore to Mackinac; and northeast to the Ottawa, and down that river to the St. Lawrence. The right of the English king to such a territory as this dated back, as the English claimed, to an alleged deed of sale in 1701, when the Iroquois ceded these hunting-grounds to English jurisdiction, in addition to their ancestral lands. It was, as they claimed, a title supplementing that of their sea-to-sea charters. When the French cited the treaty of Ryswick (1697) as giving them sway over the river basins where they held the mouths, and claimed this as paramount to any rights the Iroquois could bestow, the English fell back on these territorial charters as the most ancient and valid claim of all.

If the English charter claims were preposterous, this supplemental one was, in even some part of contemporary opinion, equally impudent and presumptuous. There was by no means an undivided sentiment among the colonists upon this point; and history has few more signal instances of tergiversation than when, at a later day, the English government virtually acknowledged the justice of the French claim in urging the passage (1774) of the Quebec Bill. "We went to war," said Townshend, in the debates on this bill, "calling it Virginia, which you now claim as Canada."

We read in Franklin's statement, in 1765, before the Stamp Act Committee, that the Virginia Assembly seriously questioned the right of the king to the territory in dispute. George Croghan, on the contrary, in a communication to Secretary Peters of Pennsylvania, wondered how anybody could doubt that the French on the Alleghany were encroaching upon the charter limits of Pennsylvania.

The French were more unanimous in their view; but it was only gradually that they worked up to a full expression of it. Bellin, the map-maker for Charlevoix, had drawn in his early drafts the limits of New France more modestly than the French government grew to maintain, and he was soon instructed to fashion his maps to their largest claims. In like manner the earliest English map-makers slowly came to the pitch of audacity which the politicians stood for, and Bollan, in 1748, complained that Popple (1732), Keith (1738), Oldmixon (1741), Moll (at several dates), and Bowen (1747) had been recusant to English interests. It was not till Mitchell produced his map in 1755 that the most ardent claimant for English rights was satisfied.

The French denial.

The instructions of Duquesne, in 1752, say that "'t is certain that the Iroquois have no rights on the Ohio, and the pretended rights through them of the English is a chimera." In the negotiations of the treaty of Utrecht, in 1713, the English had succeeded in getting an admission from the French which required all the resources of French diplomacy to qualify. This was an acknowledgment of the English sovereignty over the Iroquois. The French at a later day, when they felt better able to enforce their views, sniffed at the obligation, and called the phrase "a simple enunciation" in words of no binding significance, — a summary way of looking at an obligation which could demolish any contract. When they condescended to explain what they sniffed at, they insisted that the Iroquois themselves never acknowledged such a subjection. Sir William Johnson was frank enough to call the connection of the English and Iroquois one of alliance rather than subjection. The French further pointed out what was true, that the Iroquois did not always consider it necessary to consult the English when making treaties or declaring war. Again, when forced to other explanations, the French maintained that the subjection of the Iroquois in their persons did not carry sovereignty over their lands. If it did, they said, the Iroquois who occupy lands at Caughnawaga would be equally subject in land and person, and that would involve the absurdity of yielding to the English jurisdiction territory at the very gates of Montreal.

There was another clause in this treaty of Utrecht which the French were hard put to interpret to their advantage. This was the clause by which the French acknowledged the English right to trade with all Indians. The minutes of instruction given to Duquesne show how this was interpreted. "The English may pretend that we are bound by the treaty of Utrecht to permit the Indians to trade with them; but it is sure that nothing can oblige us to allow this trade on our own lands." This, in the light of the French claim to the water-sheds of the St. Lawrence and the Mississippi, would debar the English from trading at Oswego and on the Ohio.

The Indian trade.

In 1726, by a treaty made on September 14, and which Governor Pownall prints in his *Administration of the Colonies*, the English had secured a fresh recognition by the Iroquois of their guardianship over them. By this compact the Senecas, Cayugas, and Onondagas, falling in with the concessions of the Mohawks and Oneidas in 1684, surrendered a tract from Oswego to Cuyahoga (Cleveland), with an extent inland of sixty miles.

A score of years and more passed thereafter before the French became fully sensible that they must forcibly contest their claim to the Ohio. By this time their plan had fully ripened of connecting Canada and Louisiana by a chain of posts, and of keeping the English on the seaward side of the Alleghanies. In this, they were convinced, lay a riper future for New France rather than in crossing the Mississippi and disputing sovereignty with the Spaniard. This accomplished, they hoped to offer a barrier against the English effective enough to prevent their wresting from Spain the silver mines beyond the Mississippi.

The French had always claimed priority on the Ohio, and when Céloron was sent in 1749 to take formal possession

NOTE. The opposite map is from Mitchell's *Map of the British Colonies* (1755). It shows the Wabash country, and gives the contemporary claims as to the Iroquois rights.

The Six Nations have extended their Territories to the River Illinois, ever since the Year 1672, when they subdued, and were incorporated with, the Antient Chaouanons, the Native Proprietors of these Countries, and the River Ohio: Besides which they likewise claim a Right of Conquest over the Illinois, and all the Missisipi as far as they extend. This is confirmed by their own Claims and Possessions in 1742, which include all the Bounds here laid down, and none have ever thought fit to dispute them.
The Ohio Indians are a mixt Tribe of the Several Indians of our Colonies, settled here under the Six Nations, who have allways been in Alliance and Subjection to the English. The most numerous of them are the Delawares and Shawnoes, who are Natives of Delaware River. Those about Philadelphia were called Sauwanoos whom we now call Shawanoes, or Shawnoes. The Mohickans and Minquaas were the Antient Inhabitants of Susquehanna R.
Kaskaskies
1040 m.
C. St. Anthony
Great I.
the Missisipi
River Ohio about 1 m. broad & 5. or 6. fathom deep
to the falls
A Fine
Wabache R.
Little Wiaut
Great Wiaut
Wauwaughtanes
Pyan
The first Settle
on the R. Ohio
ghany 30 Years
have extende
Shenango

along its banks, by hanging royal insignia on trees and burying graven plates in the soil, that officer professedly made "a *renewal* of possession of the Ohio and all its affluents," — a possession originally established "by arms and treaties, particularly those of Ryswick, Utrecht, and Aix-la-Chapelle." There was urgency for such a "renewal," for Céloron found that the English were already in possession of the country, so far as the friendly sanction of the natives signified it. Thus, the Iroquois claim to that extent had proved effective, and Colden has distinctly expounded it in his *History of the Five Nations.* It was also clearly traced in maps by Jefferys in 1753, and by Mitchell and Huske in 1755.

On the Ohio.

It was, therefore, a necessity for the French to use force, if they were to make good their claims by holding the valley. Accordingly, we find, in 1751, La Jonquière instructed "to drive from the Beautiful River [Ohio] any European foreigners, and in a manner of expulsion which should make them lose all taste for trying to return." With the usual French diplomatic reservation, that governor was further enjoined "to observe, notwithstanding, the cautions practicable in such matters."

There is a *Mémoire* of 1751 which sets forth the French anxiety lest the English, by securing a post on the Ohio, should be able to keep the Indians in alienation from the French. Such English success would mean a danger to French communications with the settlers on the Mississippi, who stood in particular need of Canadian assistance in the war which was waged against them by the Carolina Indians, instigated by the English there. Without such a bar to their progress as the French possession of the Ohio, the English could easily advance, not only upon the French posts among the Illinois, but they could endanger the portage of the Miami, which was the best route from Canada, and which if lost might involve the abandonment of Detroit.

The conclusion of this complaint is twofold: Detroit must be strengthened by a farming population about it for its support, in order to preserve it as the best place to overawe the continent. The Illinois country must be protected; its buffalo trade fostered; that animal's wool made marketable; and the custom of salting its flesh prevail so that the necessity of depending on Martinico for meat be avoided.

The movement of the French on the Alleghany in 1754 had put an end to temporizing. Albemarle, who was England's ambassador at Paris, was a butterfly and a reprobate, and he was little calculated to mend matters, now easily slipping from bad to worse. War the result.

A tough and sturdy young Yankee, then keeping school in Worcester, Mass., John Adams by name, represented the rising impatience of the colonists, who had not forgotten their yeoman service at Louisbourg. He looked forward to the complete expulsion of "the turbulent Gallicks!"

The year 1755 opened with events moving rapidly. In January, France proposed to leave matters as they were and let commissioners settle the dispute in details. England in response fell back on the treaty of Utrecht. In February, France proposed as a substitute that all east of the mountains should belong to England, and all west of the Alleghany River and north of the Ohio should fall to France. This left as neutral territory the slope from the mountains to the Alleghany and the region south of the Ohio. In March, England assented to this, provided the French would destroy their posts on the Alleghany and Ohio. This would make a break in the French cordon connecting Canada with the Mississippi, and would give the English an advantage in the control of the neutral country. So France refused the terms. In June, England again resorted to the conditions of Utrecht, and insisted on the validity of the Iroquois claim. France reiterated her denial of such a claim as regards the territory, but acknowledged it in respect to persons of the confederates. England insisted, as well she might, that this was not the interpretation put upon similar provisions in other treaties. Her ministers now reminded Braddock of this provision in the treaty of 1726, and instructed him to act accordingly. This brought the business to the pitch of war, though both sides hesitated to make a declaration. Galissonnière held it to be the testimony of all maps that France was right in her claim, and her possession of what she strove for was now to be settled by sterner methods.

Danville and the other French map-makers had been brought to representations that kept Galissonnière's statement true. The English cartographers had done equally well for their side, and Mitchell could be cited to ad- Maps of the Ohio country.

vantage. His *Map of the British and French Dominions in North America* was based on documents which the English Board of Trade thought best enforced their claim, and the publication, when made, in 1755, was dedicated to their secretary. In an accompanying text the English claim was pushed to its utmost, and every old story was revamped which served to bolster pretensions of the English preceding the French in exploring the country, reviving the antiquated boast that New Englanders had even preceded the French in crossing the Mississippi, and had really furnished the guides for La Salle's discoveries.

Perhaps the best knowledge which was attainable at this day of the valley of the Ohio had been reached by Christopher Gist, who, in his wandering, had corrected the supposed curves and trends of that river. Lewis Evans, in June, 1750, made his proposals to visit and map the country under disguise as a trader, and in the pay of the province of Pennsylvania. His map of the *British Middle Colonies* was published at Philadelphia just in time to be of use to Braddock. Washington later said of it that, "considering the early period, it was done with amazing exactness." The governor of Pennsylvania was satisfied that Evans had mapped the Alleghanies correctly, and contended that this new draft showed how much would be lost if the English made these mountains their bounds.

Of the country in dispute, Evans's map in one of its legends represents: "Were nothing at stake," it reads, "between the crown of Great Britain and France but the lands in the Ohio, we may reckon it as great a prize as has ever been contended for between two nations, for this country is of that vast extent westward as to exceed in good land all the European dominions of Great Britain, France, and Spain, and which are almost destitute of inhabitants. It is impossible to conceive, had his Majesty been made acquainted with its value and great importance, and the huge strides the French have been making for several years past in their encroachments on his dominions, that his Majesty would sacrifice one of the best gems in his crown to their usurpation and boundless ambition."

The opinion of James Maury, that whoever was left at the end of the war in possession of the Lakes and the Ohio would control the continent, was not, at this time, an unfamiliar one in the public mind. It was, moreover, not unconnected with the belief that in the time to come a route west by the Hudson or the Potomac, connecting with these vaster water-ways of the interior, would make some point on the Atlantic coast "the grand emporium of all East Indian commodities." We have lived to see the prophecy verified, but by other agencies.

CHAPTER XVI.

THE ANXIETY AND PLANS OF 1754.

War existed, and there had been no declaration of hostilities. In the autumn of 1754, there was anxiety all along the barrier country.

Population of Pennsylvania, Germans, Scotch, English.

Of the 190,000 whites now composing the population of Pennsylvania, more than half were Germans. They were a gregarious, industrious people. They had been little accustomed in their European past to the kind of freedom which they enjoyed in the American wilds. They brought with them to the New World the homely life of the Old. Their existence was invested with a certain picturesqueness of light and shade, in the broidery which the modern student calls folk-lore. It rendered them superstitious rather than imaginative. Franklin could give them no more attractive name than "Palatine boors," for they had mainly come from the Palatinate.

As compared with the English and Scotch, they had little of that adventurous hardihood which subdues the earth under all conditions. The Scotch particularly had been far less solicitous about the soil they sought. Boswell tells us that when Arthur Lee once spoke of a colony of Scotch in Virginia, who had settled upon a sterile tract, Dr. Johnson assured him that the Scotch would not know the land to be barren.

If the Germans had better instincts as agriculturists, they were far less prompt to defend their lands than their Scotch neighbors. Sharpe of Maryland said they were too apathetic to bestir themselves against an enemy, unless war was at their very doors. As settlers, therefore, side by side with the Scotch-Irish, the confused mixture of blood formed an incongruous community when to the German phlegm was added the passionate temper and immovable prejudice of the Celt. This ethnic incompatibility had indeed become so obvious, that of late those who controlled the settling immigrants in the province had endeavored to keep the Teutonic element as much as possible in the east, letting the more active Scotch-Irish appropriate the country toward the west.

There were political considerations also which obtruded upon the prudent, when it was considered what violent haters of papists the Scotch were, and what unbending sectaries the German Catholics were. Dinwiddie, a Scot himself, expressed solicitude at this influx of German Catholics, and Franklin discloses a prevalent fear when he says: "The French, who watch all advantages, are now themselves making a German settlement back of us in the Illinois country, and by means of these Germans they may in time come to an understanding with ours; and indeed, in the last war, our Germans showed a general disposition that seemed to bode us no good." At Fredericton, on the Maryland frontier, a German colony had been recently increased by many French from Alsace and Lorraine, not without raising a suspicion that some of them taken prisoners by the French from the Ohio would prove useful to the foe as informers and spies upon the English. In fact, there had already begun to be the apprehension, which Burke later expresses, that Pennsylvania at least might be eventually lost to the English by the vast preponderance of its alien races.

German Catholics and the French.

It had been a condition of Washington's capitulation at Fort Necessity that the English would not for a year erect any buildings on the western slope of the mountains. Dinwiddie, with the same blunt indifference to obligations which made him abandon the hostages which Washington gave, had no intention to abide by such terms. His self-will was greater when he heard by rumor that the French intended to build forts on the Greenbrier, Holston, and New rivers in what is now eastern Kentucky and Tennessee. The story went that they intended to bring up for this purpose a force from the Mississippi. Sharpe had heard similar reports, and was transmitting them to Calvert, his English master. All this served to irritate Dinwiddie, and he gave his House of Burgesses a touch of his spleen when he prorogued them on September 5. "I thank God," he said, "I have never before

Dinwiddie and the French.

had to do with such wrong-headed people." The fact was, they had pointedly foiled him in some of his plans, particularly in refusing to support parties of observation, which the governor had wished to send toward Duquesne, so as to be ready for prompt action in the spring, before Contrecœur could be reinforced.

Dinwiddie, though of a stubborn and rather narrow nature, was by no means destitute of prevision, and had a clear perception of what the maintenance of English power on the Ohio demanded. While he was endeavoring to force or cajole his assembly into action, he was communicating with De Lancey of New York, and with no very clear sense of the geographical possibilities, was expecting him to prevent relief parties of the French passing Oswego. Turning to his nearer neighbor, Sharpe of Maryland, he urged him to occupy one of the mountain passes and stand ready at that point to push a force into the valley at a moment to be agreed upon. It was Sharpe's belief that the weather would prevent the French reinforcement reaching Contrecœur before the beginning of April, and that to secure a pass was about all that could be done. Croghan had already reported on the information of an Indian that recruits were even thus early coming to Fort Duquense at the rate of two hundred a day. "This Indian is to be believed, if there can be any credit given to what an Indian says," was Croghan's assurance.

Western movements. Autumn, 1754.

As the autumn advanced (1754), the feeling improved. A few families at Draper's Meadows — the modern Smithfield — had ventured to push forward and settle west of New River. The House of Burgesses in October voted £20,000, and Dinwiddie took courage. Sharpe was beginning also to take heart. He even cherished a scheme of a winter attack on Duquesne, with the hope of seizing an island near by and fortifying it as a base for further operations in the spring. The stories which he heard of the French intention of harrying the frontier during the winter made him more eager. In December, he wrote to Dinwiddie that eleven hundred French and seventy Adirondacks were already at Duquesne, while a force said to number four hundred French and two hundred Caughnawagas and Ottawas were preparing to join them. He had also heard that three hundred French families were taking home lots among the Twightwees at the remoter end of Lake Erie. The governor of Pennsylvania was repeating similar stories to his assembly, hoping thereby to lift them from their apathy. The entire force of French now available for the next campaign was thought to be two thousand, white and red. With such stories the public mind was filled. But the Quaker and German elements in Pennsylvania listened with little emotion, and the assembly, or at least some part of it, dared to inquire if the Indians did not own this territory, which they were asked to protect. At least, they said, it concerned the king and not them, for the Board of Trade map showed that it was beyond their charter bounds.

The signs of a violent rupture with the Delawares, Shawnees, and Munseys were becoming apparent. We possess in Charles Thomson's *Enquiry* a dispassionate contemporary account of the colonial tergiversations which had provoked these tribes. The friends of colonial honor cannot to-day read it with complacency, nor without a measure of sympathy with Teedyuscung, the chieftain, who was endeavoring to right the native wrongs. At this juncture, the Indian leader called the Half-King died, and the English lost in him a good mediator. His dying was attributed to what was called "French witchcraft;" but Governor Morris discredited the charge, and with good reason. The last scene occurred at Paxton on October 4, 1754, and Croghan was soon recording that he was endeavoring "to wipe away the Indian tears by presents to the amount of £20."

Rupture with the Indians.

Half-King dies.

Governor Morris was having quite as weary a time with the Pennsylvania Assembly as Dinwiddie had had with his burgesses. His distant friends commiserated him. Shirley wrote from Boston: "I have no leaf in my book for managing a Quaker Assembly. If I had it should be at your service." His predecessor Thomas, now at Antigua, wrote: "You must either drive the French back to their lakes or they will drive you into the sea; and if the northern colonies do not speedily unite they will carry their point" in securing an Atlantic port. For years the French had longed for this Atlantic harbor to relieve their wintry imprisonment on the ice-bound St. Lawrence. Morris was perhaps

The Pennsylvania Assembly.

The French seek an Atlantic port.

less inclined than the neighboring governors to belittle the obstacles in view, for he rather credulously believed that the French had already gathered five or six thousand regulars at Duquesne. Croghan was sending him word that the Ohio Indians were ready to assist an English expedition, but they would only do so on the English supplying clothing and other necessaries to their squaws and children. Croghan seemed loth to believe that the dissatisfaction of the Indians was widespread; but he was conscious that the French blandishments had done much. No doubt a part of the savage uneasiness was traceable to the backwardness of the English movements, for the Indian is taken with quick and bold determination. Accordingly, Croghan urged upon the Pennsylvania authorities to draw the tribes over the mountains and settle them along the Susquehanna, where they could be more easily watched and supported. Conrad Weiser had already been working to this end among the Ohio Indians, and had counseled them to settle at Aughwick, east of the divide. He quickly formulated for the governor a speech in which the savages were told that "after the king of Great Britain had tried all fair means to remove the French from their Ohio forts, he would take his foes by the arm and fling them across the lake where they came from."

Croghan and the Indians.

Conrad Weiser.

In December (1754), notwithstanding a speech "calculated to rouse his assembly from their supineness," Morris wrote to Dinwiddie that he had not been able to induce them to vote a single farthing; but within ten days he adds a postscript, to say that the legislature had at last voted £5000 "to help his Majesty's forces."

Pennsylvania votes money.

Farther south, the governor of North Carolina was waxing warm in his dealings with his assembly. He told them that the French, being unable in Europe to overpower the House of Austria, had turned to America in the hopes of dividing its magnificent spaces with Spain for the benefit of the House of Bourbon. He had much to say of "hellish missionaries" stirring up the Indians; of the seizing of strategic points on the Ohio and Mississippi, and of "schemes batched in hell and supported by the court of Rome." He ended by an appeal to the colonies to unite and drive their foes to "inhospitable Canada and the hot sands of Louisiana."

North Carolina.

Early in the summer of 1754, it was hoped that a movement had been inaugurated which would have brought a more confident spirit to grace the closing year. This was to follow the fruition of a scheme for uniting the English colonies in a political bond. For a long time, schemes of union had been in the air, and they embodied a general propitiation of the Indians and a combination to check the French. The proposers generally had small thought of the effect which such a union might have on the mother country, but the home government could hardly be counted upon for a like indifference.

Hopes of uniting the English colonies.

To manage the Indians as the custom went required money and the practice of some virtues, with a due apportionment of the vices of deceit and cajolery. Neither French nor English lacked in a selfish emulation in these respects. Governor Osborne of New York had, in 1753, brought over from England thirty silver medals, showing the stolid head of George III. By using these to decorate the leading chiefs of the Iroquois and remoter tribes, it was hoped to appease them. There was need of this, especially among the Onondagas and Senecas, whom the French were craftily enticing. On the other hand, Duquesne and Piquet were by no means sure of all the vagrants who had sought the mission of La Présentation, since among the seeming neophytes they much suspected there were spies of the English.

Management of the Indians.

In the autumn of 1753, the governor of New York had received a circular from the home government, directing him to call a meeting of commissioners from the several colonies at Albany to take existing affairs under consideration. Governor Shirley of Massachusetts had come back from Europe after his futile services in Paris in trying to settle differences with the French. He had brought with him a young Catholic wife, daughter of his landlady in Paris, to introduce her with considerable hazard into the conservative social circles of Boston. This town had, indeed, lost a good deal of its Puritanic rigor, but it had gained little in admiration of "French Papists." There was some fear that Shirley's adherence to Protestant and English views might prove to be somewhat weakened. It did not take long, it proved, to dispel the suspicion, and it seems to have been at Shirley's instigation

A congress called.

Governor Shirley.

that these orders for the Albany convocation were issued. Among the colonists there grew a prevalent opinion that if any union was consummated, Shirley was the fittest man to preside over it.

The congress at Albany, June, 1754.

The meeting was fixed for June 14, 1754, but it was the 19th before the delegates assembled. They came from New Hampshire, Massachusetts, Rhode Island, Connecticut, New York, Pennsylvania, and Maryland. Conspicuous among them was William Johnson of New York, whose success in dealing with the Indians was everywhere recognized. Not less influential was Thomas Hutchinson of Massachusetts, a stickler for the royal prerogative, but who deserved well of his province for having led it out of the sloughs of an irredeemable paper currency. Stephen Hopkins of Rhode Island and Roger Wolcott of Connecticut were men of mark. Most conspicuous of all, however, was Benjamin Franklin of Pennsylvania.

Questions considered.

The questions before them were manifold, and that of conciliating the Indians was to many minds paramount. The Lords of Trade had not long before administered a rebuke to the New York Assembly for its neglect of opportunities to this end. This neglect was now showing fruits in the unamiable mood which the assembled Indians evinced. Promises had been given out that there would be a distribution of gifts, which was usually sure to increase the savage following in case of conferences. The announcement, however, had had no very marked effect at this time, and the commissioners reckoned it a "melancholy consideration" that scarce a hundred and fifty Indians appeared. But there was a conspicuous chieftain among them in Hendrick the Mohawk, whose eloquence made a mark.

Hendrick the Mohawk and other speech-makers.

"You have thrown us behind your backs," said the savage to the assembly, "and disregard us, whereas the French are a subtle and vigilant people, ever using their utmost endeavor to seduce our people." The Mohawk spokesman taunted the English with not getting new permissions to build in the Indian territory, as they had done when they built their trading-house at Oswego. He told them they were women in not preparing, like the French, for the inevitable war.

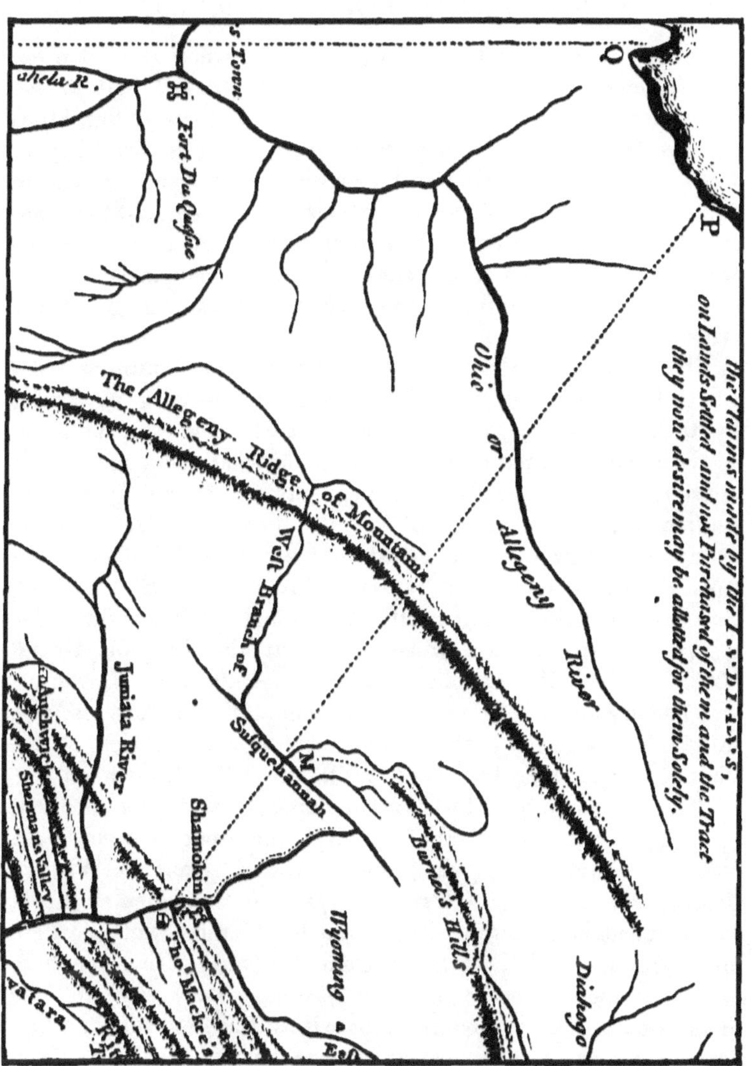

[From Charles Thomson's *Enquiry*, etc.]

Other chiefs did not avoid a plain truth when they charged the traders at Albany with selling powder and ball to the French, to be used against the English and their Indian allies on the Ohio. The traders at Oswego, they further alleged, were supplying the Montreal merchants with goods to sell to the remoter tribes. These allegations were truer than the English would acknowledge. Nor would they allow that the lands wrested by professed treaty from the Shawnees and Delawares were attained by artifice, and without the knowledge of the tribes on the soil.

This violated territory lay westward of a line running from Shamokin — the forks of the Susquehanna — in a northwest by north direction to Lake Erie. It was thus the intention of the buyers to secure an Indian fee in what remained unpurchased of the charter limits of Pennsylvania, though no consideration was to be given till it was taken up by settlements, section by section. The grant was made under deceit and pressure by unauthorized representatives of the Six Nations, and covered lands to which other tribes had a better right. The fraud was so transparent that the Iroquois Grand Council at Onondaga refused to confirm it. This injustice had led to the confederated movement under Teedyuscung, and Johnson urged that nothing short of a revocation of the claim could assuage the savage irritation at the despoilment.

Disputed land titles.

This was complicated with other claims, by which Connecticut became the rival of Pennsylvania under her sea-to-sea charter, as against the interposed grant to William Penn. To a similar interposed grant to the Duke of York, Connecticut had bowed without much difficulty; but she had, in 1753, chartered the Susquehanna Company, with seven hundred members, mostly her own people. They were to take possession of the Wyoming lands within the Pennsylvania limits, but not as yet occupied by that province. Governor Hamilton had made a protest to the governor of Connecticut, and had asked Johnson to interfere, when it became evident that the agents of the Susquehanna Company were going to take advantage of the assembly of tribes at Albany to consummate a purchase of the Indian title. These agents succeeded in getting the Indians to sign a cession on July 11, and if the Pennsylvania representatives are to be believed, it was done by mak-

Connecticut claims.

ing the grantors drunk, an act not more nefarious than some of their own performances when the Quaker province, or its masters, coveted the Indian lands. This transfer, the ground of long litigation between the two claimants, included the Wyoming valley, and extended westward to the sources of the Allegheny, and stretched from latitude 41° to 42°.

Thus the Indian problem, by the cupidity of distant Connecticut, was becoming more embarrassing on the Ohio, through the forced immigration of the Pennsylvania Indians over the eastern barrier of the Great Valley.

Union of the English colonies proposed.

The settling of the vexed question of the relations with the savages was closely connected with that other problem which the conference was more confidently expected to solve, and this was the presenting of an indomitable front to the French by the banding together of the Atlantic colonies.

Rival populations.

It is not easy to reach a positive conclusion as to the numerical strength of the rivals now struggling to usurp control of a continent. It is certain that the French were far more homogeneous; in fact, they were almost perfectly so. The English colonies, on the other hand, had been the refuge of the hunted Huguenot and the down-trodden German. There were few of the uneasy hordes of Europe which had not sent over their discontents. It is probable that the population of the Atlantic slope subject to the British monarch reached some twelve or thirteen hundred thousand, and possibly it may have reached a million and a half. The French, in all their posts and settlements from Acadia to the Mexican gulf, numbered not over ninety thousand, perhaps not more than eighty, of which there may have been twenty-five thousand too far distant from the Ohio country to be of much account in the struggle. These remoter settlements were near the St. Lawrence and Mexican gulfs.

With this great disparity between the two peoples, the French had relied on a unity of organization and celerity of movement to make them oftener than otherwise, in the past, superior to their rivals. To offset this, the English had found the alliance of the Indians not always sure, and sometimes treacherous. The last resort was to make a combination of power which could be wielded with something of the singleness of purpose which had so long served the French.

Franklin easily led the deliberations of the congress in this respect. He did not decry the English rights under their sea-to-sea charters; but he saw the practical disadvantages of these illimitable western extensions with a comparatively contracted front on the coast. The shape of these colonies, he said, was "inconvenient for the common purposes of government," and he urged that the Alleghanies be accepted at once as the western bounds of the existing colonies. This was to pave the way for new colonies to be set up as military barriers beyond the mountains, — bulwarks, indeed, against the French. He had first learned in Boston, thirty years before, how to use the press in fashioning public opinion, and it served him now. He advocated in a pamphlet the planting of one of these colonies on Lake Erie, and the other on the Ohio. Governor Pownall's views, as later developed, were much the same in spirit; but while he centred the western defense in a single colony, — preferably an Indian one dependent on the English, — he urged a second on the upper Connecticut as needful for the protection of New England. But Franklin's desire for a double colony to the west was to make them converge like a wedge, and cleave the French cordon of posts which united Canada and the Mississippi. Of these two barrier colonies, he would have the one on Lake Erie depend for supplies on Pennsylvania by the passes to the Alleghany River, while the other, on the Ohio near the Scioto, would naturally maintain its communications by the Kanawha with Virginia. The scheme also involved a good fort at Niagara and a flotilla on the Lakes, so as to maintain an ingress by the Iroquois country.

Franklin's influence in the congress.

He urges the forming of barrier colonies.

Pownall's views.

The evil of allowing the French to succeed in their plans appealed to Franklin strongly on the social side. He could but think that developed French colonies over the mountains would be sure to offer an asylum to outcasts and runaway servants from the English, and increase an inimical and neighboring population. He wrote to Whitefield that he hoped he might be able, if his plan succeeded, to settle a religious and industrious people in these colonial outposts,

Franklin's views.

and to bring a new and healthy influence upon the Indians. The packmen, he contended, had so far proved a vicious company, and demoralized the tribes by carrying as servants into the wilderness a multitude of transported Irish and other convicts. Not much that was better could be said of many of the frontiersmen in their isolated cabins.

Traders and frontiersmen.

It was apparent that Franklin's plan of barrier colonies promised more effective administration than any other yet advanced. A scheme which Archibald Kennedy had suggested in 1752 was deficient in concentrated force. He would have allotment of the over-mountain lands made by established proportions among the existing colonies. He proposed to lay out the territory in townships after the New England pattern. They were to be large enough to support sixty families each, with occasional forts for protection, while the Indian trade should be regulated by a general authority. But all such western combinations were necessarily subordinated to a comprehensive plan, by which the entire Atlantic seaboard could act in harmony for military results.

Franklin's and other plans contrasted.

Dinwiddie was in favor of two unions, one at the north, the other at the south. Few, however, could see that the protection of western pioneers could be so well assured by any severance of the colonies as by some grand union of them all. Franklin's ideas on the whole prevailed, and the proposed union gave its government the power to regulate the Indian trade; to buy for the crown all lands not within the bounds of established colonies, "or that shall not be within their bounds when some of them are reduced to more convenient dimensions;" to make new settlements on such lands by grants in the king's name, reserving a quit-rent to the crown for the general treasury; and to make statutes for such settlements till the crown shall form them into particular governments.

Protracted sessions of the congress brought about at last a unanimous acceptance of these measures, though there was undoubted lukewarmness on the part of some of the members, particularly those of Connecticut.

The document was finally signed on July 4, 1754, just at a date when Washington, under the capitulation of Fort Necessity, was withdrawing the English flag from the very territory they were seeking to preserve.

A plan agreed upon, July 4, 1754.

The members went to their respective homes, and submitted the measure to their several assemblies. Every colony rejected it. De Lancey sent it to the Lords of Trade, who laid it, October 29, before the king, without comment. Here, also, it was rejected. The colonial assemblies thought that the commissioners had failed in making a strong union, and had erred in placing the royal prerogative in sufficient subordination. The king in council thought the union ominously powerful, and that the plan boded no good for the royal authority. The prerogative party in the colonies found a spokesman in Governor Morris, who wrote to the Earl of Halifax: "The plan is very inadequate, and his Majesty and ministers were to have less power in the united legislature than they have in the several separate ones, which might answer some purposes here, but would not have answered the ends of government, or at all contributed to have kept these provinces in that dependence upon the mother country, so necessary for the interests of both."

but finally rejected by colonies and king.

So no one in the end profited by the labor of the congress. Those who were prophetic might discern that it harbingered those other and more directly fateful convocations of 1765 and 1774.

Franklin took the failure characteristically: "The different and contrary reasons of dislike to my plan makes me suspect it was really the true medium." The king, in rejecting the plan, had in fact stood for English rather than colonial interests.

Franklin told the truth bluntly, eleven years later, when he underwent his examination before the Stamp Act committee. "As to the Ohio," he said, "the contest began there about *your* right of trading in the Indian country, a right you had by the treaty of Utrecht, which the French infringed. They seized the traders and their goods, which were *your* manufactures. They took a fort which a company of *your* merchants and their factors and correspondents [Dinwiddie acted under orders from England] had erected there to secure that trade. . . . The trade with the Indians, though carried on in America, is not an American interest. It is a British interest, carried on with British manufactures, for the profit of British merchants and manufacturers. Therefore the war, commenced for the defense of a territory of the crown

Franklin's later testimony.

[Nova Scotia] and for the defense of a trade purely British, was really a British war."

Nevertheless, the colonists were the principal sufferers, and this rejection of the Albany plan preserved to their enemies their old advantage. The French still stood their former chances of brightening the Indian chain of friendship and severing the English rope of sand. The setback did not diminish Franklin's hope that the destinies of North America were yet to be settled by an English-speaking people, and the question was now to be solved over the mountains in efforts to hold and pass beyond, in military array, the two chief eastern portals of the Great Valley.

Advantage to the French, by its rejection.

CHAPTER XVII.

THE ALLEGHANY PORTALS.

1755.

In a paper which William Johnson laid before the Albany congress, he had hinted at a more systematic use of the Six Nations in thwarting the French schemes. He was not skillful at composition, and one is somewhat puzzled at his lack of precision. His plan was to possess their counsel and interests in the completest manner by planting military posts everywhere among them. He advised particularly making the most of the advantages which the English already had at Oswego, as a place of watch and ward. It was here, too, that the English could easiest subject the Iroquois and the more distant tribes to the influence of gifts. He counted upon what he felt sure was the fact, namely, that the tribes preferred to have the English rather than the French obtain a footing in the Ohio country; and that the Senecas and Onondagas were most likely to be approached by the French agents, and should be overawed in the first instance by forts placed among them. As opportunity offered, he contended that the English supervision should be pushed toward Detroit.

Johnson's plan for using the Iroquois.

When it became evident, toward autumn, that the plan of union devised at Albany was to be set aside, there was little chance for cautionary provisions to take new forms before a rumor came over the sea that the government had made up its mind to strike some sort of a blow, with two regiments of regulars that were to be ordered from Ireland to America. It was very likely now that measures more active and comprehensive than Johnson had outlined were to constitute the plan for a new campaign.

A campaign expected.

Dinwiddie, when he heard these reports, was quite as much

perplexed to provide for this royal force, in victualing and transportation, as he had been with his assembly's apathy. His neighbor, Governor Sharpe, who had had a sort of transient leadership in military matters, was by no means certain that regular troops could be trusted in a forest campaign, with such adept woodsmen on the other side as the French possessed. Besides, there was evident uneasiness among the frontier savages, and no one could say what they aimed at. The French custom of buying prisoners from the Indians made hunting the English quite as exciting as, and more profitable than, chasing game. The bad faith of the Pennsylvanians in their treaties was, in Johnson's opinion, accountable in part for the savage vindictiveness. Conrad Weiser, who was not a bad judge of the Indian temper, did not share the apprehension of Johnson, and he felt certain that the French could not command entire obedience from the tribes when the outbreak came. If the French on the Ohio were to encounter any such treachery from the natives, the English had had their share of perfidy in the Acadians, a race far removed from that guileless simplicity which attracts the poet's verse.

Temper of the savages.

Still, as ever, the French could be trusted in the trial of blandishments. "The American strength of France," says an English observer of the time, "compared with ours, is quite contemptible in all respects but one, and that is the wisdom and prudence with which it is directed." It is very clear that the French had a marked advantage in the far greater loyalty of their backwoods traders, and we encounter in the contemporary reports of the French officials but few instances of distrust of their packmen, lest they convey intelligence to the enemy. Dinwiddie was quite sure the English plans were sometimes betrayed by the English traders; and Sharpe was as confident that the colonies could not be depended upon to garrison the forks of the Ohio, if they should be retaken. The reason of his distrust was that the average provincial felt that any success against the French inured to the benefit of the British merchant rather than to the interests of his own life.

English and French traders.

So, with the failure at Albany, and with the environment of distrust and solicitude, the new year (1755) came on. The

Shawnees were active along the border, and it became necessary to make a show at least of vigilance, if the contagion of their temerity was not to spread to the Susquehanna and Shenandoah.

The Shawnees raid the borders.

Dinwiddie accordingly dispatched Major Andrew Lewis, with a force composed partly of rangers and partly of Cherokees, to patrol the frontiers. For this and other service the Virginia burgesses had, as we have seen, made a grant the preceding October. No other assembly was as active, and what Pennsylvania did a little later depended on the exertions of Franklin.

Authority had come for raising two American regiments in the crown's pay, but as the colonels designated were Shirley and Pepperrell, both carrying after ten years the laurels of Louisbourg, it was likely the recruiting would have to be done in New England. The most that Dinwiddie could hope was that these Royal Americans would be used in a diversion from the north toward Canada, so as to prevent any large reinforcement being sent to Duquesne.

Shirley's and Pepperrell's regiments.

The tidings which reached Virginia from the south were not so helpful. Governor Glen of Carolina was looking for hot work along his own frontiers, and told Dinwiddie that the attack on Virginia would be a feint, while the greater force of the enemy would ascend the Tennessee and overrun Carolina. Dinwiddie felt he needed all the help he could get, if Contrecœur had, as he supposed, already assembled sixteen hundred men at the forks.

Carolina threatened.

During January (1755), it became known in Virginia that General Edward Braddock, who had received his instructions in November, had been selected for the American command. At the time that this intelligence was fresh in Virginia, Braddock's ship was leaving the English coast. The two cabinets on each side of the English Channel had been trying to find out each what the other really meant behind the outward craft which cloaked their designs. A certain Irish medical man, settled in London, probed, as it proved, the cabinet secrets in London better for France than any one could do in Paris for the English ministry. It was professed that Braddock had no purpose to be hostile in America unless attacked. The French were likewise equipping an armament for equally innocent ends, as was rep-

Braddock to command.

The French and English cabinets.

resented. It was the real purpose of the French to gain as much time as they could, and so they shuffled in diplomatic phrases.

Just at the time when Braddock was landing at Hampton in Virginia, Machault was writing to Duquesne that the French king was persuaded the English did not intend to come to a rupture, but if they did attack, it would be on the Ohio. The Canadian governor was warned to be prepared to repel force by force, but not to strike the invader until he had been summoned. Further reinforcement with Bigot and Vaudreuil would not be long behind.

Before the end of March, Braddock's two regiments had joined him, and their movements were begun. Dinwiddie and Sharpe had already got the campaign planned for him, and their objective point was Niagara, certainly for the French the best entrance to the Ohio country. Fort Duquesne was to fall as a matter of course, and then Braddock was to advance up the Alleghany, take the forts on the way to Presqu' Isle, and proceed to Niagara. Thence he was to skirt Ontario to Oswego, where Shirley and Pepperrell were to join him in an advance on Crown Point.

The English plan of campaign.

But Braddock was determined to parcel out the glory rather than monopolize it. In order to arrange some concerted action, he summoned on March 10 a meeting of the colonial governors. Dinwiddie, meanwhile, was trying to enlist the Indians, and Braddock himself wrote to Morris of Pennsylvania, in the hopes that the tribes in that province who had lived on the Ohio would consent to join him. The southern Indians proved averse to joining the expedition, and Dinwiddie charged their defection upon French emissaries, though not unlikely they shared Governor Glen's apprehension of raids upon their own territory. It curiously happened that Dinwiddie's effort to enlist such aid, coming to the knowledge of the Six Nations, they also held back, and gave for a reason the fear of awaking broils with their old southern enemies, if they embarked on the same campaign with them. So it seemed likely that Braddock was not to profit much, if at all, by the Indian aid. It has been affirmed that he showed that he despised their assistance, and so alienated them. That he put little dependence on them was very likely true, but he certainly endeavored to do his best to placate them, though he had little success. The few who joined

The Indians to be used.

him stole away when he wanted them most. "One needs the patience of an angel to get on with them," he said, and the historical student who to-day tries to fathom their natures in the wearisome records of Indian councils which he finds, for instance, in the *Pennsylvania Archives*, may well wonder if anybody who treated with them had any patience left. Unfortunately one cannot have a much better opinion of the whites with whom the Indians dealt.

It was on April 14 that the governors met the English general at Alexandria. The outcome of their deliberation was a plan to give simultaneous alarm at all the points which Dinwiddie and Sharpe had wished to attack in succession. Braddock was to march upon Duquesne, Shirley upon Niagara, and Johnson upon Crown Point, while New England was to keep the Acadians too busy for them to afford any help farther west. If all went well, it was thought not unlikely that Braddock, meeting Shirley and Pepperrell at Niagara, would be able to go to Johnson's assistance if it was needed.

Braddock's character.

The character of Braddock, moulded by more than forty years' service in the Coldstream Guards, was hardly suited to the environments of the wilderness. He was only lately become a major-general, having been gazetted a few months before he was assigned to the American field. Those who knew him best never doubted his courage or his routine skill as a soldier, but they knew him to be desperately immoral, easily brutal, and obstinate in his opinions. A variety of witnesses of his disposition have left us the mosaics of his character. Walpole and Mistress Bellamy gossip about him as they knew him in England. Shirley, his secretary, had no admiration for him. Washington saw his failings. Franklin thought him disqualified for his task. The Virginians found him imperious, and thought him little open to the experience of woodsmen. He somehow easily wounded the sensibilities of the colonists, and it was found difficult, with such a man in command, to hold the English in the Virginia regiment to the coming task. They did not see with complacency "raw, surly, and tyrannical Scots," who were creatures of Braddock, taking the places which belonged to them. Maury evidently refers to Braddock when he speaks of the rudeness and insolence of an officer of rank which were not resented because of the common cause.

There was certainly much in what Braddock had to encounter to disgust an officer accustomed, as he was, to rigid discipline and accountability, and it should serve in some degree to exculpate him. He could ill brook any comparison of the frontier ranger with his redcoats. The refusal of the Pennsylvanians to make his efforts easier was very trying, and he would doubtless have been hardly better satisfied with New England men, who seemed at a distance to be his ideal of what provincials should be. It has been the custom of American writers to charge the dreadful miscarriage of the campaign upon this haughty and untactful general, and he very likely deserves a large share of the blame. Kingsford, the latest and best Canadian historian, has pushed his defense of Braddock as far as it will bear, if not farther, in denying that he alienated the Indians, and in insisting that the regulars behaved as well in the fight as the Virginians.

Pennsylvania and the campaign.

In Pennsylvania the Quakers and Germans united to defeat all measures that would sustain the alien general, and it was only the personal exertions of Franklin, in gathering pack-horses and wagons, that produced any assistance at all.

Contrecœur at Duquesne.

In May, 1755, Contrecœur had completed the defense of Duquesne. He had made a log fort, with walls sixteen feet thick. Trunks of trees were placed transversely, with a parapet above. A ditch lined the walls where the confluent streams did not protect it.

Braddock at Will's Creek.

Braddock was now at Will's Creek on the Potomac. Washington had joined him (May 16) on a special invitation to act as aide. The Virginia Assembly had at last been brought to regard the support of the campaign as incumbent on them as Britons.

Braddock's route.

Here at Fort Cumberland the route to be pursued became a question. Early in the year, the governor of Pennsylvania had directed the survey of a road over the western mountains of that province; but it progressed slowly, and was finally stopped when Braddock no longer needed it. It was an easier route than that to the Monongahela, and through a country affording better supplies; but other reasons prevailed, and the passage to the Youghiogheny, which Washington had

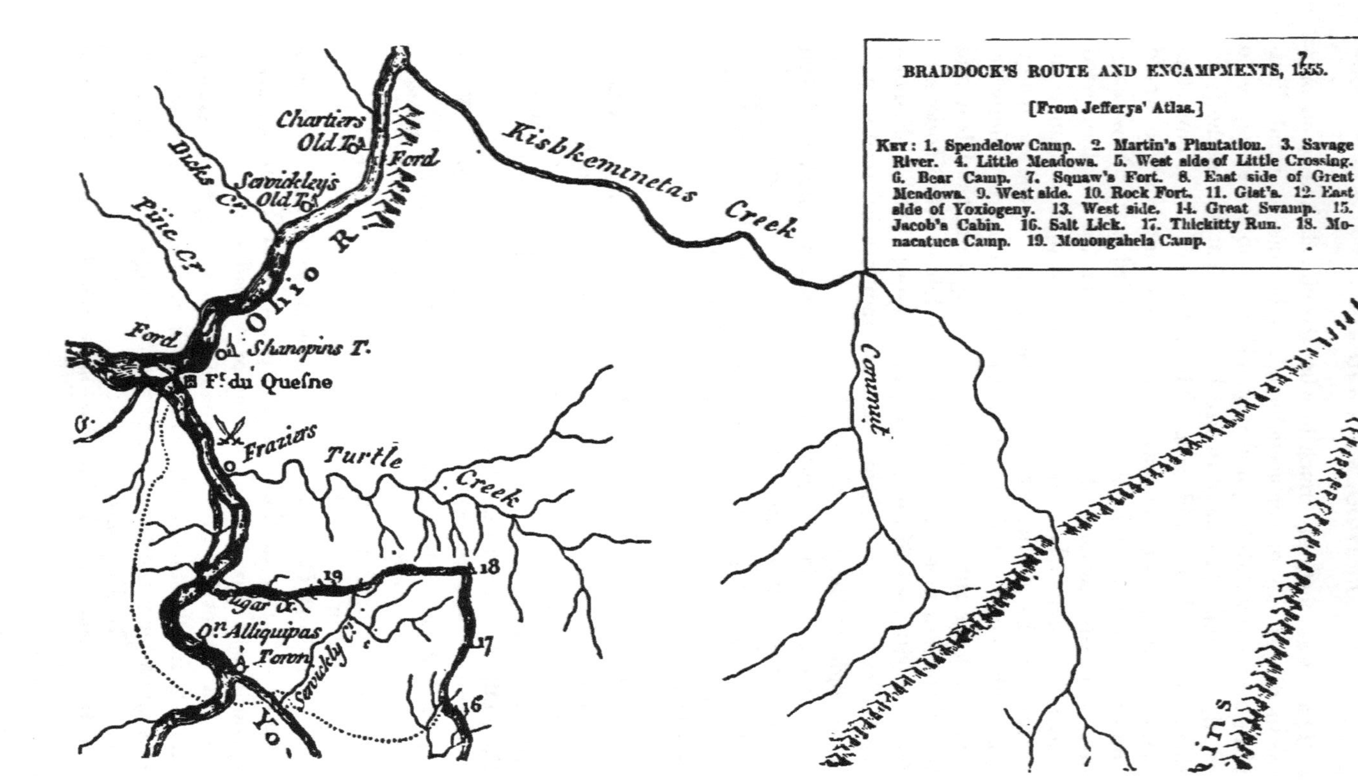

BRADDOCK'S ROUTE AND ENCAMPMENTS, 1555.

[From Jefferys' Atlas.]

KEY: 1. Spendelow Camp. 2. Martin's Plantation. 3. Savage River. 4. Little Meadows. 5. West side of Little Crossing. 6. Bear Camp. 7. Squaw's Fort. 8. East side of Great Meadows. 9. West side. 10. Rock Fort. 11. Gist's. 12. East side of Yoxiogeny. 13. West side. 14. Great Swamp. 15. Jacob's Cabin. 16. Salt Lick. 17. Thickitty Run. 18. Monacatuca Camp. 19. Monongahela Camp.

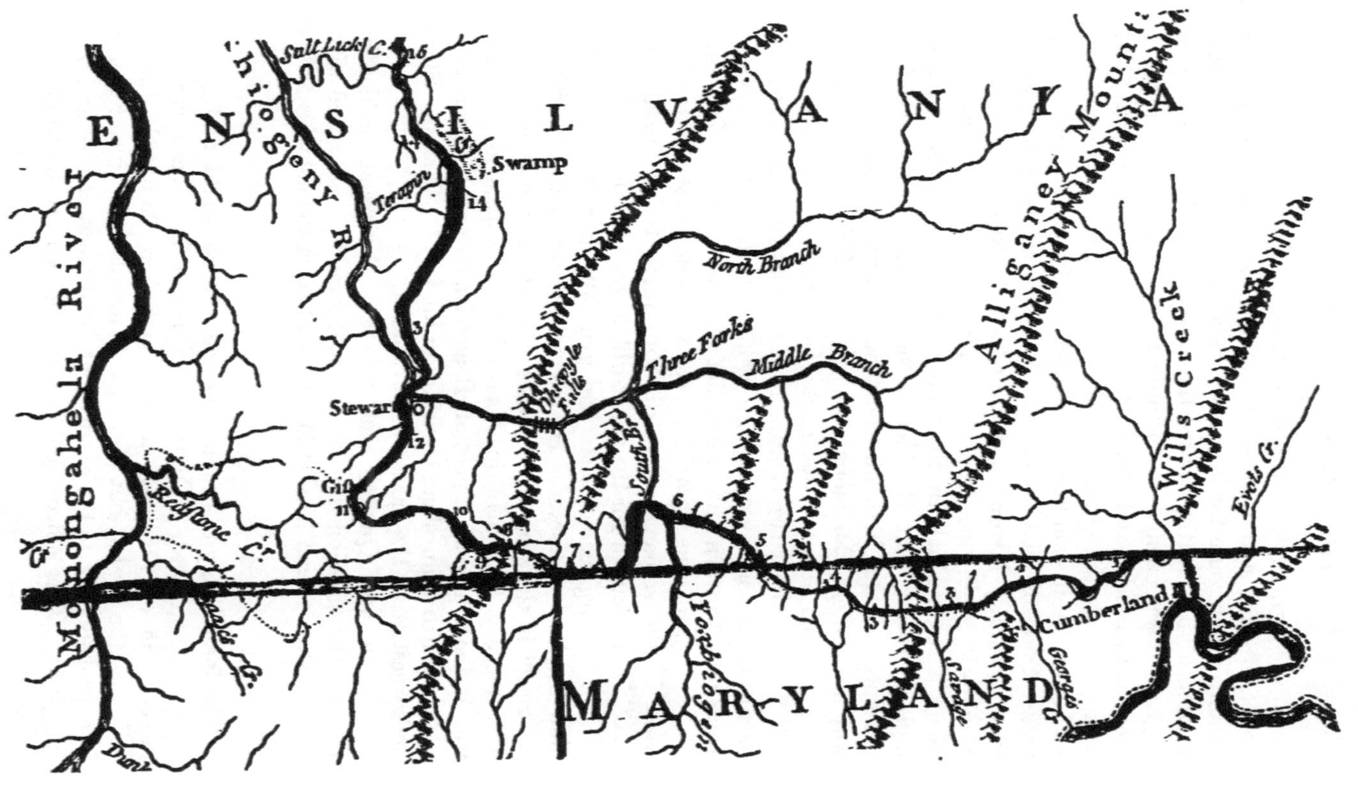
E N S I L V A N I A
chiogeny R
Salt Lick C.
Swamp
Terapin
North Branch
Three Forks
Middle Branch
Alligany Mount
Wills Creek
Evols C.
Stewart
Gist
Ohiopyle Falls
South Br.
Monongahela River
Redstone C.
Yoxhiogeni
Cumberland
Savage
Georges C.
M A R Y L A N D
Dunk

already roughly laid out, was preferred. This was partly, no doubt, because the ulterior advantage to Pennsylvania from establishing a route for her settlements was not to be considered in view of her apathy toward the expedition. Perhaps a more cogent reason existed in the influence which one Hanbury, a London merchant and shareholder in the Ohio Company, had over the weak and ignorant Duke of Newcastle. Hanbury had no hesitation in exercising this influence for the benefit of the future trade of that company. Washington, from his experience, naturally favored a route which he knew the best, and Braddock readily acceded to his aide's advice. It was thus along a route which in the main corresponds to the traveled highway to-day, that Braddock's van penetrated the gap four miles west of Cumberland, where the Baltimore and Ohio railway now enters the mountains. By the 10th of June, when this advance was made, Braddock's column consisted of about two thousand men. Confident that scouting parties of the enemy could slip by him, the general had advised Dinwiddie to warn the county lieutenants. The Virginia governor was doing his best to arouse enthusiasm; but the responses were discouraging. He confessed that he longed for the spirit which since the days of Louisbourg the colonists had generally associated with the New England character. He knew that Shirley was fearful of the result if the southern colonies did not show more alertness. When every fifth man in Massachusetts responded in 1745, was it too much to expect of Pennsylvania and Virginia that every twelfth man should spring to his feet? This was Shirley's question to the harassed Dinwiddie.

Braddock's advance.

The Virginians and Pennsylvanians apathetic.

German and Quaker and tidewater Virginian evidently thought the question impertinent, and Braddock advanced with less assistance than he should have had from the colonies at his back.

The force likely to be encountered was no doubt unduly exaggerated. Contrecœur's forces had been reduced in all his posts to less than four hundred during the winter, but some small details had since reached him, probably not to the extent that Bradstreet, at Oswego, had imagined. This officer sent a warning express to Braddock,

Contrecœur's force.

which could hardly as yet have reached that officer. At this time there were really in Duquesne a few companies of French regulars, a small body of Canadians, and perhaps eight hundred Indians. Some of these latter were a contingent from the tribes of the northwest, led by Charles de Langlade, and it has been said that Pontiac was among them.

French garrisons at the west.

Already the French had begun to withdraw their forces from the extreme northwest, and during the ensuing war their flag was nowhere flying beyond Mackinac except at the Sault Ste. Marie. They had left a small garrison at Fort Chartres on the Mississippi, now just rebuilt in substantial style.

Contrecœur and Beaujeu.

It is certain that Contrecœur had no hopes of doing more than to impede the British march. He had, in fact, not yet received the detail originally intended for Presqu' Isle, which Vaudreuil had ordered to Duquesne. Beaujeu, a subordinate officer under Contrecœur, had manifested an eagerness to confront the approaching enemy, but his commanding officer was averse to letting him. A rush of volunteers at once showed that the men had confidence in Beaujeu, and so he was permitted to lead out a body of eight or nine hundred men, mostly painted Indians, but including two hundred and more regulars and Canadians.

Beaujeu had hoped to reach the ford which Braddock must pass in season to secure it. In this he failed, but at a piece of hillocky ground along a defile, masked by thick leafage, he had just time to dispose his men before the pioneers of the British were startled at discovering them.

Braddock's force.

We must now follow Braddock's approach. He had left Colonel Dunbar some distance in his rear with a force to guard his trains. Up to his parting with Dunbar, his advance had been slow. His lumbering army had stretched three or four miles along a narrow, tortuous road, bristling with stumps and half cleared of stones. There was a motley show of the red Britisher and the blue Virginian. There were scattered, clanking cavalry and rumbling guns. His pioneers stopped to build bridges and level mole-hills where Washington saw little need of it. His flanking parties did not scour so thoroughly but that the enemy's scouts got into his camps.

Leaving Dunbar, the general now pushed on with the most available part of his army in light order and in fighting trim. He passed unopposed the ford where Beaujeu had hoped to confront him, and with almost an air of parade the red and blue, with their canopy of glancing steel, moved steadily on within the fatal defile.

It was the 7th of July. A volley at the front showed that the trial had come. Gage, the later general of the Revolutionary epoch, was in advance, and wheeling his guns to the front, their booming discharge and the rattling volley of musketeers threw the foe at first into confusion. The French leader, Beaujeu, fell. The Indians scattered and the Canadians wavered. At this moment, a commander on the English side such as Bouquet later proved himself to be might have turned this hesitancy of the enemy into a rout. The Indians, never easily rallied under discouragement, might have drawn the French into flight. Braddock hastened to the front, and the time lost in arranging a line and massing his troops in an order suited to open spaces gave the successor of Beaujeu a chance to rally his men. From every vantage-ground of rock and thicket, most of the time unseen, the French and their Indians poured into the thickened British ranks such ceaseless and irregular volleys, that the ground was soon so strewn with the dying that the tactical movements of the English were impeded. Each Virginian sought the shelter of a tree, and used up his powder upon marksmen as unseen as himself. Braddock strove hard to keep the line of the redcoats steady, but it was in vain. He had had four horses shot under him, when he gave orders for falling back. Governor Shirley's son, who was the general's secretary, was killed. Washington barely escaped on the third horse which he had mounted. Gage and Gates were wounded. Patrick MacKeller, the chief engineer, was more fortunate, and to his trained eye and calm observation amid it all we owe the plans of the battle, still existing, which are so necessary in comprehending it.

The fight July 7, 1755.

The English fly.

There could be no more trying ordeal for European troops than the incessant cracking of shots, with a man falling for each, and no one to be seen behind the white puff. Just as the recoil was most confused, the general was struck from his horse, and Washington was left in command. The young American tried to prevent the retreat from becoming a disordered rout. The attempt was useless. There was a headlong, bewildering scamper for the rear. The mass bore everybody along. It was nothing but a dispirited rabble surging before an infuriated horde of savages. In this way the fugitives, in wild confusion, enveloped the guard which was bearing off the dying Braddock. The ford which had been crossed so confidently was regained. Only when the wearied survivors huddled together for a while on the other side of the river was there a moment of respite. No attempt was made by the victors to pass the stream and harass the flying English longer; but savage and French scattered themselves along the defile and slopes, robbing the dead and despoiling the dying.

What there was left of this shamefully defeated army, now that the river was between them and their enemy, and a brief respite had followed, was soon hurried once more into a mad precipitancy, which showed little abatement till Dunbar's camp was reached. This officer, now assuming command, seems never to have given a thought to the possibility of intrenching himself, that he might save his supplies and dispirit Contrecœur enough to prevent his planning other movements. On the contrary, this Scottish colonel ordered the immediate destruction of his wagons and stores, and then led the miserable runaways in further flight.

The flight.

It was in the midst of this desperation that the almost speechless Braddock died. They buried him in the road, so that his men could trample out the signs of his grave. It was not till the fugitives reached Fort Cumberland, that there were returning signs of composure. Even then Dunbar was too agitated to do his palpable duty, and hurried on to Philadelphia, leaving the Virginians to defend what was now the most exposed of the English posts.

Braddock dies, and is buried.

So the first battle of the English in the Great Valley had been fought, with this dismal result. Three fourths of the officers had been killed or disabled and two thirds of the men, an average of not much short of two for each contestant on the other side.

The English loss.

France, with no one left to oppose her, had for a time at least made good her hold upon the broad areas beyond the mountains. Her control extended everywhere to the ridge of the Alleghanies, except at one point. The little settlement at Draper's Meadows still contained its sturdy company of loyal Scotch-Irish, guarding the sources of the Kanawha; but on the day following the defeat of Braddock, a party of Shawnees had fallen upon it and carried off some of the women. It was the first of a direful series of murderous raids along the luckless frontiers of Virginia and Pennsylvania. The furious savages now pushed over the outer mountains, and at times ravaged the banks of the Cowpasture River.

Draper's Meadows attacked.

The earliest acknowledgment of Braddock's defeat was in a circular which Colonel Innes sent by express from Fort Cumberland on July 11, four days after the battle. Two days later, he dispatched further particulars to both Sharpe and Dinwiddie. The latter got his first tidings on the 14th, the very day on which Shirley and Johnson at the north were congratulating themselves that Fort Duquesne must have fallen. Orme, one of Braddock's staff, sent off a letter from Fort Cumberland on the 18th, and a copy of this, sent north by Sharpe, was in Governor Hopkins's hands in Rhode Island on August 2, and it was not far into August before the chief centres of colonial life along the seaboard were informed of the disaster. Naturally, it was known in England before the French government heard of it, and intelligence from over the Channel reached Paris on September 5, about two months after the event.

News of the defeat spreads.

The victory caused hilarious excitement at Duquesne, as we know from the testimony of an English prisoner confined there, but it was followed by a period of trepidation, when it was feared that the British would recover, and with Dunbar's reserve advance again. What rendered the situation worse was the difficulty of communicating with Canada, and a little later such tidings as they got at the forks were far from assuring, for the wheat crop had failed on the St. Lawrence, and last year's store was brutally used to exact money from the people. Montcalm, on hearing from Duquesne, during

Effect at Duquesne.

the autumn, described the fort as "not worth a straw, and as having been recently nearly swept away by a freshet." All this time, while the English leaders were getting nothing but harrowing details from the frontiers, they might have taken some heart, could they have known the truth. In the latter part of October, Sharpe was complaining that they had not been able to learn anything about the condition of Duquesne.

The months immediately following Braddock's defeat were very anxious ones for the English. The direful catastrophe had let loose a fiendish swarm of savages along the borders. The Dinwiddie and Sharpe letters and the numerous reports from local observers, which are preserved in the printed volumes of the *Pennsylvania Archives* and *Records*, show us the gloom of the hour. The anxiety was mixed with bitterness at the pusillanimous conduct of Dunbar, in sacrificing the munitions which had cost them so dearly.

The borders raided.

Washington was soon put in command of a regiment of borderers at Winchester in the Shenandoah valley. Captain Lewis's journal of his march with these troops reveals the number of deserted houses throughout that region, whose occupants had fled before the Indian prowlers. It needed all of Washington's alertness, with the activity of his patrols, and the vicinage of Dinwiddie's fort on Jackson River, to keep this country along the eastern foot of the Alleghanies within the pale of frontier life.

Washington in the valley of Virginia.

North of the Potomac matters were even worse. The Delawares, centring at Kittanning on the Alleghany, were crossing the mountains in hordes, and skipping in fiendish fury from hamlet to hamlet. Andrew Montour was sent to the Great Island on the west branch of the Susquehanna to appease the Indians, and forestall the French in their evident purpose to seize Shamokin (now Sunbury) and make it the centre of French influence in this region. Conrad Weiser had his scouts out to watch their movements, and at one time he reported that with their French allies, not less devilish than they, fifteen hundred savages were pouring upon the side valleys along the Juniata and the west branches of the Susquehanna. Among the Mohawks, Johnson was endeavoring to make the Iroquois maintain their supremacy over these Alleghany tribes and check their incursions, but with little

The hostile Delawares.

The Iroquois.

success; nor was he more prosperous in trying to make the renegade neophytes at Caughnawaga remain neutral.

The protection of the border in Pennsylvania was much complicated by an untimely quarrel of the assembly with the Proprietaries of the province. These grandsons of William Penn had few of his winning traits. The peaceful tenets of the Quakers were also hard to overcome. "There is so great a majority of Quakers in the house," wrote Governor Morris, "that no warlike preparations are to be expected from them, being, as they pretend, contrary to their principles;" and it seemed for a while as if the Scotch-Irish and the Germans among them, who constituted the adventurous settlers of the west, were to be left to their fate by the sluggish Quakers of the east. Franklin suspected "that the defense of the country was not disagreeable to any of them, provided they were not required to assist in it." He gives us an amusing instance of the way in which they finally consented to participate in the common zeal, by voting allowances "for wheat and other grain," whose kernels they expected to be interpreted to mean powder. As matters grew worse, the assembly was at last induced to grant, "as aid to the crown," an appropriation of fifty thousand pounds to be assessed as a tax on all estates. The Proprietaries demurred, as this would include their own reserved territory within the province. The assembly would not retreat, and it was finally compromised by placing the Proprietaries' liability at five thousand pounds.

Troubles in Pennsylvania.

The Quaker element.

Disputes with the Penns.

But there was something more than money necessary, and Franklin was doing the best he could to arouse a martial spirit. In November, when even New Jersey, east of the Delaware, had become uneasy, and the mayor and principal citizens of Philadelphia were not without apprehension, as new incursions were reported from the north, Franklin was enabled to overcome the Quaker repugnance and secure the passage in the assembly of a militia act of no great stringency. If any still held that the trans-Alleghany country, being the crown's, was no concern of theirs, they could agree with Franklin that now, at least, the colony itself was attacked. It was no longer a question of protecting British trade, but of the

Pennsylvania militia act.

preservation of their own lives. They saw all this in the flocks of settlers coming into York from the distant and demoralized Cumberland County, and in the bewildered families which Weiser was conducting from over the mountains within the protecting lines of the inner forts. The valley of the Juniata had become almost entirely deserted. Maury tells us that it was short work in these painful months to withdraw the border settlements a hundred and fifty miles, thus interposing a desert on the English side of the Alleghany portals.

Frontier settlers driven back.

We have seen that while Braddock was following the Monongahela, it had been expected that along the shores of the Lakes other aggressive movements would secure an entrance to the Ohio valley in the north.

The campaign at the north.

As early as January, 1755, Shirley had matured plans for attacking Crown Point and invading Canada, — a scheme which would have seriously affected the French purpose on the Ohio. He presented this scheme to the council at Alexandria, which modified it so far as to divide the movement, Johnson undertaking the attack along Lake Champlain, while Shirley himself was to assault Niagara. Shirley's route lay from Albany to Schenectady, up the Mohawk by boat, making a portage at Fort Stanwix to Wood's Creek. Thence he was to find his way to Oswego by the traders' route, and on the lake he was to gather a flotilla and skirt the shore to Niagara.

Niagara menaced.

Shirley and Johnson were at Albany when the news of Braddock's defeat reached them, and fearing its effect upon their own men, they tried for a while to conceal the tidings. The death of Braddock had made Shirley the ranking officer on the continent, but he did not receive his new commission till the season's work was at an end. His elevation was not fortunate, and Hutchinson tells us that "friends saw the risk he was running, and wished he had contented himself with a civic station." His friends were wise. His career had been a striking, and in many ways a successful one, and he shared with Pepperell the glories of Louisbourg. His diplomatic career at Paris had brought him credit, and he had been linked with his Louisbourg associate as the two native leaders for the royal American regiments. His merits, however, were those of a politician, and not of a soldier. In some

Shirley's character.

ways he "knew how to stoop to what he understood," and he had faculties which gained the respect of Franklin, but at the same time there was a certain light air about him which Parkman calls "an element of boyishness." His career has never been adequately studied.

Unfortunately, he and Johnson were not in accord, and mutual jealousies perplexed their common aims. Johnson spoke of his rival's "causeless jealousy and unmerited resentment," and wrote bitter complaints to the Lords of Trade. On the whole, Shirley, who had pushed Johnson into the paths of military glory, secures our sympathy in the quarrel, though he was less prudent than usual in interfering with Johnson's power as superintendent of the Indians. De Lancey, a politician of a type produced by evil days, did also what he could to embitter Shirley's existence.

His disputes with Johnson, and De Lancey.

It was in March (1755) that the English government announced in Parliament that a French war was inevitable. It had learned that the French were equipping a large naval force at Brest and Rochelle, and that an attendant fleet of transports was to carry an army under Dieskau to Quebec. It mattered little that the two countries were preserving the formal intercourse of peace, and on April 27, Admiral Boscawen, possessed of an understanding of the cabinet's wishes, rather than committed to instructions, put to sea in order to intercept the French armament. A week later (May 3), the French fleet was on its way, taking not only the new general, but a new governor, Vaudreuil, to succeed Duquesne. Two only of the French ships fell into Boscawen's hands. Consequently, by June 19, the safe arrival of the rest of the fleet added three thousand French regulars to the thousand already at Quebec. This made a pretty effective addition to the eight thousand militia which Canada was drilling for the campaign.

French and English preparations for war.

During the spring, Johnson was doing the best he could to hold the Iroquois steady in their allegiance, and no doubt spending wisely the ten thousand pounds with which he had been intrusted for that purpose. In this business he was at his best, and his twenty years in the Mohawk country looking after the landed interests of his uncle,

Johnson and the Iroquois.

Sir Peter Warren, — the same who commanded the fleet that helped Pepperrell at Louisbourg, — had thoroughly schooled him in the arts of Indian diplomacy.

During the summer at Albany, he had been busy organizing the forces which he was to lead against Crown Point. General Phineas Lyman, of Connecticut, his second in command, had built a fort at the carrying place towards the lake, and this post was made the base of operations. There were among Johnson's other trusted lieutenants not a few who were later famous in this and the Revolutionary war, — Israel Putnam, John Stark, Seth Pomeroy, and Ephraim Williams among them.

The Crown Point expedition.

Dieskau moved up Lake Champlain, and was preparing to attack the fort which Lyman had built. It was now September (1755), and the impending struggle was to decide if the English were to be driven back to Schenectady and Albany by a disaster equal to that by which they had recoiled to Fort Cumberland on the Potomac.

Hendricks, the Mohawk, and Williams, the founder of the college of that name, were in command of a flying camp, watching the French advance. The French planned an ambush and enticed this too unwary body into it. The suffering of the deceived party was for a while much like that which Braddock had experienced on the Monongahela, but a vigilant woodsman, Nathan Whiting of Connecticut, finally extricated the English, after Williams and the friendly chief had fallen. Whiting did more, for he managed to keep the eager foe sufficiently long in restraint for Johnson, who was near the head of Lake George, to build a barricade of wagons and boats. It was in an onset against this improvised bulwark that the French general soon found his match. The repulse was steady and vigorous. Johnson was early wounded and borne from the field. Lyman, who succeeded to the command, turned the repulse into a rout. Dieskau was left on the field sorely but not mortally wounded, but the great body of his troops managed to fly beyond pursuit.

Battle of Lake George.

Johnson's opportunity was to have permitted so good a leader as Lyman had proved himself to be to deal a finishing stroke by advancing upon the disorganized fugitives. Perhaps he turned from the chance through something like

Johnson and Lyman.

that jealousy which he saw so readily in Shirley. Lyman's friends long contended that it was a base spirit in Johnson which prompted him later to take Lyman's name from the defensive works which the Connecticut soldier had built, and bestow upon it that of Fort Edward. Johnson's friends assert that it was more prudent for him to give over a pursuit and fortify the head of the lake by building what became known as Fort William Henry. This defense was placed so as to guard what Johnson now rechristened Lake George, after the English king, an appellation which easily supplanted the original name given by the French.

Johnson holds a conference, September 11, 1755.

Here, on September 11, he held a conference with the Indians, and for some weeks he was busy with these interviews, giving time for the French to strengthen themselves at Ticonderoga. The two armies were thus left facing each other in intrenchments, from the opposite ends of the lake, but on November 27 Johnson withdrew the main part of his forces to Albany for winter quarters.

Winter quarters.

Johnson a baronet.

The battle of Lake George, if not all that it might have been, was a cheery contrast to the miserable failure near Fort Duquesne, and Johnson was the fortunate recipient of a baronetcy and a grant of five thousand pounds. Shirley's friends claimed that this money was simply subtracted from the grant which Parliament had made for the war, and so diminished the resources which could give it vigor.

Shirley's failure.

Meanwhile, Shirley had reaped no laurels for his military ambition. Braddock's papers, taken in the fight, had revealed Shirley's intended attack on Niagara, and though there were many delays in the movements of Contrecœur, from his needless fear of Dunbar and from his intercepted communications, Shirley was so conscious that the French could effectually reinforce the point of his intended attack that he became timid. In August, he learned from spies that no troops had yet arrived at Niagara from Duquesne. He dallied at Oswego till the season of gales on the lake was impending, and on September 27 he and his council of war decided to abandon the campaign. In October, Shirley and his men were back in Albany.

A hesitating action, induced very likely in part by the unsympathetic relations of the two northern commanders, and increased, it is probable, from the setback which Braddock had received, and from the dilatory support of the colonial legislatures, had made the year, on the whole, a disastrous one for the English. The French, with the aim of driving their enemies out of the two great valleys, had practically succeeded. The little hamlet at Draper's Meadows and the posts at Lake George and Oswego still indeed remained in English hands; but there was little hope now of barrier colonies, and a plan which Samuel Hazard outlined, and which the Connecticut assembly fostered, of a new colony beyond the confines of Pennsylvania, and extending beyond the Mississippi, vanished in the air. Franklin's hopes of a Pennsylvania colony on Lake Erie, and a Virginia one by the Ohio, had passed into the limbo of forgotten things. The forty miles' breadth of bottom lands which lined the course of the Scioto was to be left to blossom under a new government in the next century.

The year disastrous for the English.

CHAPTER XVIII.

TWO DISMAL YEARS, 1756, 1757.

Plans for a new campaign. 1756.

THE year 1756 opened with the French holding the English at arm's length from the sources of the Ohio. Early in December (1755), Shirley had been confirmed in his position as commander-in-chief by the receipt of his commission. A few days later, he held a council of war at New York, and laid before it the royal instructions. These outlined a plan of campaign not greatly unlike that of the previous year, which had so woefully miscarried. Troops were to be gathered at Will's Creek, to confront the force which it was supposed France would send up the Mississippi to defend Duquesne. Indeed, Franklin, who had now been commissioned to defend the frontiers of Pennsylvania, was confident that the main French purpose was to carry the war into that province. Another army was to gain Niagara and the Lakes and secure this entrance to the Ohio valley, while ships were to be built to patrol Lake Ontario. Shirley pointed out that Oswego must be held at all hazards, for he, better than those to whom he later resigned the control, understood how it was the key of the northern route. He anticipated perfectly just what did happen, — that its fall would push the English frontiers back upon Schenectady, if not upon Albany. To retain Oswego meant to Shirley an attack on Frontenac, which his displacement put off for two years. Success at Frontenac was to be followed by a movement upon Mackinac, and Shirley estimated that a force of six thousand men would carry out this part of the campaign. Half as many, with the aid of the southern Indians, he thought would secure Duquesne; and another six thousand were enough to succeed at Crown Point. New England would take care of a feint upon Quebec by the Chaudière, for which two thousand troops would suffice.

Oswego. 1756.

The scheme was brilliant enough to animate Shirley's martial ambition, and Governor Belcher might well hope, if it were successful, that "Canada would be rooted out."

To organize such a complicated undertaking kept Shirley busy for the winter in Boston, while his old rival, Johnson, acting under Shirley's instructions, was endeavoring to check the Indian ravages which still continued along the Susquehanna and the Juniata. Franklin, at the same time, had every occasion for his activity in pushing forward defenders and their supplies. Teedyuscung, the Delaware leader, was still defiant, and nothing that Johnson could do was able for a time to induce the Iroquois to interpose as a shield for the whites. The Senecas absolutely refused, and the Delawares were satisfied with the opportunity of unpetticoating themselves, as their Indian phraseology went. The spring, with its uncertainties, led the Pennsylvania government to a declaration of war, while Teedyuscung maintained himself, both with the Six Nations and the English, in a way to show how he stood on a vantage-ground.

Dangers in Pennsylvania.

The Delaware war.

The Pennsylvania government, despite the lukewarmness of the Quaker assembly, established a line of palisaded posts from the Delaware to the new road which had been opened to the mountains. About eight hundred men were scattered among these forts as garrisons, while patrols were kept skirring about in the interspaces. As a sort of base for these operations, a new fort was built at Shamokin, where the two main branches of the Susquehanna met. These enterprises had about used up the sixty thousand pounds raised on the credit of the province. They had also given the Delawares new grounds for apprehensions lest these military structures had put new liens on their territory. It was a current belief that this fresh discontent was fostered "by vile, rascally deserters, Irish Roman Catholics, who were employed by the French."

Frontier forts.

Along the Potomac and south of it, Sharpe and Dinwiddie were scheming to keep up the courage of the people. The conditions were not inspiring. There was a space of two hundred miles between the tolerably settled tidewater country and the scattered hamlets of a frontier three hundred miles in extent. Here Washington was trying to organize a defense against a persistent horde of invaders.

The Maryland and Virginia frontiers. 1756.

He was only able to promise his rangers and garrisons eightpence a day against the eighteenpence which the same service received in Pennsylvania. Such a disparity of remuneration did not prevent Dinwiddie wishing that the Pennsylvanians would become as ardent bushfighters as his Virginians. Nevertheless, the 173,318 whites in Dinwiddie's province did far less than his zeal wished of them. He himself labored to hold the Cherokees fast in their alliance. It had long been a pet belief of the Virginian governor that a line of fortified posts from Crown Point to the Creek country was of the first importance, and he would have them built and maintained by a tax imposed by Parliament. The Albany plan of union having failed, Pennsylvania had taken up the undertaking on her own soil, under Franklin's urgency. It had been found that the Indians had learned from the French the art of firing stockades. So Sharpe of Maryland had continued the line beyond Fort Cumberland by planting Fort Frederick on the North Mountain, near the Potomac, and spent something like a thousand pounds in making it of masonry, — not altogether without inciting charges of extravagance. There were two hundred men put in it, and an equal number of men ranging beyond it. On the Virginia border, Washington had been instructed to run a line of stockaded posts, twenty or thirty miles apart, southward from Fort Dinwiddie, to depend on a fortified magazine, which, during the summer, he built at Winchester. These forts were convenient rallying-points; but they were much too far asunder to guard the contiguous valleys from hostile depredators.

Dinwiddie's views.

Fort Frederick. 1756.

The Virginia forts. 1756.

In February, Dinwiddie was hoping that Shirley's plan of an advance from Fort Cumberland would be attempted. He was urging Morris of Pennsylvania, now occupied with establishing his fortified barriers, to place one of them at least beyond the mountains. Washington, taking advantage of a lull in the enemy's movements, had gone to Boston to consult with Shirley. He was directed on his way back to confer with Morris in Philadelphia, and see if some plan of concerted action among the southern colonies could not be entered upon. Shirley figured out what the quota of these colonies would be under the schedule of 1754, and found it to be 7,284 men. Of these he thought 4,000 might, with the aid of a

English preparations. 1756.

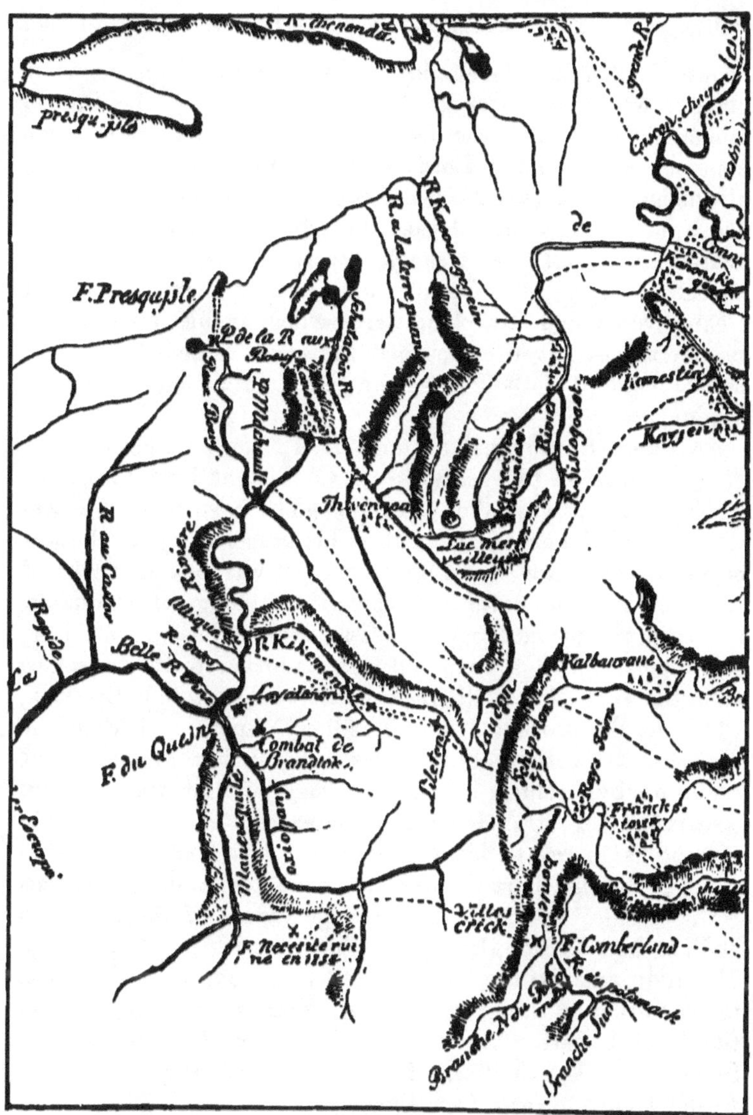

THE FRONTIERS.

[From Pouchot's *Mémoire de la dernière Guerre.*]

thousand Cherokees be employed against Fort Duquesne, while the rest would do better service north in severing the French communications with the Ohio. Dinwiddie was at the same time urging upon the Lords of Trade his plan of fortifying the mountain passes. No peace could be had, he was sure, till the French were expelled from the Ohio, and he recommended that a Protestant colony should be maintained as a barrier on the Ohio lands. The German and Irish Roman Catholics of Pennsylvania and Maryland were seldom in his mind but as hostile aliens. It was reckoned that at this time there were twelve hundred Catholics in Pennsylvania of an age to take the sacraments.

Attack planned on Duquesne. 1756.

In March, Shirley had commissioned Sharpe to head an attack on the forks of the Ohio, or at least to make a diversion in that direction. The movement gave Dinwiddie encouragement in his despondency, for he was eager for something to be done, and yet was not confident of success. He feared that Dumas, now in charge of Duquesne, had been reinforced from the Mississippi, and some time later was reporting that a thousand men had come to its assistance from the Wabash. Still, an advance would create a diversion, which would prevent Dumas's aiding Niagara, and leave the northern task easier. Dumas was doing his best to conceal his condition by keeping his raiders busy, and Sharpe was constantly hearing of their pushing in between the Pennsylvania forts so as to ravage his own borders. His scouts, forty miles beyond Fort Cumberland, were encountering the enemies' rangers. The savage rancor of these French Indians had already driven the pioneers back from the South Mountain, and left the German settlements exposed. This was the condition of things, with no organized movement made on the English part, when news of the fall of Oswego came in September. It was at once feared it might be the signal for a fresh advance in force from the Ohio.

Indian ravages. 1756.

While these alternating scenes of trepidation and preparation were following each other east of the Alleghanies, the English made two really aggressive movements beyond their passes, but neither of them effected a lodgment in the Great Valley.

In April, Andrew Lewis led a body of Virginians and Cherokees against the Shawnee towns, two hundred and fifty miles beyond the Virginia frontiers. The party was absent for a month. They experienced bad weather, and lost their provisions in crossing a stream. In its main purpose Lewis failed of success, but he captured some vagabond French. They were supposed to be a party of the exiled Acadians, who were trying to find their way from the coast to Duquesne. On the return march, his Cherokees, weary of foot, seized some horses belonging to frontiersmen. This was viewed as an outrage, and the Indians were promptly punished, but at the risk of their alliance.

Lewis's expedition against the Shawnees. 1756.

Late in August, Colonel John Armstrong started from Fort Shirley with a body of Pennsylvanians, and crossing the mountains fell upon Kittanning, the rallying-point of the hostile Delawares, situated on the Alleghany. Armstrong devastated the settlement, rescued a few English whom the Indians held as prisoners, and safely returned. He had delivered a scourging blow, but it had small effect upon the progress of events, except that it taught the enemy that there were blows to take as well as to give. The French accounts slur the matter, but the English thought it quite equal in boldness and celerity to the raids of the French. It gave occasion for Dinwiddie to offer congratulation to Governor Denny, very shortly after his succeeding to Morris in the executive office of Pennsylvania.

Armstrong attacks Kittanning. 1756.

During the summer, the French on the Ohio had been preparing for the worst. In the spring, Vaudreuil congratulated himself particularly in being able to provision Duquesne from New Orleans and the Illinois. Though this involved tugging at tow-ropes and poling bateaux against the current, it was less laborious than attempting such succor from the St. Lawrence. Vaudreuil recognized the risks from flanking parties of the English at the rapids near the modern Louisville, which necessitated a wearisome portage, and he considered that, to secure the transit, a fort at that point was necessary.

Duquesne provisioned. 1756.

Thus sure of his supplies, Dumas, the commander at the forks, pursued a policy of harrying the English to keep them busy. He was conscious that his own defenses could not stand an attack of artillery, if the enemy were given time for such an assault.

Dumas anxious. 1756.

Fearing lest this was intended, he was alert to discover any purpose of the kind, and kept out his patrols in the direction of Fort Cumberland, whence the blow must come. It was on such a scouting party that Céloron, who had buried the plates on the Ohio, was killed during the summer.

Dumas and his raiders. 1756.

Dumas had found that he must satisfy himself with the moral rather than with the physical help which had been sent to Canada in the spring. The reinforcement which had reached Quebec in May had brought Montcalm, Lévis, Bourlamaque, and Bougainville, but the troops were assigned to the more vital points of Frontenac, Ticonderoga, and Niagara, — the latter particularly. As Vaudreuil expressed it, the chief interest of the French lay here, for with Niagara wrested from them, Duquesne was but a burden. Weiser, the Pennsylvania agent, was confident that at one time Dumas had not more than two hundred men with him; but his flying squads were abundantly supplying him with scalps, as he assured his superior at Quebec.

Shirley recalled. 1756.

The general course of the war during the year had afforded little comfort to the English. The ministry, under color of his being able to give them advice, had recalled Shirley in the spring, and the intimation which was given of a new military leader caused Morris to think that the interest of the war was likely to centre in America. Shirley had already suspected that he was to be superseded, but it was not till June, after he had got his plans well matured, had placed General Winslow of Massachusetts in command of the chief army of invasion, and had had a struggle with the intrigues of Johnson and his cabal, that he received his definite orders. Some of the better men, like Livingston and Franklin, had not lost confidence in Shirley, and received the intelligence with regret, though Franklin thought that Shirley was little averse to the relief. Webb and Abercrombie had come in advance of the supreme commander, but on July 23 Shirley received his immediate successor in New York. This irritating and irritable nobleman, the Earl of Loudoun,

Loudoun in command. 1756.

lost no time in advising the colonial governors of his arrival. Shirley outlined his plan for the campaign, and the earl promptly countermanded Shirley's orders. There was indeed a new aspect to the war. The diplomats of England and France had doffed their polite caps, and in May and June respectively the two countries had declared war. Governor Hardy received the word at Albany four days after Loudoun's arrival. The news reached Dinwiddie in Williamsburg on August 7, and Washington knew it at Winchester on the 17th.

War declared. 1756.

Meanwhile, there had been a glimmer of good fortune, owing to Shirley's prevision. He had recruited a body of whalemen from New England, and put them under the command of Lieutenant-Colonel Bradstreet, to man a flotilla of bateaux and protect the communications with Oswego. In July, this amphibious little army had valiantly defeated a body of French who were trying to interrupt those communications. This success availed little, however, for a few weeks later the spirited Montcalm had invested the forts at Oswego, and was using upon them the batteries which Braddock had lost on the Monongahela. By the middle of August, the post was in French hands. The result might have been different if Loudoun had followed Shirley's advice and thrown two regiments into the forts. As it was, the French success virtually settled the year's campaign. It alarmed the English at Albany enough to paralyze their other movements. It released Montcalm so that he hastened to Carillon (Ticonderoga) and kept watch upon Winslow at Fort William Henry. With this obstruction of the English plans the season ended. The result of all was that the French had maintained themselves on Lake Champlain, and had obtained a footing on the southern shore of Ontario, strengthening the barrier in this direction against the English advance into the Great Valley.

Bradstreet's success. 1756.

Montcalm takes Oswego. 1756.

Montcalm at Carillon. 1756.

If Shirley had been shelved, his rival had been given no new chance of martial distinction. Johnson had indeed been put to the service in which he shone most. There had been for a long time ominous rumors that the Six Nations were treating with the French, and

Johnson brings Teedyuscung over to the English.

had gone over to the enemy. By an adroit bearing, Johnson was at last in a position to treat at Onondaga with the concurrence of Teedyuseung, and on July 21 the Iroquois and the Delawares were brought round to the English interests at a conference, which was strengthened by later conciliations at German Flats in August and September.

Meanwhile, the Delaware chieftain was negotiating an independent understanding with the Pennsylvanians at Easton. They might have made a peace, as it looked, if Loudoun had not interfered on the ground that Sir William alone was authorized to make Indian treaties. This interruption came at a time when it was looking black on the Pennsylvania border. Fort Granville, one of the exposed stockades, had been taken (July 30), and it seemed as if the frontiers were recoiling everywhere, and communications with Forts Lyttleton and Shirley were growing precarious. The war appeared to be assuming fresh violence, and it must be met; but after a while a lull came, and the public mind adjusted itself to new movements when the assembly, after much persuasion, had made an appropriation of thirty thousand pounds, "for the king's use," as their language of subterfuge put it.

The Delawares and the Pennsylvanians.

The Pennsylvania borders.

George Croghan, whose trading interest had suffered by the war, was relieved from the immediate perils of bankruptcy by the Pennsylvania Assembly in their anxiety to have so influential a friend sent among the Indians along the frontier. He had not disappointed expectation, unless in the lavish use which he made of the money appropriated for appeasing the Indians. The government of the province did not treat him in just the spirit he thought he deserved, and he resigned his commission. It seemed a fortunate thing, both for the crown and his province, when Johnson recognized his value, and some months later, on November 24, made Croghan his deputy in the management of the savages in Pennsylvania and on the Ohio.

George Croghan.

The events of the next year (1757) were even more discouraging for the English. There had been quiet along the borders of Pennsylvania and Virginia during the winter; but in the early spring rumors were rife of a gathering of French at Fort

Machault (Venango) for an attack on Shamokin. The French, however, were too much engrossed with a counter-solicitude, for any such desperate purpose. Vaudreuil, in April, was issuing anxious orders and urging De Ligneris, now in command at Duquesne, to strengthen that post. An extreme scarcity of provisions prevailed in Canada. The posts on the Ohio so suffered from this cause that the men were scattered to pick up subsistence. Later in the spring and in the early summer, rumors of a French advance thickened along the frontiers, and the nimble scouts kept the borderers anxious. Discordant stories about the force which De Ligneris had with him probably arose from his habit of sending out his scalping parties in a body, to be broken up when well within the enemy's borders. These parties coming and going kept the force in the fort inconstant in numbers, and this accounts for the irreconcilable figures which were from time to time reported to Sharpe or Dinwiddie. Occasionally there were stories of flotillas from the Mississippi bringing munitions and men to the French. Whenever a French prisoner was taken, he was pretty sure to magnify such recruiting. These exaggerations served to dismay the English, particularly if the prisoner could add that parties from the Illinois had come in to De Ligneris, besides occasional squads of Cherokees and Creeks.

Shamokin. 1757.

Fears of a French advance. 1757.

Such was the summer's history, — rumor and counter-rumor; and it ran well on into the autumn. By October, however, it was feared that the French successes at the north had given them the opportunity to hurry forward a contingent from Niagara, which rendered an advance from the Ohio more than probable. Upon such recurrent reports the garrison at Fort Cumberland was astir. The Indians, usually friendly, had become emboldened. The Cherokees and Catawbas were wandering about in a sulking mood, and in some places the neighboring Indians had proved so unruly that the militia was made ready for an emergency.

The southern Indians.

The same untoward condition of the English projects at the north had fostered fresh discontent among the Six Nations and the dependent Delawares. The fleeting months make a long record of conferences which only postponed the end. The Iroquois could not, or would not, restrain

The northern Indians.

their young warriors from scalping expeditions. Johnson labored with the Shawnee and Delaware embassies with little effect. The Senecas and Cayugas were unmistakably hostile, and interposed to prevent the Delawares of the Ohio from uniting with their Susquehanna brothers in any peaceful plan. By midsummer, Johnson began to have some success in keeping a part, at least, of the tribes in a neutral disposition. His immediate neighbors, the Mohawks, with the Oneidas and Tuscaroras, were more easily held.

Croghan and Teedyuscung.

His deputy, Croghan, had at the same time a passing success with Teedyuscung, who, "considering how he loved strong liquor, behaved very well." Croghan managed during the summer, by wheedling the Delawares and cajoling the Senecas, to bring that wary chieftain into one of those intermittent spasms of peace which the Indians were prompt to exhibit to those who would pay for it. They were always pretty sure to leave their brothers on the Ohio untrammeled for other negotiations of a like kind. Much the same sort of truce was purchased for a while with the Cherokees.

Pitt in power.

Any successful negotiation with the savages was at such a period remarkable, and testified to the skill of Johnson and his deputies. Pitt, of whom no one had greater expectations than himself, had, indeed, in the early summer, come into power; but hardly in time to effect much change in the American plans before another season. These were still doomed to mismanagement through the fussy imbecility of Loudoun. Early in the spring, the colonial governors, meeting him at Philadelphia, had learned that his military strategy was centred in a movement north, in connection with another toward the Gulf of St. Lawrence. It was apparent that the passes of the Alleghanies were to be left to their fate, a scant protective force looking out for the border as well as it could.

Loudoun's plans.

Rigaud foiled at Fort William Henry.

The actual campaign opened in March with a bit of good luck for the English. Rigaud, a brother of Vaudreuil, and distrusted by Montcalm, was foiled in an attempt to surprise Fort William Henry by stealing upon it over the frozen lake. Meanwhile, Loudoun sailed away from New York to do great things at Louisbourg. While he was

NOTE. The opposite map is Emanuel Bowen's map of the country of the southern Indians, 1764.

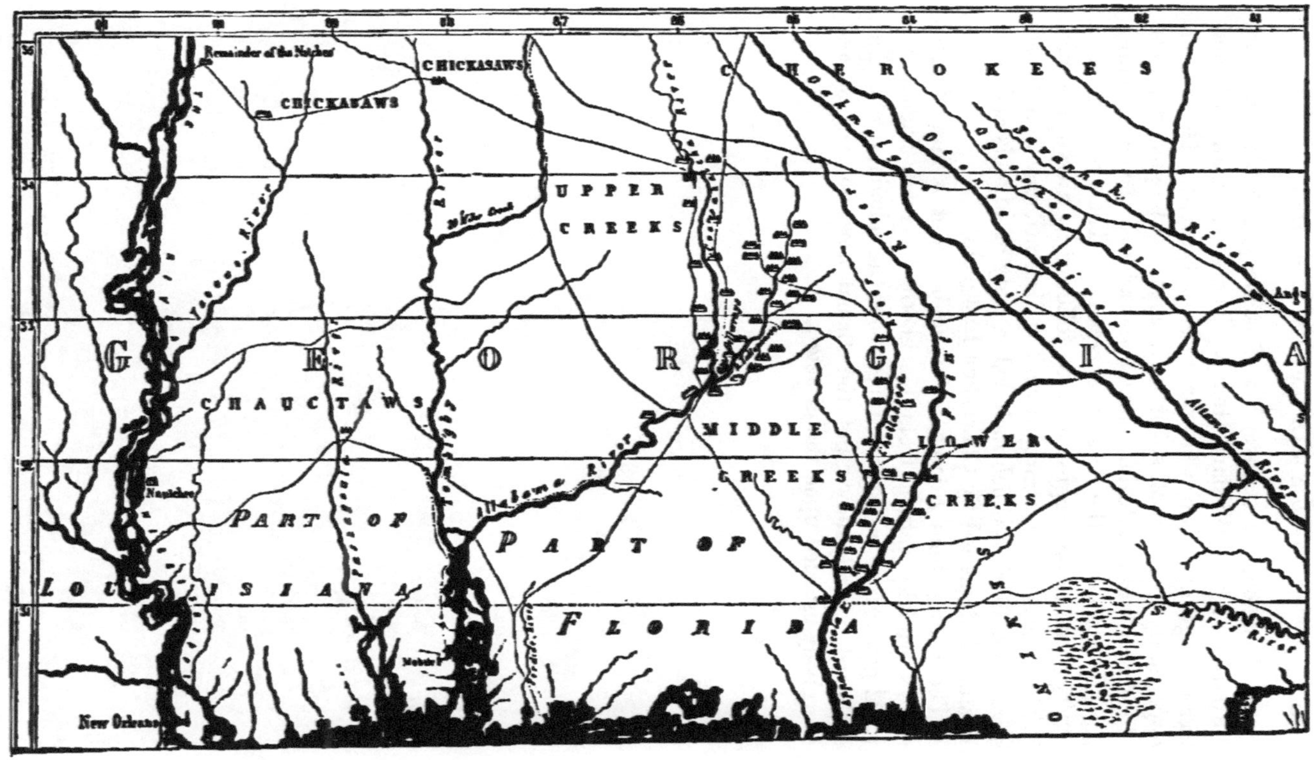

Remainder of the Natches
CHICKASAWS
CHICKASAWS
CHEROKEES
UPPER CREEKS
MIDDLE CREEKS
LOWER CREEKS
CHAUCTAWS
GEORGIA
PART OF LOUISIANA
PART OF FLORIDA
Savannah River
Ogeechee River
Oconee River
Oakmulgee River
Altamaha River
Flint River
Alabama River
Yazoo River
St. Mary's River
Natches
Mobile
New Orleans

gone, Montcalm, by a clever bit of strategy, got between Fort Edward and Fort William Henry. There was small skill and less courage in Webb, who was in Fort Edward. He had an opportunity to act with spirit, and chose to be pusillanimous. He played into Montcalm's hands, and advised the commanding officer at the lake to surrender. The red flag came down on August 9, to be followed by a revolting massacre, perpetrated upon the disarmed garrison by the savage auxiliaries, which included a body of Miamis and some western Indians led by Charles de Langlade.

Fort William Henry falls. August, 1757.

The young John Adams, when he heard of it and of Loudoun's panicky return from his bootless errand, likened the royal generals to millstones hung about the colonial neck. The seaboard, up and down, got the dismal news in August, and everybody brooded upon the disasters.

CHAPTER XIX.

THE OHIO AND ST. LAWRENCE WON.

1758–1759.

THE winter of 1757–58 in Canada was one of ill-advised confidence and gayety. For two years the French had held their own and more. Success brought its harpies, and peculation had rotted the commissariats. The falsities of life were sapping the future.

Winter, 1757–58. French and English hopes.

During the same season, among the English, there was need of buoyant prophecy to keep off grim despair. Two years of miserable conduct of affairs had done their work. Amid the depression, there was a latent hope of something better in a winter expedition; but such woodsmen as Croghan shrunk from the wild rigors of the northern winter, and had little faith that officers of European habits could endure the suffering. Pownall wrote to Pitt that nothing but an overwhelming force thrown into Canada could turn the tide. That minister, already addressing himself to the military problem, had wisely propitiated the provincials by removing discriminations which had favored the royal commission, and by making the provincial a sharer of the advantages of his rank. If Pitt had been as wise in selecting the leader to be trusted, all would very likely have been well; but when he chose Abercrombie to lead, and gave him his appointment at the very end of the woeful year of 1757, he rounded out its record of disaster. The plans for the new year were not much different from what had long been the military scheme. Fort Duquesne was restored to the prominence of a goal, as it had been in Braddock's year, and General John Forbes was selected for its reduction. This was the extreme western flank of a comprehensive plan, which left to Amherst and Wolfe the movement on the

Pitt.

Abercrombie chosen general. 1758.

Plan of the campaign. 1758.

eastern flank in an attack on Louisbourg, while Abercrombie, with Lord Howe as second, was to advance upon Ticonderoga and Crown Point.

By July, the campaign was at an end, as far as these latter movements were concerned. The rather sluggish tenacity of Amherst had gained Cape Breton, from which he returned to Boston, to start at once for Albany to support the central army, after its great catastrophe. The weakness, if not poltroonery, of Abercrombie had made the fifteen thousand men who had with flaunting parade floated down Lake George struggle back from Ticonderoga two thousand less, after having inflicted only a fifth of that loss on the French. Amherst met a dispirited army, which had lost its idol, Lord Howe, in a futile skirmish, and found Abercrombie undone. It was apparent that the catastrophe must be neutralized elsewhere.

Amherst at Cape Breton. 1758.

Abercrombie's defeat. 1758.

In August, the current changed. Bradstreet, who had in the previous year managed his whaleboat men so adroitly on the Onondaga, had unexpectedly slipped across the lake to Fort Frontenac. He had with him three thousand men, and when it became known down the St. Lawrence that the fort with all its guns, provisions, and goods was lost, and that the nine vessels in its harbor with their armaments were captured, there was reason for consternation, for it meant to the French that the command of the lake was gone, and no supplies could be got through to Niagara and Duquesne. What to do was a difficult problem, and Vaudreuil and Montcalm, never in harmony, were more than ever disagreed. It was already feared that Duquesne had been taken. "It is idle to flatter ourselves any longer," was the talk. "Canada is lost, if peace is not made this winter. The English have sixty thousand regulars and provincials in America. We have not five thousand. The English colonies can furnish two hundred thousand men; Canada at the best can supply only about ten thousand, and with it all the Indians are everywhere turning against us." There may have been more discouragement than truth in such figures, but they were disheartening in any event.

Bradstreet at Fort Frontenac. 1758.

Results of the fall of Frontenac.

We turn now to consider the direct assault of the English

upon the defenses of the Ohio. The pacification of the Indians in this region before Forbes began to move was of great importance. To do this fell largely to the assiduity of Croghan. He had in the previous December complained of the way in which the Quakers were encouraging the savage discontent. "They must be mad," he said. Their conduct was having its effect through the winter, and the French at Duquesne were not without knowledge of it. In January, Sharpe had heard that De Ligneris had from two to three hundred men in the fort, who were by relays working on a stronger post over the river, "a small distance above." While this was going on, he kept out about six hundred Indians, and it was mainly through them and their scouting that the French commander was able to report to Vaudreuil how the Pennsylvania borderers were clustering about their forts for protection.

Forbes's advance. 1758.

The Quakers and the Indians.

The southern Indians were restless also, and Fort Chissel was built to overawe them. This was at a point over the divide from the valley of Virginia and near the New River, where the trails from Philadelphia and Richmond met and advanced two hundred miles farther to Cumberland Gap.

The southern Indians.

Fort Chissel.

During March, it seemed as if Teedyuscung was to fall into one of his intermittent moods of quiet. The farmers of Pennsylvania were not so easily satisfied as the savage. They had not been paid for their assistance in helping Braddock move his army, and Sharpe bluntly told Forbes, now in Philadelphia, that he must supply ready cash if anything was to be done.

Forbes, a man of imperturbable energy, passed the spring in Philadelphia, giving what strength he had — for he was a sick man — to the task of organizing his army. He had some good lieutenants in Bouquet and others, but Washington, who joined him, did not wholly possess his confidence, and he found that Grant, who commanded some Highland Scots, was not to be trusted. His commissary, Sir John Sinclair, was not a fortunate choice. One hardly knows whether he was imbecile or simply vexatious. The service of his department in supplying stores and securing transportation was doubtless a trying one. The country people were provoking, and the friendly Indians tedious in negotiation. Forbes

Forbes in Philadelphia. His officers. 1758.

himself, generally temperate in his utterance, was prompted at times to berate the dilatory and self-seeking Pennsylvania boor.

The force which was gathering for Forbes was heterogeneous enough. Beside the Highlanders, there was a body of royal Americans — mainly German-Americans — and whatever provincial rangers and militiamen could be got together by robbing the garrisons of the frontiers from the Susquehanna to the Altamaha.

His force.

It was the last of June when Forbes himself left Philadelphia, and in his weakness he had to be borne in a litter. The question of the ultimate route over the mountains was one in which Forbes and Bouquet differed from Washington. The Virginian argued ardently for the Braddock route, because it was already opened, and its difficulties were understood and could be met. The alternative passage, which would lead the army by Carlisle, Bedford, and so on to the Pennsylvania passes, was shorter, and would have to be made ready. Bouquet talked over the advantages of each with Washington, but neither could convince the other. Bouquet thought the Virginia colonel "had no idea of the difference between a party and an army." There were very likely some counter-views based upon the future trade of the rival provinces. Virginia did not care to have a better road for trading purposes opened north of the Potomac to increase the facilities of Pennsylvania. Pennsylvania was not content to be dependent on one south of it, constructed for the behoof of Virginia. Whatever the inner secrets, Bouquet prevailed, and Forbes was to advance over the Pennsylvania passes. In July, Major Armstrong, with his pioneers, was hewing trees and leveling obstructions. Grant with his Highlanders and Lewis with a body of provincials followed for support.

Forbes's route.

In August, General Forbes had not gone on farther than Carlisle, and here he learned by letter from Abercrombie himself of his rueful failure. The fallen soldier was as confused in his recital as he could well be, though he could not disguise what seemed to have been an irretrievable disaster. There was more comfort in the story of Amherst's success at Louisbourg, which came about the same time, and Forbes caused the camp to make merry over it.

Forbes at Carlisle.

The general's health, meanwhile, was the subject of grave

apprehension. Some days he gained apparently; on others he grew worse; but he was patient. Though this advance of his army seemed slow, he was satisfied with it, for postponed action was, as he felt, the best disorganizer of the Indian allies of the French. Impatience always loosens the Indian bonds. Forbes was accordingly anxious to give, by delay, more time for this influence to work.

Forbes's health.

It was a sad mischance for the French that some one of their emissaries at Detroit had spread the report that the Iroquois were doomed to be annihilated, in order to remove the great bulwark of the English. The boast reached the Delawares, and had already been repeated to the Senecas. It was just one of those blunders that Johnson was on the watch for, and he used the story to great advantage. Not uninfluenced by it, Teedyuscung was also quieted on the Susquehanna.

The French and the Indians.

With this influence at work, affecting the French interests, there was a chance for a skillful and courageous English agent to do good deeds among the Ohio tribes. Governor Denny found the best man for the task in Christian Frederick Post, an honest and fearless Moravian, who had for years familiarized himself with the savages, and married two wives among them. He kept a journal on his expedition, and we can follow him step by step, only to be captivated by the guileless simplicity and straightforward confidence of the man.

C. F. Post on the Ohio. 1758.

He left Philadelphia on July 15, and on September 9 he had turned homeward. In less than two months he had accomplished his purpose of making the Ohio Indians ready to give a welcome to the army led by Forbes. The warriors protected Post even in going boldly into the French camps at Venango and the forks.

It was some days after Post had started homeward, when Grant marched his Highlanders rapidly ahead of his support into the vicinity of Duquesne. He was seemingly actuated by the hope of making a sudden capture of the fort. "His thirst for fame," said his general later, "brought on his own perdition." The French sallied from their defenses (September 15), and of his eight hundred plaidsmen, Grant left three hundred on the field. His defeated force then re-

Grant's defeat. 1758.

treated upon the supports. It was a stupid act, and when, two months later, the news of it reached Montcalm, he thought Duquesne had been saved for a time, even though the difficulties of succoring it might compel its abandonment in the spring.

Indian conference at Easton. October, 1758.

This heady venture of Grant had its bad effect on the Indians, and the Pennsylvanians entered upon a new conference at Easton in October with a certain disadvantage. They went farther, however, than some of the over-mountain land companies were inclined to allow. They pledged faith to the Indians that the trans-Alleghany spaces should be sacred to the savage for his hunting-ground, and no one should occupy them except with the tribes' permission. There were at this time at least three million acres of these very lands alienated to different companies. Only recently the Greenbrier Company had patented a hundred thousand acres on the river of that name. There were of course rival claims in behalf of more than one colony for these western wilds; but it was the misfortune of the Indian never quite to comprehend the white man's rivalries.

Land companies.

Post's second mission.

Post was again sent out with a new wampum belt which expressed this immunity for the Indian lands. He now added to his earlier success in winning the hesitating tribes.

Forbes at Loyalhannon. October, 1758.

After this, Forbes had little to fear from the Indians, and when he reached Loyalhannon in October, where Bouquet had formed a camp, he sent forward a messenger to warn the Indians to keep west of the Alleghany, lest they should be involved in the battle which was to come.

While the camp was at Loyalhannon, the enemy's scouts hung about, and at one time ventured upon an attack, but without success. The weather, however, was bad, making the roads heavy, and the advance was delayed. The poor general, up and down with his malady, was now within fifty miles of his goal. He waited till the 18th of November, and then, taking twenty-five hundred picked troops in light marching order, he pushed rapidly ahead, himself still borne by his men. His van was startled on the 24th by a heavy, rumbling sound, long-drawn out. Presently, his pioneers came upon the stark bodies of the slain Highlanders of Grant, and a ghastly row of heads was stuck on poles along the way. The sight inflamed the passions

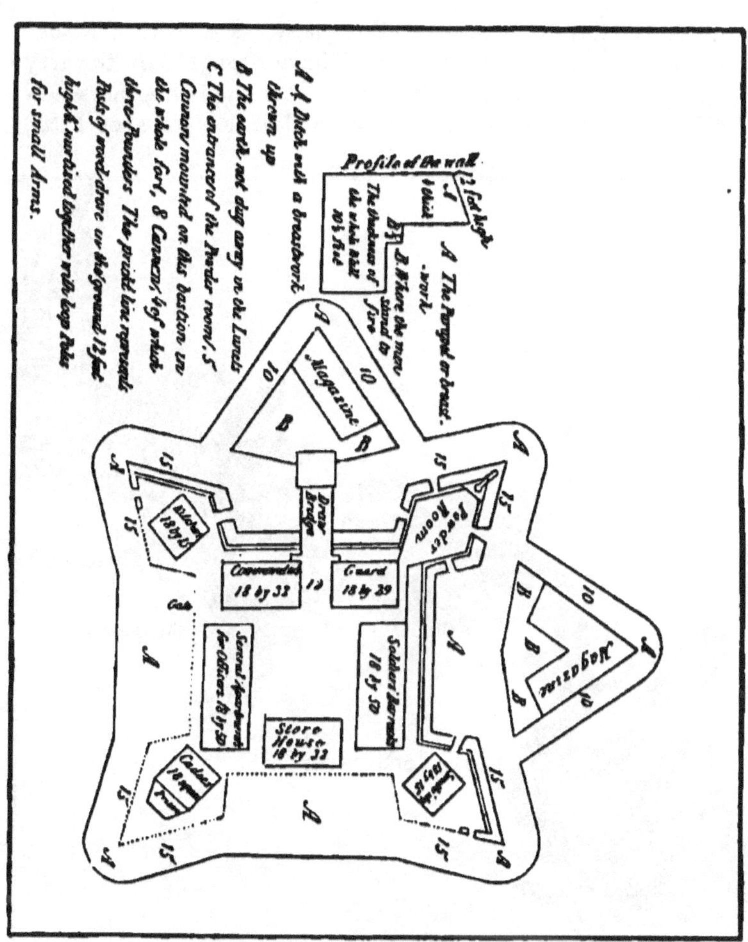

FORT DUQUESNE.
[From the *Pennsylvania Archives*, 1790, App. p. 430.]

of the men, but when the fort was reached there was no one upon whom to wreak vengeance. The dull boom had accompanied the blowing up of the fort, and its garrison was in flight. The English had marched an average of ten miles a day, and it was November 25 when they entered the ruined fort. On the 26th, Forbes wrote to Governor Denny, announcing that he had invited the headmen of the Indians to a conference, and he hoped "in a few words

Duquesne destroyed. 1758.

and in a few days to make everything easy. I shall then set out [he adds] to kiss your hands, if I have strength left to carry me through the journey." This unquailing hero hutted his men about the ground, called the spot Pitts-

Pittsburgh named.

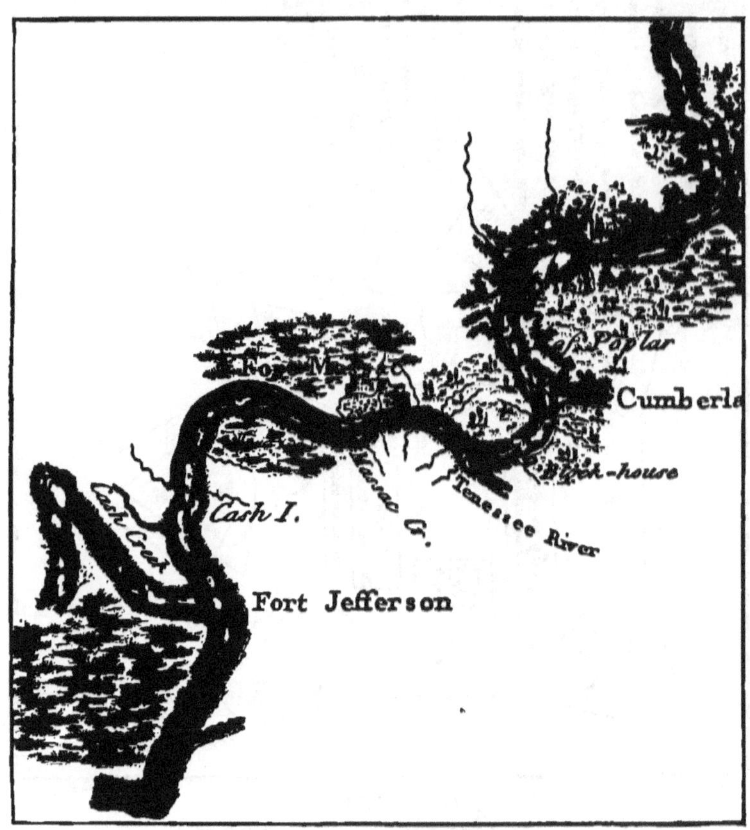

FORT MASSAC AND VICINITY.

[From the general map of the Ohio in Callot's *Atlas*, 1826.]

burgh, after the great minister, and placing Lieutenant-Colonel Mercer in command, left for Philadelphia.

The fugitives from Duquesne.

The fugitive French went off in detachments. De Ligneris led the best fighting material to Fort Machault at Venango, and soon after began to send out his emissaries to win back the Indians. Aubry conducted the

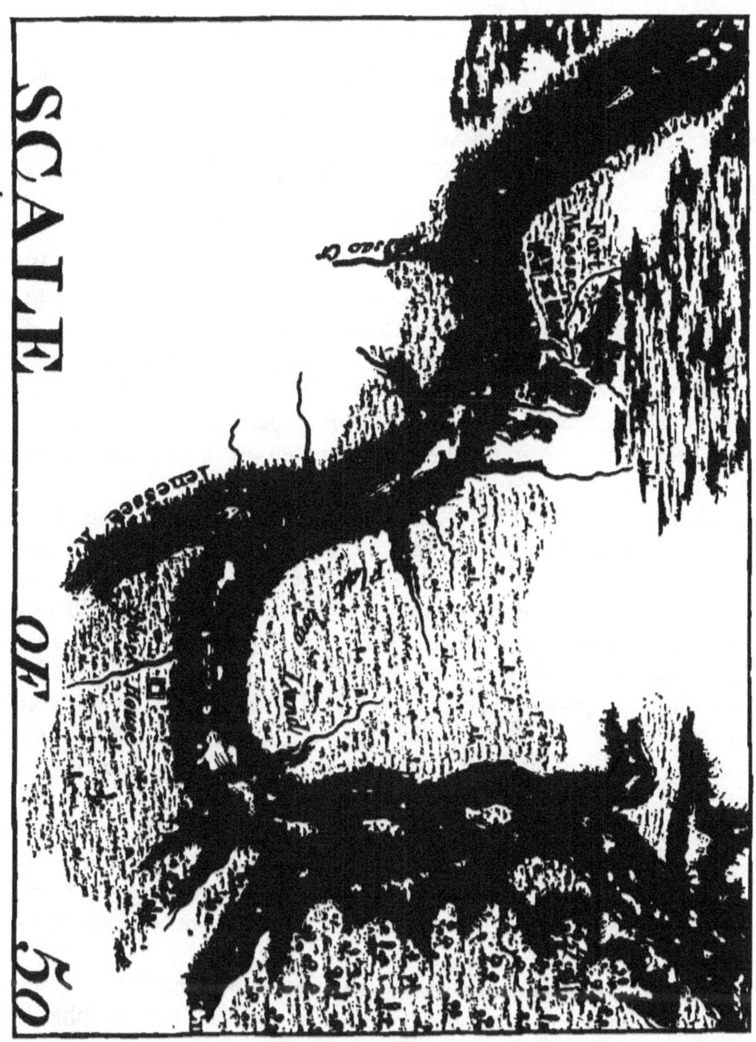

THE LOWER OHIO.

[Showing Fort Massac and the mouths of the Tennessee and Cumberland rivers. From Collot's *Atlas*, Pl. xi.]

rest in boats down the Ohio. Thirty or more miles before the Mississippi was reached, this officer stopped to rehabilitate an old stockade known as Fort Massac. Placing a garrison in it, he went on, bearing most of his cannon, and finally found rest at Fort Chartres.

Forbes dies.

Forbes reached Philadelphia, but did not long survive. In March, 1759, he died, with the satisfaction that he had done in his feebleness a heroic action, and had restored the red flag to the Great Valley. "The capture of Louisbourg is the more striking," said Bouquet, "but the capture of Duquesne is the more important." The English hold on the Ohio had been secured; it was yet to be gained on the St. Lawrence.

Campaign of 1759.

There was little doubt from the beginning that the campaign of 1759 would paralyze the military power of the French and render easy its ultimate destruction. The only hope of Montcalm was that a defeat in Canada would not carry the surrender of Louisiana. He hoped it might leave debatable the country of the Illinois, which had been alternately considered a part of Canada and of Louisiana. There was at one time a chance that Louisiana could be saved by landing a French force in Carolina to divert the English attention from a northern campaign. It was a belief that if this incursion failed to maintain itself, it could fight long enough to work its way to the Mississippi, and so unite with any remnant that might be left of the Canadian defenders. But the plan was too hazardous, and the record of the project is of interest only as a symptom of desperation.

Canada disheartened. 1759.

At the end of the last campaign, Vaudreuil had warned the home government of the inevitable catastrophe if France did not succor her colony. With a population of 82,000, and only 20,000 able to bear arms, — militia, woodsmen, and Indians, — Canada could not expect to maintain the unequal contest. Langlade might indeed bring a hundred or two of the western Indians to the rescue, but what was that to the entire defection of the Miamis? Except the Delawares, there seemed hardly a prominent tribe left to be involved in this final struggle, which had not been swung over to the English side.

The Indians.

In their intestine affairs the Canadians were no more fortunate. The governor and Montcalm had never agreed, and now that they were on the brink of ruin, their disputes grew hotter. Bougainville had been sent over to France to represent the gravity of the situation, and in the spring of 1759 he had returned without a word of encouragement. There were no soldiers to be spared for the colony. If there were and they were sent over, they would be intercepted by the English fleet. If this should not happen, they could not be provisioned. Such were the disheartening alternatives. The only ray of better fortune was that the government had recognized the necessity of placing Montcalm in an independent position as the military leader, and when Bougainville delivered to that gallant soldier this new commission, it was the only hope with which he was charged. "Our general would like to multiply us and send us everywhere," was the feeling; but with Quebec, Niagara, and the Ohio to defend, and with forces insufficient for the defense of any one of them, the struggle could not last long. "Canada will be taken," wrote Montcalm on April 12, "this campaign, or assuredly during the next, if there be not some unforeseen good luck, or a powerful diversion by sea against the English colonies, or some gross blunders on the part of the enemy." In the same letter he charges the French commissaries on the Ohio as disturbing by their peculations the relations with the Indians. "If the Indians had a fourth part of what is supposed to be expended for them, the king would have all of them on his side, the English none."

Intestine affairs of Canada. 1759.

With the English there was as much confidence as there was disheartenment on the side of the French. In Europe, England's ally, Frederick of Prussia, had indeed passed the bounds of success, and was desponding at the turn of affairs; but Pitt felt that the war was to be won in America. On December 29, 1758, he had outlined the campaign to Amherst, who was to do the work, or at least to be held responsible for it. He himself was to take charge of the direct northern attack by Lake Champlain. By the end of June, he was at Lake George with eleven thousand men, half regulars. After beginning a fort, he started with a flotilla down the lake on July 21. Bourlamaque retired before him

The English confident.

Amherst in charge. 1759.

from Ticonderoga and Crown Point. The modern tourist sees to-day at Crown Point the heavy ruins of the fort and barracks which Amherst tarried to build. He was timing his progress to join before Quebec an auxiliary force ascending the St. Lawrence. Of this army he had been anxiously awaiting intelligence, but the scouts whom he had sent north were foiled, and had escaped capture by flying down the Connecticut valley. There was another but very circuitous way to learn how Wolfe, in charge of this other force, had succeeded, and to convey to him the story of Amherst's own progress. This was by dispatching a messenger to Boston, who should then reach Quebec by the Kennebec and Chaudière valleys, — the route by which Arnold conducted his unfortunate expedition sixteen years later. From Crown Point Amherst sent such a messenger to say that he was preparing the flotilla in which he expected to advance against the French vessels, which were at Isle aux Noix. There was a long delay in getting this armament ready, and when everything was prepared in October, Amherst feared the autumnal storms and never started. The French, however, blew up their vessels, rendering easier the next year's advance by that way.

If the campaign had accomplished nothing more than the commander-in-chief had carried out, Pitt might well have wondered if hopes and outlay had been repaid. Fortunately, the campaign had been decided at Quebec and Niagara, on the two flanks.

The lesser of these two auxiliary movements reacted on the greater, and we need to follow them both connectedly. In May, Wolfe was at Halifax making his preparations. He next transferred his force to Louisbourg, having three brigadiers under him, — Monckton, Townshend, and Murray. During June, the fleet of Admiral Saunders conveyed Wolfe's transports up the St. Lawrence.

Wolfe's campaign. 1759.

Montcalm, with his army in Quebec and along the river below the town, was preparing for the attack, with about fourteen thousand men of all sorts and over a hundred guns. He had some armed boats and had improvised fire-ships, which in the end failed of their purpose in several trials against the English vessels. Vaudreuil, still obstinate, knew that Wolfe had landed nine thousand men on the island of Orleans, and he thwarted

Montcalm's purpose to fortify Point Lévis, opposite the city, on the south side of the St. Lawrence. This mischance Wolfe took advantage of, and seized that commanding ground, so necessary to his fleet. The movement was in some respects a hazardous one, for it divided his army, and placed a deep river between the two parts; but he knew that his own fleet controlled that river. This naval supremacy again induced him to make a third division, and place a force on the northern shore of the river, below the Falls of Montmorency.

While the situation on the St. Lawrence was thus in a considerable degree one of peril, events happening at Niagara had decided the fate of the Ohio country. We must glance at them before showing their effects both on Wolfe and Montcalm.

It was the English plan to save the Ohio at Niagara. Military critics have sometimes urged that the force sent against Niagara could have been more effective as a part of Amherst's army, but it is doubtful if that general could have gained celerity by an increase of force. If he was capable of such acceleration, it is possible the capture of Montreal might have taken place a year earlier, and the battle of Ste. Foy been avoided. It would have risked, however, the hold that Forbes had secured on the Ohio, and perhaps have aided that escape to Louisiana which was the ultimate hope of the Canadians.

The attack on Niagara. 1759.

In March, 1759, Bouquet had succeeded in temporary command of the department, which included the Ohio, pending the arrival of Stanwix, who had been ordered to Philadelphia. There were about a thousand men at the forks, and it was quite possible that the French, if bound to recover it, could bring a much larger force against it. What policy to pursue, if attacked, Bouquet and Amherst were not agreed upon. Bouquet was for retreating before an attack in force; Amherst for acting defensively till the post could be relieved from Fort Ligonier and the other Pennsylvania stockades. In April, all was quiet along the Alleghany, but before the month closed, the governor of Pennsylvania thought it prudent to send the Moravian, Post, to the Senecas to see if any mischief was hatching.

Bouquet's command. 1759.

That the French had intended to regain the forks seems certain, as Croghan believed, but the English advance toward Niagara had disconcerted their plans, and by early July it had been necessary, under orders, for the French to abandon the Alleghany in the hope of aiding in the defense of Niagara. The river was too low to transport the heavy stores, and they were sacrificed. Such portions as were not acceptable to the Indians were piled in the fort at Venango, and the whole was fired. The boats that had been prepared for a descent upon Fort Pitt were destroyed, and their swivels were buried. The fugitive garrison made its way by Le Bœuf, where a similar destruction took place, to Presqu' Isle, and there a new surprise awaited them.

The French abandon the Alleghany. 1759.

Prideaux, one of Amherst's brigadiers, keeping his communications open through Oswego, — which La Corne vainly tried to destroy, — had advanced upon Niagara in force, while Pouchot, the commander of that fort, was awaiting reinforcements from the western posts. Prideaux being killed early in the attack, the command fell to his second in authority, Sir William Johnson, who completed the establishment of the besieging lines. Hearing now of the approach of Aubry and De Ligneris with the western party, Johnson promptly passed up the river to confront them. It happened that the same day saw the fort surrendered, and its succoring force hurled back by Johnson. The fugitives fled to Presqu' Isle, where they were joined by those who had abandoned Venango. The united bodies continued their flight to Detroit.

Niagara attacked. 1759.

Niagara, the long-coveted entrance to the Ohio valley, was now in the hands of the victor, and Fort Pitt was safe. Such were the tidings which in these midsummer days reached the rival generals on the St. Lawrence, and were a cheer to one and disheartenment to the other. The effect on Wolfe was to spur him on to greater risks. He sent a frigate to run by the batteries of Cape Diamond, while his men dragged boats overland from Point Lévis, and embarked above under the protection of the frigate. This was a fourth partition of his army, and the risks were quite commensurate with the stakes. The desperation of Montcalm, to whom the tidings of Niagara had also come, was equaled only by that of Wolfe. Both commanders were playing their game at fearful odds ; and

Wolfe and Montcalm at Quebec. 1759.

but for his isolation, the French general might very well expect a victory as Frontenac did, when the fleet of Phips dotted the broad basin before him. The season was rapidly slipping away. Montcalm was perhaps losing the most by the delay, but neither the spirit of the English general nor the constancy of his troops could endure much longer without a trial of arms. He hoped to force an engagement near the Montmorency, but his effort failed. He withdrew his men at this point, and it was done with great good luck. Almost aimlessly, or at least without knowing precisely how to employ them, Wolfe pushed larger bodies of men up the river, and Admiral Holmes, with a part of the fleet, went up to support them. Bougainville was patrolling the river bank above the town, watching the enemy, and covering supply-trains that descended to Montcalm and the town. He had about fifteen hundred men with him. Admiral Holmes had a grim satisfaction in seeing these devoted Frenchmen grow footsore and weary, as he let his ships float carelessly up and down with the tide, while Bougainville followed abreast to prevent a landing. All the while, Montcalm had Lévis out, with another flying body of troops, to watch for Amherst, who was expected to be plodding down from Three Rivers instead of building barracks at Crown Point. By August, the French general, learning the truth about Amherst, was relieved of maintaining this wearisome watch. It was not far from the first of September when Wolfe also learned of Amherst's position by the arrival of the messenger from the Kennebec. The news was not encouraging, and it was apparent that if Quebec was to be taken, Amherst could have no hand in it. The weary weeks that had passed bid fair to be followed by as many more, closing with the failure of accomplishing anything before preparation must be made to escape an ice-bound river. But suddenly a crisis was precipitated.

Wolfe, doubtful how to turn, was one day scanning through a glass from Point Lévis the opposite precipice. There was a fair field for an encounter above; but the sheer and rugged steep above the water seemed to offer no chance whereby to gain the top. His scrutiny at last revealed what looked like a ravine, cutting into the precipice, and worn by the rains. He conjectured that it probably gave chances for a foothold. The French seemingly recognized the chance it offered to the enemy, but deemed it small, for, as Wolfe counted the tents of the guard at the head of the ravine, he saw that the force was scant. One Stobo, a provincial, who had been a captive in Quebec and had escaped, confirmed Wolfe's supposition as to the practicability of the ascent, if the men had bold leaders.

Two things favored a movement by this ravine. Bougainville, who was likely to confront the attempt if openly made, was easily carried up the river, out of support of its French defenders, by the oft-tried manœuvre of Holmes, whose ship under a favoring wind could be borne beyond the strength of the rising tide. The other advantage was fortunately revealed to Wolfe, when he learned that Bougainville was intending to send down a flotilla of supply-boats to the beleaguered town the first dark night, trusting to the deep shadows of the bank concealing them from the watchful English. The French guards and batteries along the shore were informed of the project, and would have their suspicions quelled at any similar procession of boats. Wolfe therefore determined to anticipate the French project. Arranging that Saunders with his ships below the town should divert attention by feigning an attack on Beauport, a suburb below the St. Charles, Wolfe was ready when the darkness deepened to shove his boats, with their thirty-six hundred men, directly under the bank. The long file of boats moved silently down, and every hail from the shore was treacherously answered, so that not a suspicion was aroused. The ravine was reached and his van was at the summit before the alarm was sounded. A foothold secured, details were sent up the river to capture the guns that might annoy the rear portion of his flotilla, and this prompt action secured for Wolfe a position on the field with all the troops which he had intended to handle.

On the Plains of Abraham.

Montcalm's headquarters were across the St. Charles, this minor stream forming with the St. Lawrence the promontory of Quebec, and when the day dawned, the red line of the British, stretched across the plain, was conspicuous beyond the valley to the startled gaze of the French. Montcalm saw that a crisis had come. To allow Quebec to be taken by assault on its land side would insure the turning of its captured guns upon his own camp. It has been held that Montcalm's safer course would have been to throw reinforcements into the town, and while it stood the attack, to worry the English flanks. Such a plan did not well suit the celerity and pluck of such a soldier as Montcalm, and he adopted the bolder alternative of fighting, line against line, before the gates of the town.

Both sides thus cast the die, and at ten o'clock in the morning the hostile lines were advancing face to face. The clash was a brief one. Just as the French were recoiling before the British impact, Wolfe was stricken down by a bullet, and died. The surging mass of the French was rolling back upon the gates, when Montcalm also fell. He was carried into the town to die. The French fell back within the walls and secured the gates.

The battle.

After a while the tumult had reached Bougainville, who hurried back to fall upon the English; but the rearguard under Townshend presented so solid a front that the French thought it prudent to retire. The English thus had opportunity without further molestation to secure their position before the town. They passed the succeeding night in making preparation. The morning revealed that the troops' which Vaudreuil had kept with him beyond the St. Charles had fled in the dark, leaving their tents standing. The fugitives made a forced march to Cape Jacques Cartier, thirty miles up the St. Lawrence. Here, as if chagrined at his precipitancy, the governor sought to lead his men back; but he learned on the way that Ramezay had surrendered Quebec, and the British were now everywhere in possession.

Vaudreuil flies.

Thus, on the 13th of September, fifteen minutes of heady and riskful conflict on the Plains of Abraham had practically settled the fate of the St. Lawrence valley. We have seen that a combat, not much longer protracted, coming in the nick of time, had near Niagara determined the future of the Ohio basin. The campaign had been epochal.

The valleys gained.

Munitions were thrown into Quebec, Murray was placed in command, and by the middle of October Saunders, anxious to get his ships out of the river before the ice formed, sailed away, bearing the body of Wolfe. The victory of the Plains of Abraham had indicated, but did not constitute, the end. Before another English fleet with reinforcement returned in the spring of 1760, the English garrison in the town had been put to severe trials. A luckless battle

Murray commanding in Quebec.

had taken place at Ste. Foy, one of the suburbs in which Murray had taken risks, which came near causing a redeeming success for the French, since but for the opportune appearance of the English fleet, as the spring opened, Quebec might have again been under the French flag.

Battle of Ste. Foy.

CHAPTER XX.

THE TRANSITION FROM WAR TO WAR.

1760–1762.

When, on May 9, 1760, the leading ship of an English fleet hove in sight from the citadel of Quebec, Murray saw that he was not to suffer all the evils which his ill-advised and headlong onset at Ste. Foy might well have prepared for him. Lévis, who, having pushed his opponent within the walls of Quebec, was now keeping up an artillery duel with the town, saw with dismay the English ships destroy and scatter his auxiliary force upon the river. He accordingly fled with precipitation, leaving guns and stores behind him. He had inflicted upon Murray the loss of about a third of the English force, and he now found himself hurrying to Montreal, painfully conscious that his own sacrifices had gained him little beside the well-earned laurels of Ste. Foy.

Lévis retires from before Quebec.

Pitt had hardly counted on such folly as Murray had shown, but the fleet which he had ordered up the river at as early a moment as the ice would permit showed his purposes to make the success of Wolfe something more than a barren victory. The minister now looked to Amherst to sweep the remaining French from the valley. That commander was already laying his plans to converge upon Montreal with all the forces at his disposal, and in April he had instructed Monckton at Pittsburgh to make sure of his communications with Niagara, and then to send forward to that post a force sufficient to hold it, so that its regular garrison could join the general advance upon the St. Lawrence.

The campaign of 1760.

It was evident that Vaudreuil and Lévis were now segregating all available forces at Montreal. They were keeping out small corps of observation down the river and toward Lake Champlain, and were determined to stand on

The French plans.

the defensive as long as they could, in the hope that the English combinations would miscarry, or some blunder be made by which the French could profit. The English plan of closing in upon Montreal upon three sides was pretty sure, if well timed, to force its surrender; but the chances of war are always open to an alert antagonist held at bay, and watching for breaks in his adversary's plans.

Amherst's plans.

Amherst, himself commanding one of these aggressive forces, had rendezvoused at Oswego about eleven thousand men, including a force of Indians under Johnson. Amherst's part was to advance through the Thousand Islands, capture Fort Lévis near the head of the rapids, and approach Montreal on the up-river side. Murray was to advance from Quebec with twenty-five hundred men, strengthened with a force of thirteen hundred, which Lord Rollo had brought from Louisbourg. The third army, which was to advance north upon Lake Champlain, had had the way opened for it the previous season when the threatening front of Amherst had forced the French to burn a part, at least, of their flotilla.

These lesser movements were reasonably well timed. Bourlamaque, who was watching Murray, fell back as that English officer advanced, and Haviland, commanding on Lake Champlain, easily forced Bougainville down the Sorel. These two French forces found no difficulty in joining Vaudreuil in Montreal, so that the way was clear for Murray and Haviland to put themselves into communication. When all this was done, Amherst had not yet appeared above the town. The interval was seized by the French to send off Langlade in charge of two companies of English deserters. His instructions were to lead them west and send them down to New Orleans, out of reach of the enemy in the event of disaster.

The French in Montreal.

The French now in and about Montreal numbered, all told, scarcely more than twenty-five hundred effectives. With such a force there was little chance in measuring strength in the open field with Murray and Haviland, while Amherst was close at hand. The French accordingly abided developments. There was not long to wait. Amherst soon arrived, and, joining all the forces, he held an army of seventeen thousand men in his circumjacent lines. There was some hesitation on the part of Vaudreuil in approaching his doom, mainly for the sake of show; but on September 8, the capitulation was signed. It gave up not only Montreal, but all Canada and its dependencies. All troops, wherever they were stationed, were to become prisoners of war, later to be transported to France in British ships. The exercise of the Catholic religion was guaranteed, and private property was to be respected. Vaudreuil had contended for the preservation of the French code; but Amherst was stubborn, and English law was hereafter to govern the conquered territory. The British general did not forget the sad experience of his government with the Acadians, and the folly of anything short of an absolute dominion was not to be repeated. So something like sixty-five thousand French were at a moment swung beneath the folds of the banner of St. George, as subjects of George the Second. The news did not reach England in time to gratify the old king, who had intrusted so much to Pitt. On October 25, George had swooned in his bedchamber, and fallen against a chest of drawers. Thus he died. The tidings did not reach Boston till December.

Montreal and Canada surrendered. September 8, 1760.

George II. dies. October, 1760.

Precisely what the area was that Vaudreuil's capitulation covered very likely neither he nor Amherst cared to determine too exactly. At all events, the terms given and accepted were open to later dispute. It was two years and more before the diplomatic disputants of the two governments agreed upon the final result.

Area of the conquest.

Amherst hastened to get control of as much of the west as he could, and did not wait long before dispatching Robert Rogers, the well-known partisan scout, with about two hundred men in whaleboats, — George Croghan was in the party, — to proceed along the Lakes and receive the surrender of the distant posts. Passing by Niagara River, Rogers entered Lake Erie and tarried for a while at Presqu' Isle, so as to communicate with Monckton at Pittsburgh. On October 17, this officer notified Governor Sharpe of Maryland that on the previous evening he had received Amherst's orders to send forward garrisons for Detroit and the other western stations. He further informed Sharpe that he needed militia to take the place of the royal Americans, whom he was to detach to Rogers's

Monckton and Rogers.

command. By November 7, Rogers, still following the southern shore of the lake, had reached the mouth of a river not easily identified, but probably near the spot where the modern Cleveland stands. Here a band of Ottawas confronted him and manifested some distrust, which was soon, however, overcome. Rogers in his journal does not mention that Pontiac was on the spot, though in another publication which passes under his name, *The Concise Account of North America*, Pontiac is not only represented as being present, but as bearing himself rather insolently at first. Parkman and historians generally have accepted the narrative of the *Concise Account* as a trustworthy development of the cruder statements of the journal; but Kingsford, not without reason, had been led to suspect that the *Account* was more likely than not an embellished narrative, worked up as a catchpenny venture by the publisher. This view, if accepted, throws not a little doubt over the scene, in which it has been ordinarily held that Pontiac for the first time — barring his conduct in the defeat of Braddock — stands forth in American history.

Rogers and Pontiac.

As Rogers approached the western end of the lake, rumors began to reach him that Bellestre, who commanded in Detroit, was endeavoring to arouse the Indians about him, so that he could resist the English. Rogers took occasion to send ahead a French prisoner, whom he chanced to have, who could give Bellestre assurances of what had happened at Montreal. He was also prepared to inform that officer of the instructions for his guidance which Vaudreuil had intrusted to Rogers's care. The warning had a good effect, and Rogers, landing below the town, was politely received and suffered to send forward a detail to take possession of the post. It was on November 29, 1760, that the English flag replaced the Bourbon, and a crowd of seven hundred capering savages vociferously greeted the change.

Rogers and Bellestre.

Detroit occupied.

Detroit was now a stockaded settlement of about one hundred houses, given up to the domiciled French and to the vagrants who huddled about the post. Perhaps half a hundred farmsteads, with their rude buildings, were scattered up and down the river bank. Various Indian villages dotted along the stream showed how attractive the trading-post had become to the savage rover. There was a reminder of less

Its condition.

prosperous times, when the English saw the horses which were put to service in the neighborhood, for they learned that they were the descendants of animals that had been taken on Braddock's field.

Parties were now sent off to secure the forts which the French held at the portages of the Maumee and Wabash, and open the trail to Vincennes. There were, perhaps, at this period some three thousand French in the Illinois country, but the question of their allegiance was to be left to the diplomats. Of the posts at Mackinac, Green Bay, St. Joseph, and the Sault Ste. Marie there was no such question, and Rogers started to go to them. The season, as it happened, was too far gone, and it was no easy task to buffet with the ice of Lake Huron. He accordingly returned without accomplishing his object. Putting Captain Campbell in charge of the post at Detroit, Rogers started east on December 21, and on January 23, 1761, he reported to the commander at Fort Pitt.

Other posts occupied.

Rogers returns east. December, 1760.

When the spring set in, Alexander Henry, a trader, starting from Montreal, and wearing the garb of a French-Canadian, pushed on with canoes by the Ottawa route, and established himself at Mackinac. He found the Indians about that post discontented with the prospects of English rule. A few days later, a force which Campbell had sent from Detroit to take possession of Mackinac arrived. Within a few months, one after another of the posts on the upper lakes saluted the English flag, and before the season closed, not a French banner was floating throughout the valley of the St. Lawrence and the Lakes.

Alexander Henry at Mackinac. 1761.

The English flag everywhere along the Lakes.

The feeling which Bellestre had manifested at Detroit, and which Henry had found at Mackinac, showed that the Indian problem was by no means settled with the vanishing of the Bourbon emblems. The relations of the English and the Indians were not much changed by the French becoming subjects of Britain, and by ceasing to be rivals, for if the jealousies of the French were no longer open, they were more dangerous from being insidious and stealthy. The English had produced a few men who were the equals of the French in tactful management of the savage. Johnson was

The Indian problem.

Johnson and Weiser.

still a power, but unfortunately Conrad Weiser had just died (July 13, 1760), — a man of sixty-two, who had given much of his life to pacifying the Indian. No one better than Weiser appreciated the influence of gratuities in compassing the savage wiles. English and French had long outbid each other in this distribution of gifts, and the tribes had reaped the harvest. Without the stimulation of French rivalry, it was likely the English would fall off in their gifts. Such a relaxation meant but one thing, — a weakening of the hold upon the Indians. Nor was it only this. The English trader, having no longer a rival in the French, would find himself relieved of the necessity of fostering a sympathetic address, and would relapse into that churlish temper which belonged so naturally to him, and was particularly irritating to the Indian. In this respect the English trader was as a rule a remarkable contrast to the French. Kalm tells us that while there are numerous instances of the Frenchman becoming more Indian than the savage, there is not one of the Indian becoming a Frenchman. The half-breed took much more naturally to the race of the wild mother than to the associations of the white father.

The English, French, and savage.

If Weiser was no longer to play the part of mediator, he left behind a hardly inferior intercessor in George Croghan. Adair speaks with amazement of Croghan's successful daring in face of the greatest danger. He wonders at the way in which Croghan succeeded in "pleasing and reconciling the savages." Such a man, Adair contended, was worth more than a garrison in troublous times. The truth unfortunately was that the English traders were not commonly prudent, and the French made the most of the defect. It was mainly a question of better trade with the English and of better neighbors with the French. So it was that in disasters which had now overtaken the French, the Indian saw that he was deprived of a friend who respected his rights to his ancestral lands, and in the success of the English he saw no help to keep his heritage from vanishing.

George Croghan and the Indians.

This preservation of his hunting-ground was still to be as it had been, the most vital interest of the savage. The treaty of 1758 at Easton had been an agreement on the part of the Pennsylvanians to prevent settlers

The Easton treaty of 1758.

passing the mountains. It had been approved by his majesty's ministers, and so had all the validity of a general statute, though the provinces of Maryland and Virginia had not formally acceded to it.

Monckton, who in May, 1760, had succeeded in command of the southern department, under an appointment from Amherst, had so far prevailed with the Indians of the Ohio as to get their consent to the founding of posts in the wild country, with only so much land about the stockades as would support the garrisons. In this both red and white found their advantage; but it was quite otherwise with the unauthorized settlements of the frontier vagrants. Of this latter class the Indians complained bitterly. That their complaints were justified we have the evidence of Sir William Johnson, at the north, and of Stuart, the agent of the government at the south. It was notorious that these frontier miscreants were debasing the savages with liquor, and then pretending to purchase their lands. Bouquet, now in immediate command at Fort Pitt, represented to the governor of Virginia that "vagabonds, under pretense of hunting, were making settlements of which the Indians made frequent and grievous complaints." Bouquet was a man of high character, and not very tolerant of wiles, as his letters show, and it was his aim as well as his duty to protect the rights of these savage wards. Such a purpose was hardly reconcilable with the intentions of the Ohio Company, or at least with the aims of some of its agents. That body, now that peace was in sight, was preparing to profit by the grants which had been made to it south of the Ohio, and its agents, whether authorized or not, were undertaking to secure the influence of Bouquet. Colonel Cresap, representing that company and detailing to Bouquet what this officer calls a "bubble scheme of settling the Ohio," offered to him in July, 1760, a share of twenty-five thousand acres in the company's grant. Bouquet was polite but wary, and significantly referred to the obligations of the treaty of Easton. He pointed out how sure a way it was to bring the confiding Germans and Switzers, who were counted upon to fill up the land, into unmerited grief by setting up a colony without first providing a government for their protection in a region too remote for support from the established colonies. The

Frontiersmen and the Indians.

Bouquet and the Ohio Company.

correspondence ended in Bouquet declining the bribe. During the next few months, Bouquet was doing what he could to remove all interlopers along the Monongahela, acting under the express orders of Monckton. His efforts failing of what he wished, in October, 1761, he issued a proclamation, prohibiting all settlements beyond the mountains without the permission of the general or of the governors of the provinces. Such licenses were to be lodged with the commanding officer at Fort Pitt. When this document reached Williamsburg, it created not a little uneasiness, especially as it placed offenders beyond the operation of the civil law, and made them amenable to martial law. On January 17, 1762, Governor Fauquier wrote in protest not only to Bouquet, but to Amherst. It could have been no satisfaction to the Virginians that Bouquet was much more inclined to open communication with the Ohio by the Susquehanna than by the James. Bouquet, however, claimed no purpose of interfering with patented rights, further than to establish formal requirements for registration; but announced his purpose to deal stringently with all unauthorized invaders of this western territory. Amherst stood by his subordinate in the position he had taken, but cautioned Bouquet to be discreet, for "no room must be given for the colonies to complain of the military power." Bouquet was not without suspicion that this apprehension in Williamsburg was to be traced to the discontent in Virginia at his thwarting the purpose of Washington when he caused Forbes to take his line of march, in 1758, through Virginia rather than by the Pennsylvania gaps. Already, on December 11, 1761, orders had been issued to the colonial governors absolutely forbidding them to make any grants of land at variance with the Indian rights.

Bouquet's proclamation. October, 1761.

The prospect of peace was already inciting a new movement farther south. Daniel Boone first crossed the mountains in 1760, and carved his name on a beech-tree near the Watauga River, where it is to be seen to-day if report is true. He returned to give a glowing account of the promise which the valley presented. Everywhere the deciduous trees betokened to such an eye as his the richness of the soil. It was to him a harbinger of a future landscape spotted with girdled trees, with corn waving between

Daniel Boone crosses the mountains. 1760.

the stumps, and smoke curling from the open roof of the settler's cabin. There was to come the house of logs with a clay chimney, and the woodsman teaching his boy to shoot squirrels in the head so as to save their skins. In the year following Boone's venture, Walker is said to have led a party of nineteen to hunt along the Tennessee, and year after year others penetrated farther into the wilderness.

The French and the Creeks.

Still farther south, the influence of Louisiana had not been affected by the surrender at Montreal. Governor Bull of South Carolina complained that the French from New Orleans were pushing their trade hard upon his frontiers, and were using goods which had been obtained from Rhode Island. The French were believed to be urging the Creeks to commit depredations upon the English, and the Mortar, the most powerful leader of these Indians, was making bold to assault one of the frontier forts. The Upper Creeks having declared war, it was a question whether anything could be done to prevent the defection spreading to the Lower Creeks and Cherokees. Two traders, George Galphin and Lachlan M'Gilwray, were sent to stay the mischief. But the Cherokees had become implacable. They had never forgotten the castigation they had received from the Germans of the valley of Virginia, when fallen upon as they returned from the Forbes campaign, on the supposition that they had been stealing horses at the frontier. This tribe had now been reduced to between two and three thousand warriors, but they were wary fighters, and were rendering existence along the borders of Carolina a succession of miseries. It took two years to bring them to terms. Governor Lyttleton forced them one season to go through the form of yielding, but they rallied. Others who swept through their country laid villages waste, but were balked at last. The Indians captured Fort Loudon, a post on the Cherokee River, and broke faith with its garrison, a part of which was murdered after surrendering. Amherst was finally forced into sending against them a body of twenty-six hundred Highlanders under Grant. He scoured their country west of the mountains for thirty days, and succeeded in forcing them to a peace. His treaty with them pushed the frontier forward seventy miles, and

The Cherokees.

Grant's treaty with the Cherokees.

made it run along the heads of the streams flowing into the Atlantic. Timberlake, an officer who was in these movements, printed some memoirs a few years later, in which he tells how he ventured boldly among them after the peace, and found that the French had acquired a firm hold upon them, and that it was only the allurements of the English trade that finally brought them to a peace.

But a far greater difficulty was brewing at the north, destined to convert the valley of the Ohio into a bloody arena. The distrust and apprehension which the trader, Henry, had found among the Indians at Mackinac was soon apparent to Campbell among the tribes by which his post at Detroit was surrounded. He was so convinced of the coming danger that he dispatched messengers to the other posts beyond him, advising their commandants to be alert. When the demand was made upon the tribes scattered along the straits to give up their English prisoners, they nearly all readily complied, but the Wyandots persisted in a surly demeanor. With the rest, Campbell was beguiled into dealing out ammunition on the plea that they were anxious to lend the English assistance by marching against the Cherokees. But this profession soon passed, and it became evident that emissaries of the Iroquois were exercising spells upon them which boded no good. Such was the condition when Sir William Johnson appeared on the scene (1761), bound to restore confidence if he could. It seemed for a while as if he had succeeded. Croghan felt that the interviews had been successful, for in October, 1761, he reported to that effect to Bouquet, who was now at Fort Pitt. But the repose was a snare. The influence of the French was deeper seated than was suspected, and it was nursed by the sympathy of their compatriots at New Orleans and in the Louisiana settlements. The French on the lower Mississippi were already looking to Spanish support, and the Indians were circulating reports that France and Spain were only waiting the fitting moment to recover Quebec. What was a rumor seemed to be confirmed, when, in the spring of 1762, it became known that England, early in January, had declared war against Spain. The news had reached Boston in March, when Han-

The Indian discontent at the north.

Johnson at Detroit. 1761.

England and Spain at war. 1762.

cock sent an express to Amherst in New York, and by May, Bouquet had transmitted the necessary warnings to the western posts. The Spaniards were a new enemy for the English in the interior, but the ease with which they had come from New Mexico by the branches of the Missouri was a warning that what was now territory in English possession on the upper Mississippi and Lake Superior might be open to Spanish incursions. The English were prompt to send a detachment to protect the traders in the region of the present Minnesota, and in August, Gladwin, commanding at Detroit, was directed to establish a post on Lake Superior.

Danger to the extreme western posts.

Croghan and others, who were watching the darkening moods of the Indians, were now becoming confirmed in the belief that an Indian war could not be avoided, and that the hostilities would be widespread.

When the Iroquois had overcome the Andastes and absorbed the survivors of them in their own villages, these adopted children had amalgamated with their victors, and had migrated to the Ohio. Here the conglomerate body had acquired the name of Mingoes. Affiliating in their new home with the Delawares, other dependents of the Iroquois, they were nursing a long-felt hatred of the English. Alexander McKee, a trader, was reporting in November, 1762, that they and their neighbors were making ready for an outbreak. Back of the Mingoes there was the powerful influence of the Senecas, at present the most aggressive of the Iroquois confederacy. They were probably largely responsible for the spread of the savage antipathy which was now imperiling the English. With their thousand warriors, these Indians had a firm hold upon the Shawnees, Delawares, and Wyandots, who numbered together perhaps as many more fighting men. The prospect was so alarming that Sir William Johnson was urging the policy either of removing all settlers from the unpurchased lands of the Iroquois, or of making compensation for them. The Twightwees of the Wabash region had remained so far reluctant to break with the English, and the thousand warriors which they and the other parts of the Miami confederacy could throw into the scale against the French influence constituted a ground for hope which the English were glad to cherish.

The Mingoes uneasy.

The Iroquois and Miamis.

Johnson computed that the united Iroquois could put on a war-footing not far from four thousand men, and that the western tribes could offer nearly twice as many more, making in the aggregate about twelve thousand warriors. The estimate is certainly large enough, and Parkman doubts if, in all the country east of the Mississippi, north of the Ohio, and south of the latitude of Lake Superior, more than ten thousand fighting Indians could at this time be gathered. Perhaps the most effective force among all these peoples was the Ottawas. They occupied what is now known as the southern peninsula of Michigan, and their influence stretched into the area southeast of Lake Erie. They had been strong contestants for their territorial rights, and had been taught by the French to make pretty constant dependence upon gifts for favors rendered. The change of power at Detroit had interfered with this supply of gratuities, and they had grown to believe that they were to expect nothing hereafter for their concessions. Strong in the alliances of the Foxes, Sauks, and other tribes about Mackinac, they could lend to any warlike purpose something like three thousand warriors. For their vigilance and intrigue the Ottawas were most to be feared of all the western tribes. It was Johnson's belief that what is known as Pontiac's war found its first impulse among this tribe. When Pontiac stood under the great council elm of his tribe, near the portage of the Maumee, and harangued his followers and the delegates from his allies, he was, in Johnson's view, if not the originator, the conspicuous embodiment of a rising power that was to strike terror along the English border.

Extent of warriors.

The Ottawas.

The Pontiac war.

But there were new political developments destined to crown the ambition of Pitt, and which gave England a portentous position in North America, and especially in the valley of the Mississippi, that intervened before the actual outbreak of this impending war. We need now to consider the work of the diplomats.

CHAPTER XXI.

THE TREATY OF PEACE.

1762–1763.

THE campaign of 1760 had convinced France that the end was near. She had lost Canada, and with the ill success attending her arms elsewhere, she had little hope by victories on other soils to regain her American possessions. With England, war and trade had joined for her colonial aggrandizement; with France, war had not strengthened her colony, nor had trade developed it. It was the necessity of France to enter into negotiations for peace. She might yet try by diplomacy to regain as much as she could. The vagueness of the territorial terms of Vaudreuil's surrender at Montreal was something by which her negotiators might possibly profit. It might, perhaps, enable them to throw as much territory as possible within the bounds of Louisiana, and thus place it outside the limits of the English conquest. Vaudreuil had evidently intended to leave just this chance to the diplomats. The definition of the bounds of what he surrendered was vague. In the sequel, he claimed to have included in his capitulation nothing south of the territory bounded by the height of land at the head of the streams flowing into the basin of the Great Lakes. This seems to agree with what is shown in the *Atlas Moderne* (Paris, 1762), in a map by Janvier. The understanding of the English was, or at least when the negotiations began, they claimed, that Canada included not only the basin of the Lakes, but also that of the Wabash to the Ohio, and all west to the Mississippi.

France and England in the war.

The territory surrendered at Montreal.

When, on July 15, 1761, France proposed terms of peace to England, she offered to cede Canada as Vaudreuil surrendered it, with bounds on Virginia and Louisiana. The British cabinet in their reply, July 29, insisted upon their

Peace proposals. 1761.

own definition of Vaudreuil's surrender, and would not admit that the Ohio country was included in Louisiana, or that Louisiana abutted on Virginia. On August 5, the French in a communication shifted their ground, and while agreeing to cede Canada "in the most extensive manner," proposed to interject along the western verge of the Alleghanies a neutral strip for the

[This extract from Jefferys' map shows the proposed neutral territory, being the gourd-shaped area stretching from Carolina to the north of Lake Erie.]

use of the Indians and for serving as a barrier. This neutral region is shown in two maps by Jefferys of the British, French, and Spanish settlements in North America, as "proposed by M. de Bussy in 1761." It included the peninsula north of Lake Erie, western New York, eastern Ohio, and the eastern portions of Kentucky and Tennessee. In one of the maps the southern shore of Lake Erie is not taken in, and in the other it is for a larger part made a portion of this Indian reservation. This scheme of a neutral barrier-land, much like another talked of twenty years later, in the preliminary discussions of the treaty of 1782, was now promptly rejected on August 16 by the British government. They insisted unreservedly on the limits of Vaudreuil's surrender as abutting on territory which they had always claimed, east of the Wabash and south of the Ohio. They would in no sense consider this to be neutral, holding it to be already under the protection of the English by virtue of treaties both with the Iroquois and the southern Indians. Nearly a month later, on September 13, France yielded to the English claim for the bounds of Canada, but not enough in other ways to satisfy Pitt.

Pitt resigns from the ministry.

This minister was now reaping the penalty of his success, and the aggrandizement of the Commons, which the new king's friends thought he was effecting, raised up an opposition in the king's council, which in October forced his resignation. Pitt had surmised the purpose of an offensive alliance of France and Spain, and had desired to precipitate action to forestall its results. This was one of the test questions in which he found himself balked by the friends of the king; but within three months Bute, succeeding to Pitt's office, was forced by developments, which Pitt had keenly anticipated, to declare war with Spain on January 4, 1762.

War with Spain. 1762.

Shall Canada be annexed to the British empire?

Negotiations for peace having so far failed, public interest was turned once more to a question which had been in controversy for two years. Ever since the fall of Montreal, it had been apparent that there was growing up in England among influential classes a conviction that after all it was a questionable policy which would in the final treaty wrest Canada from the French. It was claimed by such doubters that more would be gained by retaining the island of Guadeloupe, which had fallen into the British hands among their West Indian conquests.

or Guadeloupe?

Franklin and Burke.

To one who, like Franklin, held a strong faith in the great domain which the fall of Montreal had secured, the intimation of any abandonment of the results of the long war was a painful thought, and the strong feelings which he harbored made his advocacy of the retention of Canada the most notable of a large swarm of controversial pamphlets, called forth by the dispute. The tracts on the other side, which showed equal ability, sprung probably from the able pen of William Burke, assisted very likely by his more distinguished brother.

Their arguments.

Franklin at one time said of England that the little island had "scarce enough of it to keep one's shoes dry," and her contracted insularity had hardly fostered as yet any dreams of imperial range. She could scarcely appreciate, he thought, the boundless possibilities of such a territory as now lay open for her colonization. The ardent American looked forward, with the population doubling every quarter of a century, to a time when the vast interval between the Alleghanies and the Mississippi could ultimately house and feed a hundred millions of people. To part with this for the paltry island of Guadeloupe was simply, as he urged, the interest of a sordid and unimaginative mercantile spirit, which looked to the present profits of the sugar trade, and was unjust to the American colonies. "To leave the French in the possession of Canada, when it is in our power to remove them, and to depend on our own strength and watchfulness to prevent the mischief that may attend it, is neither safe nor prudent." "Canada in the hands of the French," he says again, "has always stunted the growth of our colonies," and it was no welcome thought to apprehend that in the future, Canada, still under the French, could render the peace of America dependent upon the hazards of European complications.

It was one of the arguments of the discontents that with the retention of Canada the growth of the seaboard colonies westward would nurture "a numerous, hardy, and independent people, who would become useless and dangerous to Britain," while with Canada restored to the French, the colonists would find that "a neighbor who keeps us in awe is not always the worst of neighbors." Such arguments as these intimated the revelations that the same generation was to discover in the relations of the mother country and her colonies. Franklin met them by pointing out the slender chance of danger to England with colonies whose jealousies had always prevented united action in the face of the greatest necessity for it. But he added, with an air of prescience, "When I say such a union is impossible, I mean without the most grievous tyranny and oppression." He further argued that this spreading westward meant the fostering of an agricultural people, not a manufacturing one, who would be buyers and not rival makers of English handicraft products. The dissentients also alleged that it could not be profitable for Great Britain to hold possessions two hundred miles beyond the coast and back of the mountains, because the expense of carriage would make merchandise too costly to be sold. To this Franklin replied, with a clear perception of what the Mississippi might become, that the Ohio to a sea power like England was really nearer to London than the remote provinces of France and Spain were to their home manufactures. The arguments of Franklin were to prevail.

In the interval of suspended negotiations, and amid the financial distress of France, and with no military success illuminating the gloom, Choiseul was beginning to think that if he could not make war, he could at least bring peace. With a party in England thinking that this making of war had taught them how to find a peace, there was no impediment to the resumption of negotiations in September, 1762. In the conferences which thus hastened to a result, Bute, now British minister, had shown that he was willing to accept less than Pitt had demanded, but nothing except exactions which were still stringent could have satisfied the lurking determination of the British people to make France drink deep of her humility. Feeling the debasement keenly, France finally agreed to preliminaries on November 3. The approval of the terms was under discussion in the Commons on December 9, when Pitt, coming in late, wrapped in flannel, and leaning on a crutch, made one of his histrionic speeches, in condemnation of the leniency of the ministry. It was without avail, and the House approved the terms. It might not have done so, however, if it had known that on the same day, at Fontainebleau, November 3, Choiseul and Grimaldi, the representatives of the crowns of France and Spain, had agreed that what was left of Louisiana west of the Mississippi, but including the island of New Orleans on the east bank, should be transferred from the flag of France to that of Spain. On the 13th and 23d, respectively, this secret cession was approved at the Escurial and by Louis, though it was not to be known to the world for fifteen months.

Peace negotiations resumed, September, 1762.

Preliminaries of peace. November 3.

Secret cession of the west bank of the Mississippi.

It was January 21, 1763, when Amherst, in New York, hearing of the preliminary treaty, announced to Bouquet, now at Fort Pitt, the cessation of arms. The Duke of Bedford acting for England, Choiseul for France, Grimaldi for Spain, and Mello for Portugal, the terms of the treaty were made definitive at Paris on February 10, and the ratifications were exchanged among the contracting powers a month later. The promulgation of it was made on May 4, and on July 31, Gage, at Montreal, informed Egremont that he had issued the proclamation of peace.

Cessation of arms. January 21, 1763.

Definitive treaty. February 10, 1763.

New France had disappeared, and not a foothold was left to the French Bourbons on the continent of North America. France had represented to Spain that it was for Spanish interest to encourage her American ambition, because New France could stand between the mines of Mexico and the greedy English. Now she had brought the Spaniard and the Englishman face to face across the Mississippi, but the world did not as yet comprehend it. England had never before been so great relatively as in this hour of her triumph. Pitt's dream of a greater Gallic degradation could hardly have raised higher the fortunes of England. In America, at least, she had reëstablished successfully all that she had ever gained by every treaty from Westphalia in 1648 down, and she had added to it. She had renounced, indeed, the sea-to-sea pretensions of her colonial charters, but she had silenced all opposition as far west as the Mississippi. At the north she had acquired apparently forever the region of Acadia, and it was no longer of any moment what its "ancient limits" were. She had left to France what the treaty of Utrecht had originally secured for that country, the two small islands of St. Pierre and Miquelon, "to serve as a shelter to her fishermen," — a pitiful reminder to France of her continental aspirations. We learn, however, what other use she could make of them when we find, in September, that these islands were full of French goods, waiting to be smuggled into Canada.

New France disappears.

England's greatness.

Spain, in return for the restoration of Cuba, had been forced to yield to England another British conquest, namely, all those lands lying east and southeast of the Missis-

Florida ceded by Spain.

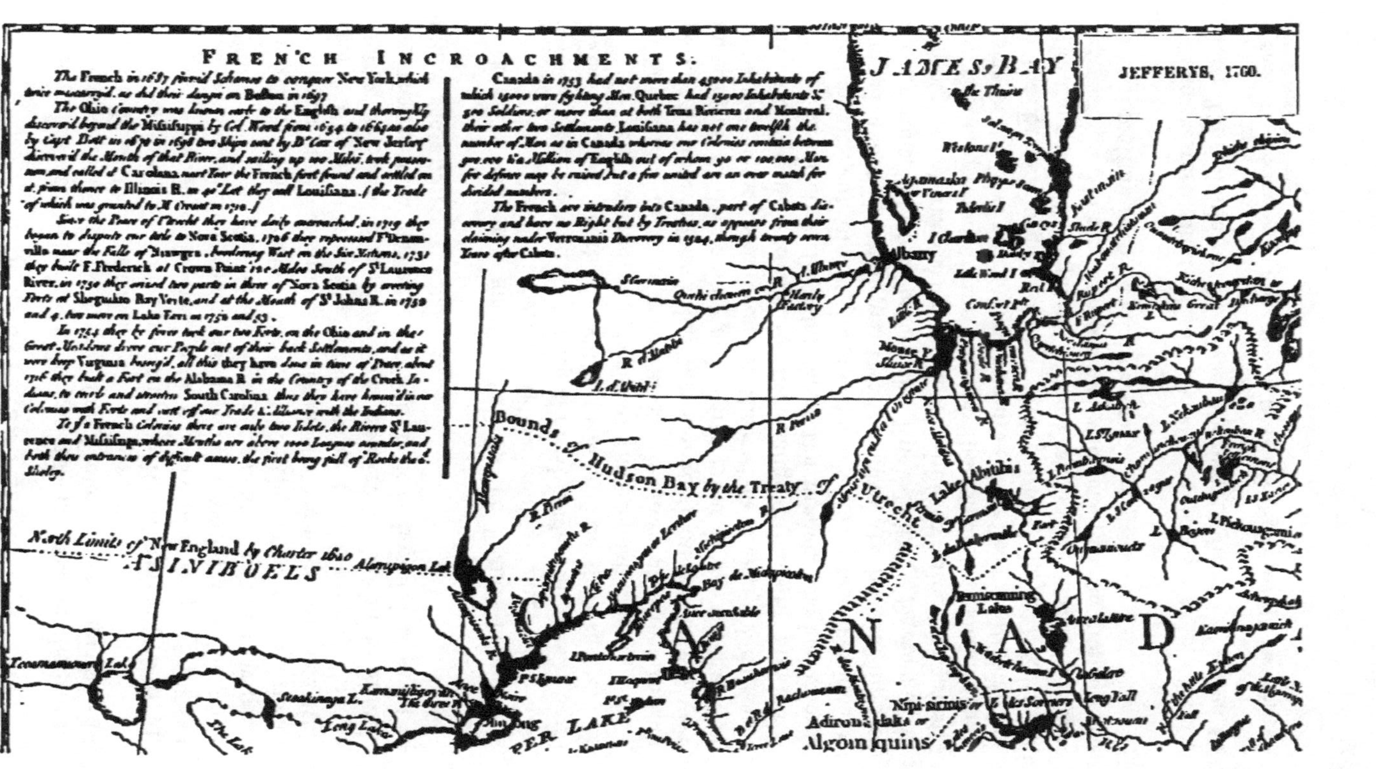
FRENCH INCROACHMENTS:
JEFFERYS, 1760.
JAMES'S BAY
Albany
Moose R.
Lake Abitibis
Bounds of Hudson Bay by the Treaty of Utrecht
North Limits of New England by Charter 1620
ASINIBOELS
Alempigon Lak
C A N A D A
Temiscaming Lakes
Nipi-sirinis or Lakes Sorcerers
Adirondaks or
Algonquins
Long Lake
The Lak
PER LAKE

sippi which were called Florida, and any pretensions she had to the parts about Mobile Bay, which France had occupied, — all lying below 31° of latitude.

Canada and Hudson's Bay.

In the north, Canada came into the British empire, "with all its dependencies," and "in the most ample form and manner without restriction," making, with the territory of the Hudson Bay Company, an uninterrupted stretch of land toward the Arctic pole, as in the Floridian peninsula she had almost touched the tropics. No one welcomed this northern acquisition more than Governor Arthur Dobbs, who saw in the boundless contiguity the chance of finding the western passage, "which I have hoped [he says] to attain these thirty years."

French Canadians under the new conditions.

It was of course a question how far the French inhabitants of the St. Lawrence valley would change their allegiance, and they were allowed under the treaty eighteen months in which to determine their future. If they stayed, the "rites of the Romish Church" were to be assured to them "as far as the laws of Great Britain permit." It was found that the change of allegiance was very distasteful to the nobility and clergy; but it was thought that the lower classes would console themselves easily. This social diversity was not strange, for the change of lordship brought a change of society little palatable to the French, who had known the amenities of life in the old country. The feudal seigneur, hedged about by privileges, free to control the life and limb of the peasant, vanished before the English law. Egremont, in writing to Murray, August 13, told him to watch the priests, for the subjection of the rites of their church to such curtailment as the laws of England required had been a bitter potion to the French negotiators. "Every priest," he added, "must take the oath of allegiance. The French king cannot interfere between his Majesty and his new subjects, and no interference in civil matters is to be allowed from any priest."

The western limits of the cession were by "a line drawn along the middle of the river Mississippi from its source to

NOTE. The opposite map is from a *Carte de la Nouvelle France*, made for the Compagnie Françoise of the West.

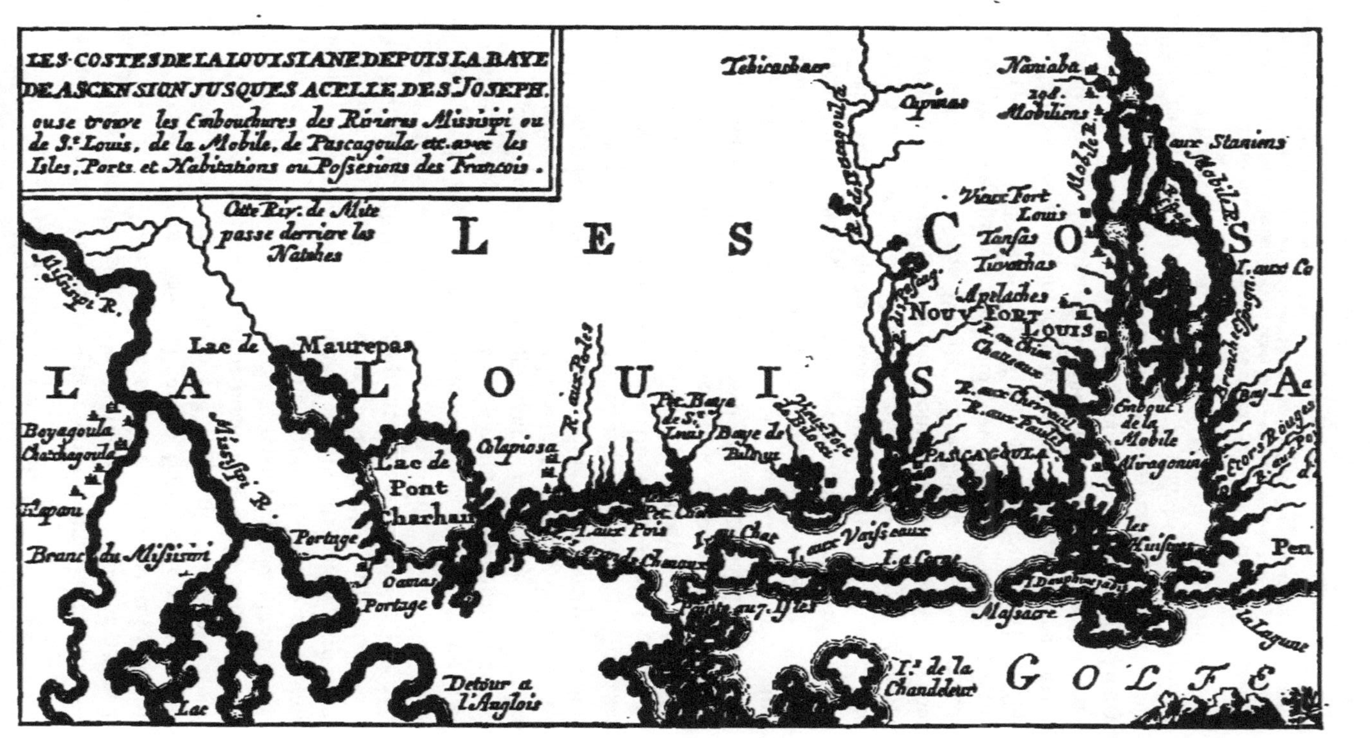
LES COSTES DE LA LOUYSIANE DEPUIS LA BAYE DE ASCENSION JUSQUES A CELLE DE S.t JOSEPH.
ouse trouve les Embouchures des Rivieres Missisipi ou de S.t Louis, de la Mobile, de Pascagoula etc. avec les Isles, Ports et Habitations ou Possesions des François.
LES COSTES
LA LOUISIA
GOLFE
Lac de Maurepas
Lac de Pont Charhain
Colapiosa
R. aux Perles
Baye de Biloxy
PASCAGOULA
NOUV. FORT LOUIS
Vieux Fort Louis
Tansas
Tuvoshas
Apelaches
Naniaba
Mobiliens
Mobile R.
I. aux Staniens
Chataux
Mobile
Aliragonins
Branche Espagn.
Les Huistres
La Corne
I. aux Vaisseaux
Massacre
I.s de la Chandeleur
Detour a l'Anglois
Portage
Oumas
Bayagoula
Missisipi R.
Tchicachas
I. aux Pois
La Laguna
Pen
Lac

the river Iberville, thence by said river through lakes Maurepas and Pontchartrain to the sea." The navigation of the Mississippi was to be free to the subjects of Great Britain as well as to those of France in its whole extent, from its source to the sea, and vessels of either nation were not to be stopped or made subject to the payment of any duty. This was of course agreed to by England in ignorance of the transmission of the rights of France to Spain, made on the day of the signing of the preliminaries, and that transmission produced later complications with Spain.

The Mississippi as a boundary.

The bed of the Iberville, except at high water, was above the surface of the Mississippi, so that the "island" on which New Orleans stands did not always exist; but this condition was not embarrassing. It was quite otherwise at the other end of the Mississippi, and ignorance of the geography of its source remained an obstacle to a clear definition of bounds twenty years later, under the treaty of 1782. When the upper waters of the Mississippi were not at this time supposed to be connected with the water-system of Hudson's Bay, the contemporary cartographers placed the river's source anywhere from latitude 45° to 55°. Jefferys thought it somewhat above 45°. Samuel Dunn, helping himself from Carver's views, put it, a little later, under 46°, and he clusters several lakes about the source. Buache, the French map-maker, working up the earlier drafts of Delisle, now forty years old, places the fountain at 46°, among the Sioux. A map based on Danville, and using material gathered by Governor Pownall, puts the source in a lake at 47°, due south of the Lake of the Woods. The Dutchman, Vander Aa, in 1755 puts the springs doubtfully at 55°, but in 1763 he finds reason to place a little group of three lakes, out of which the river flows from a triple source, under 49°. A French map, prepared for the Company of the West, establishes the head under 50°. Bowen, in a map produced to show the treaty bounds, says the position of the source is uncertain, but that the Indians report it under 50°, and in a marshy region. Robert Rogers, in his *Concise Account*, says that the Mississippi rises

Source of the Mississippi.

Map.

NOTE. The map on the opposite page is from Vander Aa's *Canada* (Leyden). It shows the supposed source of the Mississippi in three lakes in lat. 49°; the Rivière Longue of La Hontan; the river near La Hontan's lake supposed to flow to the West Sea; and another river with a similar course rising in the Lac des Pauls.

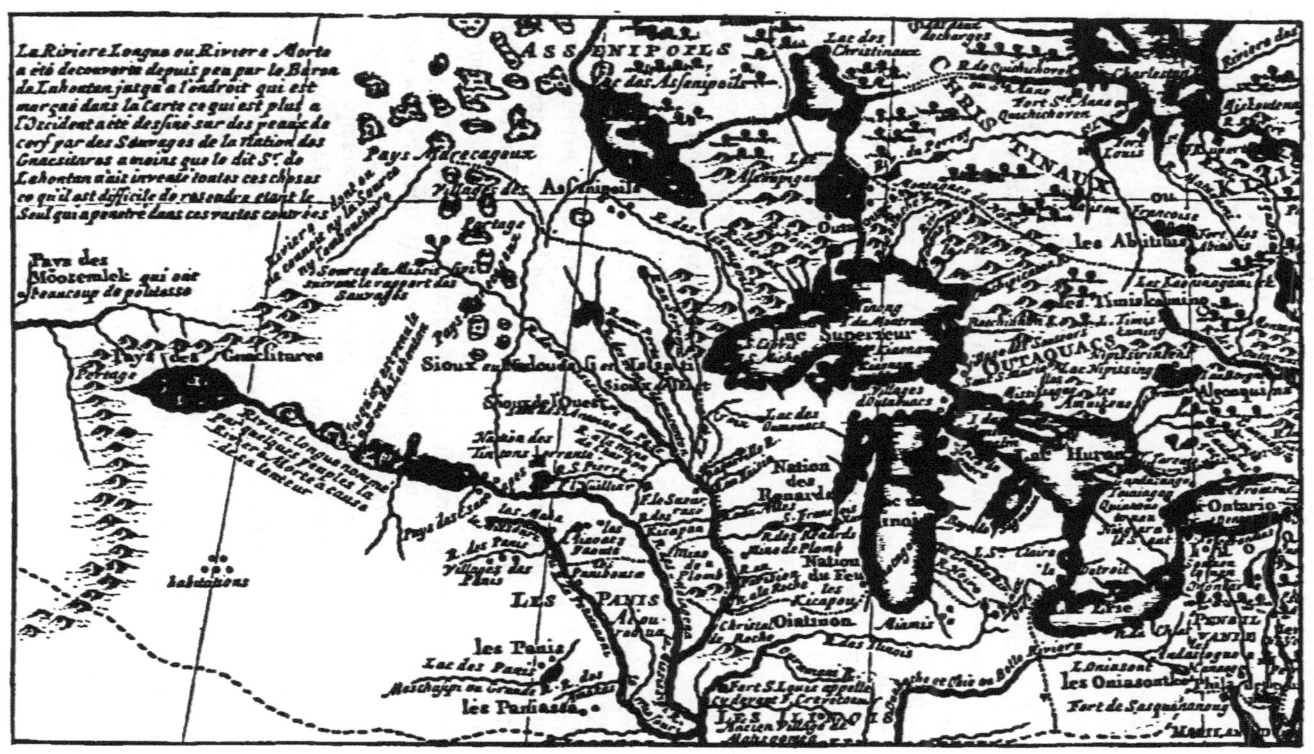
La Riviere Longue ou Riviere Morte a été decouverte depuis peu par le Baron de Lahontan jusqu'a l'endroit qui est marqué dans la Carte ce qui est plus a l'Occident a été dessiné sur des peaux de cerf par des Sauvages de la Nation des Gnacsitares a moins que le dit Sr. de Lahontan n'ait inventé toutes ces choses ce qu'il est difficile de rasendre étant le Seul qui a penetré dans ces vastes contrées
Pays des Mooзemlek qui ont beaucoup de politesse
Pays des Gnacsitares
Portage
Riviere longue nommée par quelques Peuples la Riviere Morte à cause de sa lenteur
habitations
Pays Marecageux
Villages des Assenipoils
ASSENIPOILS
Lac des Assenipoils
Lac des Christinaux
Sioux
Nation des Renards
Lac Superieur
OUTAOUACS
Lac Nipissing
les Abitibis
Lac Huron
Ontario
Erie
Le Detroit
Oiatinon
Miamis
LES PANIS
les Panis
Lac des Panis
les Paniassa
Villages des Panis
R. des Panis
Les Ilinois
Fort de Sasquahanoug
les Oniasontke
Maison Francoise
Fort St. Anne
R. de Quichichoven
Rivière des

in a lake "of considerable bigness," into which flows a stream through a notch in the mountains, carrying a red substance.

Added to this great variety of opinion respecting the position of a distinct source of the river, there were other views prevalent among geographers, who still clung to an older notion of interlinking inland waters, flowing in different directions. It was common for these to connect the upper waters of the Mississippi with a reticulation of lakes and streams, having a dependence upon Hudson's Bay, and sometimes upon that mysterious channel which formed a union with the western sea. Roberts, an English cartographer, in 1760, makes the Mississippi rise in Lake Winnipeg. Palairet, a French map-maker, embodying the joint results of Bellin, Danville, and Mitchell, connects the sources with Lake Winnipeg, though he acknowledges the upper parts of the channel are little known. He adds that some suppose there is a connection between the Mississippi or Missouri and the Manton [Mandan] River, which he represents by a dotted line as flowing ultimately into the Sea of the West. This same device of an uncertain dotted line is used by Emanuel Bowen, in 1763, to join the upper Mississippi with the Red River of the North. The *Neptune Française* has no hesitancy in connecting the Mississippi with Lake Winnipeg, and a most wonderful network of waters is supposed by Vander Aa on a map of 1755, where the Mississippi, Winnipeg, Lake Superior, and Hudson's Bay are all brought into a single system of communication. A few years later (1776), Jefferys connects Winnipeg with a fanciful inlet on the Pacific coast, which D'Aguilar is supposed to have entered in 1603, forming that water-way to the Sea of the West so long sought. Explorers in this region were still beguiled by the increasing Indian tales of the connection of the Missouri by means of a string of interjacent lakes with the South Sea, and there were stories among the Dacotahs which shortly after this induced Carver to believe that the Shining Mountains [Rockies] stretched from about 48° north latitude toward the south, and divided the waters flowing into the gulfs of Mexico and California. He suspected that north of 48° there was a water-system somehow connecting Hudson's Bay with the Pacific, and lying somewhere thereaway were the Straits of Anian, "which hav-

Passages to the western ocean.

[From the *Gentleman's Magazine*, December, 1755. It shows the popular notion of the Mississippi having its rise in the latitude of the southern end of Hudson's Bay, and indicates the supposed River of the West.]

ing been discovered by Sir Francis Drake belong of course to the English."

Such was the vague knowledge of this northwest region when, on October 7, 1763, the English king in a proclamation, issued with the concurrence of his council, and in disregard of the sea-to-sea charters, — which Kitchin, in his map made to mark the conditions of the peace, had been prompt to revive and extend as far as the Mississippi, — established as crown lands, to be held for the benefit of the Indians, all this vast region between the Alleghanies and the Mississippi, wherever in the north its source might be.

Royal proclamation of October 7, 1763.

Crown lands.

This proclamation had set up three new governments in North America, outside the preëxisting seaboard colonies. Two of these new provinces were carved out of the accessions yielded by Spain along the Gulf of Mexico, to be respectively East and West Florida. They were to be bounded north by the thirty-first parallel, and to extend from the Mississippi, with some deflections, to the Atlantic. By this a region which had been in dispute between Georgia and Spain, embracing the territory from the St. Mary's River to the Altamaha, was added to Georgia. The settling of this and other vexed questions long subsisting between the Carolinians and the French soon had the effect to force the Indians of the gulf water-shed to conclude a peace. Later, in 1764, the western part of the northern line was removed from 31° north to the parallel of the mouth of the Yazoo, the source of future difficulties.

The two Floridas.

In Canada, the new province of Quebec was a good deal curtailed from the extent which had constituted what Vaudreuil had governed. The definitions of bounds given in the proclamation do not agree with modern geography; but the province was confined approximately on the north by the water-shed of Hudson's Bay. The northern line then extended west to Lake Nepissing, taking in the Ottawa up to the portage to Lake Huron. It was bounded on the south by a due east line, which, in crossing the St. Lawrence and Lake Champlain, was supposed to follow the forty-fifth parallel, the

Bounds of Quebec.

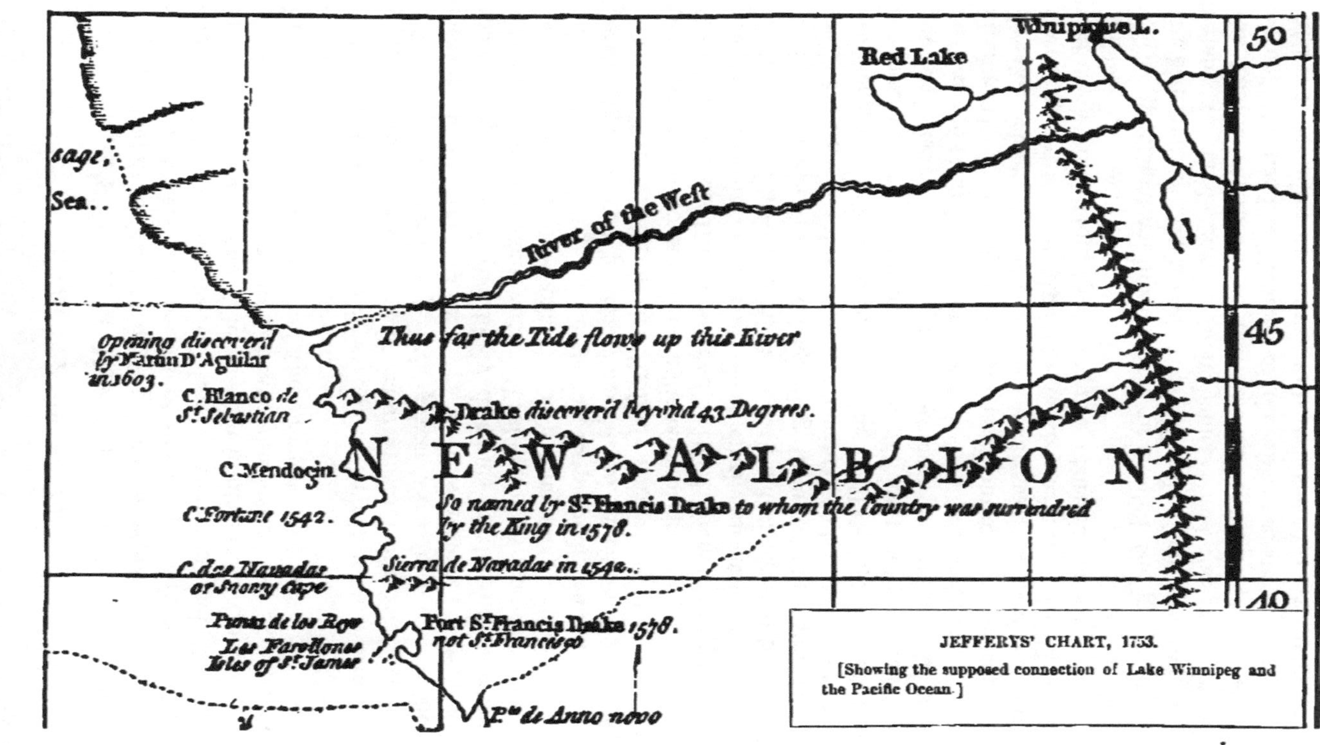

JEFFERYS' CHART, 1753.

[Showing the supposed connection of Lake Winnipeg and the Pacific Ocean.]

present northern limits of New York and Vermont, till it struck a height of land along the heads of rivers flowing into the St. Lawrence,—the source of disputes, which were only ended by the compromise of Lord Ashburton and Webster in the treaty of 1842. The western limitation of Quebec was contrary to the advice of Murray, who desired the Mississippi for the farther boundary of the province, but his views were overruled in the king's council.

The object of the council was, as we have seen, to make this western expanse an area of crown lands, "for the use of the Indians *for the present*, and until our further pleasure is known." There was in this reserved possibility some recognition of the likely demands of the future, which Franklin had foreshadowed. Washington is known to have looked upon the proclamation as a temporary expedient for quieting the Indians. Nevertheless, its promulgation was unexpected, and was very generally considered an affront to the colonies, and an interference with their natural right to subdue the earth. The conservative adherents of the crown regarded it simply as a needful protection to the Indian. The party of progress called it a tyrannous check on the inevitable expansion of the race. There was right on both sides. It had been the policy of France from the beginning, in preserving game-fields, really to put restraint upon settlements, and it had been the great cause of her misfortunes. The English had not failed to comment in their own favor on the different policy which had governed their progress. It was not now pleasant for the colonists to see their home government slide into what was recognized as the French system. Edmund Burke, representing the aversion which this new policy had aroused in England, protested against such an attempt "to keep as a lair of wild beasts that earth which God, by an express charter, has given to the children of men."

The crown lands.

The proclamation, in set terms, prohibited the governors of Quebec and of East and West Florida from granting any patents for lands beyond their bounds; and the governors of the Atlantic colonies were restrained from allotting any lands beyond the heads or sources of the rivers which fall into the Atlantic Ocean, or upon any lands reserved to the Indians, and not having been ceded to, or purchased by, the king. The edict also made reservation of all land not included in the three new governments and in the Hudson Bay Company's possession, and lying westward of the sources aforesaid, "for the use of the Indians, and no one could, under pain of the king's displeasure, take possession of any such reserved lands without the king's leave, and all persons having already done so were required to remove. All private persons were forbidden to buy lands of the Indians;" but if at any time any of the Indians were inclined to sell, it should only be to some one representing the crown.

There was doubtless in all this a number of objects to be gained. One was to limit the old colonies by the mountains, and to discredit the old charters. Another was to keep the population within easy reach of the British trade. A third was to keep the populace under the restraint of the seaboard authorities. Hillsborough, when put to the question in 1772, made no secret that this was the purpose, though regard for the Indian was made the essential object then, and has been held to have been so since. It is quite natural to suppose there was a large interfusion of various reasons.

The purpose of the king.

We shall next see that as a measure of pacifying the Indians it was too late and of little effect.

CHAPTER XXII.

THE EFFECT UPON THE INDIANS.

1763–1765.

THE uneasiness among the western Indians, of which mention has already been made, had, in the spring of 1763, become threatening. There was a rising determination on the part of the tribes to forestall renewed encroachments on the Indians' hunting-grounds, which to the savage mind seemed inevitable while the English were unchecked masters of the field. Johnson thought the readiest means of counteracting a hostile rising was to define with exactness some property line, beyond which the Indians' possessions should be sacred; but even this, in his judgment, could not maintain the peace without some systematic plan of gratuities for propitiating the tribes. He urged at the same time that steps should be taken to buy from the natives the country along the east bank of the Mississippi, from the Ohio to the Illinois, and to make it a centre of trade, in order to prevent the Indians following the French to the western side of the river. He was not alone in urging this project, for he had the countenance of Croghan.

Western Indians uneasy. 1763.

Sir William Johnson's views.

When this entire region north of the Ohio came into the British hands, there were in it a few thousand French residents, traders in the main, the validity of whose rights to the soil was recognized by the victors. The estimates of their numbers are various, but it is probable there were about twelve hundred adults and eight hundred children. Making part of their communities were also about nine hundred blacks. A movement had naturally and very soon begun among them to seek the cover of their own flag across the Mississippi. This impulse was in entire ignorance of the secret transfer of that country by France to Spain. It was in August, 1763, that

The east bank of the Mississippi.

Laclède, representing a fur company, and a party of followers left New Orleans with the expectation of establishing a post in the Illinois country. Arrived there in 1764, and hearing of the provisions of the peace, he had determined upon placing his station on the western side of the Mississippi. On the spot where now stands the city of St. Louis, two Frenchmen, Chouteau by name, had set up a trading-lodge in the previous winter, and here Laclède established his new station. It was not long before a third part of the whites and a greater proportion of the negroes left their old villages on the eastern side of the river, and gathered under the Bourbon flag at this spot. Hutchins, a little later, spoke of the new settlement as "the most healthy and pleasurable situation of any known in this part of the country. Here the Spanish commandant and the principal Indian traders reside, who, by conciliating the affections of the natives, have drawn all the Indian trade of the Missouri, part of that of the Mississippi (northward) and of the tribes of Indians residing near the Ouisconsin and Illinois rivers, to this village."

Laclède and St. Louis. 1763-64.

This exodus of the French from what was now British territory was not lost upon the western Indians, and they were become more than ever conscious that it was with the English cupidity for land they were thus left to deal, and without French support. The discontent thus increased became a savage revenge when stories, told them by the French, disclosed the English purpose to possess their country by exterminating its rightful owners.

The Indians incensed.

The British government was not long in getting intelligence of this condition at the west, while at the same time it was learning of disturbances every way similar among the southern Indians, fostered, as was believed, by the French at New Orleans and its dependent posts. As a help to counteract this mischief, a large amount of gifts, to the value of some four or five thousand pounds, had been sent over to Charleston. There was no such liberal policy pursued with the western Indians, and Croghan complained in the spring of 1763 that Amherst had pursued a too niggard policy with the savages. Croghan explained the situation to Bouquet in May: "Since the reduction of Canada, the several Indian nations this way have been very jealous of his Majesty's growing power in

Croghan's views.

this country, but this last account of so much of North America being ceded to Great Britain has almost driven them to despair. . . . You will find the Cherokees our enemies, though they seem very quiet on the frontiers of Carolina. What obliged them to be so is nothing else than the war which the western nations have carried on against them with great spirit this two years past. They have been this winter endeavoring to accommodate matters, which if they should do may give us more trouble than we expect." The trouble was already at hand throughout the entire northwest.

Just before this, Croghan had written to Amherst that the Indians about Detroit rebelled at the audacity of the French in ceding the Indian lands to the English. Just at the critical moment, the general replied rather haughtily that it was of no consequence what the Indians thought. They should understand, he said, that it is for their interest to keep quiet. This was precisely what they did not intend to do. Gladwin, who commanded at Detroit, was quite aware of the rising rebellion, and in April had sent words of warning to Sandusky and other posts. On the 27th of that month, Pontiac was in council with the warriors which his runners had assembled from far and near. The Ottawas, — his own people, — Ojibways, and Pottawattamies were particularly subservient to his powerful will. Pontiac was now a man of fifty, and his pleadings had had their effect as far south as the lower Mississippi, and as far east as the Iroquois country. It was here that the Senecas had yielded to the movement, if indeed they had not been the first, or among the first, to give it impetus.

Gladwin at Detroit.

Pontiac in council.

The plan which the conspiring tribes had agreed upon was to make a simultaneous attack on a given day upon all the forts from Pennsylvania to Lake Superior. The stroke was to fall in May. The war for a single season (1763) was vigorously pushed. It affords the student some of the most striking episodes in savage warfare. It was carried on with an animated spirit of desperation. Never before had the frontier settlements been pressed so rancorously. Two thousand settlers are said to have been killed along the borders, outside the armed posts. The savage foe burst through passes of the mountains too numerous to be guarded. Every white

Pontiac war. 1763.

man was driven from the Ohio and its upper tributaries. Every post that the French had spared along the river was destroyed, and all the settlements within reach of Fort Pitt were uprooted.

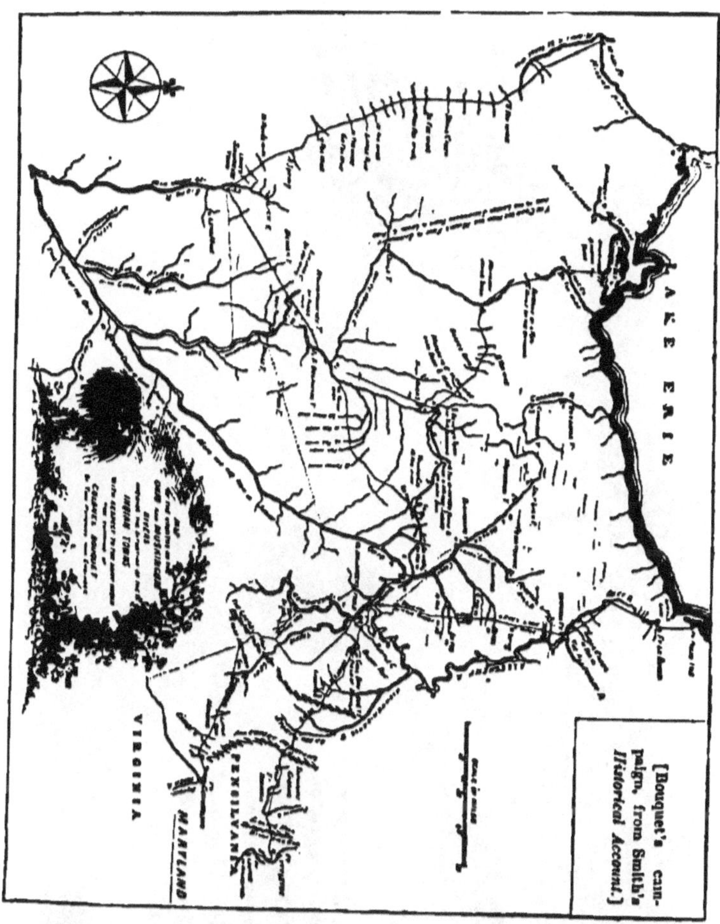

[Bouquet's campaign, from Smith's *Historical Account*.]

There is no occasion to repeat a story so graphically told in its striking details by Parkman, and it answers our present purpose merely to show how the English were awakened to a sense of their insecurity. By the last of May, rumors had reached Fort Pitt of the fall of the stockade at Sandusky, and within a month reports came in of devastations

The English alarmed.

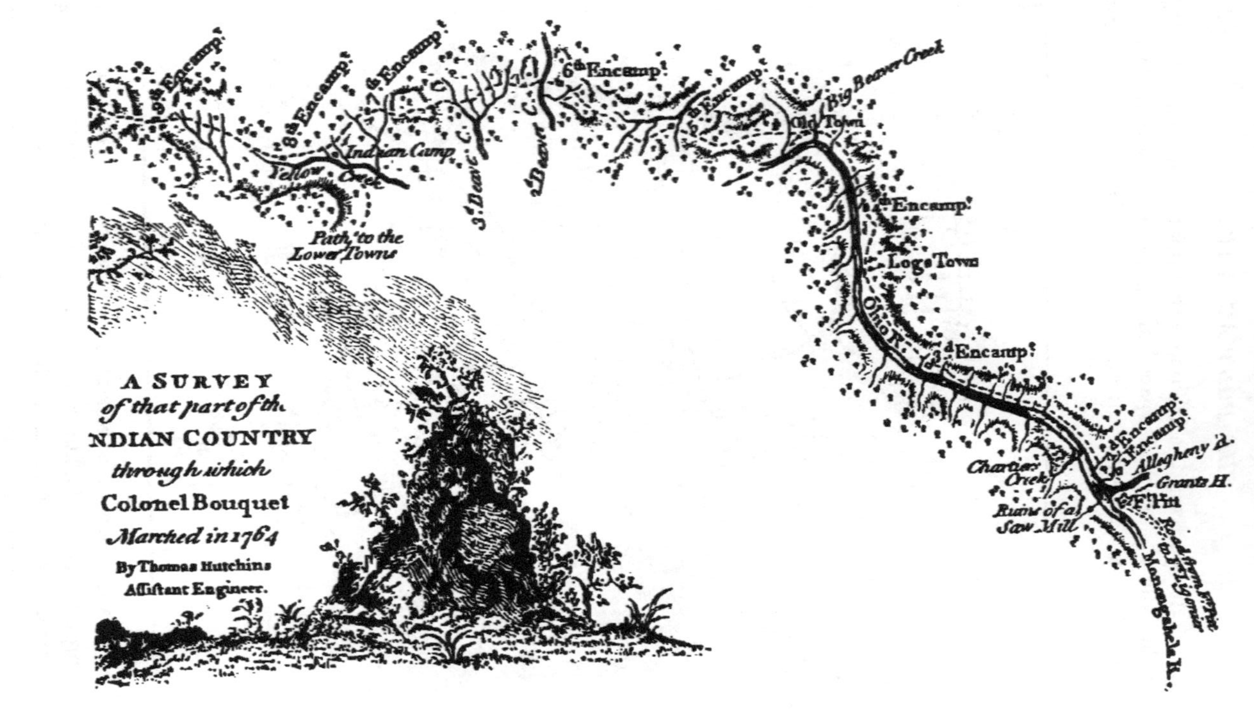

A SURVEY
of that part of th
NDIAN COUNTRY
through which
Colonel Bouquet
Marched in 1764
By Thomas Hutchins
Assistant Engineer.
6th Encamp.
Big Beaver Creek
Old Town
Logs Town
Ohio R.
Indian Camp
Yellow Creek
Path to the
Lower Towns
Charties Creek
Ruins of a
Saw Mill
Allegheny R.
Grants H.
Monongahela R.

Note. The cut on the opposite page attaches to this one at the left hand edge.

all along the Pennsylvania borders. Early in June, Croghan, then at Carlisle, reported that the Delawares, who had been waiting developments, had gone over to the enemy.

It was Croghan's belief that the French were the real instigators of this outbreak, not so much with the hope of making it successful as with the expectation that the beaten savages would seek an asylum under the Bourbon flag beyond the Mississippi. They could thus sustain the trade they were trying to build up by wresting much of it from the English. In June, a pack of huddled settlers were crouching before an attack upon Fort Ligonier, and Fort Bedford was preparing for the worst. The lesser posts near Fort Cumberland were pouring their people into that refuge.

Bouquet, now in Philadelphia, heard of the rising, but the stories were so contradictory that he was perplexed what to believe. Amherst thought it nothing but a rash attempt of the Senecas. By June 12, both Bouquet and the general had found that they must accept the worst. Croghan, at Fort Bedford, while communication was cut with Fort Pitt, believed this latter post to be invested. The truth was that on the next day after Croghan wrote, Le Bœuf had been abandoned (June 18). Presqu' Isle and Venango were also taken, and their garrisons massacred. On June 23 and 24, a sharp attack had been made on Fort Pitt itself, but without success.

Forts taken.

During July, Bouquet was struggling to organize a relieving force, but he found the loss of Presqu' Isle had disarranged his plans, and the occupation of the passes by the enemy prevented his getting needful information of their movements. To harass him further, the Pennsylvania authorities, who had gathered a force for the borders, refused to put it under his control.

Marching from Carlisle, Bouquet was attacked at Edge Hill, near Bushy Run, twenty-six miles from Fort Pitt, where he suffered a loss of sixty men. He had gained some advantages, chiefly by the good behavior of the forty-second regiment. They had shown that regulars could meet the savage with his own tactics. At the day's close, Bouquet had written to Amherst, not in the best of spirits, regretting that his train prevented his following up what advantages he had gained, and expecting the battle to be renewed in the morning. The day brought the savage host once more upon him.

Edge Hill and Bushy Run.

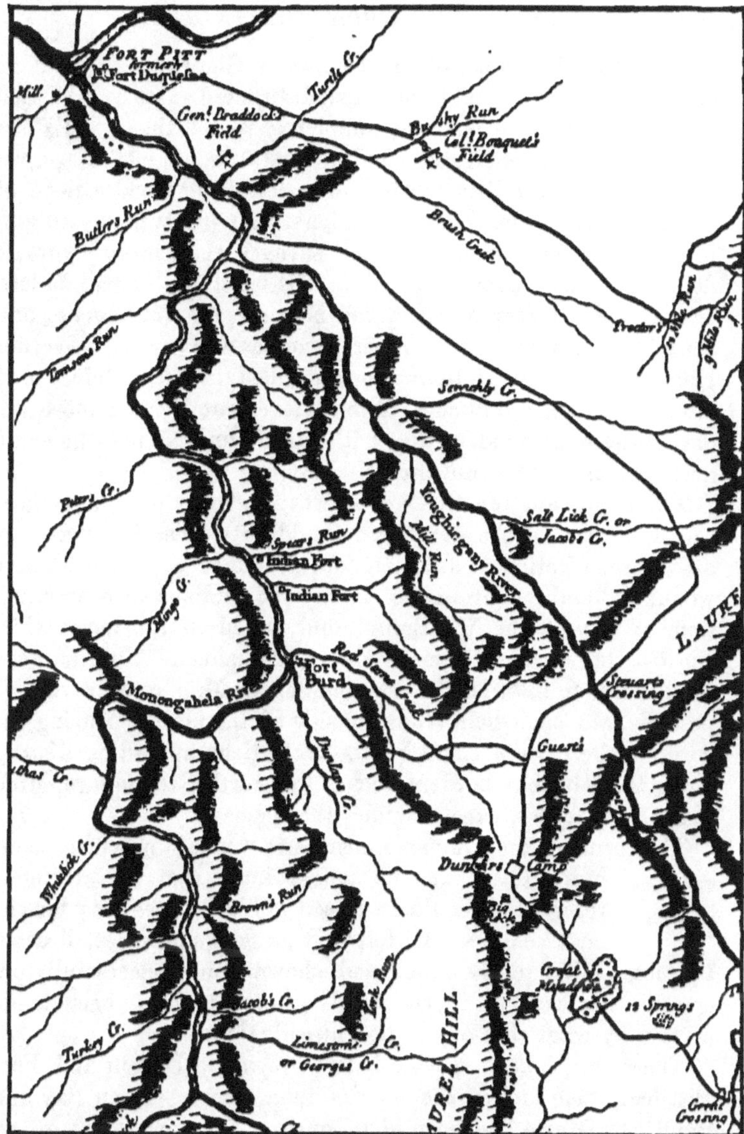

[From the *Map of Pennsylvania, chiefly from the Map of W. Scull, 1770* (London: Sayer and Bennett, 1775), showing the place of Bouquet's fight. Croghan calls Scull's map a deception, and says that Fort Pitt was put in it thirteen miles farther north than its actual situation, in order to place it on the same parallel with the bend in the Delaware at Easton, and so bring it within the five degrees west from that river which constitute the western extension of Pennsylvania under the charter.]

He now found it to consist of Delawares, Shawnees, Wyandots, and Mingoes. He lured them into a disordered onset by a feigned retreat, and then turned and completely routed them. His loss for the two days was one hundred and fifteen, and on August 11 he was at Fort Pitt, which had successfully stood a siege of five days. Here he wrote to Amherst that his two days' fighting at Edge Hill had given the savages the "most complete defeat they had ever received in the woods." It had indeed cleared the country of every foe between the settlements and Fort Pitt. Later, in September, Bouquet reported to Governor Hamilton that the Indians were stunned by their defeat, and later still, as the influence of his movement became more apparent, he was confident that with seven hundred men he could drive the enemy beyond the Mississippi.

The campaign for the season was evidently over, but there was no hope that the next year would not reveal the necessity of vigorous action. Johnson told Amherst that the French would no doubt continue to supply the Indians with ammunition, by way of the Mississippi, and would in the mean while engross the western trade by the same channel. This induced the general to instruct the commander at Mobile to prevent, if possible, any such help from the side of the Gulf. During the autumn, there were small packs of Indians spreading dismay along the Virginia borders, but at the north Croghan reported that all was quiet, except among the Senecas.

The results of the summer's war.

The result of the summer's hostilities was in a measure assuring. There was no longer doubt that the strongest force which could be raised would be necessary for the next year's work; but that an adequate force, directed by such ability as Bouquet had shown, could successfully encounter the savages in the woods seemed to have been made certain by what that officer had already done.

There was, indeed, a wide field to regain. Detroit and Fort Pitt had alone braved the attacks upon them. Green Bay and Sault Ste. Marie had been abandoned. The garrison at Mackinac had been massacred. When, in August, the survivors of the most western stations reached Montreal, not a British flag was left flying west of Detroit. The forts at Sandusky, Miami, St. Joseph, Ouiatanon, Presqu' Isle, and Venango had all been captured by the conspirators.

The news of the proclamation of October 7 was not received till it had become necessary to suppress rather than pacify the Indians, and it was likely to have little effect, except upon the whites. In November, Amherst had sailed from New York for England, and the command in America now devolved on Thomas Gage. He had recently been in authority at Montreal. His plans were soon laid for pushing forces into the Mississippi region, using both Fort Pitt and Mobile as his bases. But he soon found his hands full of other duties.

The proclamation of October 7, 1763.

Gage commander-in-chief.

Late in January, 1764, he wrote to Bouquet to come to New York and determine upon plans for the summer's campaign. By April, the plans were well in hand. Gage had put Bouquet in charge of all forces in Philadelphia and south of it, and had urged the governors of Virginia and Maryland to put their local militia under his direction.

Campaign of 1764.

To prepare the way for a northern advance, Johnson, on April 3, brought the Senecas to a peace, by which the crown secured a large tract of land on the Niagara River. This opened a route toward Sandusky by the southern shore of Lake Erie, and this part of the western advance was intrusted to the command of Colonel Bradstreet. He took along with him a force sufficient to give the Indians the effective chastisement which was expected of him. Bradstreet had enlisted a contingent of French Canadians in the hope to convince the Indians of the hopelessness of a French defection. He lingered at Niagara in order to protect Johnson, who was still negotiating with the neighboring tribes, and in August pushed on to Erie.

The northern advance under Bradstreet.

At Presqu' Isle, on August 12, evidently in the expectation of reaping the glory of closing the war, he agreed to a peace with an irresponsible party of Shawnees and Delawares. These scheming savages had planned to quiet Bradstreet by some sort of treaty, while their confederates farther south were to gain time for renewed excesses along the border. By the pliant terms of the treaty, the Indians ceded the existing posts, and granted sites for any others which the English might find it desirable to build. The whites were to have adjacent tillage lands, extending as far as a cannon-shot could reach. The savages gave hostages, and promised to deliver all

Bradstreet's treaty.

murderers of the English at Fort Pitt, and within twenty-five days to surrender at Sandusky all prisoners then in their hands.

On Bradstreet's pushing on to Sandusky, there were no signs of the expected prisoners. The Indians, pursuing their beguiling policy, promised more definite agreements at Detroit. Arrived here, the little army relieved the weary garrison, and sent forward detachments to take possession of Mackinac, the Sault, and Green Bay. On September 10, Bradstreet arranged a new conference; but Pontiac was sulking at the Maumee rapids, and would not come to it. Those who came made a feeble outward show of submission, which satisfied Bradstreet, and then he started east.

Bradstreet at Detroit.

On August 23, Grant, at Fort Pitt, had heard of the Erie treaty, and dispatched messengers at once to Gage and to Bouquet. Neither of these officers approved it, and each was confident that Bradstreet had been too precipitate in coming to even a promise of peace till the Indians had felt the blow which it was the purpose of Gage to give them. It was September 2 when Gage received the news, and he immediately sent orders to Bradstreet to quit parleying with the Delawares, for they were still ravaging the frontiers. Meanwhile, Bouquet, who had also heard of the treaty, hoped the tidings would not be confirmed, and was pushing on into the wilderness in disregard of it, but quite ready to find occasion to punish the tribes for any breach of its provisions on their part. He thought the fact that the Senecas had submitted was more likely to awe the Delawares than this trumped-up treaty was to mollify them.

Gage disapproves the treaty.

Bouquet was not a man of dallying compunctions. He had urged the Pennsylvanians to employ dogs to track the savages, if the province would not help him with men. He had given out that with three or four hundred good woodsmen, he could burn every Indian village in the Ohio country. No matter what spirit he showed, the neighboring governments were slow in coming to his aid. He had found himself held back by this apathy, with the mountains still before him, when he supposed Bradstreet was punishing the Wyandots and Delawares in the region of Sandusky.

Bouquet and his advance.

It was not till the 1st of October that Bouquet crossed the

Ohio, with a definite purpose of forcing a peace of his own imposing which should relieve the regions east and south of the Ohio of the tribes, and preserve the navigation of the Ohio itself. He had advanced into the Muskingum valley, when, on

HENRY BOUQUET.

the 17th of November, the Indians hovering about thought it wise to sue for peace. Bouquet would make no terms until every prisoner among them was surrendered. It took nearly a month to gather in these unfortunates. One among the forest exiles had given birth the previous spring to offspring supposed to be the first white child born in what is now the State of Ohio.

Having imposed his terms, Bouquet broke up his camp on the 18th, and ten days later was at Fort Pitt. Not long afterwards, Sir William Johnson congratulated him on his success. "Nothing but penetrating into their country could have done it," said the Indian agent.

Johnson's view of the campaign.

There was some disposition on the part of the Shawnees, backed by French influence and strengthened by French supplies, to hold out; but the pressure of the Iroquois finally brought them to terms. During December, Bouquet sent off messengers from Fort Loudon to inform the governors of the nearer provinces of the peace. Gage promptly approved the treaty, and advised Bouquet to do what he could to appease Pontiac. There was not a force available to make a successful march to the Illinois, and Gage had been for some time suspicious of St. Ange's influence in that region. He accordingly directed Bouquet to get a Shawnee escort for a messenger to the Illinois, in anticipation of detaching a sufficient force later, to occupy the posts still in the hands of the French. The outcome of this intention will appear in the final chapter.

The results of Bouquet's treaty were for the next ten years far from satisfactory, but it does not concern us here to enter upon the details of the irrepressible irritation of both red man and white. It led to the treaty at Fort Stanwix, and the practical annulment of the king's proclamation, before the strife of the colonies with the mother country broke up all restraints. One result of the Bouquet treaty was to draw the savages still more from the occupancy of the regions south of the Ohio, and facilitate the settling a few years later of what are now the States of Kentucky and Tennessee. Very soon after Bouquet's conference, the last of the Shawnees who lingered in that country crossed the Ohio. Another result was the sending of Croghan to England, at the instance of Sir William Johnson, to advise with the government. Croghan recommended that a line be drawn from the head of the Delaware to the mouth of the Ohio, so as to reserve for an Indian hunting-ground all to the north and west, while a fair purchase was made of all territory between such a line and the settlements. The recommendation resulted in a plan devised at Fort Stanwix four years later. By that time, Pontiac and the west-

Results of Bouquet's treaty.

ern chiefs had presented themselves at Oswego, where Johnson had concluded a treaty with them.

This harmonized interests pretty well at the north; but the troubles in Virginia kept on, and were only turned to new channels by the outbreak of the Revolution. The exhaustion of the tidewater soils, incident upon the culture of tobacco, had always incited a movement westward to find new ground, and this played not an unimportant part in the earlier advance to and beyond the mountains at the south, compared with the movement at the north. This southern exodus was painfully restrained at times by the barbarous inroads along the frontiers, and we have the testimony of Maury, the Huguenot, that this unsettled condition of life was starting emigration from Virginia into the more southern colonies, where a quieter existence seemed to be assured by the interposed barrier formed by the Cherokees and Catawbas. Maury tells us that three hundred persons passed in one week by Bedford Court House into Carolina, and in October, 1764, he says that five thousand crossed by the Goochland Court House on the same errand.

The western movement north and south.

Virginians move south.

But the movement was by no means confined to a southerly direction. The trader had long since become familiar with the mountain passes, and the pioneer was sure to succeed to the trader's routes. The Moravians were opening the way. Already, in 1761, the missionary, Post, had penetrated to an upper branch of the Muskingum, and built him a cabin there on the north side of the Tuscarawas Creek,— in what is now Stark County. It was probably the first white man's house in the wilds of Ohio.

The Moravians in the wilderness.

The British Parliament soon after, in 1763, passed a law for the naturalization of Protestant foreigners who had served in the royal army in America, and had bought land and settled. This gave a new strength to the alien population, and it proved impossible to restrain them within the limits imposed by the proclamation of 1763. The routes which had been opened over the mountains by Forbes and Braddock were dotted with the moving wagons. It has been estimated that from 1765 to 1768 some thirty thousand whites settled beyond the mountains.

Aliens naturalized.

Settlers beyond the mountains.

This had not been done without spasmodic efforts on the part of the king's officers to stop it. Repeated instructions were sent to the colonial governors to interpose restraints. Threats had been made to leave all adventurous and law-breaking settlers to the mercy of the Indians, if they persisted in entering the crown lands. Nothing of threat or prohibition had much effect. Soldiers were sent to eject such settlers on Red Stone Creek and the Cheat River, but the dispossessed squatters soon returned to their old haunts in larger numbers, recruited among their friends. Even Washington sent out his agents and surveyors through the Ohio region, who picked out desirable tracts, and blazed their bounds. It was his intention to patent them, as soon as the restrictions of the proclamation became, as every one foresaw they must become, a fruitless provision.

The story of this occupation, and the movements in which Franklin took a leading part to bring these Ohio regions within the range of civilized prosperity, with a promise finally realized by a free people, belongs rather to another volume than the present. It only remains now to show how the western posts came finally into the victor's hands.

CHAPTER XXIII.

OCCUPATION COMPLETED.

1764, 1765.

WHILE New Orleans and Louisiana were still lingering deceitfully under the flag of France, the doom of the Jesuits had been decreed in Paris. This religious order had with a remarkable prescience marked out both in the upper and the lower basins of the Mississippi what those regions could do for mankind. They had introduced the sugar cane at the south and planted wheat in the Illinois country. The Superior Council of the province had already much restricted their powers, when a general decree in Paris put an end to their work everywhere in the French dominions. It meant that the marvelous power of the Jesuit in regulating intercourse with the savage along the Great River must come, for the present at least, to an end. The settlements at Kaskaskia and in the upper country had been what the Jesuits had made them.

The Jesuits doomed.

The treaty of 1763 had drawn a sharp and natural line of demarcation between the English and the French, along the channel of the Mississippi. This meant a distinct abandonment upon the part of the British government of the old sea-to-sea claim of the early English charters. The idea of such abandonment was not a grateful one to many of the English patentees. They held that by the treaty the claim suffered only a suspension, and not a dissolution. A variety of pamphlets was sprung upon the public to enforce this view. They made the most they could of what they alleged was the avoidance by England in the treaty to guarantee to France the possession of the trans-Mississippi country. To strengthen the territorial pretension of these

The treaty of 1763 and the sea-to-sea claim.

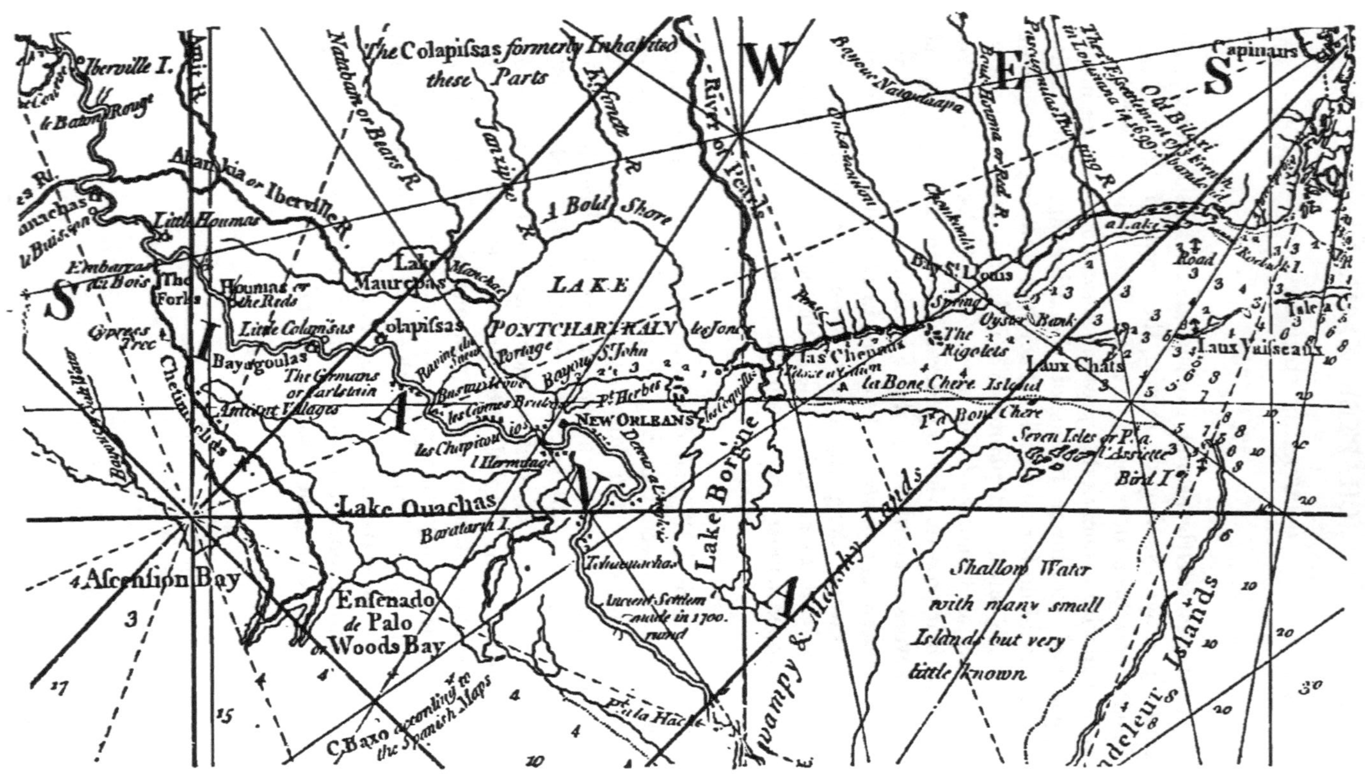

The Colapissas formerly Inhabited these Parts
Iberville I.
le Baton Rouge
Amit R.
Natabam or Bears R.
Tanzipao R
Kifimete R
A Bold Shore
River of Pearls
Bayouc Natanbaapa
Bouk Houma or Red R.
Pascagoulas R.
Old Biloxi
The first Establishment of the French in Louisiana in 1699
Capinaurs
Ascantia or Iberville R.
Little Houmas
Embarras de Bois
The Forks
Houmas or the Reds
Lake Maurepas
Manchac
LAKE
PONTCHARTRAIN
Little Colapissas
Colapissas
Cypress Tree
Bayagoulas
The Germans or Carlstein
Ancient Villages
Chetimachas
Portage
Bayou St. John
Pt. Herbert
NEW ORLEANS
les Chapitoulas
l'Hermitage
Detour a l'Anglois
Lake Ouachas
Barataria I.
Ascension Bay
Ensenado de Palo or Woods Bay
C. Baxo according to the Spanish Maps
Tchaouachas
Ancient Settlem made in 1700. ruind
Pt. a la Hache
Lake Borgne
Swampy & Marshy Lands
Bay St. Louis
Road
Oyster Bank
The Rigolets
las Chenaux
Laux Chats
Laux Vaisseaux
la Bone Chere Island
Pt. a Bone Chere
Seven Isles or P.a l'Assiette
Bird I.
Shallow Water with many small Islands but very little known
Islands

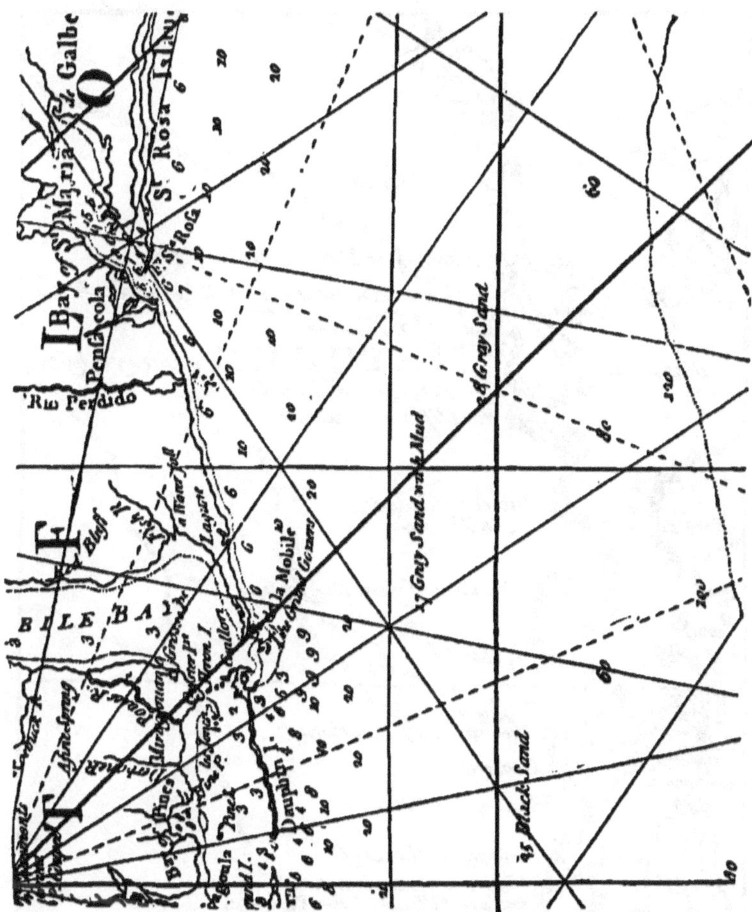

NOTE. A part of Jefferys' map, 1768, showing the vicinity of New Orleans and the Gulf coast. The section on the opposite page attaches to this part on the left hand.

[From *The Course of the Mississippi, by Lieutenant Ross, improved from the Surveys of the French*, London, 1775. It shows the point where Loftus was driven back.]

[From Callot's *Atlas*, Pl. 34.]

pamphleteers, it was necessary to depend upon English explorations as well as upon the right to issue the sea-to-sea charters. Story after story of early wanderings of the English along and beyond the Mississippi were rehabilitated in the public mind. Such were the unsupported narrative of the adventures of Colonel Wood in 1654 and 1664. The discredited journals and maps given by the younger Coxe, which carried in 1676 the roving explorers sent out by the father up the Mississippi to the Missouri, were once more cited. The fabulous party of New Englanders who went overland to New Mexico in 1678, and whose guides were represented as afterward leading La Salle down the Great River, was again created as a veritable record.

But the ambitious and seductive pretense availed nothing, and the bounds of Carolana, like those of Virginia and the other colonies having a western extension, were clipped at the Mississippi forever. England thus not only abrogated her sea-to-sea claims, but the short-sightedness which made crown lands of her acquisitions beyond the Alleghanies laid open the way for the new Republic in 1782, by virtue of having wrested them from the crown itself, to include them in its nascent realm.

It was in 1764 that efforts were first made by the English to take possession of the left bank of the Mississippi. In that year, some wanderers from Roanoke in North Carolina came to Baton Rouge and entered upon a contraband trade with the French. In the previous February, Major Arthur Loftus, with about four hundred English troops, which had come from Mobile, already taken possession of, entered the Mississippi, with the purpose of proceeding to the upper waters and receiving the surrender of Fort Chartres and the other French posts. On February 27, the detachment of Loftus left New Orleans in the ascent. Some weeks later, on May 20, the flotilla, which was making a laborious progress, was suddenly attacked at Davion's Bluff (Fort Adams). The English, surprised, were driven back with a small loss. There is some reason to believe that this attack, made by the Indians, had been encouraged by French residents, though the French officers in authority are

Carolinians at Baton Rouge. 1764.

The English driven back on the Mississippi.

FORT OF THE NATCHEZ.

[From Callot's *Atlas*.]

probably to be exonerated. Loftus, however, and his officers remained convinced of such connivance. The spot where it occurred was two hundred and forty miles from New Orleans, as is indicated in a map of the Mississippi made in a later ascent by Lieutenant Ross of the thirty-fourth regiment, in which is marked the place "where the Twenty-second regiment was driven back by the Tonicas." Andrew Ellicott also marks it in a map which accompanies his more recent journal.

St. Ange at Fort Chartres.

A few weeks later, Neyon de Villiers, who commanded at Fort Chartres, summoning St. Ange from the Wabash, left that officer in charge, and started down the Mississippi with six officers, over sixty soldiers, and about eighty French residents in his train. He reached New Orleans on July 2, finding the French still in control, and with no suspicion of the sudden shock which they were to experience three months later (October, 1764), when the provisions of the secret Fontainebleau treaty became known. A letter from the French king, dated in April, had revealed their destiny. D'Abadie, now in the governorship in succession to Kerlerec, had been in office since June, 1763. He was a man who soon commanded respect by his uprightness, but the execrable condition of the finances of the province had proved too much for even an able administrator, and he was beginning to lose ground in health and spirits under the pressure of his duties. Champigny tells us how disheartening and even appalling an effect the news which D'Abadie was compelled to disclose had made upon a community who could but feel that they had been betrayed in exigencies which little concerned them. D'Abadie suffered mortification and a revulsion of feelings with the rest, and did not live to turn the province over to the Spanish governor, whom he was instructed to receive. He died, weighed down and disconsolate, on February 4, 1765; and it was not till March, 1766, that Ulloa, the Spanish representative, arrived in the river, to treat with Aubry, the successor of D'Abadie, for the surrender of the province. This change of destiny, which fell with so distressing a blow upon D'Abadie and the faithful Louisianians, came also like a blight to a people who had shown in many ways their devotion to the Bourbon crown of France.

The secret treaty divulged by D'Abadie. October, 1764.

D'Abadie dies; Ulloa comes.

Early in 1765, some of the restless and wandering Acadians, now for ten years unwelcome and unwilling denizens along the Atlantic seaboard, had begun to arrive in New Orleans. These and later comers in part took up their home lots along the reaches of the river still known as the "Cajean Coast." They had left the English colonies with the hope of living once more under the French flag; but found they had come to a distracted land. Others, already planning for the change, were stopped by hearing of the new conditions, and, turning to seek other asylums, found their way to San Domingo, Cayenne, and even to France and Corsica. Some of these same exiles, who had started west to descend the Mississippi, met the disastrous news at Detroit, and tarried there, where they are still represented by descendants.

Acadians in Louisiana.

Since the promulgation of the proclamation of 1763, there had been an increasing disaffection among the English traders in finding themselves debarred from traffic beyond the Mississippi. In what were now the crown lands, wars and removals had sensibly thinned the native population, and it had become evident that the future of the Indian trade must be west of the Great River. The tidings of the Spanish accession to this distant territory, in that it opened new channels for English enterprise, and was not likely to cultivate the same degree of rivalry as with the French, came with new encouragements to the trader. We find this expressed in a letter of February 26, 1765, from Governor Dobbs of North Carolina, one of the last he wrote, for he expired about a month later (March 28). The English can now extend, he says in effect, their trade beyond the Mississippi, and reach the Spaniards of new and old Mexico, "by pushing on our discoverers and traders by the Missouri and the rivers west of the Mississippi," and so secure "an open trade to the westward American ocean." The gain, however, was not to be all on one side, for both Spanish and French traders were pushing east of the Mississippi, and were carrying off furs from points within sixty miles of Detroit, and Kaskaskia was filled with goods from New Orleans.

English traders and the new conditions.

French traders east of the Mississippi.

It was evident that the English, if they would retain the Indian trade, could not long delay possession of this Illinois and Wabash country. The approach was now to be made overland from the east. We have seen that Gage, at the end of Bouquet's campaign, had instructed that officer to send messengers to the Illinois. Early in 1765, Lieutenant Fraser had been dispatched from Fort Pitt to prepare the tribes and the French for the English force which was to follow. He reached the Illinois villages, where the French traders conspired to take his life. He owed his deliverance to Pontiac, now disposed to make his peace with the inevitable masters. Fleeing finally in disguise, Fraser left the field open by descending in June to New Orleans.

Troops to be sent overland.

Lieutenant Fraser sent west.

The mission was soon to be pursued by a different man, for the lot had fallen to George Croghan, the best choice possible, and favored by Bouquet, though he was not in all ways above suspicion when the Indian trade was in question. Under instructions from Sir William Johnson, Croghan left Fort Pitt about the middle of May, 1765. He had two boats, with several white companions. A small party of Delawares, Shawnees, and Iroquois soon joined him. He went prepared to note the country and plot the windings of the Ohio. The early geographers of this valley owed something to him, though his scale of distances proved subject to considerable errors. Fortunately, his journal has been preserved, and we can see in his narrative how the river banks were at this time alive with the buffalo and other wild game.

George Croghan sent west. 1765.

Croghan had sent out messengers to summon the French traders to meet him at the mouth of the Scioto and take the oath of allegiance, and the Indians helped to bring them in. By the 6th of June, he was at the mouth of the Wabash, where he found the Indians less tractable than the Shawnees had been higher up the valley. He now dispatched messengers to St. Ange to warn him of his approach; but his advance was brought suddenly to a stop. On the morning of June 8, a body of Kickapoos and Mascoutins, on the pretense that his Indians were Cherokees, attacked and captured him. The savages carried their prisoner to Vincennes, and arrived there on the 15th. Croghan reports this town to have at the time some eighty French habitations (occupied, to his eyes,

The Kickapoos attack. June, 1765.

by an idle and lazy population), with Indian huts scattered among them. Croghan himself was treated with respect, and was sent up the river to Ouiatanon, where he was released. Here he received a letter from St. Ange, promising a courteous reception. He now met Pontiac, and at a concourse of the neighboring tribes held at Ouiatanon, Croghan speedily brought them to terms. The Twightwees gave up their English prisoners, and hoisted the English flag upon the banks of the St. Joseph, a branch of the Maumee. That the Indians of the upper Ohio valley had already succumbed seemed to help Croghan with the more distant tribes, and Pontiac's good offices became important. Croghan, in the report which he made to Johnson, spoke of the Ottawa chief as "a shrewd, sensible Indian of few words, who commands more respect among his own nation than any Indian I ever saw." Croghan adds that Pontiac seemed to understand the late contest as a "beaver war," stirred up for profit. The chief spoke for peace, but he demanded powder and lead for his people, and begged that they might-be dismissed with a plenty of rum! It was further the opinion of Croghan that the French hold upon the Indians was still strong, and that the English must not expect a speedy revulsion in their favor.

Treaty at the Maumee portage.

Pontiac.

Croghan made concessions enough to accomplish his purpose, and early in August started down the Maumee in the confident expectation that the march of the English, later on, to Fort Chartres would be permitted without restraint. On the 17th, he was at Detroit, and repeated his success with the new savage hordes which greeted him there, and then, securing Pontiac's promise to seal the peace with Johnson at Oswego, he started for Niagara.

Croghan in Detroit.

Croghan's report being made, Captain Thomas Stirling started from Fort Pitt with a hundred and twenty Highlanders, and, meeting with no obstructions, the expedition reached Fort Chartres, and on October 10, in the presence of Stirling and his Black Watch regiment, the French flag was hauled down, and St. Ange gave up his authority. There was not now a Bourbon symbol flying anywhere throughout the English conquest. The threats of resistance which early in the spring the adjacent

Stirling marches west.

Fort Chartres given up. October 10, 1765.

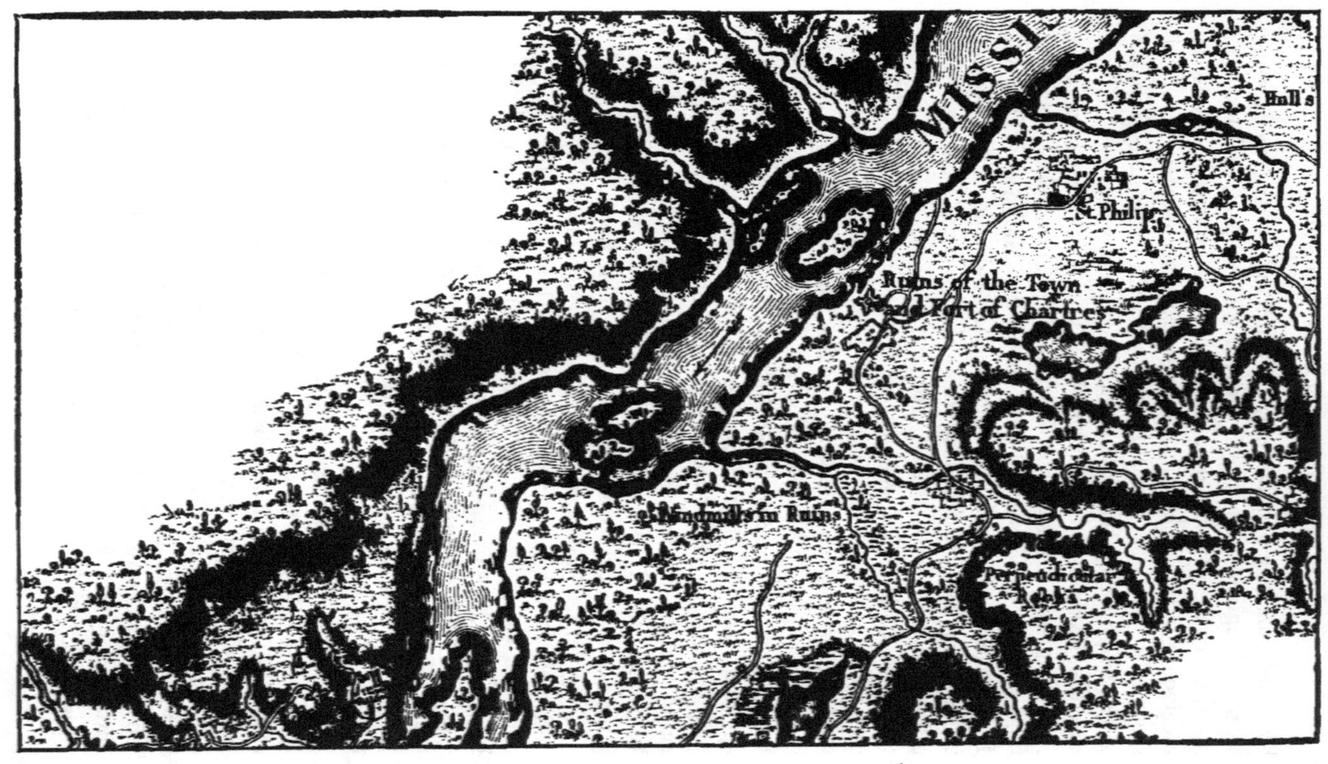

MISSI
Hull's
St. Philip
Ruins of the Town
and Fort of Chartres
Windmills in Ruins
Perpenchonar
Rocks

[From Callot's *Atlas*, Pl. 28.]

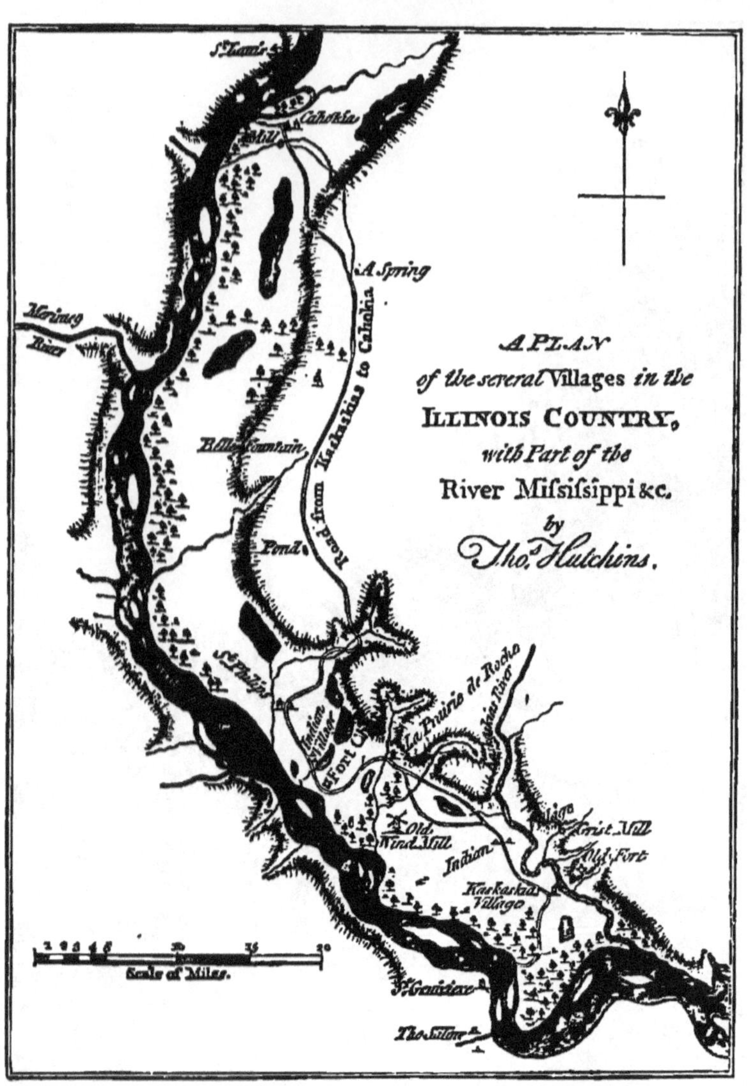

A PLAN
of the several Villages in the
ILLINOIS COUNTRY,
with Part of the
River Misſiſsippi &c.
by
Thos. Hutchins.
Cahokia
Mill
A Spring
Road from Kaskaskias to Cahokia
Merimeg River
Pond
St. Philips
Indian Village
Fort Cha
La Prairie de Rocher
Kaskaskias River
Old Wind Mill
Indian
Grist Mill
Old Fort
Kaskaskias Village
Scale of Miles.

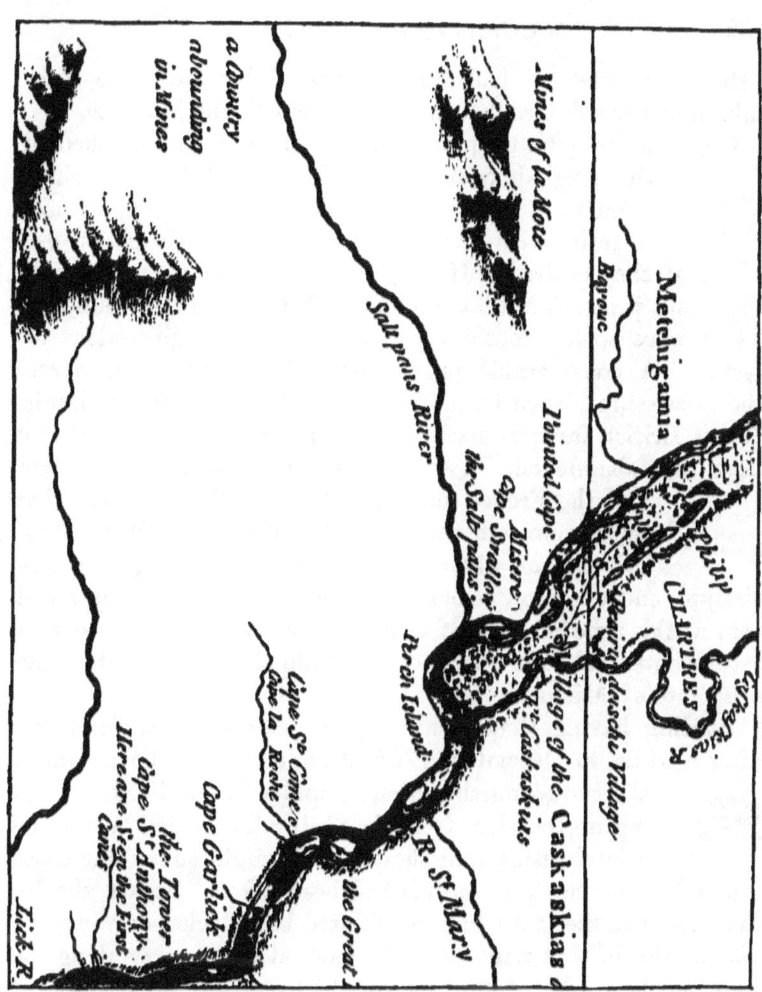

FORT CHARTRES AND KASKASKIA.

[From Lieutenant Ross's *Course of the Mississippi, improved from Surveys of the French,* London, 1775.]

tribes were making had been succeeded by the same quiet submission which Croghan had compelled on the Maumee.

Gage had prepared a proclamation, which was now issued by the English commander. It assured the French of security in their religion, and gave them opportunity to retire with their property to New Orleans, or elsewhere if they desired. If they remained, they were promised the same protection that was accorded to British subjects. There were some thousand French whom these provisions affected. A considerable proportion followed St. Ange across the Mississippi, when he moved his headquarters to St. Louis. A few British families succeeded to some of the farms that had been thus abandoned. Two years later, it was estimated that half the French settlers had crossed the river, and that there were something over two thousand left on English soil, of whom three fourths were along the Mississippi, and a quarter remained on the Wabash. It is supposed that at this time hardly half as many French occupied these new settlements, and they were mostly within the limits of the modern State of Missouri.

The English proclamation.

The French depart or remain.

Stirling having thus secured quiet possession, his force was after a while, in December, 1765, strengthened by the arrival of the thirty-fourth regiment under Major Farmer, coming up the river from the Gulf. There had been some apprehension that these troops might suffer like those under Loftus; but precautions had been taken. Stuart, the Indian agent in the south, had propitiated the Chickasaws by gifts, and parties of that tribe not only scoured the country along the river on the flanks of the flotilla which carried the troops, but a body of their hunters kept the little army supplied with game. There had been some fear that perhaps the minor tribes along the river would yield to French intrigue, and harass the British, but the Choctaws restrained them. The Arkansas on the western bank proved also friendly, and Stuart indulged a hope that their peaceable disposition might yet conduce to their crossing the river. With them, the Natchez, and the Alibamons, the English might command some six hundred warriors to protect the free navigation of the Mississippi. While these precautions had made the movements of the troops safe in the lower valley,

British troops ascend the Mississippi.

A FRENCH HOUSE AMONG THE ILLINOIS.

[From Callot's *Atlas*, Pl. 21.]

a body of Cherokees had been sent to the Illinois country, where their motions proved a distraction to the French and Indians. With these plans for protecting its flanks, the English regiment at last, after a toilsome passage of five months and more, entered quietly within the defenses at Fort Chartres, and the English possession of the country was completed.

INDEX.

71

www.ingramcontent.com/pod-product-compliance
Lightning Source LLC
Chambersburg PA
CBHW032012110726
47901CB00004B/1054

* 9 7 8 3 3 3 7 0 6 0 3 2 9 *